Fodor's 07

BELIZE

**Where to Stay and Eat
for All Budgets**

**Must-See Sights
and Local Secrets**

Ratings You Can Trust

Fodor's Travel Publications   New York, Toronto, London, Sydney, Auckland
www.fodors.com

FODOR'S BELIZE 2007

Editors: Sarah Sper, Christina Knight

Editorial Production: Linda Schmidt, Aviva Muse-Orlinoff
Editorial Contributor: Lan Sluder
Maps: David Lindroth, Ed Jacobus, *cartographers*; Rebecca Baer and Bob Blake, *map editors*
Design: Fabrizio La Rocca, *creative director*; Guido Caroti, *art director*; Moon Sun Kim, *cover designer*; Melanie Marin, *senior picture editor*
Production/Manufacturing: Angela L. McLean
Cover Photo (coral reef): Jeff Hunter/The Image Bank/Getty Images

ISBN-10: 1–4000–1673–8

ISBN-13: 978–1–4000–1673–0

ISSN: 1559–081X

SPECIAL SALES

This book is available at special discounts for bulk purchases for sales promotions or premiums. Special editions, including personalized covers, excerpts of existing books, and corporate imprints, can be created in large quantities for special needs. For more information, write to Special Markets/Premium Sales, 1745 Broadway, MD 6-2, New York, New York 10019, or e-mail specialmarkets@randomhouse.com.

AN IMPORTANT TIP & AN INVITATION

Although all prices, opening times, and other details in this book are based on information supplied to us at press time, changes occur all the time in the travel world, and Fodor's cannot accept responsibility for facts that become outdated or for inadvertent errors or omissions. So **always confirm information when it matters,** especially if you're making a detour to visit a specific place. Your experiences—positive and negative—matter to us. If we have missed or misstated something, **please write to us.** We follow up on all suggestions. Contact the Belize editor at editors@fodors.com or c/o Fodor's at 1745 Broadway, New York, NY 10019.

PRINTED IN THE UNITED STATES OF AMERICA

10 9 8 7 6 5 4 3 2 1

Be a Fodor's Correspondent

Your opinion matters. It matters to us. It matters to your fellow Fodor's travelers, too. And we'd like to hear it. In fact, we *need* to hear it.

When you share your experiences and opinions, you become an active member of the Fodor's community. That means we'll not only use your feedback to make our books better, but we'll publish your names and comments whenever possible. Throughout our guides, look for "Word of Mouth," excerpts of your unvarnished feedback.

Here's how you can help improve Fodor's for all of us.

Tell us when we're right. We rely on local writers to give you an insider's perspective. But our writers and staff editors—who are the best in the business—depend on you. Your positive feedback is a vote to renew our recommendations for the next edition.

Tell us when we're wrong. We're proud that we update most of our guides every year. But we're not perfect. Things change. Hotels cut services. Museums change hours. Charming cafés lose charm. If our writer didn't quite capture the essence of a place, tell us how you'd do it differently. If any of our descriptions are inaccurate or inadequate, we'll incorporate your changes in the next edition and will correct factual errors at fodors.com *immediately.*

Tell us what to include. You probably have had fantastic travel experiences that aren't yet in Fodor's. Why not share them with a community of like-minded travelers? Maybe you chanced upon a beach or bistro or B&B that you don't want to keep to yourself. Tell us why we should include it. And share your discoveries and experiences with everyone directly at fodors.com. Your input may lead us to add a new listing or highlight a place we cover with a "Highly Recommended" star or with our highest rating, "Fodor's Choice."

Give us your opinion instantly at our feedback center at www.fodors.com/feedback. You may also e-mail editors@fodors.com with the subject line "Belize Editor." Or send your nominations, comments, and complaints by mail to Belize Editor, Fodor's, 1745 Broadway, New York, NY 10019.

You and travelers like you are the heart of the Fodor's community. Make our community richer by sharing your experiences. Be a Fodor's correspondent.

Happy traveling!

Tim Jarrell, Publisher

CONTENTS

ABOUT THIS BOOK

Our Ratings

Sometimes you find terrific travel experiences and sometimes they just find you. But usually the burden is on you to select the right combination of experiences. That's where our ratings come in.

As travelers we've all discovered a place so wonderful that its worthiness is obvious. And sometimes that place is so unique that superlatives don't do it justice: you just have to be there to know. These sights, properties, and experiences get our highest rating, **Fodor's Choice**, indicated by orange stars throughout this book.

Black stars highlight sights and properties we deem **Highly Recommended**, places that our writers, editors, and readers praise again and again for consistency and excellence.

By default, there's another category: any place we include in this book is by definition worth your time, unless we say otherwise. And we will.

Disagree with any of our choices? Care to nominate a place or suggest that we rate one more highly? Visit our feedback center at www.fodors.com/feedback.

Budget Well

Hotel and restaurant price categories from ¢ to $$$$ are defined in the opening pages of each chapter. For attractions, we always give standard adult admission fees; reductions are usually available for children, students, and senior citizens. Want to pay with plastic? **AE, D, DC, MC, V** following restaurant and hotel listings indicate whether American Express, Discover, Diner's Club, MasterCard, and Visa are accepted.

Restaurants

Unless we state otherwise, restaurants are open for lunch and dinner daily. We mention dress only when there's a specific requirement and reservations only when they're essential or not accepted—it's always best to book ahead.

Hotels

Hotels have private bath, phone, TV, and air-conditioning and operate on the European Plan (aka EP, meaning without meals), unless we specify that they use the Continental Plan (CP, with a continental breakfast), Breakfast Plan (BP, with a full breakfast), or Modified American Plan (MAP, with breakfast and dinner), or are all-inclusive (including all meals and most activities). We always

list facilities but not whether you'll be charged an extra fee to use them, so when pricing accommodations, find out what's included.

Many Listings

★	Fodor's Choice
★	Highly recommended
⊠	Physical address
↔	Directions
⌖	Mailing address
☎	Telephone
🖷	Fax
⊕	On the Web
✑	E-mail
🎟	Admission fee
☉	Open/closed times
►	Start of walk/itinerary
Ⓜ	Metro stations
▭	Credit cards

Hotels & Restaurants

🏨	Hotel
⟲	Number of rooms
♨	Facilities
🍽	Meal plans
✗	Restaurant
⌕	Reservations
🏛	Dress code
⤢	Smoking
⚏	BYOB
✗🏨	Hotel with restaurant that warrants a visit

Outdoors

🏌	Golf
⚠	Camping

Other

☗	Family-friendly
🛈	Contact information
⇨	See also
⊠	Branch address
☞	Take note

WHAT'S WHERE

BELIZE CITY 	Belize City is probably the first place you'll see in Belize, and often it doesn't make a good impression. The predominantly Creole city, with a population of less than 80,000, is hardly more than an overgrown town. Its reputation for crime and street hassles isn't totally without foundation. The city's ramshackle commercial center, with narrow streets, unpainted storefronts, and boys on bikes yelling "gimme dollar" could qualify Belize City as a stand-in for a run-down West African town. (In fact a movie set in Africa, *The Dogs of War,* was filmed here.) But first impressions aren't everything. Under Belize City's not-so-pretty skin is an interesting old character. This is the business, media, financial, transportation, cultural, social, and—despite the capital being almost 50 mi away—political hub of Belize. Things are happening here—parties, live music, good conversation, and good food. Areas of the city, such as the waterfront along the harbor, have been spruced up and actually look inviting. Charming old colonial buildings dot the Fort George area. Houses are being painted, signage is being improved, and streets are being cleaned. Tourist police are running off hustlers. Cruise ships have brought a new bustle to downtown. It's not New York, but Belize City has a raffish charm that grows on you the more time you spend here.
THE CAYES & ATOLLS 	Though Belize has hundreds of islands in the Caribbean, only a handful are set up for visitors with hotels, restaurants, and tours, and the majority are in this area. The two largest and most populated cayes (pronounced *keys*) are Ambergris (*Am-bur-griss*) Caye, with around 8,000 people, and Caye Caulker, population 1,000. They're just a few hundred feet inside the Belize Barrier Reef. The Caribbean ambience and signature Belizean accent of Ambergris Caye make it the country's most popular place to visit. Though it's pretty touristy for Belize, it's nowhere close to the craziness of other Caribbean beach towns like Cancun and Playa del Carmen. The tallest buildings are only three stories, many of the streets are sand, and golf carts are the most common kind of transportation. Why go to Ambergris? You can dive, snorkel, swim, and fish to your heart's content, or stroll the streets of San Pedro, Ambergris Caye's only town. San Pedro, immortalized in Madonna's "La Isla Bonita," has tons of restaurants and is the only place in the country with decent nightlife options. North Ambergris, finally connected to town by a new bridge over the river channel, is beginning to flourish as an area for upscale beach resorts and vacation homes.

WHAT'S WHERE

Caye Caulker is Ambergris Caye's sister island—smaller, less developed, and a cheaper date. Caulker (whose name comes from *hicaco*, the Spanish word for coco plum) has the kind of laid-back, sandy-street, low-key island charm that travelers pay thousands to experience. Here, you can have it for peanuts.

Farther offshore, three South Pacific–style atolls—Lighthouse, Glover's, and Turneffe—have pristine waters and fabulous diving but little else save a few dive and fishing lodges. Also off the coast are many small, remote cayes. Two, Tobacco and South Water, each have a handful of small hotels, and several others have a single lodge or hotel.

NORTHERN BELIZE

Northern Belize is the "Sugar Coast" of Belize, land of sugarcane and sweet places to visit. Corozal Town, up against the Mexican border, is one of the undiscovered jewels of Belize. There's not a lot to do, but it's a great place to do it. Go ahead: slow down, relax, and enjoy life. The weather's gorgeous (there's less rain here than anywhere else in Belize) and the fishing's excellent. Orange Walk Town doesn't have many attractions, but it's a gateway to the big, wild tracts of land in the northwest. Northern Belize is home to several top-notch jungle lodges and a half dozen notable Mayan sites, including Lamanai, with its stunning setting on the New River Lagoon, the largest body of fresh water in Belize. Sarteneja, in the northeast, is a sleepy fishing village on the sea, with only two tiny hotels. It's just waiting to be discovered by travelers who like to wander off the beaten path.

THE CAYO

The Cayo, in western Belize, has a lot going for it: wide-open spaces, few bugs, and friendly people. The major towns are San Ignacio–Santa Elena (population about 16,000), about 10 mi from the Guatemala border, and Belmopan City (population about 9,000), the sleepy little capital of Belize. The town of Benque Viejo del Carmen sits at the edge of Guatemala, a little more than an hour-and-a-half drive from the marvelous ruins of Tikal. About 20 years ago, the first small jungle lodges in the Cayo began operation around San Ignacio. Now, there's a flourishing mix of hotels, cottages, and jungle lodges in all price ranges near San Ignacio, on both the Macal and Mopan rivers, and in the Mountain Pine Ridge, a pine forest area that looks more like the southern Appalachians than the tropics. The area's loaded with natural attractions and packed with potential for outdoor activities—caving, canoeing, hiking, horseback riding, and mountain biking, to name a few. Several of the country's most accessible Mayan ruins are here, including Caracol, the premiere Mayan site in Belize, and Actun Tunichil Muknal, the Mayan cave that many call the highlight of their trip. Belmopan, between Belize City and San Ignacio, is the downsized capital of Belize, but there's not much to see or do within the town. The Belize Zoo is nearby, as are several excellent jungle lodges. Along the scenic Hummingbird Highway south of Belmopan are barely explored caves, rivers, and national park areas.

THE SOUTHERN COAST

Want beaches? The best on the mainland are in Placencia, an appealing seaside alternative to the bustle of Ambergris Caye. The peninsula has some 16 mi of beachfront along the Caribbean, a backside lagoon where manatees are frequently seen, and a few dozen hotels and restaurants. In recent years, several of Belize's most deluxe resorts have opened on the peninsula, and a real estate boom is underway. Most of the seafront property's already been sold to American baby boomers dreaming of a Caribbean retirement, and more than 1,000 condos are planned, but when you drive down the peninsula on the muddy unpaved road, you wouldn't know it. Between Dangriga and Placencia is Hopkins, which has new small seaside hotels and clusters of condos. Although the sand flies can eat you alive here (bring bug spray with DEET, like Deep Woods Off), you can get in some excellent fishing and beach time, take a day trip to the nearby Cockscomb Wildlife Sanctuary jaguar reserve, boat out to the reef, or enjoy some good snorkeling and diving.

TOLEDO & THE DEEP SOUTH

Rainy and lush, beautiful and remote, Punta Gorda in far southern Belize is the jumping-off point for the unspoiled Mayan villages of Toledo District and for onward travel to Guatemala and Honduras. Over the next few years, as the final few miles of the paving of the Southern Highway to Punta Gorda is completed and the road is extended into Guatemala, this area is expected to take off, so now's the time to see it. PG, as it's known, is Toledo's main city, but it's small—fewer than 5,000 people live here, mostly Garifuna, local Maya, and immigrants from Guatemala. Mayan villages, hardly changed for centuries, are dotted around PG. Ancient Mayan ruins here have architectural and construction styles quite different from Mayan settlements in other parts of Central America. Lovely cayes, the southern end of the barrier reef, and near-pristine waters offer terrific fishing, diving, and snorkeling.

QUINTESSENTIAL BELIZE

Belikin Beer

No matter where you are in Belize—whether you're seated at a seaside restaurant or perched on a bar stool in San Pedro—ask for a beer, and you'll be presented with a small dark bottle with an illustration of a Mayan temple on the front (in case you were wondering, that's the Temple of the Masonry Altars at Altun Ha). This is Belikin, Belize's national drink. You may find, like we did, how deliciously addictive this hoppy, malty lager is.

You'll soon notice the way it's served in bars and restaurants: the bartender folds a little white napkin and wraps it around the top of the bottle. No glass—you drink the beer straight from the bottle. If you like a darker beer, try the Belikin Stout.

The Jewel

Belizeans frequently talk about "the Jewel." They say, "Get yourself a piece of the Jewel." Or, "When are you coming back to the Jewel?" By Jewel, they simply mean Belize. And, of course, Belize is a Jewel. It's a place of incredible natural beauty, of mint-green seas and emerald-green forests, of the longest barrier reef in the Western or Northern hemispheres, with more kinds of birds, butterflies, flowers, and trees than in all of the United States and Canada combined. Massive ceiba trees and graceful cohune palms stand guard in rain forests where jaguars still roam free and toucans and parrots fly overhead. Rivers, bays, and lagoons are rich with hundreds of different kinds of fish. And Belizeans themselves are Jewels. The country is a gumbo of cultures—African, Hispanic, Mayan, Asian, European, and Caribbean—all getting along better than anyone would expect. Belize? It's a Jewel.

If you want to get a sense of life in Belize, start by familiarizing your-self with some of its simple pleasures. Here are a few highlights that will send you home saying, "Ah mi gat wahn gud guf taim" (I had a good time).

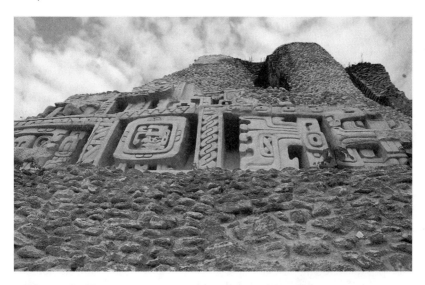

Bird-Watching

Once you see toucans at Tikal or the hard-to-find motmot in the Cayo, you, too, might get caught up in the excitement of searching for some of Belize's 600 species of birds. Many Belizeans know all their local birds (although the names they have for them may differ from those in your birding guide) and where the best places are to find them. Crooked Tree, Chan Chich at Gallon Jug, the New River and New River Lagoon near Lamanai, and much of the Toledo District in the Deep South are wonderful areas for bird-watching; keep your eyes peeled to the treetops and don't forget your binoculars.

Archaeological Treasures

Though the ancient Mayan empire—which once occupied much of present-day Guatemala and extended into Belize, Mexico, Honduras, and El Salvador—began to collapse around AD 900, it still left one of the richest cultural and archaeological legacies in the world. Only a fraction of the thousands of Mayan ruins have been excavated from the jungle that over the centuries has swallowed the splendid temples and sprawling cities. Evidence of the Maya is everywhere in Belize, from the lagoon-side temples of Lamanai to the caves of Actun Tunichil Muknal. All together, Belize has about a thousand Mayan sites, most small and unexcavated, with likely hundreds or even thousands still to be discovered.

WHEN TO GO

Belize is a year-round destination, but some times to visit are preferable to others. Belize, like much of Central America and the Caribbean, has two basic seasons: the rainy season, and the dry season. The rainy season is June through October, extending in some areas through November or even December. The dry season runs from December through May. However, by "dry season" Belizeans usually mean the months in late winter and spring, February through May, before seasonal rains begin in June, when temperatures inland may reach 100°F.

If you want to escape crowds and high prices and don't mind getting a little wet, visit in the rainy season. Though some restaurants may close and hotels may offer limited facilities, reservations are easy to get, even at top establishments, and you'll have the Mayan ruins and beaches to yourself. The busiest time in Belize is the Christmas–New Year's period, followed by Easter, but most hotels count the high season as mid-November through April.

The dry season can be a less attractive time for inland trips, with dusty roads and wilting vegetation, but this is a good time to visit the coast and cayes, with their cooling winds from the sea.

Scuba enthusiasts can dive all year, but the water is clearest from March to June. Between November and February cold fronts from North America can push southward, producing blustery winds known as "northers" that bring rain and rough weather and tend to churn up the sea, reducing visibility. Water temperatures, however, rarely stray far from 80°F, so many people dive without a wet suit.

Climate

Belize is a small country, but there's considerable variation in weather from north to south, and also from the cayes to the mainland. Rainfall, for example, varies dramatically depending on where you are: the Deep South gets as much as 160 to 200 inches of rain each year, but the rest of the country gets a lot less, as little as 50 inches in Corozal. The cayes generally get less rain than does the mainland.

The rain is not continuous; sudden thunderstorms are followed by sun. Often the rains come during the night, leaving much of the day for outdoor activities. The rainy season doesn't mean monsoons, but, rather, seasonal rains that green the countryside.

The dry season, generally January or February to May, is usually hot as well as dry. In late spring—April is usually the hottest month of the year—temperatures inland can reach 100°F (38°C).

Belize's Caribbean coast often gets sweltering humid weather with soaring temperatures, especially in summer, while the Mountain Pine Ridge, with elevations up to almost 3,700 feet, is cooler and less humid. In the Pine Ridge, on some nights in November to February, a fire in the fireplace can feel good.

Overall, however, Belize's subtropical temperatures generally hover between 21°C and 29°C (70°F and 85°F), much like the weather in south Florida. It's the high humidity that'll make you sweat. Remember to drink plenty of bottled water to avoid dehydration.

The western Caribbean's hurricane season is from June through November. September and October are the two prime months for tropical storms and hurricanes in Belize. Over the past century, about 85% of storms to hit Belize arrived in those two months; hurricanes, however, are relatively rare.

The chart shows average daily maximum and minimum temperatures for Belmopan City, Belize.

🛈 **Forecasts** When you check weather forecasts for Belize, keep in mind the variations in weather around the country. It may be raining in Belize City but sunny in San Pedro, 36 mi away. The Belize National Meteorological Service's Web site is a good source for accurate weather information across the country.

Belize National Meteorological Service ☎ 225/2012 ⊕ www.hydromet.gov.bz/.

Weather Channel Connection ☎ 900/932–8437 95¢ per minute ⊕ www.weather.com.

Central America

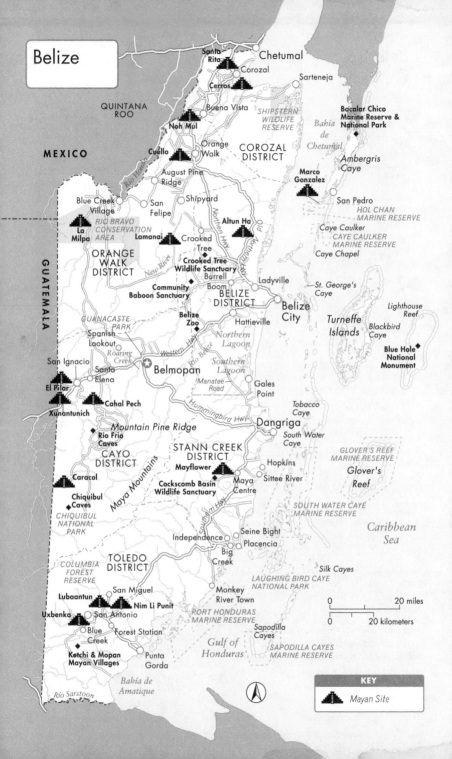

IF YOU LIKE

Luxury Resorts

Deluxe duvets. 1,200-thread-count sheets. Your own villa on a private island or a jungle hideaway with fine wines and gourmet dinners. You may be traipsing around Mayan ruins or diving the Blue Hole during the day, but at night you can look forward to indulgent pampering at Belize's luxury jungle lodges and beach resorts.

Azul Resort, North Ambergris Caye. It's all top of the line at this hip and exclusive beach resort. Kick back with a killer frozen Mojito at the seaside Rojo Lounge.

Blancaneaux Lodge, Mountain Pine Ridge. Francis Ford Coppola's riverside jungle lodge hints of Beverly Hills.

Caye Chapel Island Resort, Caye Chapel. Super-size beach villas next to a challenging seaside 18-hole golf course? No, you're not in Boca Raton—you're on a private island.

Cayo Espanto, near Ambergris Caye. Really want to splurge? A stay on this small, private island will cost you almost as much as a Toyota Prius, but you'll have your own butler, personal chef, and gorgeous views of the sea.

Inn at Robert's Grove, Placencia. Imported steaks, a wine cellar, tennis, and hot tubs on the roof—who needs Hilton Head?

The Lodge at Chaa Creek, Cayo. Soak up the carefully tended landscaping, deluxe garden suites, spa, Cuban cigars, and expensive cognac.

Turtle Inn, Placencia. Francis Ford Coppola hand-picked the Balinese furniture and art in these thatch cabanas, but that's not even the best part. Just wait until you see the garden showers.

Fishing

Some of the world's most exciting sport-fishing lies off Belize's coast and cayes. Go for the "grand slam" of tarpon, bonefish, permit, and snook on the shallow flats between the mainland and the reef. Sailfish, wahoo, marlin, and barracuda abound farther out to sea. Several specialty resorts and fishing camps, such as Turneffe Flats and El Pescador, cater to the angler, but most hotels can help you organize excellent fishing trips.

Turneffe Atoll. Bonefish, tarpon, permit, snappers, jacks, barracuda, wahoo, dorado, and billfish all ply the waters.

Glover's Atoll. Shallow tidal flats around the atoll make for plenty of bonefish; there's also permit, jack, and barracuda.

Placencia. If you don't want to ante up the big bucks that the resorts charge farther north, head here—it's become one of Belize's main fishing centers. Budget hotels start around BZ$50 a night. Permit's the number one catch inside the reef, or cast a line in the Placencia Lagoon or the deep sea beyond the reef.

Punta Gorda. If you're serious about fishing, this is where you need to be. The waters off PG are world-famous for permit fishing, and the Port Honduras Marine Reserve has at least 100 species of fish.

Ambergris Caye. There's surprisingly good saltwater fishing on the northern cayes—look for bonefish, permit, and tarpon.

Chetumal Bay. Your chances of coming home with something are best at this large fishery in northern Belize. Myriad bonefish, tarpon, and permit await.

IF YOU LIKE

Caving

One of the most exciting ways to tour Belize is to head underground—there are hundreds of caves all over the country. You can canoe down subterranean rivers in some, ducking under low-hanging rock stalactites and dodging bats while keeping your eyes trained for Mayan artifacts. The easiest caves to visit are in the Cayo; you don't need a guide to visit open caverns such as Rio Frio and St. Herman's. Before you head out to cave, make sure to find out if it's open to the public, if you need a guide, and, if the cave has a river, if the water level is low enough for visitors.

Actun Tunichil Muknal. Go here for amazing limestone formations, many undisturbed Mayan artifacts, and calcified human remains. It's the top caving experience in Belize.

Barton Creek Cave. Canoe about a mile on an underground river through Barton Cave, which has some Mayan artifacts and skeletal remains.

Rio Frio Cave. Though it's more a natural tunnel than a cave, it's still worth a visit for its large entryway and path above the Cold River.

Che Chem Ha. This cave, once used by the Maya for grain storage and ceremonial rituals, is on private land about 25 minutes from San Ignacio in the Vaca Plateau.

Caves Branch Caves. The Caves Branch River cave system has become a popular place for cave tubing. You float on an inner tube on an underground river through the caves, the only light coming from your headlamp.

Scuba Diving & Snorkeling

Don your scuba or snorkeling gear and soak up the cast of aquatic characters offshore and around the Barrier Reef. One moment you may come upon an enormous spotted eagle ray; the next you may find the feisty little damselfish, a bolt of blue no bigger than your little finger. Bloated blowfish hover in their holes like nightclub bouncers; lean and mean barracuda patrol the depths; and queen angelfish shimmy through the water with the puckered lips and haughty self-assurance of supermodels. Graceful sea fans and great chunks of staghorn coral add to the exhilarating underwater experience.

Hol Chan Marine Reserve. Snorkel with nurse sharks and stingrays at Shark-Ray Alley and keep your eyes peeled for moray eels in the reserve.

Glover's Reef. This is probably the least visited and arguably the most pristine dive and snorkel area of Belize. You can see nurse sharks, eagle rays, and manta rays, and go wreck diving.

Turneffe Islands. Mangroves line a shallow lagoon, creating a rich nursery for sea life where snorkelers and divers alike can see reef sharks, dolphins, eagle rays, large green moray eels, and turtles.

Blue Hole. The underwater sinkhole, one of the most famous dives in Belize, forms a perfectly round, deep blue circle.

South Water Caye. If you want to shore snorkel, come here. The beach is sandy and the island is one of Belize's most beautiful.

Sapodilla Cayes. Fringe reefs and patch reefs in shallow water around the cayes support tropical fish like spadefish and parrotfish.

GREAT ITINERARY

RUINS, RAINFORESTS & REEF

Sample the best of all that Belize offers—ruins, rainforests, and reef—in only seven or eight days. If you have only five days, shave off some time in the Cayo by visiting just one Mayan ruin and heading to Actun Tunichil Muknal on Day 2 instead of Day 3.

Day 1: Arrival

Fly into the international airport near **Belize City** and immediately head out to the **Cayo** in Western Belize, about two hours by road from the airport. Stay at one of the superb jungle lodges, such as the Lodge at Chaa Creek or duPlooy's, or, for less money, Black Rock or Crystal Paradise.

Logistics: The best way to see the mainland is by rental car. Pick up a car at one of seven car rental agencies in kiosks just across the main parking lot at the international airport. If you'd rather not drive, you can arrange a shuttle van, take a bus, or ask your hotel in the Cayo to pick you up. Buses don't come to the international airport—if you're taking one, you have to take a taxi into town (BZ$50). There's currently no scheduled air service to the Cayo. (⇨ Smart Travel Tips A to Z)

Day 2: Exploring the Cayo

On your first full day in Belize, get out and explore San Ignacio and the beautiful hill country around the Cayo. Among the top attractions are the small but interesting Mayan ruins at Xunantunich, Green Hills Butterfly Farm, the Rainforest Medicine Trail at Chaa Creek, and the Belize Botanical Gardens at duPlooy's. Save a little time for walking around and shopping in San Ignacio.

After a full day of exploring, have cocktails and a good dinner at your lodge.

Logistics: You can do all four attractions and San Ignacio in one day, if you have a rental car and if you don't dawdle. Sans car, you can hire a taxi for the day, or opt for your hotel's tours.

Day 3: Actun Tunichil Muknal (ATM)

Prepare to be wowed by the ultimate cave experience. Go into the mysterious and beautiful Mayan underworld and see untouched artifacts dating back thousands of years.

Logistics: You must have a guide for ATM, so book your trip the day before with an authorized tour guide. It's an all-day event, and you'll get wet—bring a change of clothes and wear walking or tennis shoes, not sandals. If you're badly out of shape or have mobility issues, this isn't a tour for you.

Day 4: Tikal

Tikal, very simply, is the most awe-inspiring Mayan site in all of Central America, rivaling the pyramids of Egypt and the ruins of Angor Wat in Cambodia. It's well worth at least two days and nights, preferably staying in one of the three lodges at the park, but even on a day tour, you'll get a sense of the majesty of this Classic-period city.

Logistics: Although you can go on your own, the easiest and most stress-free way to see Tikal is on a tour from San Ignacio—you'll leave around 6:30 AM and return in the late afternoon; lunch is usually included.

Day 5: Caracol & the Mountain Pine Ridge

You can't pass up a trip to Caracol, the most important Mayan site in Belize. The trip there is part of the fun—you bump along winding roads through the Mountain Pine Ridge, past the Macal River, and through broadleaf jungle. If you've seen enough Mayan ruins, skip Caracol and spend the day exploring the Mountain Pine Ridge—there's the Rio Frio cave and numerous waterfalls. A bonus: the higher elevation here means it's cooler and less humid than other parts of Belize. If you don't mind packing and unpacking again, for your last night in Cayo consider switching to one of the four lodges in the Pine Ridge. Our favorites are Blancaneaux and Hidden Valley Inn.

Logistics: From Blancaneaux or Hidden Valley, it's around a two-hour drive to Caracol, and about an hour longer from most lodges around San Ignacio. The road can be near-impassable after heavy rains, so check locally for the latest conditions.

Day 6: San Pedro

Return to Belize City by car, bus, or shuttle van. Then fly or take a water taxi to San Pedro (Ambergris Caye) for fabulous eating (our favorites are Rojo Lounge at Azul Resort, Rendezvous, and Casa Picasso) and water activities (like snorkeling Shark-Ray Alley).

Alternative: San Pedro's a bustling town, so if you want a more laid-back experience on the coast, stay on Caye Caulker instead. You still have access to the same snorkel and dive sites.

Day 7: Blue Hole

Take a day trip to dive or snorkel the Blue Hole at Lighthouse Reef atoll. Dive boats also stop at Half Moon Caye for other dives (or snorkeling) besides the Blue Hole.

Logistics: A trip to the Blue Hole involves a full day on the water, so bring seasick medicine and plenty of sunscreen. Dive boats to Lighthouse leave early, usually before 7 AM.

Day 8: Departure

Return to Belize City by plane or water taxi for your international flight.

Logistics: Plan on arriving at least two hours ahead of your international flight. Luggage is hand-inspected by security and there's often a long line at check-in.

TIPS

1. If you have a rental car, you may have time to stop at the Belize Zoo or make a trip down the Hummingbird Highway (Belize's most scenic drive) en route to the Cayo.

2. Ask locally about road conditions in the Mountain Pine Ridge if you're driving to Caracol or Tikal.

3. Internal flights to and from the municipal airstrip in Belize City are cheaper than to and from the international airport. On flights to San Pedro, you'll save about one-half the cost.

4. Water taxis are less expensive than flying, but avoid boats on rainy or stormy days, as you and your luggage will get wet.

ON THE
CALENDAR

	The top seasonal events for Belize are listed below, and any one of them could provide the stuff of lasting memories. If you want your visit to coincide with one of these occasions, be sure to plan well in advance.
WINTER Dec.	**Christmas Bird Count**, late December, usually the 30th, is the Belize Audubon Society's annual Bird Count, held in Belize City, Gallon Jug, and elsewhere. Another count is held in the spring.
Jan.	**Horse Races**, New Year's Day, are traditional at Burrell Boom.
SPRING Mar.	A grueling, multiday canoe race, **La Ruta Maya** is the longest race of its kind in Central America. Held in early March, (it's scheduled to begin March 9 in 2007 and March 7 in 2008) it runs 170 mi (279 km) from San Ignacio to Belize City on the Belize River over the course of four days.
	Baron Bliss Day, celebrated on the second Monday in March, is when Belize City locals give three cheers for Baron Henry Edward Ernest Victor Bliss, a wealthy English sportsman who offered Belize an immense estate in return for a holiday devoted to sailing and fishing.
	San Pedro is one of the few places in Belize where **Carnaval** gets any attention. It's not Rio or New Orleans, but the town puts on parades, music, and street dancing performances during the week before Lent. On Fat Tuesday, it's paint day, and anyone on the streets might be splashed by a mixture of water and paint.
Apr.	Bring a picnic lunch to Sarteneja on **Easter Sunday** for the sailboat regatta and races, when the usually sleepy fishing villages come alive with visitors and boaters. San Ignacio also has a two-day Easter Fair, with music, games, and sports.
May	In Belize, Crooked Tree celebrates the local cash crop with the annual **Cashew Festival**. Held the first weekend of the month, the festival includes sale of jams, jellies, juices, preserves, and other delicacies produced here. On May 24 the country celebrates **Commonwealth Day**, which commemorates the birthday of Queen Elizabeth II, with a bicycle race from Belize City to San Ignacio.
SUMMER June	The **Día de San Pedro**, a three-day festival honoring St. Peter, is celebrated June 27–29 in San Pedro. The early morning boat parade, usually on the 29th, is the highlight.
	Lobster Festivals are held in Caye Caulker and Placencia to celebrate the beginning of the lobster-fishing season (June 15). The dates of the festivals vary from year to year.

Aug.	The Mopan Maya village of San Antonio in Toledo observes the Día de San Luis Rey in August (early September some years) with religious ceremonies and the Deer Dance. A similar festival including the Deer Dance is celebrated in San Pedro Columbia, a Ketchi village, on Easter. The San Pedro Costa Maya Festival, held in mid-August, is a four-day multicultural bash with musical concerts, a beauty pageant, and other events that takes place on Ambergris Caye.
FALL Sept.	The Battle of St. George's Caye celebrates the David-and-Goliath defeat of the Spanish navy by a motley crew of British settlers, buccaneers, and liberated slaves. This week of merrymaking in Belize begins September 10. Guatemalans around Tikal and nationwide celebrate their Independence Day on September 15 with traditional music, dances, and costumes. September 21 is National Independence Day in Belize, honoring the country's independence from Great Britain in 1981.
Oct.	Thousands of dollars in prizes are awarded at the Belikin Spectacular: Blue Water Fishing Tourament, in San Pedro for the largest marlin, sailfish, wahoo, barracuda, tuna, and other fish caught on Pan-American Day in mid-October.
Nov.	On All Saints' Day, also known as Day of the Dead, is celebrated November 1, in Guatemala, but much less so in Belize. Some Maya villages in Toledo observe All Saints' Day and also, on November 2, All Souls' Day. Garífuna Settlement Day, November 19, marks the arrival of Black Carib settlers, known as Garífunas, from the West Indies in 1823. Processions and traditional dancing are held throughout Belize, especially in Dangriga, and increasingly in Punta Gorda and also in Hopkins and elsewhere.

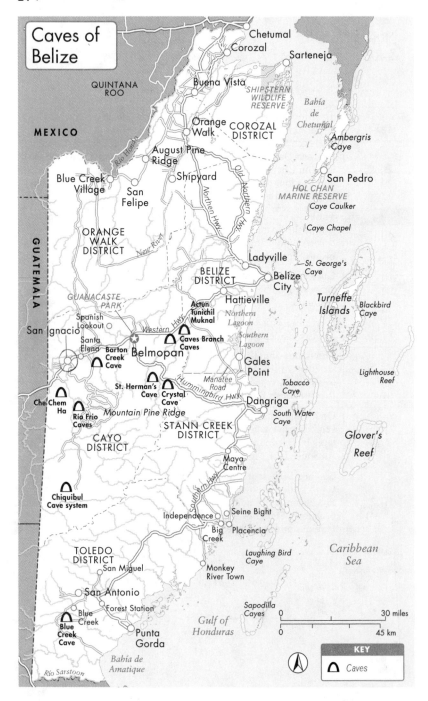

Caves of Belize

MEXICO

QUINTANA ROO

Chetumal
Corozal
Sarteneja

Buena Vista

SHIPSTERN WILDLIFE RESERVE

Bahía de Chetumal

Orange Walk
COROZAL DISTRICT

Ambergris Caye

August Pine Ridge

Shipyard

Rio Hondo

Blue Creek Village

San Felipe

San Pedro

Northern Hwy

Old Northern Hwy

HOL CHAN MARINE RESERVE

Caye Caulker

Caye Chapel

ORANGE WALK DISTRICT

New River

Ladyville

St. George's Caye

BELIZE DISTRICT

Belize City

Turneffe Islands

Blackbird Caye

GUANACASTE PARK

Spanish Lookout

Hattieville

Northern Lagoon

Actun Tunichil Muknal

Western Hwy

Santa Elena

San Ignacio

Barton Creek Cave

Belmopan

Caves Branch Caves

Southern Lagoon

Gales Point

Lighthouse Reef

St. Herman's Cave

Crystal Cave

Manatee Road

Hummingbird Hwy

Tobacco Caye

Che Chem Ha

Río Frio Caves

Mountain Pine Ridge

Dangriga

South Water Caye

Glover's Reef

CAYO DISTRICT

STANN CREEK DISTRICT

Maya Centre

Chiquibul Cave system

Southern Hwy

Independence

Seine Bight

Big Creek

Placencia

Laughing Bird Caye

Caribbean Sea

TOLEDO DISTRICT

San Miguel

San Antonio

Forest Station

Monkey River Town

Sapodilla Cayes

0 _____ 30 miles
0 _____ 45 km

Blue Creek

Blue Creek Cave

Punta Gorda

Gulf of Honduras

Bahía de Amatique

Río Sarstoon

GUATEMALA

KEY
⌂ Caves

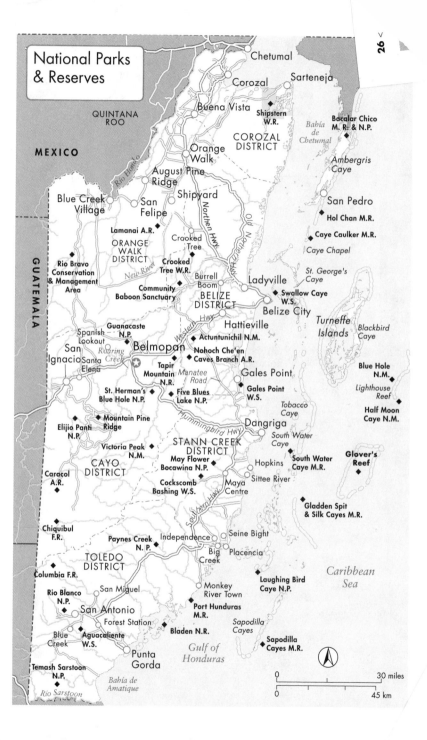

National Parks & Reserves

MEXICO

QUINTANA ROO

GUATEMALA

Chetumal

Corozal

Sarteneja

Buena Vista

Shipstern W.R.

Bahía de Chetumal

Bacalar Chico M.R. & N.P.

COROZAL DISTRICT

Ambergris Caye

Orange Walk

August Pine Ridge

Shipyard

Rio Hondo

Northern Hwy

San Pedro

Hol Chan M.R.

Caye Caulker M.R.

Caye Chapel

Blue Creek Village

San Felipe

Lamanai A.R.

Crooked Tree

ORANGE WALK DISTRICT

New River

Old Northern

Rio Bravo Conservation & Management Area

Crooked Tree W.R.

Burrell Boom

Ladyville

St. George's Caye

Community Baboon Sanctuary

BELIZE DISTRICT

Swallow Caye W.S.

Belize City

Turneffe Islands

Blackbird Caye

Hattieville

Guanacaste N.P.

Spanish Lookout

Belmopan

Western Hwy

Actuntunichil N.M.

San Ignacio

Santa Elena

Roaring Creek

Nohoch Che'en Caves Branch A.R.

Tapir Mountain N.R.

Manatee Road

Gales Point

St. Herman's Blue Hole N.P.

Five Blues Lake N.P.

Gales Point W.S.

Tobacco Caye

Blue Hole N.M.

Lighthouse Reef

Half Moon Caye N.M.

Elijio Panti N.P.

Mountain Pine Ridge

Hummingbird Hwy

Dangriga

South Water Caye

Victoria Peak N.M.

STANN CREEK DISTRICT

May Flower Bocawina N.P.

Hopkins

South Water Caye M.R.

Glover's Reef

Caracol A.R.

CAYO DISTRICT

Cockscomb Bashing W.S.

Maya Centre

Sittee River

Gladden Spit & Silk Cayes M.R.

Chiquibul F.R.

Paynes Creek N.P.

Independence

Seine Bight

Southern Hwy

Big Creek

Placencia

Caribbean Sea

Columbia F.R.

TOLEDO DISTRICT

Rio Blanco N.P.

San Miguel

Monkey River Town

Laughing Bird Caye N.P.

Blue Creek W.S.

Aguacaliente W.S.

San Antonio

Forest Station

Port Hunduras M.R.

Sapodilla Cayes

Bladen N.R.

Sapodilla Cayes M.R.

Temash Sarstoon N.P.

Punta Gorda

Bahía de Amatique

Rio Sarstoon

Gulf of Honduras

0   30 miles

0   45 km

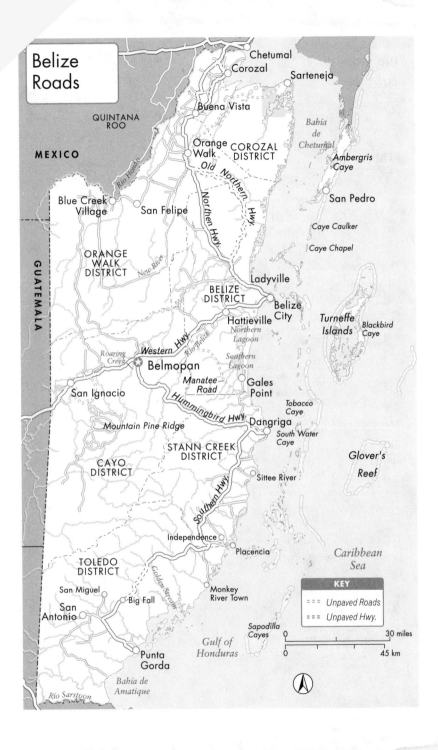

Belize Roads

QUINTANA ROO

MEXICO

GUATEMALA

Chetumal
Corozal
Sarteneja
Buena Vista
Orange Walk
COROZAL DISTRICT
Old Northern Hwy.
Northern Hwy.
Bahía de Chetumal
Ambergris Caye
Blue Creek Village
San Felipe
San Pedro
Caye Caulker
Caye Chapel
ORANGE WALK DISTRICT
New River
Ladyville
BELIZE DISTRICT
Belize City
Hattieville
Northern Lagoon
Turneffe Islands
Blackbird Caye
Roaring Creek
Western Hwy
Río Belize
Southern Lagoon
Belmopan
Manatee Road
Gales Point
San Ignacio
Hummingbird Hwy
Dangriga
Tobacco Caye
South Water Caye
Mountain Pine Ridge
STANN CREEK DISTRICT
Glover's Reef
CAYO DISTRICT
Sittee River
Southern Hwy
Independence
Placencia
Caribbean Sea
TOLEDO DISTRICT
Golden Stream
San Miguel
Big Fall
Monkey River Town
San Antonio
Sapodilla Cayes
Punta Gorda
Gulf of Honduras
Bahía de Amatique
Río Sarstoon

KEY

=== *Unpaved Roads*
=== *Unpaved Hwy.*

0 ____ 30 miles
0 ____ 45 km

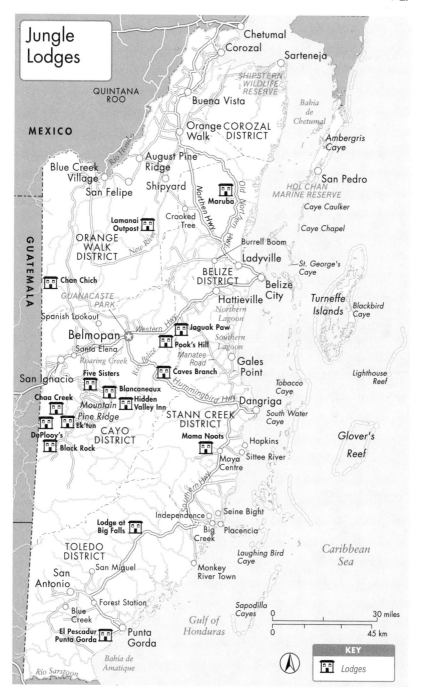

Jungle Lodges

MEXICO

QUINTANA ROO

Chetumal
Corozal
Sarteneja

SHIPSTERN WILDLIFE RESERVE

Buena Vista

Bahía de Chetumal

Orange Walk   COROZAL DISTRICT

Ambergris Caye

Blue Creek Village

August Pine Ridge

Shipyard

San Felipe

Rio Hondo

San Pedro

HOL CHAN MARINE RESERVE

Maruba

Caye Caulker

Lamanai Outpost

Crooked Tree

Caye Chapel

ORANGE WALK DISTRICT

New River

Burrell Boom

Ladyville

St. George's Caye

GUATEMALA

Chan Chich

GUANACASTE PARK

BELIZE DISTRICT

Belize City

Turneffe Islands

Blackbird Caye

Spanish Lookout

Hattieville

Northern Lagoon

Belmopan

Western Hwy.

Jaguak Paw

Southern Lagoon

Santa Elena

Roaring Creek

Pook's Hill

Manatee Road

Gales Point

Lighthouse Reef

San Ignacio

Five Sisters

Rio Belize

Caves Branch

Hummingbird Hwy.

Tobacco Caye

Chaa Creek

Blancaneaux

Hidden Valley Inn

Dangriga

South Water Caye

Pine Ridge

Mountain

Ek'tun

STANN CREEK DISTRICT

Glover's Reef

DuPlooy's

CAYO DISTRICT

Mama Noots

Black Rock

Hopkins

Sittee River

Maya Centre

Independence

Seine Bight

Lodge at Big Falls

Big Creek

Placencia

Caribbean Sea

TOLEDO DISTRICT

Laughing Bird Caye

San Antonio

San Miguel

Monkey River Town

Sapodilla Cayes

0   30 miles

Blue Creek

Forest Station

0   45 km

El Pescadur

Punta Gorda

Punta Gorda

Gulf of Honduras

Bahía de Amatique

Río Sarstoon

KEY

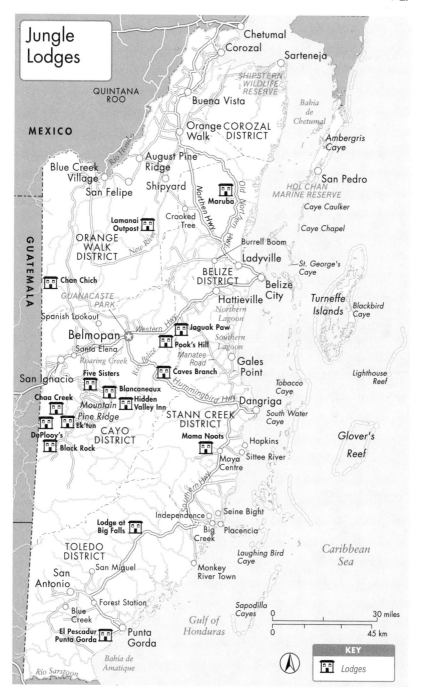 Lodges

Belize City

"Early Monday morning we finally walked around Belize City. Their zoo is nice. Very small, but nice."
—gnrbernstein

"They basically carved trails out of a jungly area [at the zoo] for visitors and put fencing up. In other words, you're walking around on jungle paths and the animals are in natural environments. There are lots of informative, creative, hand-painted signs and all of the animals are indigenous species: tapirs, several kinds of monkeys, jaguars and other cats, toucans, etc. Highly recommended."
—hopefulist

By Lan Sluder

BELIZE CITY IS MORE OF a town than a city—few of the ramshackle buildings here are taller than a palm tree, and a short distance beyond the city center, streets give way to two-lane country roads where animals outnumber people. Any dining room downtown could leave the impression that everybody knows everybody else in this town, and certainly among the elite who can afford to dine out, that's probably true.

Although on paper Belize City looks like an ideal base for exploring the central part of the country—it's two hours or less by car to San Ignacio, Corozal Town, Dangriga, and even less to Altun Ha, Belmopan, and the Belize Zoo—most old Belize hands will advise you to get out of Belize City as quickly as you can. They point to the high crime rate, similar to or higher than the rate in an inner-city area of a large U.S. city, and to the relative lack of attractions in Belize City.

That's true enough, and certainly any visitor to Belize City should take the usual precautions for travel in an impoverished urban area, but Belize City does have an energy and excitement to it. There are good restaurants, the most varied shopping in Belize, a vibrant arts community, and, outside some of the rougher parts of town, nice residential areas and a number of pleasant hotels and B&Bs. There's also an easygoing sociability in Belize City. People meet on the street, talk, joke, laugh, and argue.

Numbers in the margin correspond to points of interest on the Belize City map.

History

The Maya had long had small fishing camps—but no large cities—near the present-day site of Belize City, but they abandoned the area in the 1600s. A few English adventurers and pirates then established camps at the mouth of the Belize River and on cayes just offshore. They began cutting logwood, which was valued in Europe as a source of black dyes. In the 1700s the Bay Settlement, as it was called, received influxes of new British settlers, termed Baymen, and African slaves from Jamaica.

Spain claimed Belize as a minor backwater of its New World domain, but Spain's influence dwindled after some of its Navy ships were defeated by a ragtag group of Baymen in 1798 at the Battle of St. George's Caye 9 mi (15 km) off Belize City. Belize Town, as it was then called, became the main export center for logwood, and, later, mahogany. Belize City became the capital of the British colony of British Honduras in 1892, and by 1904 its population had grown to about 10,000.

Belize was one of Pax Britannia's most neglected colonies. The British, who were usually generous in such matters, left little of either great beauty or interest in their former colony's capital—no parks or gardens, no university, no museums. One of the clichés about Belize City is that the most

TOP REASONS TO GO

BELIZE CITY IS THE KEY TO understanding Belize. If you haven't spent time in Belize City, you won't understand Belize. Belize City is the commercial, social, sports, and cultural hub of the country. It's even the political hub, despite the fact the capital, Belmopan, is an hour west. The prime minister, former prime ministers, most of the other ministers, and nearly all of the country's movers and shakers—lawyers, judges, TV and newspaper owners, the people who run Belize's few big businesses—all live in or near Belize City.

GREAT PHOTO OPS. Belize City is highly photogenic, full of interesting faces, streets full of color, and charming old colonial houses. In short, Belize City has character.

COLONIAL ARCHITECTURE. Belize City rewards the intrepid traveler with a surprising number of interesting sights and memorable places, among them the everyday colonial-era buildings in the Fort George and Southern Foreshore sections. These are places where people still live and work. For the most part, buildings are wood, with tin or zinc roofs, and many are in need of a coat of paint or a bit of repair. However, they ooze Caribbean port-of-call atmosphere.

BECAUSE YOU HAVE TO. As a visitor to Belize, you'll almost certainly have to spend a little time in Belize City, whether you like it or not. The international airport is in Ladyville, at the northern edge of the city. Belize City is the transportation hub of the country, and most flights, buses, and car rentals originate here. If you're arriving late or leaving early, you'll have to overnight in or near the city. Make the best of it. Take care, but explore the city and enjoy it.

exciting thing that happens is the opening of the rusty swing bridge on Haulover Creek.

Belize City's rough reputation began after two devastating hurricanes caused authorities to move the capital to Belmopan. Belize City was robbed of its reason for being.

Press accounts of street crime made Belize City sound like south-central Los Angeles, though it wasn never as bad. In the mid-1990s both the government and private sector began a concerted effort to stop the hemorrhage of travelers, and thus money, away from the city. In 1995 a Tourism Police unit was created to help cut down on crime, and officers on foot or bicycle patrol are now a familiar sight. To make getting around the city easier, roads were resurfaced and traffic lights were installed. More and more colonial buildings were restored, making the Fort George area an increasingly pleasant place to stay. Casino gaming was legalized, and considerable numbers of local residents and visitors now lose their money at the Princess Hotel & Casino on the harbor front.

Late 2001 saw the unveiling of a cruise ship terminal and shopping area called Fort Point Tourist Village, and Carnival Cruise Lines plans to build a new US$50 million terminal in the Port Loyola area, with completion likely in 2007. The city now gets almost a million cruise ship passengers annually, creating new tourism jobs but raising concern that the fragile ecology of reef and rain forest could be damaged.

EXPLORING BELIZE CITY

If you're prepared to go beyond a cursory excursion, Belize City will repay your curiosity. Belizeans are natural city dwellers, and there's an infectious sociability on streets like Albert and Queen, the main shopping strips. The finest British colonial houses—graceful white buildings with wraparound verandas, painted shutters, and fussy Victorian woodwork—are on the North Shore, that is, the Fort George area, near the Radisson Fort George, the most pleasant part of the city in which to stroll.

Navigating

Belize City is defined by the water around it. The main part of the city is at the end of a small peninsula, jutting out into the Caribbean Sea. Haulover Creek, an extension of the Belize River, running roughly west to east, divides the city into the North Side and the South Side. The North Side is, to generalize, more affluent than the South Side. The venerable Swing Bridge connects the two sides, although in modern times other bridges over Haulover Creek, especially the Belcan Bridge northwest of the city center, carry more traffic. At the mouth of the river, just beyond Swing Bridge, is the Belize Harbor (or Harbour as it's written locally, in the English style).

The only routes into the city are the Northern Highway from the north, and, the Western Highway from the west. Coming from the north, follow the Northern Highway to Freetown Road and Barracks Road to reach the center. Alternatively, you can swing west on Princess Margaret Drive to Barracks Road, along the seafront. From the west, the Western Highway becomes Cemetery Road, which leads you to the center via the South Side and Orange Street. The city center itself is a confusing warren of narrow streets, many of them one way.

If you're spending time in downtown Belize City, you're better off without a car. Parking is limited, and leaving a car on the street overnight, especially with any valuables in it, is just asking for trouble. Although most residents don't own a car and get around on bicycle or on foot, even a few cars on the narrow streets can cause a traffic backup. There are a few stoplights, but often they're not working, and local drivers seem to know traffic rules that you don't know.

If you're staying in either the northern or western sprawling suburbs, a car is handy. There's no point-to-point bus system in the city, although buses (except the few express buses) going north or west will drop you almost anywhere. Taxis (recognizable by their green license tags) are plentiful. Fares within the main part of the city are inexpensive—BZ$7 for one person, plus BZ$1 for each additional passenger, to most points. Taxis aren't metered—ask what the fare is in advance. Your hotel can call a cab for you, or you can flag one down. Taxis also congregate at Market Square near Swing Bridge. It's not customary to tip taxi drivers, unless they help you with luggage or perform other services. Most drivers are friendly and are happy to point out interesting sites to visitors.

The Neighborhoods

Fort George is the "colonial" section of Belize City, with grand old 19th- and early-20th-century homes and buildings.

Marine Parade Harborfront, along the water near the Princess Hotel & Casino and BTL Park, has more open, public space than buildings, making it a pleasant escape from the bustle of the city center.

The **Commercial District,** on the South Side, mainly on Albert and Regent streets, is the commercial center of the city.

King's Park is an upscale residential area about 2 mi (3 km) north of the city center, along Princess Margaret Drive.

The **Northern Suburbs,** along the Northern Highway between the city center and the international airport, is the fastest-growing part of the metropolitan area, with middle-class residential sections such as Buttonwood Bay and Belama, along with some of the city's stores and supermarkets, plus several hotels and B&Bs.

The **Western Suburbs** is a multiuse commercial and residential area along the Western Highway, beginning at "Boot Hill" on Cemetery Road at the intersection of Central American Boulevard. Several new tourist attractions have popped up here, such as Old Belize Museum. Also, this area is on the way to the Belize Zoo, Belmopan, and the Cayo.

City Safety

Belize City earned a reputation for street crime in the early '90s, but the government has made great progress in cleaning up the problem. Crimes against tourists in Belize City are now relatively rare, and statistically as a visitor you may be safer in Belize City than in some other areas, such as near the Guatemala border in the Cayo. Still, the crime rate in Belize City is comparable to that of a distressed inner-city area in the United States. The street hustle, drug offers, and aggravation might get to you. Take the same precautions you'd take in any city—don't wear expensive jewelry or watches, avoid handling money in public, and leave valuables in a safe. Ignore offers to buy drugs. On buses and in crowded areas hold purses and backpacks close to your body. Check with the staff at your hotel before venturing into any unfamiliar areas, particularly at night. Avoid leaving your rental car on the street overnight.

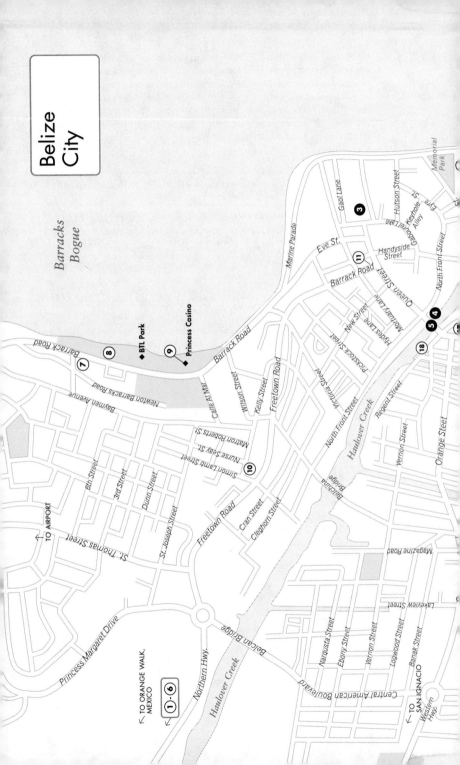

Belize City

Barracks Bogue

Barrack Road

BTL Park ◆

Princess Casino ◆

Marine Parade

Eve St.

Gaol Lane

❸

❶❶

Barrack Road

Hutson Street

Handyside Street

George Kerthole Alley

Eyre St.

North Front Street

Newton Barracks Road

❼ ❽ ❾

Bayman Avenue

Calle Al Mar

Wilson Street

Kelly Street

Freetown Road

New Street

Hyde Lane

Mortuary Lane

Queen Street

Pickstock Street

Victoria Street

North Front Street

❺ ❹

❶❽

Haulover Creek

Regent Street

Vernon Street

Orange Street

6th Street

3rd Street

Dunn Street

St. Joseph Street

Simon Lamb Street

Nurse Seay St.

Matron Roberts St.

❶⓪

Freetown Road

Cran Street

Cleghorn Street

Belchina Bridge

Magazine Road

St. Thomas Street

← TO AIRPORT

Princess Margaret Drive

← TO ORANGE WALK, MEXICO

❶ - ❻

Northern Hwy.

Belcan Bridge

Haulover Creek

Central American Boulevard

Lakeview Street

Narqusta Street

Ebony Street

Vernon Street

Logwood Street

Banak Street

← TO SAN IGNACIO

Western Hwy.

Memorial Park

KEY

► 1 Exploring Sights

1 Hotels & Restaurants

Inner Channel

Birds Isle

1/4 mile

1/4 kilometer

A GOOD
WALK

Start your tour of Belize City in the Fort George neighborhood at the **Fort George Lighthouse and Bliss Memorial ❶** ► on Marine Parade; you'll have a view of the bustling city harbor just over the promontory. West of the harbor is the Southern Foreshore. The Bliss Memorial is where Henry Edward Earnest Victor Bliss is buried. The wealthy English baron visited Belize briefly in 1926, the year he died, and bequeathed much of his fortune to a country he barely knew.

Across the street from the lighthouse and Bliss memorial is the Radisson Fort George Hotel, with its executive wing sheathed in glass. While you're here, walk a block or so northwest along Cork Street by the Radisson and the Great Hotel, a small inn housed in a notable early-20th-century colonial building. Several other good examples of colonial architecture, mostly from the 1920s, are on Cork Street.

Walk northwest on Fort Street (prominently posted signs point the way), and stop at the **Tourist Village ❷** for a rest room break (they're spotless), gift shopping, or a snack. The Tourist Village may be closed if there are no cruise ships in port, which is usually the case on Sunday. There also are several restaurants just outside the Tourist Village.

From the Tourist Village, continue on Fort Street a short distance to North Park Street. Here you'll see Memorial Park, a small V-shape grassy park swept by sea breezes. The park commemorates the 1798 Battle of St. George's Caye. On the south side of the park is the National Handicraft Center, a good place to buy Belizean-made crafts. Also adjoining the park on the north side is the Chateau Caribbean Hotel, formerly a seaside colonial mansion and private hospital.

Continue on Fort Street to North Front Street. Turn right on Gabourel Lane. You'll pass the site of the American Embassy, which is moving to Belmopan. Continue on Gabourel Lane and stop in at the **Museum of Belize ❸**, once a prison, which is now an impressive space in the Central Bank Building complex. After visiting the museum, retrace your steps on Gabourel Lane back to North Front Street. Continue on North Front Street to the **Marine Terminal ❹** from which you can take water taxis to the Northern cayes. In the Marine Terminal is the Coastal Zone Museum, which has displays on the Barrier Reef, and the Marine Museum, which has displays about the country's maritime history. Next to the Marine Terminal is **Swing Bridge ❺**, which crosses Haulover Creek, part of the Belize River. It goes into action at 5:30 AM or 6:30 PM weekdays.

Once across Swing Bridge you're on the South Side, the business and commercial part of the city. It has some unsavory sections, so don't stray far from the main drags. On your left is the Commercial Center, a market with some fruit and vegetable vendors and tourist stalls. Walk south about ⅖ mi (⅔ km) along Albert Street, lined with banks, small stores, and shops. At the end of Albert Street is **St. John's Cathedral ❻**, built by slaves with bricks that served as ballast in the hulls of ships arriving from Europe.

Turn left and walk beside the cathedral to Regent Street. Almost straight ahead, you'll see the **House of Culture** ❼, (previously called Government House), the former residence of Belize's governor-general. Walk back north along Regent Street. As you near Haulover Creek again, to your right between Church and Bishop streets, along the Southern Foreshore, is a cultural and arts center, the **Bliss Center for the Performing Arts** ❽. The renovated center overlooks the harbor and hosts the most important arts and cultural events in Belize, along with more mundane shows such as karaoke contests. Also on your right is the **Belize Supreme Court** ❾, a reconstruction of the original wooden courthouse, which burned in 1926. You'll recognize it by its clock tower.

TIMING The demeanor of Belize City, with its narrow, sunburned streets and ramshackle houses, changes little from day to day, or season to season. The exception is Sunday, when the city becomes almost a ghost town, and summer, when the flame trees with their fire-orange blossoms add a vibrant color to the town. Belize City is fairly compact, so this walk should take only two hours. Green signs posted prominently in most areas direct you to the places of interest.

Don't do the walk after dark. While Belizeans are usually friendly and outgoing, anyone who seems *too* eager to become your friend is likely to be trouble. Drug dealers and ordinary street hustlers may approach you even in daylight, though tourist police who patrol the area are making progress in getting them off the streets. If approached, just say no, but to avoid a confrontation, do so without being aggressive.

FORT GEORGE

This is the most pleasant and appealing section of the city, much of it cooled by prevailing breezes from the sea. It has stately colonial buildings that escaped the hurricanes of 1931 and 1961, several embassies (though the U.S. embassy is moving to Belmopan), upmarket restaurants such as Harbour View that attract the city's elite, and the city's best hotels including the Radisson Fort George and the Great House, plus the Fort George lighthouse, a small park, and the Tourism Village.

Sights to See

❶ **Fort George Lighthouse and Bliss Memorial.** Towering over the entrance to Belize Harbor, the lighthouse stands guard on the tip of Fort George Point. It was designed and funded by the country's greatest benefactor, Baron Bliss. The English nobleman never actually set foot on the Belizean mainland, but in his will he bequeathed most of his fortune to the people of Belize, and the date of his death, March 9, is celebrated as a national holiday. He is buried here, in a small, low mausoleum perched on the seawall, up a short run of limestone stairs. The lighthouse is for photo ops only—you can't enter it. ✉ *Marine Parade.*

Image Factory. This commercial gallery selling art prints, books, and gifts doubles as a serious art gallery, exhibiting Belize's top avant-garde

CLOSE UP

Made in Belize

For a such a little country, some of the products of Belize really pack a punch. Below is a list of some of our favorite souvenirs.

Hot Sauce One of Belize's best-known products come from a little plant near Dangriga. This spicey sauce was originally created by Marie Sharp in her kitchen in the early 1980s. It comes in a variety of heat levels, from the moderate Mild Habanero and Belizean Heat, to the fiery No Wimps Allowed, and, finally, Beware. **Marie Sharp's** also makes less dangerous products, such as jams, jellies, and other spices and sauces. Call ahead to set up an informal tour of the plant. ⊠ *3 Pier Rd., Dangriga* ☎ *522/2370 or 520/2087.*

Rum A favorite of the rum connoisseurs and a speciality of Belize, One Barrel, from **Travellers Ltd.,** has won a number of international tasting awards in the gold rum category; Duurley's, another Travellers product, is also delicious. The company is run by the Perdomo family of Belize City. For distillery tours, contact Travellers Liquors Ltd. ✉ *Box 623, Belize City* ☎ *223/2855.* A good mixing white rum, and the one you'll see in most bars, is called Caribbean Rum. It is made by family-owned **Cuellos** distillery, who offer occasional distillery tours. ⊠ *2 Miles, Yo Creek Rd., Orange Walk Town* ☎ *322/2141.* Most rum is between BZ$14 to BZ$20 a bottle.

Hardwood Furniture If the cost of shipping doesn't break your budget, the low-slung folding "Clam chairs" are a favorite and made from the regions tropical hardwood. **New Hope Woodworking, Ltd.** (⊠ Buena Vista St., San Ignacio, Cayo ☎ 824/2188)

also makes more portable, small wooden boxes. **New River Enterprises** (⊠ 14 Westby St., Orange Walk Town ☎ 322/2225) makes beautiful solid mahogany and other hardwood doors, some around BZ$2,400 plus shipping. They also make patio furniture and a nicely designed two-piece "Orange Walk chair." **Hummingbird Rattan** (⊠ 54 Hummingbird Hwy., Belmopan City ☎ 822/3164) uses bamboo, wicker and rattan, sometimes mixed with mahogany, for indoor and outdoor furniture.

Coffee Gallon Jug Estates in Orange Walk District is the only commercial coffee producer in Belize (and it is small, with only about 100 acres of coffee plantings). Made with only Arabica beans, the Gallon Jug coffees are shade-grown and don't use pesticides, herbicides, or fungicides. Whole bean and ground coffee, packed in colorful gold and green, can be bought all over Belize.

Beer With a nationwide monopoly on beer, the **Belize Brewing Co. Ltd.** is one of the countries most profitable businesses. The beer is perfect for sipping on the beach and there are four types to choose from: a lager, with 4% alcohol; Belikin Premium, also a lager, with 5% alcohol; Lighthouse, a pale lager, with 4.2% alcohol; and Belikin Stout, a dark beer with 6% alcohol. If none of these are to your liking, a few other foreign brands, such as Bud and Heineken, are available at a much inflated cost. Some cruise ship and Belize City tours include a stop at the Bowen brewery, and a half-hour tasting of the beers. For information, contact ⊠ *1 King St., Belize City* ☎ *227/2602.*

artists. Exhibit openings are usually on Friday. ⊠ *91 N. Front St.* ☎ *223/4093* ✉ *Donations accepted* ⊙ *Weekdays 9–6.*

❹ **Marine Terminal.** You can catch a boat to Ambergris Caye, Caye Caulker, St. George's Caye, and Caye Chapel, from this white clapboard building, which was a firehouse in the 1920s. Browse the two museums on the premises while you wait. The **Coastal Zone Museum** is on the main floor and has information about the reef and the creatures that live there. On the second floor is the **Marine Museum,** where you can wander among models of boats that have sailed these waters and tools used by shipwrights. One ticket gets you into both museums. ⊠ *10 N. Front St., at Queen St.* ☎ *223/1969* ✉ *BZ$8* ⊙ *Mon.–Sat. 8–5:30.*

❸ **Museum of Belize.** Debuting in 2002, this small but interesting museum was a Belize City jail from the 1850s to 1993. Displays on Belize history and culture include ancient Mayan artifacts, eclectic memorabilia, and an actual jail cell. Yasser Musa, son of the country's prime minister, runs the museum. Exhibitions change frequently. ⊠ *Gabourel La.* ☎ *223/4524* ✉ *BZ$10* ⊙ *Weekdays 9–5.*

❺ **Swing Bridge.** As you might have guessed, the bridge spanning Haulover Creek actually swings. Each weekday at 5:30 AM and 6:30 PM, four men hand-winch the bridge a quarter-revolution so waiting boats can continue upstream (when it was the only bridge in town, this snarled traffic for blocks). The bridge, made in England, opened in 1923; it was renovated and upgraded in 1999. It's the only one of its kind left. Before the Swing Bridge arrived, cattle were "hauled over" the creek in a barge. ⊠ *Haulover Creek where Queen and Albert Sts. meet.*

❷ **Tourist Village.** In the former Customs House, the Tourist Village (also called the Tourism Village) is predominantly geared to cruise ship passengers. In fact, Belizeans are often discouraged from going into the Village, or may even be denied admittance. As a visitor, to enter you may be required to show your passport. Inside and immediately around the Tourist Village are several gift shops, restaurants, a car rental agency, tour companies, and taxi stands. With the opening, possibly in 2007, of the new Carnival Cruise Line Terminal in the Port Loyola area (to the tune of BZ$100 million), the long-term future of this Tourist Village is unclear. ⊠ *Fort St.* ⊙ *Open on days when cruise ships are in port.*

SOUTH SIDE COMMERCIAL DISTRICT

This area, along Albert and Regent streets, two parallel streets running north-south from Haulover Creek, is the commercial heart of the city. It has many small stores, banks, and budget hotels, along with several places of interest, including St. John's Cathedral and the House of Culture. A third parallel street, the Southern Foreshore, hugs the waterfront along the south side.

Sights to See

⓼ Bliss Center for the Performing Arts. This building, overlooking the harbor from the Southern Foreshore, houses the Institute of Creative Arts and hosts cultural and arts events throughout the year. Renovated and expanded in 2004, the Bliss Center's 600-seat theater is headquarters for the Belize International Film Festival in February. A drama series, children's festivals, dance, art displays, and other cultural and musical performances take place at various times. ⊠ *2 Southern Foreshore, between Church and Bishop Sts.* ☎ *227/2110.*

⓻ House of Culture. Formerly called Government House, the city's finest colonial structure is said to have been designed by the illustrious British architect Sir Christopher Wren. Built in 1814, it was once the residence of the governor-general, the queen's representative in Belize. Following Hurricane Hattie, the governor and the rest of the government moved to Belmopan, and the house became a venue for social functions and a guesthouse for visiting VIPs. (Queen Elizabeth stayed here in 1985, Prince Philip in 1988.) Now it's open to the public, and you can peruse its archival records, art, silver, glassware, and furniture collections, or mingle with the tropical birds that frequent the gardens. ⊠ *Regent St. at Southern Foreshore* ☎ *227/3050* 🔁 *BZ$10* ☉ *Weekdays 9–4.*

⓺ St. John's Cathedral. On Albert Street's south end is the oldest Anglican church in Central America and the only one outside England where kings were crowned. From 1815 to 1845 four kings of the Mosquito Coast (a British protectorate along the coast of Honduras and Nicaragua) were crowned. ⊠ *Albert St.* ☎ *227/2137.*

⓽ Belize Supreme Court. Not the oldest building in the city but one of the most striking, the Belize Supreme Court building is patterned after its wooden predecessor, which had burned in 1918. An 1820 court building had also burned down. The current building, painted white, has filigreed iron stair and balcony rails between two arms of the structure, and above the balcony a four-sided clock. This being Belize, the clocks seem to all show different times. ⊠ *Regent St.* ☎ *22.*

MARINE PARADE HARBOR FRONT

This rather nebulously defined area, which stretches from the Fort George section of Marine Parade to Barracks Road and then to the beginning of Princess Margaret Drive, could eventually be Belize City's equivalent of Havana's Malecón. Only a few years ago, it was an unsightly conglomeration of old buildings and vacant lots. With cleaning up and some gentrification, the area now has several good restaurants, condominiums, a hotel-casino, and a popular park.

Sights to See

Princess Casino. Belize City's only casino is usually bustling with local residents, especially Chinese, out trying their luck. It also attracts cruise ship passengers. The gaming complex has two movie theaters (the only movie theaters in Belize) and Belize's largest hotel. ⊠ *Barrack Rd. Kings Park* ☎ *223/2670* ⊕ *www.princessbelize.com.*

BTL Park. Belize Telecommunications Ltd., the telephone company, though often maligned by Belizeans, did a fine job when they adopted this park along Barracks Road and redeveloped it as a recreational area. It attracts local families for picnics, musical concerts, and other events, and it's often jumping even late in the evening. ⊠ *Newtown Barracks.*

WESTERN SUBURBS

For visitors, this part of the metropolitan area mostly is just a place to pass through on the way to Cayo. However, local entrepreneurs have opened several businesses targeted to cruise ship passengers.

☺ **Gran's Farm.** A Belize City dentist opened this activity area that combines guided hikes along trails and walks in botanical gardens and orchards, canoe rentals on Hector Creek, and swimming. The botanical garden has some 600 species of plants and trees, including 60 types of fruit trees. Gran's Farm also has a restaurant, gift shop, and swimming pool. ⊠ *Mile 14½, Western Hwy.* ☎ *222/4219* ⊲ *BZ$12 to BZ$30, depending on which tours and activities you choose* ☼ *Tues.–Sun. 9–6.*

☺ **Old Belize Museum.** Most of the visitors here are tour groups from cruise ships, but you also can visit the museum on your own. In a large warehouse-style building, exhibits are devoted to the Maya, Garifuna, and Creoles in Belize City; the rain forest and displays on logging, chicle harvesting, and sugar production. Although the exhibits are educational, BZ$20 is a little expensive for a 45-minute walk-through. Also at the site of the museum is a marina; a restaurant, Sibun Bite Bar & Grill, where you can get a decent hamburger; gift shop; and a small man-made beach. This is the only beach near Belize City. ⊠ *Mile 5, Western Hwy.* ☎ *222/4219* ⊲ *BZ$20* ☼ *Sun. and Mon. 10–4, Tues.–Sat. 8–4.*

WHERE TO EAT

Though most restaurants here cater to locals, their number and quality rival those of tourist magnet San Pedro in Ambergris Caye. The city has inexpensive dives serving "dollar chicken" (fried chicken, a local favorite, though it no longer costs just a dollar), Chinese joints of 1950s vintage specializing in chow mein, and lunch spots for downtown office workers seeking Creole dishes such as cowfoot soup and rice and beans. Belize City also has upmarket restaurants serving the city's affluent elite. Only a couple of these are "dressy" (by Belize standards, this means a nice collared shirt for men and perhaps a long tropical dress for women) and reservations are rarely necessary.

A few restaurants around the Tourist Village target cruise ship passengers, typically for lunch and drinks but the one thing you won't find here are chain restaurants. In fact, there's only one fast-food chain restaurant anywhere in Belize, a Subway deli on Freetown Road.

WHAT IT COSTS In Belize Dollars				
$$$$	**$$$**	**$$**	**$**	**¢**
AT DINNER	over $50	$25–$50	$15–$25	$8–$15	under $8

Prices are per person for a main course at dinner, including tax and service.

★ **$$$–$$$$** ✕ **Harbour View.** For the most romantic setting in the city, ask for a table on the wraparound balcony overlooking the harbor. The friendly staff and consistently excellent food also make the Harbour View a favorite of Belize's power brokers. The seafood is especially good; try the snapper with mango chutney, cooked in a banana leaf. Pork dishes, especially Pork Picasso with a hot pepper relish, also are delicious. ⊠ *Fort St.near Tourist Village* ☎ *223/6420* ⊟ *AE, D, MC, V.*

★ **$$–$$$** ✕ **Smokey Mermaid.** On the ground floor of the Great House hotel, a small shopping gallery leads to the Smokey Mermaid, where amiable servers deliver Caribbean-influenced seafood dishes, inventive pastas, and savory barbecues. (It's not smoky in here, by the way.) The large dining courtyard has a fountain, shaded by breadfruit and sapodilla trees and big, turquoise umbrellas. The freshly grilled fish is excellent and comes from an antique, 19th-century bricked grill. There's often a live band playing Belize-style reggae. During lunchtime on days when cruise ships are in port, the restaurant is packed with day-trippers attracted by coupons touting free drinks with meals. ⊠ *13 Cork St.* ☎ *223/3400* ⊟ *AE, MC, V.*

$–$$$ ✕ **Chon Saan Palace.** A local favorite for more than 30 years, Chon Saan Palace is the best Chinese restaurant in Belize City, which is otherwise full of bad Chinese eateries. It has some 200 dishes on the menu, most Cantonese-style, such as sweet-and-sour pork. We like the Chinese-style crab legs. There's a live seafood tank with lobster and the catch of the day, kept alive until you're ready to eat it. On Sunday, the restaurant switches gear a bit and makes sushi. ⊠ *1 Nurse Seay St., at 1 Kelly St.* ☎ *223/3008* ⊟ *MC, V.*

$–$$$ ✕ **Sumathi.** Sumathi serves the best Northern Indian food in Belize City, and perhaps in all of Belize, so don't let the ugly concrete façade turn you away. The restaurant uses an authentic tandoori oven, a large clay oven with intense heat that cooks meat and seafood quickly, leaving it crispy on the outside and juicy inside. Try the tandoori chicken, with cumin, ginger, and minty yogurt, served with *naan* (Indian flatbread). There are many vegetarian options, too. Service is attentive, and portions are generous. ⊠ *190 Newtown Barracks, near Princess Hotel & Casino* ☎ *223/1172* ⊟ *MC, V.*

$–$$ ✕ **Global Spice.** It's unusual to include an airport restaurant in any listing of best restaurants, but Global Spice, near the "waving gallery" on the second floor of the main terminal, will leave you with a nice taste of Belize. In 2005 chef Jason de Ocampo won second place in the annual "Taste of Belize" cooking contest, which focuses on Belizean national and regional cooking. This is a good place to get that farewell plate of rice and beans. ⊠ *Philip S. W. Goldson International Airport, 2nd level of main terminal* ☎ *225/3339* ▭ *MC, V.*

$–$$ ✕ **JamBel Jerk Pit.** Serving Jamaican jerk-style dishes, some with a Belizean twist, Jambel Jerk Pit is a branch of the two San Pedro restaurants of the same name. Jerk chicken, lobster, and fish are the way to go here. Unless you choose lobster, you can get a big plate of food and a cold drink for BZ$15. There are only half a dozen tables inside, and the bathroom is in a separate building next door. Try to get a table in the outdoor courtyard. ⊠ *2 B King St.* ☎ *227/6080* ▭ *MC, V.*

$–$$ ✕ **Macy's.** Stewed iguana, known locally as bamboo chicken, is available on request here, but you can also try armadillo or brocket deer. Macy, the Jamaican-born proprietor of this five-table spot, says iguana is tough to prepare—it has to be scalded, then washed in lime juice and vinegar—but it's delicious to eat. Fish or chicken with rice and beans and other more traditional dishes also are served. On display is a letter from the bishop of Belize congratulating the staff on its catering feats and a photo of Harrison Ford, who commandeered the table by the door during the making of *The Mosquito Coast.* ⊠ *18 Bishop St.* ☎ *207/3419* ▭ *No credit cards.*

★ $–$$ ✕ **Wet Lizard.** Right next to the Tourist Village, overlooking cruise ship terminals 3 and 4, there's no question of the target market of the Wet Lizard. Even so, it's become a popular bar and a place to grab a sandwich or hamburger, even for those not on a cruise ship. An expansion added a gift shop and upper deck with bright green roof trim. ⊠ *1 Fort St.* ☎ *223/2664* ▭ *MC, V.*

¢–$$ ✕ **Big Daddy's Diner.** With a central location in the Commercial Center, just south of Swing Bridge, Big Daddy's is a popular lunch spot for downtown workers. The large portions served cafeteria-style come cheap, and the clean, sunny surroundings including gleaming wood ceiling, ceiling fans, and views of Haulover Creek out the big windows are extras that don't cost a thing. Come for breakfast and get a plate of fry jacks—fried bread, a bit like New Orleans beignets without the powered sugar—eggs, and delicious Belizean bacon for around BZ$8. ⊠ *Commercial Center, 2nd fl. near Swing Bridge* ☎ *227/0932* ▭ *MC, V.*

¢–$$ ✕ **Dit's Saloon.** More café-cum-saloon than restaurant, Dit's is a Belize City institution that specializes in beans and rice. (Like many older Belizean restaurants, it's got a sink right in the dining room.) Cheery striped tablecloths lend the place a homey feel. Among the must-try, sticky and sweet baked goods are the three-milks cake and the coconut tarts. The platters of eggs, beans, and toast, washed down with large mugs of tea, are an excellent breakfast value. Sip on the delicious fresh-squeezed juices. ⊠ *50 King St.* ☎ *227/3330* ▭ *No credit cards.*

¢–$$ ✕ **Nerie's.** Always packed with locals, Nerie's is the *vox populi* of dining in Belize City. The many traditional dishes on the menu include fry jacks for breakfast and cowfoot soup and *garifuna sere* (fish soup with coconut milk) for lunch. Stew chicken with rice, beans, and a soft drink will only set you back BZ$10. ⊠ *Queen and Daly Sts.* ☎ *223/4028* ⊠ *124 Freetown Rd.* ☎ *224/5199* ▭ *No credit cards.*

"Roots" Belizean

If you spend time talking with Belizeans, sooner or later conversation will turn to "roots." It's not a vegetable, but a term referring to people born in Belize who share a certain set of values. Usually, but not always, it connotes ordinary folk, not wealthy Belizeans. These are Belizeans who ride the bus instead of driving a new Ford Explorer.

"Being roots Belizean is a way of life, a mindset, and a unique set of values," says Wendy Auxillou, a second-generation Belizean who lives on Caye Caulker. Roots Belizeans enjoy the simple pleasures of life: talking with friends they run into on the streets of Belize City; skipping work or school to swim in the sea, river, or lagoon; sitting on a veranda on a hot afternoon; fishing in an old wooden skiff; raising chickens in the backyard for Sunday dinner. More recently, it's going to a local restaurant or bar for karaoke, as Belizeans have developed a genuine affection for the pastime.

Roots is about community involvement. Children are often looked after by aunts and grannies, as well as neighbors. Misbehaving children might find themselves answering to a slew of adults in addition to their parents.

It's going to the market and eating boiled corn, *dukunu* (boiled cornbread), *garnaches* (crispy tortillas topped with beans and rice), and Belizean-style hot dogs, which are wrapped in bacon and grilled with onions. It's buying bananas 20 for a dollar. It's enjoying the smell and taste of all the local fruits, like tambran, grocea, a dozen different kinds of mangoes, sapodilla, mamie, jicama, watermelon, pineapple, guava, and papaya. It's about going to restaurants with local flavor, like Caladium in Belmopan, Nerie's in Belize City, Clarissa Falls near the Cayo, and Victor's near Orange Walk Town.

"It's about eating johnnycakes or plucking chickens with your neighbor, just because," says one Belizean.

Some claim that the original and perhaps only roots Belizeans are Creoles, descendents of the rough-and-ready Baymen and freed African slaves. Others argue that anybody can be a roots Belizean, that there are roots Mestizos, roots Maya, even roots Mennonites.

—Lan Sluder

WHERE TO STAY

Belize City has the country's largest hotels, though size is all relative in Belize. The Radisson, Princess, and Biltmore Plaza each have more than 75 rooms and strive, not always successfully, for an international standard. The city also has its share of small inns and B&Bs with character, such as the Great House, D'Nest Inn, and Villa Boscardi. Although easy on the pocketbook, the city's many budget and moderately priced hotels frequently have thin, inexpensive mattresses, scratchy sheets, and amenities such as room phones may be scarce. In Belize City, safety is an issue, especially at the cheaper hotels, so be sure to check that doors and windows securely lock and that the entrance is well lighted.

Several of the city's best hotels are in the Fort George area, but there are also good choices in the northern suburbs between downtown and the international airport. The Commercial District on the South Side (south of Swing Bridge) has the largest number of budget hotels.

WHAT IT COSTS In Belize Dollars					
	$$$$	$$$	$$	$	¢
FOR 2 PEOPLE	over $500	$300–$500	$200–$300	$100–$200	under $100

Prices are for two people in a standard double room in high season, including tax.

★ $$–$$$ ✕🖻 **Radisson Fort George.** Porters in white pith helmets perpetuate a sense of British colonialism at Belize City's finest large hotel. Lush red and ocher fabrics, faux-leopard carpets, and reproduction rattan and hardwood antiques re-create the British raj of the 1880s. There are panoramic views of the sea through tinted glass from rooms in the six-story tower, while those in the executive wing across the road overlook the river and one of the hotel's two pools. Dining options include the expensive St. George's Dining Room, the Stonegrill where food is grilled at tables on heated volcanic stones, or the coffee shop, Le Petit Café. The Baymen's Tavern is one of the city's upscale watering holes. ⊠ *2 Marine Parade* ☎ *227/7400, 800/333–3333 in U.S.* 🖷 *227/3820* ⊕ *www.radissonbelize. com* 🛌 *102 rooms* ⚭ *Restaurant, room service, in-room data ports, some in-room safes, minibars, cable TV, 2 pools, gym, dive shop, marina, fishing, 2 bars, shops, laundry service, Internet room, business services, meeting rooms, car rental, travel services, no-smoking rooms* 🖃 *AE, MC, V.*

★ $$ ✕🖻 **The Great House.** Among Fort George's loveliest sights is the colonial façade of this large wooden house, across the street from the Radisson. Owner Steve Maestre converted his 1927 home into an outstanding inn. The large rooms have polished antique pine floors, with modern conveniences such as wireless Internet and dedicated fax lines. Tiers of wraparound veranda allow you to relax while taking in the sea breeze. On the ground floor there's a tiny gallery of shops and an excellent restaurant, the Smokey Mermaid *see above.* ⊠ *13 Cork St.* ☎ *223/3400* 🖷 *223/3444* ⊕ *www.greathousebelize.com* 🛌 *16 rooms* ⚭ *Restaurant, fans, in-room fax, in-room safes, refrigerators, cable TV, shops, laundry service, wireless Internet, car rental, travel services* 🖃 *AE, DC, MC, V.*

$$ ✕🖻 **Princess Hotel & Casino.** Big-time gambling arrived in Belize City when the casino opened at this sprawling hotel, the largest in Belize, in 2000. Though it's not the MGM Grand, the casino has tables for black jack, poker, craps, roulette, and more than 400 machines. Belize's only movie theaters and bowling alley are also here. Alas, the rooms and service aren't as exciting as the gaming. Even the most expensive rooms sorely

need upgrading, and new carpets, linens, and a good spring cleaning are in order. The big money is in the casino, so guest service in the hotel is often notably lacking. ⊠ *Kings Park* ☎ *223/2670* 🖷 *223/2660* ⊕ *www. princessbelize.com* ⊅ *175 rooms, 5 suites* ⚘ *Restaurant, room service, in-room broadband, cable TV, pool, gym, hair salon, dive shop, marina, fishing, bowling, 2 bars, casino, theater, laundry service, Internet, business services, meeting rooms, car rental, travel services, no-smoking rooms* ⊟ *AE, MC, V.*

$–$$ ✕🖭 **Best Western Belize Biltmore Plaza.** Under new management, this hotel staged a comeback with many improvements to its pool, grounds, and rooms. "Deluxe" and "premier" rooms, with new carpets and mattresses, are worth the extra cost. The Victorian Room (BZ$14–BZ$40), which serves entrées like stew chicken and grilled steak, is now a popular dining spot for local businesspeople. ⊠ *Mile 3½, Northern Hwy.* ☎ *223/2302* 🖷 *223/2301* ⊕ *www.belizebiltmore.com* ⊅ *75 rooms* ⚘ *Restaurant, room service, some in-room safes, cable TV,*

> **WORD OF MOUTH**
>
> I quite like the Biltmore, moderately priced hotel with a pool, rooms with a/c, cable tv, restaurant, bar, gift shop. Lively happy hour with music on Fridays.
> —KatieValk

pool, gym, 2 bars, shops, laundry service, Internet room, business services, meeting rooms, travel services, no-smoking rooms ⊟ *AE, MC, V.*

$–$$ ✕🖭 **Chateau Caribbean.** Bright Caribbean colors enliven the rooms in this colonial-style hotel, once a private home and then a hospital, where some scenes in the 1980 movie, *The Dogs of War,* were filmed. Suites have balconies overlooking the harbor. As this is Belize, don't expect everything to work perfectly—your room's louvered windows might not close, defeating the air-conditioning, and some rooms need renovation. The second-floor restaurant has ocean views, and a menu with an unusual combination of Chinese and Caribbean dishes: you can have grilled snapper with rice and beans while your dining companion tries the sweet-and-sour pork. ⊠ *6 Marine Parade* ☎ *223/ 0800* 🖷 *223/0900* ⊕ *www.chateaucaribbean.com* ⊅ *20 rooms* ⚘ *Restaurant, room service, fans, cable TV, bar, laundry service, meeting rooms* ⊟ *AE, MC, V.*

$ 🖭 **Coningsby Inn.** Named for the grandfather of the owner, the Coningsby Inn opened in 2000 as a moderately priced hotel with good security and amenities such as room phones, a perk not always available in this price category. The house with a white picket fence and veranda is on the quiet end of Regent, about a block from the House of Culture. Rooms are above average in size and well maintained, though perhaps the staff could be a little friendlier. ⊠ *76 Regent St., at south end of Regent* ☎ *227/1566* 🖷 *227/3726* ✎ *coningsby_inn@hotmail. com* ⊅ *10 rooms* ⚘ *Dining room, fans, cable TV, Internet room, travel services* ⊟ *MC, V.*

★ **$** 🖭 **D'Nest Inn.** In Belama Phase 2, a safe, middle-class suburb between the international airport and downtown, D'Nest Inn is run by a charming couple, Gaby and Oty Ake. Gaby is a retired Belize City banker, and

Oty is originally from Chetumal, Mexico. The three guest rooms are furnished with antiques such as a hand-carved, four-poster bed. With a private entrance and your own key, you can come and go as you like. The two-story house is on a canal a few feet from the Belize River. Gardens around the house are filled with hibiscus, frangipani, roses, and other blossoming plants. ⊠ *475 Cedar St., From Northern Hwy., turn west on Chetumal St., turn right at police station, go 1 block and turn left, then turn right on Cedar St.* ☎ *223/5416* ⊕ *www.dnestinn.com* ⇌ *3 rooms* ⌂ *Refrigerators, fans, cable TV, wireless Internet, travel services* ⊟ *MC, V* ⦿ *BP.*

$ ⊞ **Global Village Hotel.** New in late 2004, this Chinese-owned hotel has little atmosphere, but it's sparkling clean, with modern furniture and fixtures, and a good value at BZ$100 for a double. Near the turnoff to the international airport, the hotel has free transportation to and from the airport and a fenced parking lot with 24-hour security. ⊠ *Mile 8½, Northern Hwy.* ☎ *225/2555* ◳ *220/3000* ⊕ *www.globalhotel-bz.com* ✛ *South of the turnoff to the international airport* ⇌ *40 rooms* ⌂ *Restaurant, cable TV, bar, meeting rooms, airport shuttle, travel services* ⊟ *MC, V* ⦿ *CP.*

$ ⊞ **Villa Boscardi.** If you're edgy about downtown Belize City, this B&B in the northern suburbs might be your cup of herbal tea. Françoise Boscardi opened her quiet Buttonwood Bay area home to guests. Its rooms are bright, sunny, and stylish, with hints of both Europe and Belize in their decor. An evening shuttle to downtown restaurants can be arranged for BZ$10; airport pick-up for up to three people is BZ$40. ⊠ *6043 Manatee Dr., turn toward sea off Northern Hwy. at Golding Ave., then left on 2nd lane to 5th house on right* ☎☎ *223/1691* ⊕ *www.villaboscardi.com* ⇌ *6 rooms* ⌂ *Fans, some refrigerators, cable TV, Internet room, airport shuttle, car rental; no phone in some rooms* ⊟ *AE, MC, V* ⦿ *CP.*

¢–$ ⊞ **Embassy Hotel.** Just across the parking lot from the international airport, this is lodging for people in transit. Although there's little charm and some rooms look onto shabbier surroundings, it's safe, clean, and convenient. Not completely devoid of charm, it has a sunny roof deck where you can relax in a hammock or challenge a friend to a game of table tennis. For longer stays, consider the one-bedroom apartments, which go for BZ$600 a month, plus utilities. The hotel will store your luggage or dive gear for a fee of about BZ$2 per day. ⊠ *Philip S. W. Goldson International Airport* ☎ *225/3333* ◳ *225/2267* ⊕ *www.embassyhotelbelize.com* ⇌ *40 rooms, 7 suites, 4 apartments* ⌂ *Restaurant, cable TV, bar, meeting rooms, car rental, travel services* ⊟ *MC, V.*

¢–$ ⊞ **Hotel Mopan.** Established in 1973 by Jean Shaw, a pioneer in Belize tourism, the Hotel Mopan is well known for attracting interesting, well-traveled guests including archaeologists, adventurers, and birders. The hotel is now run by Shaw's children, who have upgraded and renovated the hotel while keeping the rates affordable. There's an Internet room, guest quarters are bright and clean, and the staff is always helpful. ⊠ *55 Regent St., at south end of Regent* ☎ *227/7351* ◳ *227/5382* ⊕ *www.hotelmopan.com* ⇌ *12 rooms* ⌂ *Fans, cable TV,*

Internet room, travel services; no a/c in some rooms, no room phones ☰ *MC, V.*

¢ 🖭 **Belcove Hotel.** Right in the middle of things, the Belcove is a popular budget hotel just south of Swing Bridge, literally at the edge of Haulover Creek. You can sit on one of the balconies of this three-story wood hotel, painted sunflower yellow, and watch the boats on the river. Some of the rooms are barely larger than the beds in them, but they're clean, and the staff is helpful and friendly. ⊠ *9 Regent St., just south of Swing Bridge* ☎ *227/30541* 🖷 *227/5248* ⊕ *www.belcove.com* 🔖 *12 rooms, 4 with shared baths* ☖ *Fans, cable TV in some rooms, travel services; no a/c in some rooms, no room phones* ☰ *MC, V.*

NIGHTLIFE & THE ARTS

Travelers who like to use their vacations to catch up on their nightlife rather than sleep will find Belize City's scene limited at best. Although locals love to party, safety concerns keep visitors away from most nightspots except hotel bars, such as the bar at the Radisson Fort George or the Calypso Bar at the Princess Hotel & Casino. Even the safer venues, such as the Putt Putt bar near the Princess, can be risky at times—a beauty pageant queen, Belize's representative to the 2005 Miss Universe Pageant, was robbed here by two armed men in mid-2005. After dark, take a taxi, or, if driving, park in a fenced and secured lot, such as at the Princess.

Karaoke is a craze among many Belizeans. A hugely popular, locally produced karaoke television show, *Karaoke TV*, has been running on Tuesday nights on Channel 5 in Belize City since 2001. Most of the hotel bars have karaoke nights once or twice a week. Even in Belize, you'll hear tried-and-true karaoke favorites such as "Crazy" by Patsy Kline and lots of Elvis and vintage Sonny and Cher, and you'll also hear songs like "Bidi Bidi Bam Bam" by Selena and "Greatest Love of All" by Whitney Houston. Singers may go from country to Motown and hip-hop to funk and R&B to reggae, ska, and Latin soca. One KTV champion, Angelo Fabrio, a teenager from Corozal, specializes in Ricky Martin and Elvis impersonations. Belizean taste in music is nothing if not eclectic. At live music shows and clubs in Belize City, you can hear an equally diverse mix of music, although rap in all its variations is as popular in Belize City as in Los Angeles.

One uniquely Belizean style of music is punta rock. It's based on the traditional punta rhythms of the Garifuna, using drums, turtle shells, and rattles of the Garifuna. In the late 1970s Pen Cayetano, a Garifuna artist in Dangriga, began writing punta songs, updating the music with an electric guitar, keyboard, and other electronic instruments. Punta rock, earthy and sexy, swept Belize and later became popular in other Central American countries, a result of the export of the music by Andy Palacio, "the ambassador of punta rock," and other punta rock stars.

For gambling, the Princess is the only casino in town.

Bars

The bars at the upmarket hotels, particularly the **Calypso Bar at the Princess Hotel & Casino,** and the bars at the **Radisson Fort George** are fairly popular—and safe—places to congregate for drinks. We also suggest two very local spots, Putt Putt and the Bamboo Bar, where you can go in safety (though occasional incidents do happen even here). If you have a layover at the international airport, you might have a beer at the nearby Manatee Lookout.

At **Bamboo Bar at Sun Spree Resort** (⊠ 1668 Seashore Dr. ☏ 223/6268), an open-air bar overlooks a small swimming pool. The crowd is mostly local young businesspeople and creative types.

Baymen's Tavern (⊠ Radisson Fort George Hotel, 2 Marine Parade ☏ 223/3333), is a spot at which to sip a rum and tonic, with live entertainment on weekends, usually a singer or a small band. There's also a more casual section of the bar, on an open-air deck, with views of a garden and the sea.

Club Calypso (⊠ Marine Parade ☏ 223/7162) at the Princess Hotel & Casino, in its own building at the Princess pier, adjoining the hotel, is busiest on weekends when it has live reggae and punta bands. You can also get a bite to eat here, mainly seafood and hamburgers.

Run by a Belizean who returned home after living in Canada, **Manatee Lookout** (⊠ Northern Hwy., on Belize River ½ mi [1 km] south of the international airport access Rd. ☏ 205/2391), a short cab ride (around BZ$6–BZ$8) from the airport, is a place to grab a beer and chicken wings if your flight is delayed. The bar has big windows and an open-air deck overlooking the Belize River, and you might in fact see a manatee. British commandos from the nearby army base at Price Barracks in Ladyville sometimes invade this bar in force, scouting rum and cokes.

Putt Putt (⊠ Newtown Barracks ☏ 203/0100), diagonally across from Princess Hotel & Casino in a semipermanent tent, attracts a mix of visitors and locals for drinks and, on weekends, live music.

Casinos

The only games in town are at the **Princess Hotel & Casino** (⊠ Kings Park ☏ 223/2670 ⊙ Noon–4 AM), which has live tables for blackjack, roulette, and poker, along with about 400 slots. Dancers from Eastern Europe and Russia put on shows, and there are free drinks and a buffet for players. It's open 365 days a year. You'll have to show your passport and register (no charge) at the reception counter before you can go in.

Theaters

The main venue for theater, dance, music, and the arts in Belize City is **Bliss Center for the Performing Arts** (⊠ 2 Southern Foreshore, between Church and Bishop Sts. ☏ 227/2110), which seats 600. As a small, provincial city, Belize City rarely attracts international headliners. It's rare to have more than one or two shows a week at the center, and most of these are local performances—a children's dance group or a young singer's debut concert. You might see a karaoke show or a performance by a Garifuna dance or music group. Concert organizers try to bring in performing talent from around the country, and on a Saturday night you could hear a Maya singer from Toledo or a marimba band from Benque Viejo del Carmen. Most shows are in English, with Creole often mixed in. Ticket prices vary but typically range from BZ$10 to BZ$30.

SPORTS & THE OUTDOORS

Belize City is a jumping-off spot for trips to the cayes and to inland and coastal areas, but the city itself offers little in the way of sports and outdoor activities. There are no golf courses, public tennis courts, or other sports facilities of note around Belize City. Unless you're on a cruise ship or otherwise have only a short time in Belize, you'll be better off going elsewhere for your sporting activities—to the cayes and Southern Coast for snorkeling, diving, and fishing, and inland to Cayo, northern Belize, or Toledo for caving, cave tubing, hiking, horseback riding, canoeing, and other activities. *See chapters on Northern Belize, The Cayo, Southern Coast, Toledo and the Deep South, and The Cayes and Atolls, and also the Beyond Belize City section below.*

Diving & Water Sports

Belize Dive Connection (✉ 2 Marine Parade ☎ 223/4526 📠 227/8808) runs trips from the Radisson Fort George dock. Dive trips to the Belize Barrier Reef, about 30–45 minutes away, cost around BZ$180 per person. Those to Turneffe Atoll cost BZ$280 per person and involve an hour to 90 minutes of travel time one way. Snorkel trips are BZ$130–BZ$200 per person.

Sea Sports Belize (✉ 83 N. Front St. ☎ 223/5505) will take you on a 30- to 45-minute trip to Goff's Caye or St. George's Caye for snorkeling (BZ$220) or to Turneffe Atoll for diving (from BZ$285).

Fishing

If you're a serious angler, you'll likely end up in Placencia, Punta Gorda, or even in San Pedro, but you can arrange fishing charters from Belize City. Both the **Radisson Fort George** and the **Princess Hotel & Casino** have marinas, and local fishing guide services and lodges operate near the city.

Belize River Lodge (✉ Box 459, Belize City, Ladyville ☎ 225/2002 📠 225/2298 ⊕ www.belizeriverlodge.com) is the oldest continuously operating fishing lodge in Belize. Six-night fishing cruises on a 58-foot Hatteras yacht, with meals, guides, and transfers start at about BZ$6,000 per person, based on four people.

Action Belize (⊠ Mile 3½, Northern Hwy. ☎ 223/2987 🖷 223/2986) has 25- and 27-foot boats and fishing guides that will take you out to try your luck with permit, tarpon, snook, and bonefish.

Sea Sports Belize (⊠ 83 N. Front St. ☎ 223/5505) has five- to six-hour deep-sea fishing trips for BZ$1,400 for up to four people, and reef fishing for BZ$1,100. Flats and river fishing expeditions for up to three people cost around BZ$800 for three to five hours of fishing.

Golf

There are no golf courses in Belize City, but there's a spectacular one at Caye Chapel, about a half hour away by water taxi, or 10 minutes by plane.

Caye Chapel Island Resort (⊠ Caye Chapel ☎ 226/8250 🖷 226/8201 ⊕ www.cayechapel.com) has an 18-hole, 7,000-yard course, beautifully laid out along the sea. At this exclusive and remote course, you don't have to worry about tee times or round limits. Unpredictable trade winds and crocodiles in the water hazards make play challenging. A day package at the island costs BZ$400 per person for all the golf you can play (8 AM–4 PM), golf cart and club rental, lunch, and use of the beach and swimming pool. Transportation to the island is additional. The Caye Caulker Water Taxis, leaving from the Marine Terminal, will drop you at Caye Chapel (BZ$35 round-trip, about 30 minutes), or you can fly to the island's airstrip, arranged through Maya Island Air or Tropic Air, for around BZ$200 per person. You can also charter a boat—check with the golf resort for information. Reservations for golf are required, and each member of the party must pay the daily golf rate, even if just lounging at the pool.

SHOPPING

Belize City has the most varied shopping in the country, but that's not saying too much. Rather than catering to leisure shoppers, most stores in Belize City cater to the local market and those from other parts of the country who need to stock up on supplies at lumberyards, home-building stores, appliance outlets, and supermarkets. Gift shops and handicraft shops are concentrated in the downtown area in and near the Tourist Village. Carved wood bowls and decorative pieces, especially from ziricote, a rare hardwood that grows well in Belize, and hot sauces from Marie Sharp and Gallon Jug Estates, are among the most popular souvenirs.

About a dozen ships per week call on Belize City, and each time the Tourist Village shops open their doors. Wednesday is usually the biggest day of the week for cruise ships in Belize City, often with three to five in port, and Saturday is another popular day. Rarely is there a ship in port on Sunday. The Web site Cruisecal.com lists the days cruise ships visit ports, including Belize City.

Most stores in the downtown area are open Monday–Saturday from around 8 AM to 6 PM. On Sunday, nearly all stores downtown are dark, although some stores in the suburbs are open Sunday afternoon.

In a misguided effort at civic redevelopment, the city did away with the old markets at Swing Bridge in the 1990s, replacing them with a modern, two-story Commercial Center just south of Swing Bridge, with stalls and shops selling food and household items. Although clean, the Commercial Center doesn't have the atmosphere, or the customer base, of the old markets.

Shopping Centers & Malls

Fort Point Tourist Village (⊠ Fort George cruise ship docks, east of Swing Bridge ☎ 223/7008 ☉ When cruise ships are in port) is packed with day-trippers when cruise ships are in port and is nearly deserted, or closed, at other times. It has around 30 gift shops, clean rest rooms, a cyber-café, a car rental kiosk, restaurants, and other services.

Commercial Center (⊠ South of Swing Bridge ☉ 7:30 AM–5 PM), in a modern concrete building, is a rather drab market. The first floor has fruit and vegetable and other food stalls, and the second level houses **Big Daddy's Diner** (*see above*) and a few small shops, including several small gift and handicraft shops.

To stock up on picnic supplies, head to **Brodie's** (⊠ Mile 2½, Northern Hwy. ☎ 223/5587 ✉ 16 Regent St. ☎ 227/7070).

Save-U Supermarket (⊠ Sancas Plaza at Northern Hwy. and Central American Blvd. ☎ 223/1291) is a good place for groceries, liquor, and sundries.

Specialty Shops

Opened in 2004, **Fine Arts Gallery** (⊠ 1 Fort St., next to Tourist Village ☎ 223/7773), quickly became one of Belize's top spots to shop for art. It has original paintings by many of Belize's best-known artists, including Pen Cayetano, Walter Castillo, and Patrick Chevailler, along with prints by Carolyn Carr and other artists.

Go-Tees (⊠ 6238 Park Ave., in Buttonwood Bay ☎ 223/4660 ☉ Weekdays 8–5) makes and sells an eclectic variety of items, from T-shirts silk screened with unique Belizean themes to Belize flags, hammocks, and sarongs.

One of Belize's premier art galleries, **Image Factory** (⊠ 91 N. Front St. ☎ 223/4151), is run by a nonprofit foundation. Its exhibitions change monthly and its store sells works by more than 20 Belizean artists.

National Handicraft Center (⊠ 2 South Park St., in Fort George section ☎ 223/3636) has Belizean souvenir items, including hand-carved figurines, handmade furniture, pottery, and woven baskets. The prices are about as good as you'll find anywhere in Belize. It faces the small Memorial Park, which commemorates the Battle of St. George's Caye and is just a short stroll from the harbor front, the Tourist Village, and many of the hotels in the Fort George area, including the Radisson, Chateau Caribbean, and Great House.

BEYOND BELIZE CITY

If you're like most visitors to Belize, you'll spend at most only a night or two in Belize City before moving on. If you're heading west to Cayo, plan to make a stop at the wonderful Belize Zoo, about 30 mi (49 km) west of Belize City. Going north or west, you can visit the Community Baboon Sanctuary, as there is road access to Bermudian Landing, where the sanctuary is located, via either the Northern Highway or the Western Highway. Other areas of interest, including Crooked Tree Wildlife Sanctuary and Altun Ha Mayan site, within an hour or two of Belize City, are included in the North Belize chapter.

Belize Zoo

★ ☙ Turn a sharp corner on the jungle trail, and suddenly you're face-to-face with a black jaguar, the largest cat in the Western Hemisphere. The big cat growls a deep rumbling threat. You jump back, thankful that a strong but inconspicuous fence separates you and the jaguar.

One of the smallest, but arguably one of the best, zoos in the world, the Belize Zoo packs a lot into 29 acres. Containing more than 125 native species, the zoo has self-guided tours through several Belizean ecosystems—rain forest, lagoons, and riverine forest. Along with the rare black jaguar and the spotted jaguar, you'll see the country's four other wild cats: the puma, margay, ocelot, and jaguarondi. Perhaps the zoo's most famous resident is April, a Baird's tapir. This relative of the horse and rhino is known to locals as the mountain cow, and is also Belize's national animal. At the zoo you can also see jabiru storks, a harpy eagle, scarlet macaws, crocodiles, and many snakes, including the fer de lance.

The zoo owes its existence to the dedication and drive of one gutsy woman, Sharon Matola. An American who came to Belize as part of a film crew, Matola stayed on to care for some of the semi-tame animals used in the production. She opened the zoo in 1983 and in 1991 it moved to its present location. She's also an active environmentalist.

⚠ Besides touring the zoo, you can also hike or canoe through the adjacent 84-acre Tropical Education Center. The center is involved in a green iguana breeding project. Dormitory accommodations, with outdoor toilets, are available at the center for BZ$32 per person, and camping is BZ$13 per person; spiffier cabins go for BZ$70–BZ$75. Overnighters can take a nocturnal zoo tour for BZ$20. For Tropical Education Center accommodations, call in advance, and be aware that the lodging area is a long hike from the zoo. Meals are sometimes available, but you should be prepared to make your own meals. ⊠ *Western Hwy, 30 mi (49 km) west of Belize City* ☎ *220/8004* ⊕ *www.belizezoo. org* ⬚ *zoo admission BZ$15* ☽ *Daily 9–5.*

Community Baboon Sanctuary

☙ One of Belize's most fascinating wildlife conservation projects is the Community Baboon Sanctuary, which is actually a haven for black howler monkeys. Spanning a 20-mi (32-km) stretch of the Belize River, the reserve was established in 1985 by a group of local farmers. The howler monkey—an agile bundle of black fur with a deafening roar—was then zealously hunted throughout Central America and was facing extinction. Today the sanctuary is home to nearly 1,000 black howler monkeys, as well as numerous species of birds and mammals. Thanks to ongoing conservation efforts, you can see the howler monkeys in a number of other areas, including at Lamanai in northern Belize, along the Macal, Mopan, and Belize rivers in western Belize, and near Monkey River in southern Belize. Exploring the Community Baboon Sanctuary is easy, thanks to about 3 mi (5 km) of trails that start near a small museum and visitor center.

There are two routes leading to the sanctuary. If you are going north on the Northern Highway, turn west at Mile 13 onto the Burrell Boom Road. Go 3 mi (5 km) and turn right just beyond the new bridge over the Belize River. Signs to Bermudian Landing mark the turn. Stay on this road approximate 12 mi (20 km) to Bermudian Landing. If going west on the Western Highway, turn north on the Burrell Boom Road at a roundabout at Mile 15 ½ of the Western Highway, and go 9 mi (14 km) to the new bridge over the Belize River. Just before the bridge, turn left. Signs to Bermudian Landing mark the turn. Stay on this road approximate 12 mi (20 km) to Bermudian Landing.

You can also use the Burrell Boom Road as a short cut between the Northern and Western highways, avoiding Belize City. When taking this short cut, you stay on the Burrell Boom Road rather than turning toward Bermudian Landing. When on the Burrell Boom Road, you may want to stop at the **Central Prison Gift Shop** at the Central Prison, on the road to Burrell Boom about 3 mi (5 km) from the Western Highway. Prisoners at the "Hattieville Ramada" make small craft items and sell them at the gift shop. ⊠ *Community Baboon Sanctuary, 31 mi (50 km) northwest of Belize City* ☎ 220/2181 ⊒ *BZ$10* ⊙ *Daily 8–5.*

Monkey Bay Wildlife Sanctuary

ᘓ ⚠ Monkey Bay is a privately owned wildlife reserve on 1,070 acres near the Belize Zoo, established by Matt and Marga Miller in the 1980s. Here, you can canoe on the Sibun River, hike a 16 mi (31 km) nature trail along Indian Creek (only partly within Monkey Bay lands), or go bird-watching—some 250 bird species have been identified in the area. It has a natural history library with some 500 books and other reference materials, which visitors can use. The sanctuary also has educational and internship programs. In 2004 the reserve started a green iguana breeding and hatching project, to release young iguanas into the wild. Overnight accommodations are available, including tent camping (BZ$15 per person), a bunkhouse (BZ$20 a person), and rooms (BZ$35 per person) in the field research station. Meals are also available at times, if an educational group is in residence. Otherwise you'll have to make your own meals. Most of the reserve's facilities demonstrate high ecological awareness. For example, the bathrooms collect methane gas for cooking. Most programs are geared for overnight or multinight visits, but you can come on a day visit. Call in advance to see what activities or facilities may be available when you want to come. ⊠ *Mile 31, Western Hwy., 31 ½ mi (51 km) northwest of Belize City* Ⓓ*Monkey Bay Wildlife Sanctuary, Box 187, Belmopan* ☎ *820/3032* ⊕ *www.monkeybaybelize.org.*

Where to Stay & Eat

Just west of the Belize Zoo, the Western Highway is home to three similar restaurants in the same area: Cheers, JB's, and Amigos. Locals disagree as to which is the best, but, truth be told, they all have cold beer, unremarkable burgers, fries, and other snacks, and all have open-air seating, with decor heavy on T-shirts and other relics put up by tourists and British army troops.

$$ ╳⊞ **Belize R Us Resort.** New in 2005, Belize R Us brings a bit of refinement to howler monkey watching. The resort perches at the edge of the Belize River, and you can launch a canoe, kayak, or powerboat from the hotel's dock, or just laze about the riverside swimming pool and thatch palapa. The air-conditioned rooms are large, with custom-made mahogany furnishings. The on-site restaurant serves good Belizean food. Rates include pick-up from the international airport. ⊠ *Burrell Boom Village, 12 mi (20 km) from Baboon Sanctuary* ☎ *225/9029* ⊕ *www.belizerus. com* ⊅ *4 rooms* ⌂ *Restaurant, fans, cable TV, pool, boating, fishing, horseback riding* ▭ *MC, V.*

$ ╳⊞ **Cheers.** Rows and rows of T-shirts hanging from the ceiling rafters may sound more like a market than restaurant, but the shirts, hung by previous guests and decorated with funny comments and traveler memorabilia, lend a colorful atmosphere to this open-air restaurant. Breakfast is served all day, and the burritos, rice and beans, and burgers will fill you up. Out back is a garden with a nice collection of orchids. Cheers recently added three air-conditioned rental cabins, with high ceilings that make them seem bigger than they are. One has a king bed and two have queens. ⊠ *Mile 31 ¼, about 2 mi (3 km) west of Belize Zoo* ☎ *822/8014* ⊕ *www.cheersrestaurant.bz* ⊅ *3 cabins* ⌂ *Restaurant, fans, refrigerators, cable TV; no room phones* ▭ *MC, V.*

¢–$ △ **Nature Resort.** You're guaranteed to see (and hear) plenty of howler monkeys at this small, Belizean-owned lodge on the Belize River. Dr. Roy Young and family provide simple, clean accommodations convenient to the Baboon Sanctuary. The resort also rents canoes and horses for exploring the area. ⊠ *Bermudian Landing Village near Baboon Sanctuary visitor center* ☎ *610/1378* ⊅ *5 cabanas; 6 rooms, 2 with shared baths* ⌂ *Restaurant, fans, boating, horseback riding; no a/c in some rooms, no room phones, no room TVs* ▭ *MC, V.*

BELIZE CITY ESSENTIALS

Transportation

For more information about transportation and other essentials, *see* Smart Travel Tips A to Z *at* the back of the book.

BY AIR

Philip S. W. Goldson International Airport (BZE) is near Ladyville, 9 mi (14 km) north of the city. The international airport is served by American, Continental, Delta, TACA, and US Airways. Tropic Air and Maya Island Air have limited service to Guatemala, and Atlantic Air has service three days a week to Honduras. There is no service to Mexico. As of this writing, the runways at the international airport are being lengthened, and nonstop charter service from Europe is anticipated. In addition to international flights, a domestic terminal at the International Airport has flights on Maya Island Air and Tropic Air to Ambergris Caye and Caye Caulker and the coastal towns of Dangriga, Placencia, and Punta Gorda. The Belize City Municipal Airport, on the seafront about 1 mi (2 km) north of the city center, has domestic flights only; Maya Island Air and Tropic Air serve the same domestic destinations from here as from the international airport. However, fares from the municipal airport are about 10%–45% cheaper, depending on the destination, than similar flights departing from the international airport.

There is an Atlantic Bank ATM near the American Airlines check-in that accepts foreign ATM cards on the Visa Electron network.

Taxis to town from the international airport cost BZ$50. Some hotels in and near Belize City also offer transfers from the airport, usually for around the same price as taxi fare. However, a few provide it gratis *(check hotel listings in this chapter for details)*. If you're renting a car, just walk out the main terminal across the small parking lot to the line of rental car offices.

BY BUS

Belize City is the hub of the country's fairly extensive bus network, so there's service to most regions and to the Guatemalan and Mexican borders. Novelo's and its subsidiaries, Northern Transport and Southern Transport, formerly were the dominant carriers in the country, but Novelo's, following a series of financial problems, shut down operations in late 2005. Smaller carriers, of which there are nearly 100 around the country, scrambled to replace service. In early 2006 the Belize government announced that it would not grant another charter for a nationwide bus company. The country was divided into three zones—northern, western, and southern bus routes—with Belize City as the hub. The Novelo's terminal on West Collette Canal in Belize City reopened for use by small bus companies, and beginning in February 2006 about 75 buses were using this terminal. Bus terminals in Belmopan and Corozal are also expected to reopen. However, in other destinations, the Novelo's terminals did not reopen. As of this writing, there is bus service in most of Belize, but schedules change frequently, and, in general, there are fewer buses, so buses can be very crowded.

🚌 **Belize City Main Bus Terminal** ✉ W. Collet Canal, Belize City.

There's no point-to-point bus service within Belize City, but local nonexpress buses will stop and drop off most anywhere on the standard route.

For example, if you're going from West Collette Canal downtown to Brodie's supermarket on the Northern Highway just north of downtown you can be dropped off at or near Brodie's.

BY CAR

For car rental information *see* Car Rental *in* Smart Travel Tips A to Z at the front of the book.

TO & FROM BELIZE CITY There are only two highways to Belize City: the Northern Highway, which stretches to the Mexican border, 102 mi (165 km) away, and the Western Highway, which runs 81 mi (131 km) to Guatemala. Both are paved and in good condition. Signs guide you to nearby destinations such as the Belize Zoo.

IN BELIZE WITH A CAR Finding your way around the city itself can be confusing. The downtown area's narrow one-way streets, sometimes without identifying signs, often end abruptly due to construction work or an inconveniently located river. However, as part of its effort to become more user-friendly for cruise ship passengers, who now number about a million a year, Belize City has added green directional signs in the downtown area. Big directional signs also are now posted identifying key turns on the Northern and Western highways. With rare exceptions—the Princess Hotel & Casino is one—hotels in and near the city center offer mostly on-street parking, and you run the risk of a break-in if you leave the car overnight. Hotels in the suburbs north and west of the city usually have fenced or otherwise secured parking. Give your nerves a break and explore the city by taxi or on foot in safer sections like the Fort George area.

BY TAXI

Cabs cost BZ$7 for one person between any two points in the city, plus BZ$1 for each additional person. Outside the city, and from downtown to the suburbs, you're charged by the distance you travel. Traveling between the international airport and any point in the city (including the businesses and hotels along the Northern Highway) is BZ$50. There are no meters, so be sure to agree on a price before you leave. Authorized taxis have green license plates. You can find taxis at Market Square or by Swing Bridge, or larger hotels will call them for you. For pick-up, call Cinderella Plaza Taxi.
🚖 Cinderella Plaza Taxi ☎ 223/0371.

Contacts & Resources

BANKS & EXCHANGE SERVICES

U.S. dollars are accepted everywhere in Belize, but if you need to exchange another currency, you can do so at one of the five banks in Belize City: Alliance Bank, Atlantic Bank, Belize Bank, First Caribbean International Bank (formerly Barclays), and ScotiaBank. Most banks have their main offices on Albert Street in downtown Belize City, with smaller branches scattered around the city. Expect to be charged a 1%–2% fee if you exchange U.S. dollars. Fees for other currencies vary, but in general it's difficult and expensive to exchange currency other than U.S. dollars, even Canadian dollars and U.K. pounds. If you must convert currency, try the Belize Bank office at the international airport, or the main offices of banks in Belize City. Guatemalan and Mexican currencies can be easily exchanged at border areas.

The biggest employer in Belize—the Belize government—pays most employees on the 14th or 15th of the month, and on those days in particular banks in Belize are jammed, with customer lines often snaking around the outside of the building. Banks are also usually busy on Friday.

Though most banks in Belize City have ATMs, some machines won't accept cards issued outside Belize. If your ATM card has a Visa or MasterCard symbol, it will work in at least some Belize ATMs, and you can generally withdraw up to BZ$500 (US$250) a day. You get your cash in Belize dollars. The ATMs of Belize Bank are your best bet. With about 15 locations around the country, Belize Bank accepts foreign ATM cards on the CIRRUS, PLUS, and Visa Electron networks. Atlantic Bank ATMs accept foreign ATM cards with the Visa Electron symbol. First Caribbean branches in Belize City, Dangriga, and Belmopan also work with non-Belize ATM cards. You should have a four-digit PIN. Try not to depend on ATMs for all your cash, as ATM systems may be down, or the ATMs may be out of cash. Most banks offer cash advances on cards issued by Visa and MasterCard for a fee ranging from BZ$10 to BZ$30.

🏦 Banks **Alliance Bank** ⊠ Princess Margaret Dr. ☎ 223/5698. **Atlantic Bank** ⊠ Freetown Rd. ☎ 223/4123. **Belize Bank** ⊠ 60 Market Sq. ☎ 227/7132. **First Caribbean International Bank** ⊠ 21 Albert St. ☎ 227/7211. **ScotiaBank** ⊠ Albert St. ☎ 227/7027.

EMERGENCIES

Karl Heusner Memorial, a public hospital, and Belize Medical Associates, a private facility, both have 24-hour emergency rooms. Brodie's Pharmacy, at Market Square and on the Northern Highway, is open daily (hours vary). Community Drug, with several locations in Belize City, is open daily, and its Farmers' Market location is open daily 8–8, including holidays. Your hotel, the U.S. Embassy or other embassies, and the hospitals can refer you to a dentist.

🏥 Hospitals **Belize Medical Associates** ⊠ 5791 St. Thomas St. ☎ 223/0303. **Karl Heusner Memorial Hospital** ⊠ Princess Margaret Dr. ☎ 223/1548.

💊 Pharmacies **Brodie's Pharmacy** ⊠ Regent St. at Market Sq. ⊠ Mile 2 ½, Northern Hwy. **Community Drug** ⊠ Farmers' Market ⊠ 18 Albert St.

INTERNET, MAIL & SHIPPING

Most midlevel and upscale hotels in Belize City, and some budget spots, have Internet access, either wireless as at D'Nest Inn and the Great House, or in an Internet room as at the Radisson Fort George and Hotel Mopan. Cybercafés are now common in Belize City, as elsewhere in Belize. The problem is that these lightly capitalized businesses frequently are here today and gone tomorrow. Your best bet is just to scout the area where you're staying for an open Internet café. Rates vary, but typically you'll pay around BZ$5 for a half hour, BZ$8–BZ$10 for an hour. The main post office is inside the historic Paslow Building, just north of Swing Bridge. It's open weekdays 8–noon and 1–4:30. Mail service from Belize City to the United States and other countries is generally fast and reliable (airmail to the United States usually takes about five days). For faster service use DHL and FedEx; both have offices in Belize City.

📶 Contacts **Click & Sip Internet Café** ✉ Fort St. in Tourist Village ☎ 223/1305. **M-Business Solutions** ✉ 13 Cork St. in Great House ☎ 223/6766 ⊕ www.officeservices.bz.
📶 Overnight Services **DHL** ✉ 38 New Rd. ☎ 223/4350. **Federal Express** ✉ 32 Albert St. ☎ 227/3507.
📶 Post Office **Main Post Office** ✉ N. Front St. at Queen St. ☎ 223/2201.

TOURS

Although Belize City is centrally located for day trips to the northern cayes and to inland areas in the middle of the country, few travelers use it as a base. The reasons include the city's reputation for street crime and hassle, and, more recently, the influx of cruise ships bringing crowds of day-trippers who crowd the area around the Tourist Village and monopolize cave tubing and snorkeling trips and tours to Mayan ruins. Except for attractions within an hour or so of the city, such as the Belize Zoo and Baboon Sanctuary, it generally makes sense to move on from Belize City.

Even so, if you're staying in Belize City you can take day trips to Altun Ha, Crooked Tree Wildlife Sanctuary, and Lamanai. You can also do day trips to nearby islands, including St. George's, Chapel, Caulker, and Ambergris cayes, either on your own or with a local tour operator. Your hotel can also arrange day trips.

S&L Travel and Tours is an established local tour operator that offers trips to Lamanai, Xunantunich, and Altun Ha Mayan sites; Belize Zoo; the Mountain Pine Ridge; and the Sibun River for cave tubing. Belize Trips's Katie Valk, a transplanted New Yorker, can organize a custom trip to almost any place in the country and also to Tikal in Guatemala. With her hotel connections she can even get you a room when everything seems booked. She's also a warden for the U.S. Embassy.

Several other Belize City–based tour companies are listed below. Keep in mind that most Belize City tour operators focus more on the booming cruise ship market, which brings customers by the thousands, than on individual travelers. Some of these cruise ship tour operators, while generally reputable, have no office and operate with a Web site and a cell phone, meeting customers at the Tourist Village. Katie Valk at Belize Trips is an exception, as she focuses on individual and small group travel.

📶 **Katie Valk, Belize Trips** ✍ Box 1108, Belize City ☎ 223/0376 ⊕ www.belize-trips.com. **Cave-Tubing in Belize** ☎ 605/1573 ⊕ www.cave-tubing.com. **Coral Breeze Ltd.** ⊕ www.coralbreezelimited.com. **D iscovery Expeditions** ✉ 5916 Manatee Dr., Buttonwood Bay ☎ 223/0748 ⊕ www.discoverybelize.com. **Maya Travel Services** ✉ 42 Cleghorn St., Belize City ☎ 223/1623 ⊕ www.mayatravelservices.com. **S&L Travel and Tours** ✉ 91 N. Front St. ☎ 227/7593 ⊕ www.sltravelbelize.com.

VISITOR INFORMATION

The Belize Tourism Board, in new quarters at the New Horizons Building at Mile 3 ½, Northern Highway, is open Monday–Thursday 8–5, Friday 8–4:30.

🛈 **Belize Tourism Board** ✉ Lower Flat, New Horizon Investment Bldg., Mile 3 ½, Northern Hwy, (Box 325), Belize City ☎ 223/1913 or 800/624–0686 🖶 223/1943 ⊕ www.travelbelize.org.

The Cayes & Atolls

WORD OF MOUTH

"We just returned from a 10-day trip to Belize and we stayed in Ambergris Caye. Just about any place you go around there has fabulous snorkeling. You can book your trips when you get there, so don't fret. It is all very laid back. Try to get on with a smaller organization or individual so you don't end up on a boat with 10 other people who have never snorkeled before in their lives."

—JanieC

By Lan Sluder   **IMAGINE HEADING BACK TO SHORE** after a day of snorkeling, the white prow of your boat pointing up toward the billowing clouds, the sky's base darkening to deep lilac, spray from the green water pouring over you like warm rain. To the left, San Pedro's pastel buildings huddle among the palm trees like a detail from a Paul Klee canvas. To the right, the surf breaks in a white seam along the reef.

You can experience such adventures off the coast of Belize, where more than 400 cayes (pronounced "keys," as in the Florida Keys) dot the Caribbean Sea like punctuation marks in a long, liquid sentence. Most cayes lie inside the Barrier Reef, which allowed them to develop undisturbed by tides and winds that would otherwise have swept them away. The vast majority are uninhabited but for pelicans, brown- and red-footed boobies, and some creatures curiously named wish-willies (a kind of iguana). Island names are evocative and often humorous: there are Wee Wee Caye, Laughing Bird Caye, and—why ask why?—Bread and Butter Caye. Names can suggest the company you should expect: Mosquito Caye, Sandfly Caye, and Crawl Caye, which is supposedly infested with boa constrictors. Several, like Cockney Range or Baker's Rendezvous, simply express the whimsy or nostalgia of early British settlers.

Farther out to sea, between 30 mi and 60 mi (48 km and 96 km) off the coast, are the atolls, which are impossibly beautiful when viewed from the air. At their center the water is mint green: the white sandy bottom reflects the light upward and is flecked with patches of mangrove and rust-color sediment. Around the atoll's fringe the surf breaks in a white circle before the color changes abruptly to ultramarine as the water plunges to 3,000 feet.

History

Because of their strategic locations on trade routes between the Yucatán in the north and Honduras in the south, the Northern Cayes, especially Ambergris Caye and Caye Caulker, were long occupied by the Maya. Then, as now, the reef and its abundance of fish provided a valuable source of seafood.

The origin of Belize's atolls remains a mystery, but evidence suggests they grew from the bottom up, as vast pagodas of coral accumulated over millions of years. The Maya were perhaps the first humans to discover the atolls, but by the time the first Spanish explorers arrived in 1508, the Mayan civilization had already mysteriously collapsed and few remained on the islands.

In the 17th century, English pirates used the atolls as a hideout, plotting their attacks on unwary ships. The most famous battle in Belize history happened on September 10, 1798, when a ragtag band of buccaneers defeated a Spanish armada at the Battle of St. George's Caye.

The economy on the islands has ebbed and flowed, as pirates were replaced by wealthy plantation owners, who were eventually usurped by lobster fisherman. The atoll's first hotel opened in 1965 and soon began attracting divers from around the world. Today, tourism is by far the top industry.

TOP REASONS TO GO

SCUBA DIVING. Dive destinations are often divided into two broad categories—the reef and the atolls. Most reef diving is done on Belize's northern section, particularly off Ambergris Caye. For a truly dramatic experience, head to the atolls for some of the world's greatest diving opportunities. One caveat: the atolls and remote cayes, usually with just one or two small lodges, are far removed from the usual resort amenities such as shops and restaurants.

NO SHOES, NO SHIRT, NO PROBLEM. The cayes are all about relaxing, as if the concept of being laid-back was invented here. "Go Slow" street signs dot the sandy roads on many of the islands, and unlike some parts of the mainland, where strenuous outdoor activities such as rappelling, hiking, and caving are prime, here you spend a lot of time lazing in hammocks or sipping beer in a beachside palapa. The islands are where Belizeans come on vacation.

SNORKELING. You don't have to don scuba gear to enjoy the colorful fish and psychedelic vistas under the surface of the sea. Some of the best snorkeling in the Caribbean is off the coast of Belize. This is one of the few places in the world where you can swim with sharks (harmless nurse sharks) and stingrays. Because there isn't much shore snorkeling here, you'll jump in a boat for a short ride out to the reef or to patch coral—it all makes the experience that much more exciting.

GOOD EATS. Because they attract so many free-spending tourists, Ambergris Caye and Caye Caulker have more restaurants than anywhere else in Belize, and some of the best, too. If you love to eat—especially fresh seafood—go to the islands. You can gorge on lobster, conch, shrimp, and fish. At least on the larger islands, there are eateries for every taste and pocketbook, from local spots with sand floors to beach barbecues and pizzerias to sophisticated restaurants where you can enjoy the creative flavors of the cayes.

BEACHES. They're not your typical wide, sandy spreads, but they're classic postcard material nonetheless, with windswept cocopalms facing expanses of turquoise, green, and purple. The quality and beauty of beaches on the cayes vary—some of the best are on small, remote cayes, like South Water. In any case, you'll usually have a front-row seat, because in Belize's cayes, beach hotels in all price ranges (with only a handful of exceptions) are actually right on the beach.

EXPLORING THE CAYES & ATOLLS

Island hopping between the Ambergris Caye, Caye Caulker, and Belize City is simple, though getting to other cayes can be more complicated. Caye Caulker Water Taxi Association water taxis—fast, open boats that hold 30 to 50 passengers—regularly connect Ambergris Caye and Caye

Caulker, and on trips to and from Belize City, also stop on demand at Caye Chapel and St. George's Caye. Other than that, you're generally left to your own devices to find transportation between islands. You can charter a small boat with driver—typically BZ$400 and up a day—or negotiate a one-way or round-trip price. Remember that distances between islands in Belize often are substantial. For example, it's more than 50 miles from San Pedro, Ambergris Caye, to the southern tip of Turneffe Atoll. Even at a rapid 20 mph clip, that's two and a half hours one way. You'll have little luck renting a powerboat on your own, as boat owners are reluctant to risk their crafts in the hands of someone without local knowledge of Belize's tricky waters.

If you're diving or snorkeling, a speedboat will take you to your destination. Power generally comes from two hefty outboards mounted on the back, and with the throttle open it's an exhilarating ride. Sit in the middle if you don't want to get splashed.

You'll generally get around by golf cart, bike, or on foot. Ambergris Caye is the only island where you'll see cars, though you can only rent a golf cart or a bike on this or any other island. Around San Pedro, taxis are usually minivans, though some hotels will transport you in a jumbo golf cart. When you're going to remote areas of North Ambergris, your resort will often provide transportation via water taxi or a boat. On Caye Caulker, the only taxis are golf carts.

When to Go

Island weather tends to be a little different from that on the mainland. Although weather varies depending on the island's location (those in the far south get more rain than those in the north), the cayes are generally drier than the mainland. Storm squalls come up suddenly, but just as quickly they're gone, leaving sunny skies behind. Keep in mind that if you see rain in the forecast for Belize City, this doesn't mean it'll necessarily be wet in San Pedro.

Health & Safety

Visiting Ambergris Caye is like a vacation in Florida—you'll face few health concerns worse than sunburn. San Pedro's water, from a treated municipal water supply, is safe to drink. On Caye Caulker, the water, usually from brackish shallow wells, often smells of sulfur. To be safe, drink only bottled water. On other remote cayes, the water usually comes from cisterns. Stick to the bottled stuff, unless you're assured the water potable. At times, the sand flies on Caye Caulker and some remote cayes can be irksome—apply baby oil or another oily lotion liberally to your feet and ankles to keep them at bay. Insect repellent with at least 30% DEET helps ward off mosquitoes.

In terms of crime risk, the cayes are among the safest areas of Belize. However, petty thefts do happen, and there are drugs on both Caye Caulker and Ambergris Caye. Ignore any offers to buy drugs.

About the Restaurants

Ambergris Caye has the biggest selection of restaurants of any destination in Belize, and among them are some of the country's best. They range from simple beach barbecue joints to upscale, sophisticated eateries, where, especially if you eat lobster, you can easily spend BZ$100 a person, including a drink or two. You have a wide choice of kinds of food on Ambergris, too: seafood, of course, but also steak, pizza, sushi, tapas, Chinese, Thai, Mexican, and French.

Caye Caulker has several small bistros where fish arrives at your table fresh from the ocean, and sometimes you find yourself eating with your feet in the sand. On other islands, you're usually limited to eating at your dive lodge or resort.

Many restaurants have sea views. Some are in thatch palapas, and others are in concrete or wood buildings that have windows open to catch the breeze. On Caulker and Ambergris cayes you won't have a problem finding places serving late-night snacks or breakfast in the morning, including the traditional Belizean breakfast of fruit, fry jacks, eggs (from brown eggs only), and delicious Belizean bacon or sausage, washed down with good Guatemalan coffee and fresh-squeezed OJ. On remote cayes and the atolls, you'll probably be at the mercy of your hotel's meal schedule, with specified hours for each meal.

The restaurants (all of which are indicated by a ✕) that we list are the cream of the crop in each price category. Properties indicated by a ✕▣ are lodging establishments whose restaurant warrants a special trip.

About the Hotels
The more budget-oriented cayes, such as Tobacco and Caulker, have mostly small hotels and simple cabins, usually built of wood and typically without any amenities beyond a fan or two. Caye Caulker, for example, has only one hotel with a swimming pool. At the other end, notably on Ambergris Caye, are deluxe condotels (condo developments where individual owners let their units on a daily basis through a management company) and an increasing number of vacation villas, usually rented by the week. Some of these are extremely upscale, with 5,000-plus square feet of luxury and the latest toys, whirlpools, plasma TVs, DVD players, and custom kitchens. Nearly all the hotels on Ambergris Caye have air-conditioning, and a majority also have swimming pools. Air-conditioning is also available at nearly all the remote caye lodges, except at the very low end.

Regardless of which caye you're staying on, lodgings have several things in common: they're small (often just five or six rooms), low-rise, and almost always on the water.

One lodging category, sadly, is becoming an endangered species: the thatch cabana or thatch hut. Why are there so few of these traditional island lodgings still around? They're easy targets for tropical storms and hurricanes; the thatch is expensive to maintain; and they're havens for creepie crawlies.

Off-season (typically just after Easter to around Thanksgiving), most island hotels, except some budget hotels, reduce rates by around 30% to 40%.

The lodgings (all indicated with a 🏠) that we list are the cream of the crop in each price category. We always list the facilities that are available—but we don't specify whether they cost extra: when pricing accommodations, always ask what's included. Properties indicated by a ✕🏠 are lodging establishments whose restaurant warrants a special trip.

WHAT IT COSTS In Belize Dollars					
	$$$$	**$$$**	**$$**	**$**	**¢**
RESTAURANTS	over $50	$25–$50	$15–$25	$8–$15	under $8
HOTELS	over $500	$300–$500	$200–$300	$100–$200	under $100

Restaurant prices are per person for a main course at dinner. Hotel prices are for two people in a standard double room, including tax and service.

About the Water Activities

The cayes are all about diving, snorkeling, fishing, sea kayaking, windsurfing, sailing, and even parasailing. Diving and snorkeling are excellent on the barrier reef and truly world-class around the atolls. There's great fishing, whether for bonefish, tarpon, or permit on the flats, or snapper, grouper or barracuda near the reef, or for sailfish, marlin, tuna, and other big fish in the blue water outside the reef. Caye Caulker is known for its excellent windsurfing, especially in spring, and the Belize cayes are famous for kayaking. Boating and sailing are good in the protected waters inside the reef. Beach swimming, however, is only fair in many areas because of the shallow waters, mucky bottoms, and large amounts of sea grass near shore. Still, most resorts have a swimming area off a pier or on a part of a sandy beach where they've cleared the sea grass. The Caribbean here is usually crystal clear and around 80°F.

Numbers in the margin correspond to points of interest on the Cayes, Atolls, & Barrier Reef map.

AMBERGRIS CAYE & SAN PEDRO

❶ *35 mi (56 km) northeast of Belize City.*

At 25 mi (40 km) long and 4½ mi (7 km) wide, Ambergris is the queen of the cayes. On early maps it was often referred to as Costa de Ambar, or the Amber Coast, a name supposedly derived from the blackish substance secreted by sperm whales—ambergris—that washes up on the beaches. Here the reef is just a few hundred yards from shore, making access to dive sites extremely easy: the journey by boat takes as little as 10 minutes. Coast and coral are farther apart as you head south, which means a greater dependence on weather. Because Ambergris Caye was the first to cater to those hoping to witness Belize's undersea world, it's generally superior in the number of dive shops, experience of dive masters, and range of equipment and facilities it offers. San Pedro even has Belize's only hyperbaric chamber and an on-site doctor to tend divers with the bends. Most dive shops are attached to hotels, where the quality of dive masters, equipment, and facilities can vary considerably.

GREAT ITINERARIES

It's difficult to recommend itineraries on the cayes, because what you do and where you go depends greatly on the island where you're staying. If you're on a remote caye or atoll, your activities and itineraries are defined partly by your interests (whether it's diving, fishing, or just lazing in a hammock), and by the lodge's daily schedule (or lack of one). Your basic itinerary might go a little like this: dive, eat, sleep, and dive.

On the other hand, if you're on Ambergris Caye or Caye Caulker, you can set your itinerary around a wide choice of daily island activities, day trips to the mainland, snorkeling or diving on the barrier reef, and day trips to the atolls.

IF YOU HAVE 5 DAYS ON AMBERGRIS CAYE OR CAYE CAULKER

Spend your first full day getting to know the island. On Ambergris Caye, rent a golf cart or bike and explore the north and south ends of the caye. Have a beach picnic or enjoy one of the many good restaurants. If you're on Caulker, which is much smaller, you can explore on foot, or, if you prefer, on a bike or in a golf cart. On your second day on either caye, take a boat trip to Hol Chan Marine Reserve and Shark-Ray Alley for snorkeling, and spend the rest of the day on the beach or just hanging out in San Pedro town or Caulker village. On your third day, take a full-day dive or snorkel trip to Lighthouse Reef, with stops at the Blue Hole and Half Moon Caye. If you're not planning to spend a few days on the mainland this trip, take a tour to the Lamanai Mayan ruins, which includes an exciting boat ride up the

New River, on your fourth day; or, for some pampering, take one of the combined day trips to Maruba Spa and the Altun Ha Mayan site. If you do plan a mainland stay, then use Day 4 to try windsurfing on Caye Caulker, parasailing on Ambergris Caye, golfing on Caye Chapel, bonefishing in the flats, or sea or lagoon kayaking. On your final day, take a relaxing daylong catamaran snorkeling trip with a beach barbecue.

IF YOU HAVE 5 DAYS ON A REMOTE CAYE OR ATOLL

On arrival, take off your shoes, take a deep breath, grab a cold drink, and relax. This is what the islands are all about, with the cooling trade winds in your hair and no decisions to make except whether you want the grilled fish or the lobster for dinner. If you're on a dive package, you typically do two to three dives a day, weather permitting. On a fishing package, you'll be out on the flats or the reef all day every day. If you're not tied to a package, get up early and watch the sunrise on your first full day. Then spend the day exploring the island: go swimming, spend some time beachcombing, or snorkel off the shore. On your second day, take a dive or snorkel trip to the nearest atoll. On the third day, hire a guide and try your hand at fishing for bonefish or permit on the flats. On your fourth day, take a catamaran sail along the barrier reef, with stops for snorkeling and a barbecue on a deserted beach. On your final day, go kayaking around the island and relax on the beach.

HOW TO CHOOSE A DIVE MASTER

Most dive masters in Belize are former anglers who began diving on the side and ended up doing it full time. The best have an intimate knowledge of the reef and a superb eye for coral and marine life.

When choosing a dive master or dive shop, first check the Web. Participants on forums and newsgroups such as ⊕ www.ambergriscaye.com and ⊕ www.gocayecaulker.com field many questions on diving and dive shops in Belize. On islands where there are multiple dive shops, spend some time talking to dive masters to see which ones make you feel most comfortable. Find out about their backgrounds and experience, as well as the actual crew that would be going out with you. Are they dive masters, instructors, or just crew? Get a sense of how the dive master feels about reef and sea life conservation.

Besides questions about costs and equipment, ask:

- How many people, maximum, go out on your dive trips?
- Is there a minimum number of divers before you'll make the trip?
- What's the ratio of divers to dive staff?
- What dive sites are your favorites, and why?
- What kind of boat do you have, and how long does it take to get where we're going?
- Who is actually in the water with the divers?
- What kind of safety and communications equipment is on the boat?
- What's the procedure for cancellation in case of bad weather?
- How do you decide if you're going out or not?
- If you're not comfortable with the answers, or if the dive shop just doesn't pass your sniff test, move on.

Water Activities & Tours

Scuba Diving & Snorkeling

Dives off Ambergris are usually single tank at depths of 50 feet–80 feet, allowing about 35 minutes of bottom time. Most companies offer two single-tank dives per day, one in the morning and one in the afternoon. Snorkeling generally costs BZ$50–BZ$60 per person for two or three hours or BZ$100–BZ$200 for a day trip, including lunch. In addition, if you go to Hol Chan Marine Reserve there's a BZ$20 park fee. Diving trips run BZ$70–BZ$80 for a single-tank dive, BZ$100–BZ$130 for a double-tank dive, BZ$80–BZ$90 for a one-tank night dive, and BZ$300–BZ$400 for day trips with dives to Turneffe Atoll or Lighthouse Reef.

Fodor'sChoice
★ The reef's focal point for diving and snorkeling near Ambergris Caye is the **Hol Chan Marine Reserve** (Maya for "little channel"), 4 mi (6 km) from San Pedro at the southern tip of Ambergris. It's a 20-minute boat ride from the island. Hol Chan is a break in the reef about 100 feet wide

Bay of Chetumal

BACALAR CHICO MARINE & NATURE RESERVE

COROZAL DISTRICT

Deer Caye

1 **Ambergris Caye**

4 **Cayo Espanto**

Marco Gonzales

San Pedro

Cangrejo Caye

HOL CHAN MARINE RESERVE

Santana

Altun Ha

Hick's Cayes

2 **Caye Caulker**

CAYE CAULKER MARINE RESERVE

3 **Caye Chapel**

B a r r i e r   R e e f

C a r i b b e a n   S e a

Montego Caye

5 **St. George's Caye**

Crawl Caye

Three Corner Caye

BELIZE

Ladyville

Belize City

Drowned Cayes

Northern Cayes

Western Hwy.

Belize Harbour

Water Caye

Douglas Caye

Blackbird Caye

7 **Lighthouse Reef Atoll**

Northern Lagoon

Middle Long Caye

Turneffe Atoll **6**

Calabash Caye

Blue Hole

Southern Lagoon

Inner or Main Channel

Alligator Caye

Deadman's Cayes

Long Caye

HALF MOON CAYE NATIONAL MONUMENT

Gales Point

Colson Cayes

Big Caye Bokel

Mullins River

Southern Long Caye

Mosquito Caye

Sandfly Cayes

Fly Range

Silk Cayes

Silk Grass

Dangriga

Columbus Caye

Cross Caye

STANN CREEK DISTRICT

Coco Plum Caye

Hopkins

Twin Cayes

Man-of-War Caye

Tobacco Reef

GLOVER'S REEF MARINE RESERVE

All Pines

Sittee Point

8 **Tobacco Caye**

9 **South Water Caye**

10 **Glover's Reef Atoll**

Bread & Butter Caye

Wee Wee Caye

Northeast Caye

Norval Caye

Southwest Caye

SOUTH WATER CAYE MARINE RESERVE

Maya Beach

Seine Bight

Placencia

Lark Caye

Big Creek

LAUGHING BIRD CAYE MARINE RESERVE

TOLEDO DISTRICT

Laughing Bird Caye

PORT HONDURAS MARINE RESERVE

Sapodilla Cayes

Gulf of Honduras

SAPODILLA CAYES MARINE RESERVE

KEY	
◿	*Dive Site*
▲	*Mayan Site*

70

Corozal District

Northern Highway

0 ___ 10 miles

0 ___ 10 kilometers

and 20 feet–35 feet deep, through which tremendous volumes of water pass with the tides.

The 3-square-mi (8-square-km) park has a miniature Blue Hole, a 12-foot-deep cave whose entrance often attracts the fairy basslet, an iridescent purple-and-yellow fish frequently seen here. The reserve is also home to a large moray eel population.

Varying in depth from 50 feet to 100 feet, Hol Chan's canyons lie between buttresses of coral running perpendicular to the reef, separated by white, sandy channels. You may find tunnel-like passageways from one canyon to the next, and not knowing what's in the next "valley" as you come over the hill can be pretty exciting.

Because fishing is off-limits here, divers can see abundant marine life, including spotted eagle rays. There are throngs of squirrelfish, butterfly fish, parrot fish, and queen angelfish, as well as Nassau groupers, barracuda, and large shoals of yellowtail snappers. Altogether, more than 160 species of fish have been identified in the marine reserve, along with 40 species of coral, and 5 kinds of sponges. Hawksbill, loggerhead, and green turtles have also been found here, along with spotted and common dolphins and West Indian manatees.

Shark-Ray Alley is a sandbar within Hol Chan where you can snorkel alongside nurse sharks and stingrays (which gather here to be fed) and even larger numbers of day-trippers from San Pedro and from cruise ships. Sliding into the water is a small feat of personal bravery—the sight of sharks and rays brushing past is spectacular yet daunting. A night dive here is a special treat: bioluminescence causes the water to light up, and many nocturnal animals emerge, such as octopus and spider crab. Because of the strong current you'll need above-average swimming skills, especially at night. ⊠ *Southern tip of Ambergris Caye* ⊠ *BZ$20.*

The **Belize Barrier Reef,** the second-longest barrier reef in the world, is off the eastern shore of Ambergris Caye. From the island, you see the coral reef as an almost unbroken chain of white surf. Inside the reef, the water is clear and shallow, and the reef itself is a beautiful living wall formed by billions of small coral polyps. Just outside the reef, the seabed drops sharply, and from a distance the water looks dark blue or purple. ⊠ *½ mi (1 km) east of Ambergris Caye.*

Development on Ambergris continues relentlessly, but the far north of the island remains pristine, or close to it. At the top of the caye, butting up against Mexico, **Bacalar Chico Marine & Nature Reserve** spans 41 square mi (105 square km) of land, reef, and sea. Here you may cross paths with whitetail deer, ocelots, saltwater crocodiles, and, according to some reports, pumas and jaguars. There are excellent diving, snorkeling, and fishing opportunities, especially off Rocky Point, and a small visitor center to get you oriented. You'll need a boat and a guide to take you here. An all-day snorkel trip to Bacalar Chico costs around BZ$170. ⊠ *North end of Ambergris Caye* ⊠ *BZ$10.*

CHARTERS,
LESSONS &
EQUIPMENT

Bottom Time Dive Spot (⊠ Barrier Reef Dr. at Holiday Hotel, San Pedro ☎ 226/2634 🖷 226/4263 ⊕ www.sanpedroholiday.com/dive.html) offers a range of local dive and snorkel trips. **Amigos del Mar** (⊠ Off Barrier Reef Dr. near Mayan Princess Hotel ☎ 226/2706 ⊕ amigosdive. com) is perhaps the island's most consistently recommended dive operation. It offers a range of local dives as well as trips to Turneffe Atoll and Lighthouse Reef in a fast 48-foot dive boat. The well-regarded **Gaz Cooper's Dive Belize** (⊠ 5 mi north of town at Playa Blanca Resort ☎ 226/3202 ⊕ www.divebelize.com) boasts that it has the island's smallest dive operation. Operated by Elmer "Patojo" Paz, who has nearly 20 years of diving experience, **Patojo's Scuba Center** (⊠ At Tides Hotel at the north end of San Pedro ☎ 226/3202 ⊕ www.ambergriscaye. com/tides/dive.html) is a small dive shop with a good reputation.

Many dive shops and resorts have diving courses. A one-day basic familiarization course costs between BZ$250 and BZ$350. A four-day PADI open-water certification course costs BZ$700–BZ$800. One popular variant is a referral course, where the academic and pool training is done at home, but not the required dives. The cost for two days is about BZ$450–BZ$550. Prices for dive courses vary a little from island to island, generally being a little less expensive on Caye Caulker. However, even prices on Ambergris Caye, which tends to have higher costs for most activities, are a little lower than on the mainland.

If you're staying on Ambergris Caye, Glover's Reef is out of the question for a day trip by boat. Even with perfect weather—which it often isn't in winter—a trip to Lighthouse Reef takes between two and three hours. Turneffe is more accessible, though it's still a long and costly day trip, and you're unlikely to reach the atoll's southern tip, which has the best diving.

LIVE-ABOARD
DIVE BOATS

If you want to hit the best dive spots in Belize and dive a lot—five or six dives a day—live-aboard dive boats may be your best bet. Live-aboards concentrate on dives around Belize's three atolls—Lighthouse, Turneffe, and Glover's—with most dives at Lighthouse and Turneffe. The boats depart from Belize City.

Expect to pay about BZ$3,000–BZ$5,000 for six days of diving. That price includes all dives, meals, airport transfers, and stateroom accommodations on the dive boat. It does not include airfare to Belize, tips, alcoholic beverages, equipment rentals, Nitrox, marine park fees, and incidentals.

The itinerary of the **Belize Aggressor** (☎ 985/305–2628 or 800/348–2628 ⊕ www.aggressor.com) has passengers embarking in Belize City on a Saturday and spending time until the next Friday at Turneffe and Lighthouse atolls, with as many as five or six dives each day. This orderly operation is run by a khaki-clad crew of five, who can accommodate up to 18 passengers. It uses a 120-foot luxury cruiser powered by twin 500-horsepower engines and equipped with ultramodern communication systems. Staterooms are spacious double-berth cabins brightened with sky-blue fabrics, lightwood trim, and multiple windows instead of small portholes. All have private baths, TVs and VCRs, plus individual climate controls.

Nekton Diving Cruises (☎ 954/463–9324 or 800/899–6753 ⊕ www. nektoncruises.com) has weekly departures from Belize City on most Saturdays from November to May on the *Nekton Pilot.* The 80-foot craft's twin hull makes it appear like it's walking across the water on four big feet. Based on the same technology that allows oil platforms to operate in the rough waters of the North Sea, the design is supposed to provide more stability and reduce the chance of seasickness. On board are a sundeck and hot tub. Most Nekton cruises visit Turneffe and Lighthouse atolls, but about a third of them, called Belize South itineraries, also include dives at Glover's Reef Atoll.

Peter Hughes Diving (☎ 305/669–9391 or 800/932–6237 ⊕ www. peterhughes.com) runs trips on the 138-foot *Sun Dancer II,* which can hold up to 20 passengers in 10 staterooms. It departs from Belize City on Saturday afternoon and moors at either Turneffe or Lighthouse atoll. For the next six days, divers explore these two atolls, diving as many as five times a day. The ship moves two or three times a day.

Sailing

Belize will probably never rival the British Virgin Islands for sailing. The shallow water kicks up a lot of chop, and hidden coral heads and tidal currents are dangerous for even those familiar with the area. When you charter a boat you have to stay inside the barrier reef, but there's a lot of beautiful territory to explore.

CHARTERS, **TMM Belize** (⊠ Coconut Dr., San Pedro ☎ 226/3026 or 800/633–0155
LESSONS & ⊕ www.sailtmm.com), which has a small fleet of catamarans (37 feet–47
EQUIPMENT feet) and one monohull, has weeklong bareboat and captained charters out of San Pedro. It has another base in Placencia. Rates vary, depending on boat type and time of year, but range from BZ$6,000 to more than BZ$16,000 a week, not including provisions, cruising fee (BZ$30 per person), and incidentals. Skippers and cooks are each an additional BZ$200 per day. Split among three to eight people, the prices are competitive with hotel rates.

Lady Sharon (⊠ O'Farrel House, next to Belize Yacht Club, San Pedro ☎ 226/2292 ⊕ www.ambergriscaye.com/ladysharon) is a 65-foot catamaran day cruiser (BZ$100, including lunch and rum punch). A sunset cruise, from 5 to 7 PM, is BZ$90; sometimes there's live music. You can also book the boat for a day trip to the Blue Hole for snorkeling; the cost is BZ$350.

Discover Cruises (⊠ San Pedro ☎ 226/2965 ⊕ www.traveltourbelize. com) has trips on a catamaran, with snorkeling and a stop either at Caye Caulker or a small island for a beach barbecue. The boat leaves at 9 AM and returns at 4 PM. Cost is BZ$150. Private and group charters are also available.

El Gato (⊠ San Pedro ☎ 226/2264 ⊕ www.ambergriscaye.com/elgato) has day cruises to Caye Caulker, with two stops for snorkeling, for BZ$100.

Fishing

Although southern Belize, especially Placencia, is the main sportfishing center in Belize, Ambergris Caye also has good opportunities for flats, reef, and deep-sea fishing. Expect to pay about BZ$450 to BZ$500 for one or two people for a day of flats fishing for bonefish, permit, or tarpon, including a guide and a boat. Reef fishing for snapper, grouper, barracuda, and other reef fish costs around BZ$450–BZ$500 a day, including a guide and a powerboat. Deep-sea fishing outside the reef for billfish, sailfish, wahoo, and tuna runs around BZ$1,200 to BZ$1,400 a day, depending on the number in your party and the size of the boat. **El Pescador** (☎ 226/2398 or 800/242–2017 ⊕ www.elpescador.com) is an upscale fishing lodge on North Ambergris. It offers fishing packages including room, meals, boat, and guide, starting at BZ$2,600 per person, double occupancy, for three nights.

For fishing that's easier on the pocketbook, you can fish for snapper, barracuda, and other fish from piers and docks on the island. No license is required. Buy bait, hooks, and tackle at small fishing tackle shacks on the beachfront in San Pedro. You can also wade out in the flats near shore on North Ambergris, just north of the river channel, and try your luck with bonefish. (Keep an eye out for the occasional crocodile.) You'll catch more with a guide and boat, but fishing on your own is inexpensive fun.

FISHING GUIDES   Here are some well-established and widely recommended local fishing guides:

George Bradley (✉ Back St., San Pedro ☎ 226/2179) specializes in fly-fishing for bonefish. **Pete Graniel** (✉ San Pedro ☎ 226/2584) has a 30-foot boat that's good for trolling. **Fishing San Pedro** (✉ Coconut's Internet Café, San Pedro ☎ 226/2835 ⊕ www.fishingsanpedro.com) is a fishing- guide service run by Steve De'Maio that works with about a half-dozen guides on the island.

Parasailing

Parasailing is terrific around Ambergris Caye. As you soar over the vodka-clear waters, suspended from a parachute and pulled by a speedboat, you can see rays, sharks, and other sea life.

Fido's Parasail Fun Sports (✉ Beachfront at Fido's on Barrier Reef Dr., San Pedro ☎ 226/3513 ⊕ www.belizeparasailing.com) has parasailing setups for one, two, or three persons. Singles pay BZ$140, doubles BZ$240, and triples BZ$330.

Windsurfing & Kite Surfing

Caye Caulker is better known as a windsurfing destination, perhaps because it attracts a younger crowd than Ambergris Caye, but the winds are equally good and consistent off Ambergris Caye. February through July sees the windiest conditions, with winds 12 to 20 knots most days. Kite surfing, combing a windsurfing-type board pulled by a large kite, is also available on Ambergris Caye.

Sailsports Belize (✉ San Pedro ☎ 226/4488 ⊕ www.sailsportsbelize. com) offers windsurfing instruction at BZ$90 an hour, with equipment

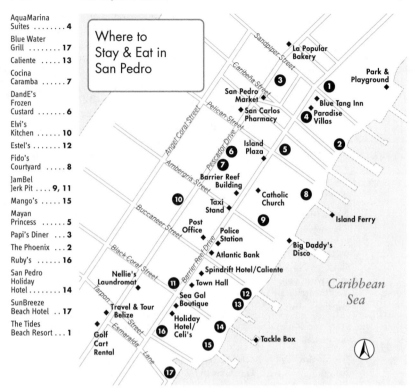

Where to Stay & Eat in San Pedro

rental at BZ$40 to BZ$50 an hour, BZ$130 to BZ$150 a day, or BZ$420 to BZ$500 a week. Five hours of intensive kite surfing instruction costs BZ$600, and your initial kite-board rental, with an instructor on hand to assist, is BZ$120 for two hours. After that, kite surfing equipment rentals are BZ$60 for a half day and BZ$90 for a full day.

Jet Skis

Karibbean Water Sports (✉ South Beach Marina, San Pedro ☎ 226/3205 ⊕ www.southbeachmarina.net) has Yamaha Wave Runners for rent for BZ$200–BZ$270 an hour.

Exploring Ambergris Caye & San Pedro

A few years ago, when you flew into the caye's main town, San Pedro, your plane's wingtips would have nearly brushed the laundry hanging in people's backyards. And once you landed, you could walk from one end of town to the other in 10 minutes. Today you need a bike just to get from one end of the airstrip to the other. Every year there are more cars, more souvenir shops, and more tourists. Ambergris will never be like Cancún, but it's the most developed—some would say overdeveloped—of the cayes. Still, only one street is paved (the rest are sand), transportation is most commonly by golf cart and bike or by foot, and the tallest building is just three stories.

At its core, the town remains unchanged: a couple of rows of brightly painted wooden houses flanked by the ocean on one side and the lagoon on the other. Old men lean over their balconies in the evenings to watch the world go by, and many people stroll down the roads barefoot. Stores and restaurants still have names like Lily's, Celi's, or Lee's. With a population of around 4,400, San Pedro is a small, friendly, and prosperous village. It has one of the country's highest literacy rates and an admirable level of awareness about the reef's fragility.

Where to Stay & Eat

One of your biggest decisions in Ambergris Caye will be choosing a place to stay. There are three basic options: in or near the town of San Pedro, in the South Beach or South End area beyond town, or on North Ambergris, beyond the river channel. Access to restaurants, bars, and other activities is easiest in and around San Pedro. Accommodations in town are generally simple and reasonably priced (BZ$30–BZ$300), but rooms on the main streets can be noisy, not so much from cars as from late-night revelers.

For silence and sand, head out of town for resort-style accommodations. To get more privacy, consider the South End. Though it, too, is developing rapidly, it's still less hectic than in town, and it's only a golf cart or taxi ride away.

If you really want to get away, choose the more remote North Ambergris, which is reached mainly by water taxi. A new bridge across the river channel, which opened in early 2006, is destined to make the north more accessible. The plan is that only golf carts, bikes, and pedestrians will be permitted to cross the bridge (though some worry that eventually cars and trucks will also be allowed to use it).

With the exception of a few budget places, nearly all of the resorts on the island are on the sea. Most are small, under 20 or 30 rooms, and all are three stories or less in height. Many are managed by the owners. The newer resorts and hotels are on North Ambergris Caye, of which the farthest-north resort, Salamander, is about 10 mi (17 km) north of San Pedro or on the South End, where the most distant resorts are around 2½ mi (4 km) south of town.

During the off-season (May–November), lodging properties often have walk-in rates that are up to a third less than advertised rates. But you'll usually have to ask for them, as otherwise you'll pay the regular rate.

CONDOTELS Besides full-service hotels and resorts, the island has condotels, which are individually owned condos managed by an on-site management company. The condo units usually are offered on a nightly basis, like a hotel, and in most cases the properties have full kitchens and most of the amenities of a regular hotel, except perhaps a restaurant.

VACATION HOMES Ambergris Caye has dozens of homes that can be rented on a weekly basis. These range from simple two-bedroom cottages that go for BZ$1,000–BZ$2,000 a week to luxurious four- or five-bedroom villas, which might rent for BZ$5,000–BZ$10,000 or more weekly. In most cases credit cards are not accepted. **Caye Management** (☎ 226/3077 ⊕ www.cayemanagement.com) is the island's oldest and largest rental management company.

Fairly new to the island are clusters of upscale homes or villas that are offered for weekly, and sometimes nightly, rental. These luxury homes, often with 4,000 to 5,000 square feet of space, or more, typically have a shared pool and other resortlike amenities. Although they usually have no restaurant, they may offer food service prepared by a chef and delivered to the guests in the homes.

TIME-SHARES Time-shares have been on the island for years. New to the island are upscale "fractional ownership" or "residential club" resorts, which sell longer-term memberships and rights to use the property, typically for two, four, or six months a year. One of these, Sueno del Mar, opened on North Ambergris in 2006.

RESTAURANTS Ambergris Caye has the largest and most diverse selection of restaurants in the country. Here you can buy cheap tacos or grilled chicken from a street vendor, eat barbecued fish on the beach, or, at the other end, dine on ceviche, lobster, and steak at upscale eateries. Even the most upmarket spots have a casual atmosphere, some with sand floors and screenless windows open to catch the breezes from the sea.

The largest concentration of restaurants is in town, but many, including some of the best on the island, are opening on the South End and on North Ambergris.

San Pedro

★ $$–$$$$ ✕ **DandE's Frozen Custard.** Dan and Eileen (DandE, get it?) Jamison, who used to run the local weekly paper, the *San Pedro Sun* opened this custard and sorbet shop in 2005. For something with an island flavor, try the mango sorbet or the sour sop frozen custard. ⊠ *Pescador Dr. next to Cocina Caramba* ☎ 608/9100 ▭ *No credit cards* ⊘ *Closed Wed.*

★ $$–$$$$ ✕ **Elvi's Kitchen.** Initially, Elvi Staines sold burgers from the window of her house in 1974. Soon she added a few tables on the sand under a flamboyant tree. A quarter century later the sandy floor is still here, and the tree remains (cut back to fit inside the roof), but everything else is changed. Enter through massive mahogany doors and you'll be tended to by a staff of a couple dozen. The burgers are still good, but Elvi's now specializes in upmarket dishes such as shrimp in watermelon sauce (BZ$34) or crab claws with garlic butter (BZ$75). For dessert, don't pass on the coconut pie. ⊠ *Pescador Dr. near Ambergris St.* ☎ 226/2176 ▭ *AE, MC, V* ⊘ *Closed Sun.*

$$–$$$ ✕ **Blue Water Grill.** Close to the beach and perpetually busy, this restaurant's seats are on a raised, covered deck with views of the barrier reef a few hundred yards away. The emphasis here is on seafood, but there's wood-fired pizza and pastas, and Tuesday and Thursday are sushi

nights. The crispy coconut shrimp sticks are great. ⊠ *Beachfront at SunBreeze Hotel* ☎ *226/3347* ⊟ *AE, MC, V.*

$–$$$ ✕ **Caliente.** Come here for a seat where you can catch sea breezes, and dig into spicy Mexican dishes with a Caribbean twist, such as margarita shrimp or *caracol al mojo de ajo* (grilled conch with garlic sauce). The local expat community often congregates here for lunch and a few piña coladas. ⊠ *Beachfront, Barrier Reef Dr. in Spindrift Hotel* ☎ *226/2170* ⊟ *MC, V* ✺ *Closed Mon.*

> **WORD OF MOUTH**
>
> In San Pedro, I'd recommend Caliente. I had a wonderful Brazilian shrimp dish, can't recall the name, but it was excellent.
> —JeanH.

$–$$$ ✕ **Cocina Caramba.** You'll quickly sense the frenetic energy of this noisy and often packed restaurant operated by Rene Reyes, who worked in restaurants in Miami and San Pedro before opening his own spot. There's nothing very fancy on the menu here—just basics like grilled snapper, fried shrimp, pork chops, and Mexican fajitas and burritos—but everything is well prepared, and the service is snappy and enthusiastic. ⊠ *Pescador Dr.* ☎ *603/1652* ⊟ *MC, V* ✺ *Closed Wed.*

$–$$$ ✕ **Fido's Courtyard.** Sooner or later you're sure to end up at Fido's (pronounced Fee-do's), sipping something cold and contemplating the ocean views, under what the owners claim is the largest thatch palapa in Belize. This casual restaurant and bar is one of San Pedro's most popular places, serving burgers, fish-and-chips, and pizza. Upstairs is the Rice 'n Roll sushi and martini bar. Fido's is open every day for lunch and dinner, and most nights, depending on the season, there's live music. ⊠ *Beachfront, Barrier Reef Dr. just north of Catholic church* ☎ *226/3176* ⊟ *MC, V.*

$–$$$ ✕ **Mango's.** Noted local chef Amy Knox moved here from Victoria House and quickly made Mango's one of the top dining choices on the island. Many of the dishes have a Mexican base but with Knox's sophisticated twist. She calls her cooking "New Wave Latin," Caribbean food infused with spicy Latin flavors from Cuba, Argentina, and Mexico—it's good enough to have earned her Belize Chef of the Year honors twice. Try the pulled pork taquitos, or the huge fish burritos (enough for two). This is also one of San Pedro's best values, with even lobster and shrimp dishes under BZ$40. ⊠ *Beachfront, Barrier Reef Dr.* ☎ *226/2859* ⊟ *MC, V.*

$–$$$ ✕ **Papi's Diner.** Atmosphere is in short supply at Papi's, as are views of the sea. Little more than a screened porch with a few wooden tables, the unpretentious diner is tucked away at San Pedro's north end. But the seafood and other dishes are expertly prepared by owner Stephen "Papi" Manuel at some of the town's most reasonable prices, and usually every table is occupied. Grilled fish is served with multiple side dishes. ⊠ *Pescador Dr. at north end of town behind Seven Seas Resort* ☎ *226/2047* ⊟ *No credit cards.*

$–$$ ✕ **Estel's Dine by the Sea.** Estella's father-in-law was a World War II flier with a squadron called Di Nah Might (his flight jacket is displayed on the wall). Not surprisingly, this is one of San Pedro's best places for a hearty American-style breakfast of bacon, fried potatoes, and freshly squeezed juice. Later in the day you can order burgers, Mexican meals, and excellent seafood dishes. The little white-and-aqua building is on the beach, as you might infer from the sandy floor and porthole-shape windows. There's a terrace outside where you can sit under a thatch umbrella and watch pelicans. ⊠ *Beachfront, Barrier Reef Dr.* ☎ *226/2019* ⊟ *No credit cards.*

$–$$ ✕ **JamBel Jerk Pit.** In the middle of town next door to Big Daddy's is this casual eatery, which blends Jamaican and Belizean cuisines (hence the name) to produce spicy jerk-style dishes. You can relax in the main dining room, where reggae is always playing, or upstairs on the roof, where it's often so windy you need to hang on to your napkin. The ocean views make it worth the trouble. There's also a new, slightly spiffier branch just down the street in the lobby of the Coral Beach Hotel. ⊠ *Barrier Reef Dr. at Central Park and Big Daddy's* ☎ *226/3303* ⊠ *Barrier Reef Dr. in Coral Beach Hotel* ☎ *226/2013* ⊟ *AE, MC, V.*

¢–$ ✕⛶ **Ruby's.** No wonder budget-minded travelers flock to this clean, simple hotel on the beach: air-conditioned rooms with private baths and balconies facing the ocean go for BZ$100, while the original rooms with fans, facing the street, are only BZ$70 for a double. Try the breakfast burritos at the hotel's little restaurant, Ruby's Café, which opens at 5 for the fishing and diving crowd. ⊠ *Beachfront, south end of Barrier Reef Dr. at Tarpon St.* ☎ *226/2063* 🖶 *226/2434* ⊕ *www.ambergriscaye. com/rubys* ⤢ *23 rooms, 21 with bath* ⚐ *Restaurant, beach, fishing; no a/c in some rooms, no room phones, no room TVs* ⊟ *MC, V.*

$$$$ ⛶ **The Phoenix.** Bold geometric forms and massive concrete walls with deeply recessed windows mark this new luxury beachfront condominium resort, designed by architect Gui Trotti (he also designed part of NASA's space station). The Phoenix is at the north end of town, on the former site of a nun's retreat; at this writing it was partially complete, with its remaining units set to open in 2007. ⊠ *Beachfront, Barrier Reef Dr.* 🖶 *226/3414* ⊕ *www.ambergriscaye.com/phoenix* ⤢ *32 2-bedroom apartments* ⚐ *Kitchens, cable TV, 2 pools, beach, Internet, travel services* ⊟ *MC, V.*

$$–$$$ ⛶ **AquaMarina Suites.** On the water at the north end of San Pedro, this suites hotel and time-share is within walking distance of everything in town. Although the junior and regular suites are on the small side, they're furnished in light, tropical colors and have queen-size beds, kitchens with mahogany cabinets, and some have private balconies with gorgeous views of the water. Note that the pool is tiny and the beach is busy, with a fair amount of walk-by and boat traffic. ⊠ *Beachfront, Barrier Reef Dr.* ☎ *226/4675, 800/641–2994 in U.S.* 🖶 *226/3414* ⊕ *www. aquamarinasuites.com* ⤢ *31 suites* ⚐ *Kitchens, cable TV, pool, beach, bar, shop, travel services* ⊟ *MC, V.*

$$–$$$ ⛶ **SunBreeze Beach Hotel.** A midsize resort across from the airstrip at the town's southern edge (but there's no issue with aircraft noise), the SunBreeze has large rooms that surround a U-shape, plant-filled courtyard. Five deluxe rooms have whirlpool baths; all are equipped for guests with disabilities. The hotel was upgraded and renovated in 2004–2005. There's a small beach area (with a seawall, though), a shaded pool, and a dive shop. ⊠ *Coconut Dr.* ☎ *226/2191, 800/688–*

0191 in U.S. and Canada ⌨ *226/2346* ⊕ *www.sunbreeze.net* ⇩ *42 rooms* ⌂ *Restaurant, some refrigerators, cable TV, pool, beach, dive shop, dock, shops, laundry service, meeting rooms, travel services* ⊟ *AE, MC, V.*

$$ ▦ **Mayan Princess.** Sitting pretty in the middle of town, this pink hotel has rattan furniture covered with pastel-color fabrics. Sliding doors open onto verandas, where you can eat meals prepared in your well-equipped kitchenette. In the low season—and sometimes even in the high season—room prices drop dramatically. It doesn't hurt to ask for a deal when making reservations. ⊠ *Beachfront, Barrier Reef Dr.* ☎ *226/2778 or 800/850–4101* ⌨ *226/2784* ⊕ *www.mayanprincesshotel.com* ⇩ *23 apartments* ⌂ *Fans, kitchenettes, cable TV, beach, travel services* ⊟ *AE, MC, V.*

$$ ✕▦ **San Pedro Holiday Hotel.** Trimmed in cheery pink-and-white colors, this spic-and-span quartet of colonial-style houses is in the center of San Pedro. Though much has changed now, it opened in 1965 as the first hotel on the island. All rooms have polished wood floors, and many have views of the in-town beach. Celi's Restaurant on the first floor has casual beachfront dining. ⊠ *Beachfront, Barrier Reef Dr.* ☎ *226/2014* ⌨ *226/2295* ⊕ *www.sanpedroholiday.com* ⇩ *14 rooms, 1 suite, 1 apartment* ⌂ *Restaurant, fans, some refrigerators, beach, dive shop, windsurfing, bar, shops, laundry service, travel services; no room phones, no TV in some rooms* ⊟ *AE, MC, V.*

$$ ▦ **The Tides Beach Resort.** If diving is your reason for being, and you don't want to spend a ton of money, you couldn't do better than this hotel, owned by Patojo Paz, one of the island's most experienced dive masters, and his wife. The three-story wood-frame structure recalls a time before everyone built with reinforced concrete. Top picks here are the second and third floor oceanfront rooms, which have balconies overlooking the beach. The hotel is north of town, but you can walk along the beach to San Pedro's bars and restaurants. ⊠ *Beachfront, Boca del Rio Dr., north of town* ☎ *226/2283* ⌨ *226/3797* ⊕ *www.ambergriscaye.com/tides* ⇩ *8 rooms* ⌂ *Fans, some refrigerators, pool, beach, dive shop, dock, bar, laundry service; no room phones, no TV in some rooms* ⊟ *MC, V* ◎ *CP.*

North of San Pedro

$$$$ ✕ **Capricorn.** Once the island's most acclaimed restaurant, Capricorn continued to thrive when new owners took over in 2003, but since one of the new team members departed in 2005, things haven't been the same. The seaside setting is still romantic, and some dishes, such as the stone crab claws, provide a glimpse of the old Capricorn, but the cooking is inconsistent, and service is spotty. Although the focus here is on the restaurant, there are three cute little cabanas, but we've

---

WORD OF MOUTH

We stayed at The Tides hotel and it has its own dive shop, Patajo's. We did most of our tours through them. It is a small family run place. Very friendly, clean, and close to the town. It isn't a big glitzy place so you feel more connected with the locals. Everyone else there loved it and would definitely go back. On our last night there the owners, Sabrina and Patajo treated some of the guests to a free BBQ'd meal.

—JanieC

Where to Stay & Eat in
North Ambergris Caye

North
Ambergris

—About 5 miles
from town

—About 2.5 miles
from town

San Pedro River

SAN
PEDRO

NOT TO SCALE

heard complaints about brackish water with a strong sulfur smell. ✉ *3 mi (5 km) north of San Pedro* ☎ *226/2809* ▤ *AE, MC, V.*

★ **$$$-$$$$** ✕ **Rendezvous Restaurant & Winery.** Belize's only Thai–French restaurant combines local seafood with Thai spices and presentation methods. The menu changes frequently, but try not to miss the chocolate truffle cake with Belizean *wongla* (sesame seed) candy. The owners, Glen and Colleen Schwenginger, who have lived and worked in Thailand and Singapore, also produce and bottle their own wines using imported grape concentrate. It's not bad. Rent the honeymoon suite above the restaurant if you can't bear the water-taxi ride back to your hotel. It's next door to Journey's End resort. ✉ *4 mi (7 km) north of San Pedro* ☎ *226/3426* ▤ *AE, MC, V.*

$$-$$$$ ✕ **Rojo Lounge.** This is the hippest restaurant and bar on the cayes. Rojo
Fodor's Choice Lounge, in a sultry open-air palapa on a beautiful beach, is definitely
★ red hot. Lunch offers a selection of sophisticated snacks like chili-dusted cold shrimp, grilled lobster salad, and conch pizza, from BZ$24 to BZ$44. Dinner is romantic and delicious, with surprising combinations such as cashew-crusted grouper stuffed with lobster (BZ$62) and guava-glaze ribs (BZ$58). The bar serves killer frozen mojitos. ✉ *Beachfront, North Ambergris, 5 mi (8 km) north of town, Ambergris Caye* ☎ *226/4012* ▤ *AE, MC, V* ☾ *Tues.–Sun. noon–10:30 PM.*

$$$–$$$$ ✕⊡ **Mata Chica.** Casitas in shades of mango, banana, and blueberry off-set by brilliant white sand give this resort a Gauguin-like quality, though on recent visits we've found the South Seas atmosphere, like the paint on the casitas, fading a bit. Inside, the fabric, artwork, and tiles echo the outdoor colors. For extra space, choose a two-bedroom villa or the 5,000-square-foot "Beach Mansion." Delectable though pricey seafood is served at Mambo. There's a new swimming pool, and the beach here is postcard pretty, although a stretch of sand nearby is littered with garbage. ⊠ *5 mi (8 km) north of San Pedro* ☏ *220/5010* 🖷 *220/5012* ⊕ *www.matachica.com* ⇘ *12 casitas, 2 2-bedroom villas, 1 beach house* ⚐ *Restaurant, fans, pool, spa, beach, snorkeling, boating, fishing, bar, Internet room, laundry service, travel services; no room phones, no room TVs, no kids under 10* ⊟ *AE, MC, V.*

$$$–$$$$ ✕⊡ **Portofino.** Even if you're not a newlywed, try the honeymoon suite at this tranquil North Ambergris resort. Inside a thatch cabana, the 800-square-foot suite has the island's best sea views and a private whirlpool. The other cabanas have four-poster bamboo beds draped with linen mosquito nets (although mosquitoes are only occasionally a problem). Three "tree house" suites are perched on wooden stilts above the sand. Le Bistro restaurant serves seafood with Caribbean and French influences and offers the option, if it's not too windy, for dining on the hotel's pier. ⊠ *6 mi (10 km) north of San Pedro* ☏ *220/5096* 🖷 *226/4272* ⊕ *www.portofinobelize.com* ⇘ *8 rooms, 4 suites* ⚐ *Restaurant, room service, fans, minibars, beach, snorkeling, boating, fishing, bar, laundry service, travel services; no room phones, no room TVs* ⊟ *AE, MC, V* ❶ *CP.*

$$$$
Fodor'sChoice
★
⊡ **Azul Resort.** This new resort has only two beach villas, but what beach houses they are! The two-level villas have an open floor plan, 20-foot ceilings, and beams of mylady wood. Custom kitchens have Viking appliances, and the stunning cabinets and most of the furniture is made of Belize's unique ziricote wood. Each villa has an Apple computer, 50-inch plasma flat-screen TV, and Bose home theater system. On the rooftop, you can laze in the hot tub or sunbathe in delicious privacy. There's a gorgeous infinity pool, and the hip Rojo Lounge is next door for drinks and some of the best food on the island. ⊠ *North Ambergris, 4 mi (6 km) north of San Pedro* ☏ *226/4012* 🖷 *220/5058* ⊕ *www.azulbelize.com* ⇘ *2 beach houses* ⚐ *Restaurant, room service, fans, kitchens, cable TV, DVDs, pool, beach, bar, Internet, travel services* ⊟ *MC, V.*

★ $$$$ ⊡ **Seascape Villas.** Six posh homes spread across 4 beachfront acres are among the island's most exclusive properties. Each 3,000-square-foot villa has a sunken living room, slate floors, an outdoor garden with hot tub, and unobstructed views of the sea. In lieu of an on-site restaurant, Glen Schwenginger, chef and co-owner of Rendezvous Restaurant & Winery next door, serves meals in your beach house (meals are not included in the price of your stay). The villas are privately owned and available for rent when the owners aren't in residence. ⊠ *North Ambergris, 4 mi (6 km) north of San Pedro* ☏ *226/5203* ⊕ *www.seascapebelizevillas.com* ⇘ *6 beach houses* ⚐ *Fans, kitchens, cable TV, tennis court, pool, beach, Internet, travel services* ⊟ *MC, V.*

$$$$ ▦ **Captain Morgan's Retreat.** Featured prominently on *Temptation Island,* this resort and time-share hasn't been shy about touting its turn on the reality show. But instead of scantily clad beauties, here you'll find a long, quiet stretch of sand lined with thatch-roof cabanas. Newer condo villas have a sitting room and kitchen. The pool surrounded by a hardwood deck offers an alternative to a dip in the ocean, which isn't at its best here. Despite the attractive setting, the aggressive time-share offerings are a turnoff, and the rates aren't much of a bargain either. ✉ *4 mi (6 km) north of San Pedro* ☎ *226/2567, 888/653–9090 in U.S.* ⊟ *307/587–8914* ⊕ *www.captainmorgans.com* ➱ *14 casitas, 12 condo villas* ⏷ *Restaurant, fans, pool, beach, dive shop, dock, bicycles, volleyball, bar, laundry service, travel services; no TV in some rooms* ▤ *AE, DC, MC, V.*

$$$–$$$$ ▦ **El Pescador.** Nearly every place on Ambergris Caye claims that it offers fishing trips, but this hotel has the best angling resources. Loosely described as a "fishing camp," the main lodge is actually a handsome colonial house with comfortable, if not luxurious, rooms with mahogany floors. Adjoining the lodge in two groupings, each with a pool, are deluxe two- and three-bedroom villas. You can enjoy a fine meal, served family style in the dining room, or a drink on the veranda. Most guests arrive as part of a fishing package; prices start at BZ$2,890 per person for three nights, including fishing guide, boat, and meals. ✉ *3 mi(5 km) north of San Pedro* ☎ *226/2398* ⊟ *226/2977* ⊕ *www. elpescador.com* ➱ *13 rooms, 8 villas* ⏷ *Dining room, fans, kitchens, 3 pools, beach, dock, boating, fishing, bar, shop, laundry service, travel services; no TV in some rooms* ▤ *MC, V* ⏽◯⏽ *All meals included.*

$$$–$$$$ ▦ **White Sands Cove.** One of the first resorts you come to after crossing the bridge across the river channel is this collection of one- and two-bedroom condos housed in octagonal-shape buildings near the beach. Suites have tile floors, cabinets and trim of cedar and mahogany, and full kitchens. There's 200 feet of beachfront, and a pier. ✉ *North Ambergris, 3 mi (5 km) north of town* ☎ *226/3528, 888/362–2683 in U.S. or Canada* ⊟ *226/3753* ⊕ *www.whitesandscove.com* ➱ *14 suites* ⏷ *Fans, kitchens, cable TV, pool, beach, spa, dock, bar, travel services* ▤ *AE, MC, V.*

$$$ ▦ **Belizean Shores.** If you're looking for a peaceful setting and well-maintained rooms at reasonable prices, this condotel with one-bedroom units is a good choice. Kick back with a cool cocktail from the 24-hour pool's swim-up bar, or stay in and cook dinner in the pretty kitchens, which have mahogany cabinets, fridges, microwaves, and small butane stoves. If you want to eat out, skip the on-site restaurant—the service's indifferent and the food's inconsistent—and head instead for one of the nearby eateries, some of the island's best. ✉ *5 mi (8 km) north of San Pedro* ☎ *226/2355* ⊟ *226/2931* ⊕ *www.belizeanshores.com* ➱ *48 suites* ⏷ *Restaurant, fans, kitchens, cable TV, 2 tennis courts, gym, pool, beach, dock, boating, fishing, bar, shop, laundry service, travel services* ▤ *MC, V* ⏽◯⏽ *All meals included.*

$$ ▦ **Salamander Hideaway.** If you want peace and quiet without frills, this spot 10 mi (17 km) north of town is for you; if you're looking for a traditional beach resort with easy access to restaurants and nightlife, look elsewhere. Choose from either the rustic thatch cabanas on the beach or the two-level jungle cabanas in the back. Don't expect luxury, or even privacy—the water for showers is brackish, and the toilets are in the bedroom. On the plus side, the food here is quite good, and if you like water sports, there's free access to kayaks, windsurfers, snorkel equipment, and small sailboats. This far north, the reef is close enough to shore that you can kayak out for snorkeling. Salamander is an "ecocentric" resort, with solar and wind power. ⊠ *11 mi (18 km) north of San Pedro* ☎ *602/1713* ⊕ *www.salamanderbelize.com* ⤳ *8 cabanas* ⌂ *Restaurant, fans, beach, dive shop, snorkeling, windsurfing, boating, fishing, bar; no a/c, no room TVs, no room phones* ▭ *MC, V.*

South of San Pedro

★ **$$–$$$** ✕ **Casa Picasso.** Belizean artists created the Picasso-inspired art on the walls of this Spanish-influence restaurant, which specializes in tapas like *gamas a la plancha* (sautéed shrimp with red pepper). Lasagna and other pasta dishes are also served, along with freshly baked rustic Italian bread. Martinis are a specialty. The restaurant has the island's largest selection of desserts, including a tangy key lime pie. ⊠ *Sting Ray St. off Coconut Dr., on lagoon side* ☎ *226/4507* ▭ *AE, MC, V.*

$$–$$$ ✕ **Tastes of Thailand.** Run by an English–Thai couple (she cooks, he waits tables), this comfortable little restaurant serves the most authentic Thai food in Belize. One dish, Hurricane Hits (BZ$48), has a mix of mussels, shrimp, and other seafood in a spicy sauce. There are a bunch of vegetarian options. ⊠ *Sea Grape St. off Coconut Dr., on lagoon side* ☎ *226/2601* ▭ *MC, V* ☺ *Dinner Mon.–Sat.*

$–$$ ✕ **Jade Garden.** Classic Cantonese dishes have a Caribbean twist at this restaurant. You'll find fish chow mein and conch kebabs on the menu, alongside American-style 12-ounce T-bone steaks and Belizean-style pork chops. The attractive restaurant fills the top two floors of a white colonial-style building just outside town. It's outfitted with handsome rattan furniture and pastel tablecloths, making this one of the caye's more comfortable restaurants. ⊠ *Coconut Dr., ¼ mi south of airstrip* ☎ *226/2126* ▭ *AE, MC, V.*

★ **$$$–$$$$** ✕▥ **Victoria House.** With its bougainvillea-filled gardens, this property 2 mi (3 km) south of San Pedro has the style and seclusion of a diplomatic residence. In the white colonial-style house with airy verandas and tile walkways are three ample suites with mahogany furnishings, steps from a gorgeous infinity pool. If a suite's not your thing, you have a wide choice of other accommodations here, from simple motel-like rooms to a five-bedroom villa. New condo units are opening in late 2006. The restaurant remains one of the island's best. ⊠ *Coconut Dr., 2 mi (3 km) south of San Pedro* ☎ *226/2067, 800/247–5159 in U.S.* 🖷 *404/373–3885* ⊕ *www.victoria-house.com* ⤳ *12 rooms, 10 casitas, 3 suites, 3 villas* ⌂ *Restaurant, fans, kitchens, pool, beach, dive shop, dock, snorkeling, windsurfing, boating, fishing, bar, laundry service, Internet, travel services; no room phones, no room TVs* ▭ *AE, D, MC, V.*

★ **$$–$$$** ✕▥ **Banana Beach Resort.** Thanks to its friendly staff's accommodating attitude, this resort has one of the island's highest guest occupancy rates. The original section, built around an interior courtyard, has one-bedroom suites; a newer section has regular rooms at bargain prices, plus deluxe "flex suites" that expand from one to four bedrooms, depending on your needs. The restaurant, El Divino (named after a beloved staffer who passed away), is a steak house and martini bar. ⊠ *Coconut Dr., 1½ mi (2½ km) south of San Pedro* ☎ *226/3890* 🖷 *226/3891* ⊕ *www.bananabeach.com* ⏎ *24 rooms, 42 suites* ⚐ *Restaurant, fans, some kitchens, cable TV, 2 pools, beach, dive shop, dock, boating, shops, laundry service, Wi-Fi, travel services, no-smoking rooms* ▤ *AE, D, MC, V* ¶◯¶ *CP.*

$$$$ ▥ **Grand Colony Villas.** These are some of the most upscale condos on the island: two-bedroom, two-bath apartments, ranging from 1,100 to more than 1,900 square feet, have tall ceilings, marble or hardwood floors, mahogany doors and cabinets, and luxurious furnishings. To top it all off, the beach here is as good as it gets on Ambergris Caye. ⊠ *Coconut Dr., 1½ mi (3 km) south of town* 226/3739 🖷 226/2768 ⊕ www. grandcolonyvillas.com ⏎ 21 condo apartments ⚐ Fans, kitchens, cable TV, pool, beach, dock, laundry service, Internet, travel services ▤ AE, MC, V.

★ $$$$ ▥ **Villas at Banyan Bay.** If you enjoy little luxuries like a whirlpool bath in your room, this red tile–roofed complex about 2 mi (3 km) south of town will suit you splendidly. You won't feel cramped here—stylishly furnished two-bedroom condos with verandas overlooking the sea have cathedral ceilings with tropical hardwoods. The kid-friendly pool is one of the island's largest, and Mar de Tumbo tops the short list of the island's best beaches. Rico's Bar & Grill has a beautiful setting on the water, though the food is only so-so. ⊠ *Coconut Dr., 1½ mi (2½ km) south of San Pedro* ☎ *226/3739* 🖷 *226/2766* ⊕ *www.banyanbay.com* ⏎ *42 apartments* ⚐ *Restaurant, fans, in-room hot tubs, kitchens, cable TV, Internet room, pool, beach, dive shop, dock, bar, laundry service, travel services* ▤ *AE, MC, V.*

$$$–$$$$ ▥ **The Palms.** Stay here for the gorgeous sea views from the oceanfront units. The one- and two-bedroom apartments are spacious with earthtone furnishings and kitchens, including full-size fridges. The tiny pool is in a shady spot at the back of the property and can be a little cool in winter. The Palms is at the south edge of town, a stroll away from most of the restaurants and activities in San Pedro, five minutes from the airport (noise is not an issue, though), and five minutes from the largest grocery on the island. ⊠ *Coconut Dr.* ☎ *226/3322* 🖷 *226/3601* ⊕ *www. belizepalms.com* ⏎ *8 2-bedroom apartments, 5 1-bedroom apartments* ⚐ *Fans, cable TV, pool, Wi-Fi, beach* ▤ *MC, V.*

$$$–$$$$ ▥ **Ramon's Village Resort.** One of the first resorts on the cayes, Ramon's has grown into one of its largest, but still retains its thatch-and-sand atmosphere. A five-minute stroll from town, the very popular resort attracts an active crowd who take their margaritas by the pool. The beachfront units are attractive, but those in the back are dark and can be noisy. You may find room prices surprisingly high for the size and amenities, but you're paying for the terrific setting and location. The 500-foot beach is among San Pedro's best, and snorkeling is pretty good off the 420-foot pier, with its artificial reef. The hotel also manages a collection of cottages across the street called Steve and Becky's Cute Little Hotel. ⊠ *Coconut Dr.* ☎ *226/2071, 800/624–4315 in U.S.* 🖷 *226/2214* ⊕ *www.ramons.com* ⏎ *61 rooms, 8 cottages* ⚐ *Restau-*

Where to Stay & Eat South of San Pedro

SAN
PEDRO

*San Pedro
Lagoon*

**Maya
Island
Air**

**Hyperbaric
Chamber**

**Sports
Arena**

Air Strip

**Tropic
Air**

❸

❹

❼

❷

❶

❺

❻

❽

❾

❿

⓫ — About 1.5 miles
from town

⓬

⓭

⓮

⓯

⓰

About 2.5 miles
— from town

TO CAYE CAULKER
& CAYE CHAPEL
↓

Barrier Reef

NOT TO SCALE

rant, room service, fans, some kitchens, some refrigerators, pool, beach, dive shop, dock, snorkeling, boating, fishing, bar, shop, laundry service, travel services; no TV in some rooms ⊟ AE, MC, V.

$$$–$$$$ ▣ **Xanadu Island Resort.** It's billed as the "world's first monolithic dome resort," a description that might appeal only to engineers. Happily, these domes look nicer than they sound and the result is a structure that can withstand winds up to 300 mph. There's a mélange of one-, two- and three-bedroom units. All are attractively furnished in earth tones and have modern amenities. Palm trees surrounding the pool make it feel nicely tropical; there's also a 350-foot pier and a stretch of sand, but it has a seawall. You also get free access to bikes, canoes, and kayaks. ⊠ *Coconut Dr., 1 mi (2 km) south of San Pedro* ☎ 226/2814 🖷 226/3409 ⊕ *www.xanaduresort-belize.com* ⇌ *18 suites* ⚲ *Fans, in-room safes, kitchens, cable TV, pool, beach, dock, snorkeling, bicycles, Wi-Fi, travel services, no-smoking rooms* ⊟ AE, MC, V.

$$–$$$ ▣ **Mata Rocks Resort.** Squeaky clean rooms at this intimate, midlevel hotel right on the beach have perfect sea views and breezes. Though Mata is a 30-minute walk from all the dining and nightlife options in town, it makes up for it with a quintessential thatch tropical beach bar and arrangements with nearby restaurants for food delivery (BZ$10 cab fee). Bikes are complimentary. ⊠ *Coconut Dr., 1½ mi (3 km) south of town* ☎ 226/2336, 888/628–2757 in U.S. and Canada 🖷226/3416 ⊕*www.matarocks. com* ⇌ *17 rooms* ⚲ *Fans, some kitchenettes, refrigerators, cable TV, pool, bar, laundry services, travel services* ⊟ AE, MC, V ⑩ CP.

$–$$$ ▣ **Caribbean Villas.** It lacks some of the perks of newer, larger properties, such as a pool or room TVs, but Caribbean Villas, with its 2½ acres of gardens, a bird sanctuary, and quiet beachfront, is a low-key alternative to some of the glitzier developments. Choose from a small studio with no air-conditioning (BZ$130) to lofted suites for families (BZ$360). All but the studio have a sea view. The dock has a small artificial reef. Minimum stay in-season is four nights. ⊠ *Coconut Dr., 1 mi (1½ km) south of town* ☎☎ 226/2715 ⊕ *www.caribbeanvillashotel. com* ⇌ *5 rooms, 9 suites* ⚲ *Fans, some kitchens, beach, laundry service, travel services; no a/c in some rooms, no room phones, no room TV* ⊟ MC, V.

$$ ▣ **Royal Caribbean Resort.** The small canary-yellow cabins lined up in tidy rows at this new resort may remind you of army barracks, except for the thatch roofs, but inside the rooms are comfortable, with tile floors, wicker furniture, and small kitchenettes. There's a pool and 400 feet of beach on 10 acres just south of Victoria House, and the price, just BZ$250 double, is right. ⊠ *Coconut Dr., 2¼ mi (3½ km) south of town* ☎ 226/4220 🖷 226/4221 ⊕ *www.ambergriscaye.com/royalcaribbean/* ⇌ *45 cabins* ⚲ *Fans, kitchenettes, cable TV, pool, beach, laundry service, travel services; no a/c, no room phones* ⊟ AE, MC, V.

$–$$ ▣ **Corona del Mar Apartments and Hotel.** One of the better values on the island, Corona del Mar has lagoon-view rooms for BZ$180, and the apartment suites for BZ$300 can sleep six. Seafront units have balconies. Though there's no pool, it's right on the beach and has the first and only elevator on the island. ⊠ *Coconut Dr., 1 mi (1½ km) south of town* ☎ 226/2055 🖷 226/2461 ⊕ *www.ambergriscaye.com/*

coronadelmar/ ⌁ *12 rooms, 4 suites* △ *Fans, cable TV, beach, dock, travel services* ▭ *AE, MC, V* ⍾ *CP.*

$ ▦ **Changes In Latitudes.** Out front, the sign depicting an igloo melting beneath a tropical sun is an in-joke about the original Canadian owner's move south to run this little B&B. The tranquil inn is near San Pedro's restaurants and bars, but isn't on the beach. Although they're all on the small side, the rooms are clean and have louvered windows to allow breezes in. The three garden-side rooms get the most light. A full breakfast is served in the common room, but you can prepare your own meals. ⊠ *Coconut Dr., ¼ mi south of San Pedro* ▦▦ *226/ 2986* ⊕ *www.ambergriscaye.com/latitudes* ⌁ *6 rooms* △ *Fans, laundry service, travel services; no room phones, no room TVs* ▭ *MC, V* ⍾ *Breakfast included.*

¢   ▦ **Pedro's Backpacker Inn.** Gregarious British expat Peter Lawrence opened the island's only hostel-style accommodations in 2003. A single bed and shared bath in this white frame house on stilts go for BZ$25, or you can get a bed, barbecue dinner, and a Belikin beer for BZ$40. ⊠ *Princess Dr. south of San Pedro* ▦ *226/3825* ⊕ *www. backpackersbelize.com* ⌁ *20 rooms* △ *Fans; no a/c, no room phones, no room TVs* ▭ *MC, V.*

Nightlife

San Pedro has the most active nightlife scene in Belize, but, still, don't expect Miami Beach. Beach bars abound, and you can get sloshed just walking from your South End hotel into town. A few spots have live music. Generally, the action starts late (after 10 or 11). Karaoke is big in Belize, and some bars and clubs in San Pedro have karaoke nights, which are more for locals than visitors. In late January and early February, singer Jerry Jeff Walker holds "Camp Belize," two weeklong events in San Pedro during which Walker puts on shows for his loyal fans.

Bars & Clubs

With live music most nights, **Barefoot Iguana** (⊠ Coconut Dr., about a mile south of town) is the island's loudest bar. Known for its burgers, **BC's Beach Bar** (⊠ South of SunBreeze Hotel) is a popular oceanfront bar that hosts all-you-can-eat barbecues on Sunday afternoon. **Big Daddy's** (⊠ Barrier Reef Dr., north side of Central Park) is the scene of much of the action in downtown San Pedro. Since it's right on the water, there's a beachside barbecue some nights. The music and real boozing don't get started until late, usually around 11.

Across the street from Big Daddy's is **Jaguar's Temple** (⊠ Barrier Reef Dr.), a popular San Pedro dance club.

Several popular bars are on piers out in the water, including **Wet Willy's** (⊠ At Hustler's pier) and **Tackle Box** (⊠ At Shark's pier). Under a giant thatch palapa, **Fido's** (⊠ Barrier Reef Dr.) is always jumping and has live music most nights. On the odd side of the nightlife spectrum is the Chicken Drop, held on Wednesday starting around 6 PM at the **Pier Lounge** (⊠ At

Spindrift Hotel, Barrier Reef Dr.). Bet a buck on a numbered square, and if the chicken poops on your square, you win the pot of US$100.

Shopping

Cobblestoned Barrier Reef Drive, formerly Front Street, is San Pedro's Street of Shopping Dreams—it's lined with souvenir shops complemented by restaurants, small hotels, banks, and other anchors of tourist life on the island. Stores with more of a local appeal are on Pescador Drive (Middle Street) and Angel Coral Street (Back Street), especially at the north end of town. Barrier Reef is closed to golf carts and vehicles on weekends, starting around 6 PM Friday, and local vendors set up shop selling locally made jewelry and wood carvings (they're also out sometimes during the week in high season). Except for these items, few are made on the island. Most of the souvenir shops sell crafts from Guatemala and Mexico, along with carved wood and slate from the mainland. Belizean hot sauces, such as Marie Sharp's and Gallon Jug's Lissette Sauce, along with local rums, make good souvenirs; they're cheaper in groceries (try Pescador Drive and Angel Coral Street) than in gift shops. To avoid worsening the plight of endangered sea life, avoid buying souvenirs made from black coral or turtle shell.

Best Shops

At the long-established **Belizean Arts** (⊠ Fido's Courtyard off Barrier Reef Dr. ☎ 226/3019), you'll find works by important local painters including Walter Castillo, Nelson Young, and Pen Cayetano. Also on display are handicrafts from the region, including hand-painted animal figures from Mexico, masks and fabrics from Guatemala, and brilliantly colored tropical fish made of coconut wood. **Ambar** (⊠ Fido's Courtyard off Barrier Reef Dr. ☎ 226/3101) offers locally made jewelry of jade, silver, and gold. **Isla Bonita Designs** (⊠ At north end of Barrier Reef Dr. ☎ 226/4258) sells original clothing made on the island. The owner of **Sea Gal Boutique** (⊠ Barrier Reef Dr., in Holiday Hotel ☎ 226/2431) has an artist's eye: most of the souvenirs here are in good taste, even the T-shirts. For gaudy geegaws and unabashedly touristy souvenirs, the **Toucan Gift Shops** (⊠ Barrier Reef Dr. ☎ 226/2431), including Toucan Too and Di Bush Toucan, all sporting the bright green, yellow, and red Toucan logo, are hard to miss. **Island Supermarket** (⊠ Coconut Dr., south of town ☎ 226/2972) has the largest selection of groceries, liquor, and beer, along with hot sauces and other Belizean-produced items. Prices generally are 30% to 75% higher than in supermarkets in the United States, except for a few items, such as rum, produced in Belize.

One of the least expensive places to buy groceries is **San Pedro Supermarket** (⊠ Pescador Dr., at north end of town ☎ 226/3446). They have free delivery and a 7% discount if you spend BZ$100 or more. **Caye Coffee** (⊠ In San Pablo residential area south of town [follow signs] ☎ 226/3568), the island's only coffee roaster, sells Belizean and Guatemalan coffees. **Wine De Vine** (⊠ Vilma Linda Shopping Center across from primary school at south end of town ☎ 226/3430) has a good selection of wines, many from Chile and Argentina, and imported cheeses, at prices (due to import taxes) roughly double the cost in the United States.

CAYE CAULKER

❷ *5 mi (8 km) south of Ambergris Caye, 18 mi (29 km) northeast of Belize City.*

A half hour away from San Pedro by water taxi and sharing essentially the same reef and sea ecosystems, Caye Caulker is very different from its big sister island, Ambergris Caye. It's smaller, with a population of around 1,200, less developed, way more relaxed, and less expensive.

Caye Caulker long has been a stop on the Central America backpacker trail, and it remains Belize's most popular budget destination. Yet, its more charming aspects are breaking through as more upscale lodgings open up in town. Flowers outnumber cars ten to one (golf carts, bicycles, and bare feet are the preferred means of transportation).

As you might guess from all the NO SHIRT, NO SHOES, NO PROBLEM signs at the bars, the living is relatively easy here. This is the kind of place where most of the listings in the telephone directory give addresses like "near football field." However, Caye Corker, as it's often called in Belize (or Cayo Hicaco in Spanish, a reference to the coco plums on the island), isn't immune to change. A new public pier opened in 2003, many hotels are adding air-conditioning, the first hotel swimming pool debuted in 2005, and the island now has cybercafés and several upmarket restaurants; there are even a couple of condos. Still, Caye Caulker remains the epitome of laid-back, and as development continues at a fevered pace on neighboring Ambergris Caye, Caulker's simpler charms exercise considerable appeal to those who seek an affordable and relaxing island experience.

Like Ambergris Caye, Caye Caulker can be used as a base to explore part of the mainland. It's only about 45 minutes by water taxi, or 15 minutes by air, to Belize City. Tours run from Caulker to the Mayan ruins at Lamanai and Altun Ha, and other tours go to the Belize Zoo and to the Caves Branch River for cave tubing.

Water Activities & Tours

When you see the waves breaking on the barrier reef just a few hundred yards from the shore, boats full of eager snorkelers and divers, and the colorful sails of windsurfers dashing back and forth in front of the island, you know you've come to a good place for water sports and activities. You can dive, snorkel, and fish the same areas of the sea and reef as you can from San Pedro, but usually for a little less dough. One area where Caulker suffers by comparison with its neighboring island is in the quality of its beaches. Caulker's beaches, though periodically nourished by dredging to replenish the sand, are modest at best, mostly narrow ribbons of sand with shallow water near the shore and, in places, a mucky sea bottom. You can swim at "the Split," a channel cut through the island by Hurricane Hattie in 1961, at the north end of the village, or from the end of piers.

Scuba Diving & Snorkeling

Hol Chan Marine Reserve at the southern tip of Ambergris Caye (*see Ambergris Caye section, above*) is a popular destination for snorkel and dive trips from Caye Caulker. At Hol Chan, you can swim with nurse sharks and stingrays and see hundreds of tropical fish, some quite large due to the no-fishing restrictions in the reserve. On the way, your boat may be followed by a pod of frolicking dolphins, and you may spot sea turtles or even a manatee. Boats from Caulker also go to Lighthouse and Turneffe atolls.

The Caye Caulker Marine Reserve north and east of Caye Caulker, with its coral canyons, is a favorite of divers, especially for night dives. Caulker has its own miniversion of San Pedro's Shark-Ray Alley, called Shark-Ray Village.

CHARTERS, LESSONS & EQUIPMENT A plethora of dive and snorkel operators offer reef tours (some of them are "cowboys"—unaffiliated and unreliable—so make sure you use a reputable company). Plan on spending about BZ$30–BZ$40 for a snorkel trip around the island or around BZ$60–BZ$90 for a six-hour snorkel trip to Hol Chan Marine Reserve.

Local two-tank reef dives typically run about BZ$120, and those to Hol Chan or other nearby areas cost about BZ$160 to BZ$180. Day trips to Lighthouse or Turneffe Atolls, with three dives, cost around BZ$230 to BZ$270. If you stop at Half Moon Caye, there's an additional BZ$80 park fee. At Hol Chan, the park fee is BZ$20, and at Caye Caulker Marine Reserve, BZ$10.

Go out for a snorkel on a sailboat with **Raggamuffin Tours** (✉ Front St. ☎ 226/0348 ⊕ www.raggamuffintours.com), which goes to Hol Chan for BZ$70, including the park entrance fee. **Tsunami Adventures** (✉ Front St. at Split ☎☎ 226/0462 ⊕ www.tsunamiadventures.com) runs full-day snorkeling trips to Hol Chan for BZ$90 including the park entrance fee and lunch. **Carlos Tours** (✉ Front St. ☎ 226/0058) runs snorkel trips to Hol Chan Marine Reserve and elsewhere, manatee spotting trips to Swallow Caye, and full-day snorkel and sightseeing trips with several stops on the barrier reef, at San Pedro, and at small cayes. Prices vary according to the destination but range from around BZ$50 to $120 per person. **Anwar Tours** (✉ Front St. ☎ 226/0327) runs snorkel trips to Sargeant's Caye, with stops to see manatees at Swallow Caye and, often, lunch at St. George's Caye. Rates for this full-day trip are around BZ$120. Anwar, like other tour operators, provides various snorkel and other tour options, depending on demand. Stops and length of trips vary depending on weather and sea conditions. If you're looking for someone to take you out to the reef for diving, **Frenchie's Diving Services** (✉ Front St., north of public pier ☎ 226/0234) is a respected local operator. For trips to the Blue Hole, Turneffe, and local dives, **Paradise Down** (✉ Front St., north of public pier ☎ 226/0437) has three well-equipped dive boats and enjoys a top reputation.

Sailing

A few small sailboats offer sailing and snorkeling trips to nearby areas. One company, Raggamuffin Tours, also offers multiday combination sailing and camping trips to Lighthouse Atoll and to Placencia.

CHARTERS, LESSONS & EQUIPMENT **Raggamuffin Tours** (⊠ Front St. ☎ 226/0348 ⊕ www.raggamuffintours. com) has day sails and sunset and moonlight sails for BZ$40 to BZ$70. Longer charter trips are also available. Two-night camping and sailing trips to Lighthouse Reef are BZ$500 per person, and two-night/three-day camping and sailing trips to Placencia, with nights at Tobacco Caye and Ranguana Caye, also are BZ$500 per person. If you want to sail your own boat, **SaylKing** (⊠ Beachfront near Split ☎ 620/6875) rents four Topaz Uno Plus sailboats and two Topaz Duo sailboats for BZ$30 to BZ$40 an hour.

Windsurfing

With brisk easterly winds most of the year, Caye Caulker is one of Belize's premier centers for windsurfing. The island gets winds over 12 knots most days from November to July. The best windsurfing is in the morning and afternoon, with lulls around midday. In the late winter and spring, winds frequently hit 20 knots or more.

CHARTERS, LESSONS & EQUIPMENT Opened in 2004 by Michael Femrite, an aerospace engineer from Minnesota, **Michael's Windsurf & Water Sports** (⊠ Beachfront, just north of main public pier ☎ 226/0457 ⊕ www.windsurfbelize.com) has an excellent selection of long and short boards, with rental rates of BZ$40 to BZ$50 an hour, BZ$90 to BZ$100 for a half day, BZ$130 to BZ$150 a day, and BZ$410 to BZ$450 a week. Lessons are BZ$70 to BZ$90. Michael's also has some kite surfing equipment. A five-hour, private introduction to kite surfing course is BZ$300. Orlando Curasco at **Orlando's Windsurfing** (⊠ At Morgan's Hotel, on beach south of public pier ☎ 226/0178) rents older equipment and offers lessons for around BZ$60 for two hours.

Deep-Sea Fishing

Caye Caulker was a fishing village before it was a visitor destination. From Caulker, you can fly-fish for bonefish or permit in the grass flats behind the island, troll for barracuda or grouper inside the reef, or charter a boat to take you to blue water outside the reef for deep-sea fishing. Blue marlin weighing more than 400 pounds have been caught off Caye Caulker, along with big sailfish, pompano, and kingfish.

For a guide and boat for flats and reef fishing, you'll pay around BZ$400 to BZ$600 a day for one or two people. Bring all the fishing gear and tackle you think you'll need to Caye Caulker, as little is available on the island. If you're a do-it-yourself type, you can fish off the piers.

CHARTERS, LESSONS & EQUIPMENT **Porfilio "Piggy" Guzman** (⊠ Calle Almendro ☎ 226/0152) is the best-known fishing guide on the island, and he may charge a little more than others. **Raggamuffin Tours** (⊠ Front St. ☎ 226/0348 ⊕ www. raggamuffintours.com) arranges full-day fishing charters with boat, guide, and spinning tackle for BZ$500, half day BZ$400. **Tsunami Adventures** (⊠ Front St. at Split ☎ 226/0462 ⊕ www.tsunamiadventures. com) offers reef, deep-sea, and flats fishing trips starting at BZ$350 for a half day, including boat and guide.

Manatee Spotting

Several operators do boat trips to see West Indian manatees. It's illegal in Belize to get into the water with the gentle sea cows, but some tour operators do permit it. Tours typically cost around BZ$70 to BZ$80 per person. Some stop at Goff's Caye, which has excellent snorkeling.

CHARTERS, **Carlos Tours** (✉ Front St. ☎ 226/0058), one of the most recommended LESSONS & tour operators on Caye Caulker, runs snorkeling trips with stops at some EQUIPMENT of the best snorkel spots near Caye Caulker, and also at Hol Chan Marine Reserve and other places, along with manatee spotting tours. **Anwar Tours** (✉ Front St. ☎ 226/0327) runs snorkel and manatee spotting trips, and also does tours to Altun Ha Mayan site. **Chocolate** (✉ Front St. ☎ 226/0151), who pioneered manatee tours, only occasionally goes out on tours.

Exploring Caye Caulker

Caye Caulker is a fairly small island, only 5 mi (8 km) long and a little over 1 mi (2 km) wide at the widest point—most of the island is only a few hundred feet wide. The island itself is divided by "the Split," the small gulf of water separating the north area and the south area. The area north of the Split is mostly mangroves and lagoons, accessible only by boat, while the only village occupies most of the area south of the Split. From the Split to the airstrip, which is at the south end of the island, is about a mile (2 km). Directions in the village usually use the public pier or dock, where you come in on the water taxi, as the reference point. Things are either north of the pier or south of it. The village has only three streets: Front, Middle, and Back (sometimes they're referred to as roads) running north and south; Back Street just runs on the south side of the village. All of the streets on the island are hard-packed sand. On the east side, you can also walk along the beachfront. Officially, the streets are named, from front to back, Avenida Hicaco, Avenida Langosta, and Avenida Mangle, but rarely does anyone use these names. There are more than a dozen short east–west streets, mostly unnamed.

The busiest part of the village is Front Street, especially around the area where the east–west street, officially Calle del Sol, comes from the public pier. Generally, the north end of the village bustles more than the south end, which is primarily residential. At the south end of the village, on the seafront before you get to the airstrip, is a small littoral forest with interpretive trails and a library and conference center operated by the Belize Tourism Industry Association. For tourist information, visit ⊕ www.gocayecaulker.com, the official site of the Caye Caulker chapter of the BTIA.

Other than a few emergency vehicles, there are no cars on the island. Most locals and visitors get around on foot, although you can rent a golf cart or bike.

North of the Split there are only a few homes, without electricity, but private land there is being sold, and more homes are planned. The Caye Caulker Forest Reserve, about 100 acres at the northern tip of the island, is a protected area consisting mostly of red, black, and white mangroves. A designated marine reserve, comprising the grassy lagoons, the barrier reef, and the sea out about a mile east of the reef, adjoins the forest reserve.

Where to Stay & Eat

Caye Caulker has more than 40 hotels, mostly small places with just a few rooms. The older budget hotels are mostly clapboard, with fans but no air-conditioning, and usually without TV or room phones. If they're not on the water where they can catch the prevailing sea breezes, they are often burning hot during the day. Hotels built in the last decade or so are generally constructed with concrete, and an increasing number have air-conditioning. Only one hotel, Seaside Cabañas, has a swimming pool.

Once your dining choice on Caulker was fish, fish, or fish, but now you can enjoy Italian, Mexican, and Thai, as well as wonderful fresh seafood and lobster. Several restaurants serve wholesome natural foods and vegetarian dishes. Prices for meals here are generally lower than on other islands, and even a lobster dinner is usually less than BZ$35.

$$–$$$ ✕ **CocoPlum Gardens.** It's a bit of a hike to this little restaurant at the island's south end, but it's worth the effort. At breakfast, enjoy wholesome breads, fresh-made granola, omelets, and whole wheat pancakes, all in a lovely garden setting (the owners also operate a nursery). At dinner there's pizza, pasta, and fish. While you're here, browse the small gallery and gift shop with Belizean-made crafts. As you're leaving, keep an eye out for the "tree cat," the Dutch owners' cat that sleeps sprawled over a limb, with legs dangling. ⊠ *Back Street, south end of island near airstrip* ☎ 226/0226 ▭ *MC, V* ☺ *Closed Fri. and Sat. No lunch.*

$–$$$ ✕ **Rainbow Grill & Bar.** To catch the sea breezes, the Rainbow is built out over the water. It serves some of the tastiest, freshest seafood on the islands—our favorites are the grilled or fried fish dishes. This place is always buzzing. ⊠ *On beachfront between public pier and Split* ☎ 226/0281 ▭ *MC, V* ☺ *Closed Mon.*

$$$ ✕ **Don Corleone Caribbean Trattoria.** If you're tired of fried seafood and beans and rice, the authentic Italian at Don Corleone is an offer you can't refuse. On the wall is a poster of the *The Godfather,* naturally, and you can get Italian wines and espresso and cappuccino. Try the pasta carbonara, cooked al dente as it should be, or the seafood linquine. ⊠ *Front St. half way between public pier and Split, on west side of St.* ☎ 226/0025 ▭ *MC, V* ☺ *Closed Sun.*

$–$$ ✕ **Habaneros.** On the front door is a hand-painted drawing of a habanero pepper plant, but you shouldn't feel threatened—not everything here is super spicy. When you taste the Snapper Santa Fe or the vegetable lasagna, you'll know why this is considered one of the best restaurants between San Pedro and Belize City. The specialty at lunch is "Mayan pizza," a thin-crusted pizza with a variety of topping options. ⊠ *Front St.* ☎ 226/0486 ▭ *AE, MC, V.*

$–$$ ✕ **Rasta Pasta Rainforest Café.** People flock to this eclectic beachfront spot, with sand floors, for owner Maralyn Gill's conch fritters, giant burritos, Thai curries, and scrumptious coconut macaroons. Service is sometimes slow. Maralyn also sells a line of spices you can take home. ⊠ *Front St. on beach north of public pier* ☎ 206/0356 ▭ *MC, V* ☺ *Closed Wed.*

Where to Stay & Eat on Caye Caulker

The Split

Lazy Lizard's Bar

Frenchie's Dive Shop

Soccer Field

NOT TO SCALE

Dock Street

Public Pier

Back Street

Middle Street

Front Street

Post Office

Airline Offices

Airstrip

$–$$ ✕ **The Sandbox.** Whether outside under the palms or indoors under the lazily turning ceiling fans, you'll always have your feet in the sand here. The names of regulars are carved on the backs of the chairs. Open from 7 AM to 10 PM, the Sandbox has a large menu, with tasty items such as lobster omelet with fry jacks for breakfast, lobster fritters or barbecue chicken for lunch, and red snapper for dinner. The chowders are also very good. Prices are reasonable, and portions are large. At night the bar gets lively. ⊠ *Front St. near public pier* ☎ 226/0200 ⊟ *AE, MC, V.*

$–$$ ✕ **Syd's.** If you ask a local resident for a restaurant recommendation, chances are you'll get a vote for Syd's. It serves Belizean and Mexican favorites like beans and rice, stew chicken, *garnaches,* and tostadas (BZ$1.50), along with (in-season) lobster and conch at prices lower than you'll pay at most other eateries. If you have a choice, dine outside in the patio rather than inside. ⊠ *Middle St., south of public pier* ☎ 226/0294 ⊟ *MC, V* ⊙ *Closed Sun.*

¢–$ ✕ **Glenda's Café.** The menu here is on a chalkboard, short and sweet, and you place your order at the window. At breakfast, when this café is most popular, you can get a hearty breakfast of eggs, bacon, beans, homemade cinnamon roll or johnnycakes, and fresh orange juice for a pittance. It opens at 7:30 AM. ⊠ *Back St. north of post office* ☎ 226/0148 ⊟ *No credit cards* ⊙ *Closed weekends. No dinner.*

$$ ▦ **Auxillou Beach Suites.** Smack in the middle of Caulker, on the beach-front north of the public pier, is this collection of eye-catching green, coral, and blue houses. Inside, the one-bedroom suites are more toned down, with neutral-color walls, tile floors, and kitchenettes. Each unit has a deck or balcony, and you're only about 50 feet from the sea. ⊠ *Front St. north of public pier* ☎ 226/0370 ⊕ *www.auxilloubeachsuites.com* ↜ *10 apartments* ⚲ *Fans, kitchenettes, beach, travel services; no phones in rooms, no TVs in some rooms* ⊟ *MC, V.*

$$ ▦ **Caye Caulker Condos.** If you want a full kitchen to prepare some of your own meals, these new condos are a good choice. The luxe units are done in cheerful tropical colors and have tile floors, full air-condi-tioning, and private verandas facing the water. Ask for a second-floor room—the view is better. Bikes are complimentary. ⊠ *At north end of island, near Split* ☎ 226/0072 ⊕ *www.cayecaulkercondos.com* ↜ *8 apart-ments* ⚲ *Fans, kitchens, beach, travel services; no phones in rooms, no TVs in some rooms* ⊟ *MC, V.*

★ **$$**   ▦ **Iguana Reef Inn.** One of Caye Caulker's most upmarket lodgings, Iguana Reef has just about everything but a concierge and a pool. The suites are colorfully furnished with handmade furniture and local artwork and have air-conditioning, which, while becoming more common, is still the excep-tion, not the rule, for the island. Upstairs suites have vaulted ceilings with skylights. The latest addition is a thatch-roof bar. Because the inn is on the island's lee side, you have the benefit of sunset views from your ve-randa, but you're not on the beach. Co-owner James Dombrowski has a lot of information about the island. ⊠ *Near end of Middle St., next to soccer field* ☎ 226/0213 ⊟ 226/0087 ⊕ *www.iguanareefinn.com* ↜ *12 suites* ⚲ *Fans, refrigerators, snorkeling, fishing, bar, travel services; no room phones, no room TVs, no kids under 10* ⊟ *AE, MC, V.*

★ **$–$$**   ▦ **Seaside Cabañas.** If your Belizean dreams include lounging poolside, Belikin in hand, get thee to Seaside, a delightful beachfront inn with the

CLOSE UP

Permanent Vacations

THAT WELL-TANNED LADY relaxing under a palm tree on the beach may not be a tourist after all. She could be an expatriate who decided to chuck it all and move to Belize. Thousands of Americans, Canadians, Europeans, and Asians have already done so or have bought property and plan to move later, perhaps after retirement.

Attracted by low real estate prices, a frost-free climate, and an awesome spectra of activities, many expats are drawn to Belize, especially to Ambergris Caye, Corozal, and the Cayo. Ambergris Caye has an idyllic Caribbean island atmosphere. Corozal Town and its environs have Belize's lowest living costs, and Mexico is right next door. The Cayo appeals to those who want land for growing fruit trees or keeping a few horses.

With houses renting for as little as BZ$400 a month (though some in San Pedro go for 10 times that amount), and land selling at prices last seen in the United States in the 1960s, retirement dollars can stretch very far here. Beachfront building lots go for as little as BZ$100,000 to BZ$150,000—still pricey, but cheap in comparison to oceanfront lots in Florida or California. There are no major restrictions against foreigners owning land in Belize. Moreover, with English as an official language and English Common Law forming the basis of Belize's legal system, Belize is very accommodating to expats.

In late 2001 the government unveiled a program called the Qualified Retired Persons Incentive Program to attract retirees to Belize. In exchange for depositing BZ$4,000 a month in a Belize bank for living expenses, and proving that you have the resources to

do so, anyone aged 45 and older can get official residency, along with the right to import household goods, a car, boat, and even an airplane tax-free. The application costs about BZ$1,500 and is relatively painless. After getting Qualified Retired Persons status, you have almost all the rights of a Belize citizen except you can't vote or work for pay. The Belize Tourist Board (BTB) administers the program, and details are available on its Web site, ⊕ www.travelbelize.org.

The BTB won't disclose exactly how many applications it's received, but they've gotten at least a few thousand so far. It's a wonder that more people haven't applied: 70 million baby boomers in the United States alone are expected to retire over the next 5 to 20 years. Many of them will be looking for alternatives to cold winters and high prices up north.

For those not quite ready to retire, it's still possible to move to Belize, although work permits are difficult to obtain, and salaries are a fraction of those in the United States, Canada, or Western Europe. The best option may be to invest in or start a business in Belize that employs Belizean workers, thus paving the way for a self-employment work permit and fast-track residency.

Of course, Belize isn't for everyone. And Belize, as seen from the perspective of a full-time resident, isn't the same as the Belize that's experienced by vacationers. Expats anywhere face culture shock, and Belize presents some special situations, including lack of high-tech medical care and a higher risk of theft and burglary than back home.

only swimming pool on the island. Seaside, which has three sunset orange–color thatch-roof buildings arranged in a U-shape around the pool, commands a prime location just south of the public pier. Bathrooms feel barebones (showers don't have curtains) but other creature comforts (air-conditioning, cable TV, and a mini-refrigerator) make up for it. Four of the rooms (numbers 1, 2, 3, and 4) have private rooftop terraces for sunning or watching the sea—they're not much more a night and worth the extra money. The Una Mas bar serves drinks and coffee. ⊠ *At public pier* ☎ *226/0498* 📠 *226/0125* ⊕ *www.seasidecabanas.com* ↪ *15 rooms, 1 2-bedroom suite* ⚓ *Fans, refrigerators, cable TV, pool, snorkeling, fishing, bar, shop, travel services; no room phones* ▭ *MC, V.*

¢–$$ 🏨 **De Real Macaw.** De Real Macaw represents the "new Caulker" trend in guesthouses: better service, bigger rooms, more amenities like air-conditioning and cable TV, and all at a good value. You have a choice of six rooms or two larger apartment suites. It's not luxurious, but it's clean and well run. ⊠ *Front St. north of public pier* ☎ *226/0459* 📠 *226/0497* ⊕ *www.derealmacaw.com* ↪ *6 rooms, 2 suites* ⚓ *Fans, refrigerators, cable TV, beach, laundry service; no a/c in some rooms, no phones in some rooms* ▭ *D, MC, V.*

✔$ 🏨 **Chocolate's.** Chocolate is a young-looking seventysomething Belizean who rents out one of Caye Caulker's best rooms—a romantic retreat with a four-poster bed, vaulted mahogany ceiling with fan, and a screened-in veranda that looks out to the sea. The tile bath has a gigantic shower (terry robes are nearby). Chocolate helped pioneer manatee-watching trips to Goff Caye and is notable for his dedication to conservation. ⊠ *At north end of island near Split* ☎ *226/0151* ↪ *1 room* ⚓ *Fans, refrigerator, snorkeling, shop; no a/c, no room phone, no room TVs* ▭ *MC, V.*

$ 🏨 **Lazy Iguana B&B.** This B&B may be the tallest structure on the caye. The views of the sunsets from the fourth-level rooftop terrace are terrific, though the hotel's location on the island's back side means you need to swat an occasional mosquito while you watch. The rooms are furnished with attractive wicker and tropical hardwood furniture. Feel free to make yourself at home in the common room, which has TV and Internet access—owner Mo Miller says no shoes are required. ⊠ *Back St. north of airstrip* ☎ *226/0350* 📠 *226/0320* ⊕ *www.lazyiguana.net* ↪ *4 rooms* ⚓ *Fans, Internet room, no-smoking rooms; no room phones, no room TVs, no kids under 10* ▭ *MC, V* ⑂ *CP.*

¢–$ 🏨 **Morning Star.** Want cozy? This quiet little budget inn about 300 feet from the beach has two smallish rooms, way up on the third floor, with a veranda offering views of the island and sea. There's also a tiny cabin at the back in the garden. The Morning Star (also called the Jaguar Morning Star) is run by a Belizean–American couple. ⊠ *Middle St. south of public pier* ☎ *226/0347* ⊕ *www.jaguarmorningstar.com* ↪ *2 rooms, 1 cabin* ⚓ *Fans, some refrigerators, travel services; no a/c, no phones in rooms, no room TVs* ▭ *MC, V.*

★ ¢–$ 🏨 **Treetops.** Owners Terry and Doris Creasey (he's British, she's Austrian) bring international flair to this seaside guesthouse, which is so well run and such a good value that it's almost always full. One room has an East African theme, with authentic masks and spears, and another has art from Malaysia and Indonesia. Two third-floor suites, Sunset and Sunrise, have king-size beds and private balconies with views of the water.

A few people rankle at the house rules and regulations enforced by the owners: rooms are cleaned at 8:30 AM, no ifs, ands or buts; no cooking in rooms, not even hot water for coffee or tea; no outside guests; checkout required by 9:30 AM. ⊠ *Caye Caulker* ☎ *226/0240* 🖷 *226/0115* ⊕ *www.treetopsbelize.com* ↩ *4 rooms, 2 with bath, 2 suites* ♻ *Fans, refrigerators, cable TV, beach, snorkeling, laundry service, travel services; no a/c in some rooms, no phones in some rooms, no kids under 12, no smoking* ▤ *MC, V.*

¢ 🖼 **Tina's Bak Pak Hostel.** If you're looking for the cheapest place to stay on the island, look no further: you can have a hammock here for BZ$16 per person. Though the two-story lodgings are very basic, you're right on the beach, and the price and location means this place is usually packed with young people. Tina Auxillou, one of the Auxillou sisters who have many tourism-related businesses on the island, runs it. ☎ *226/0351* 🖷 *226/0097* ↩ *2 rooms, 3 dorms, all with shared baths* ♻ *Fans, travel services; no a/c, no room phones, no TV* ▤ *MC, V.*

¢ 🖼 **Trends Beachfront Hotel.** One of the first things you see when you arrive at the island's pier is this little hotel, painted tropical pink and turquoise. Thanks to its location and bright rooms, it's often booked full. TVs are available on request. ⊠ *Near Front St. at public pier* ☎ *226/ 0094* 🖷 *226/0097* ⊕ *www.trendsbze.com* ↩ *6 rooms, 1 cabana* ♻ *Fans, refrigerator; no a/c, no room phones, no TV in some rooms* ▤ *MC, V.*

Vacation Home Rentals

A handful of privately owned homes are available for rent on the island, either daily or by the week. Expect to pay around BZ$80 to BZ$200 a night or BZ$800 to BZ$1,200 a week. In most cases, credit cards are not accepted.

One of the larger rental agencies, **Caye Caulker Rentals** (⊠ Front St. ☎ 226/0485 ⊕ www.cayecaulkerrentals.com) has more than a dozen houses for rent, some daily from BZ$80 a night, and others, including beachfront houses, from around BZ$800 a week. Owned by Diane Auxillou Kuylen, **Diane's Beach House** (⊠ Front St. ☎ 226/0083 ⊕ www. staycayecaulker.com/beachhouse.html) has two nice suites—a one-bedroom and a two-bedroom—in a mango-color house with views of the sea. Rates are BZ$260 to BZ$300 nightly. **Heredia's Apartments & House Rentals** (⊠ Calley del Sol, about a block from public pier ☎ 226/ 0132)has several budget apartments and houses on the lagoon side, most under BZ$500 a week.

Nightlife

You don't come to Caye Caulker for the hot nightlife, but the island does have its share of laid-back bars.

Knock back a Belikin or two to the beat of reggae music at **I&I Reggae Bar** (⊠ Off Front St. south of public pier, go south on Front St. to dead ends, then turn right ☎ No phone). Swings hang from the ceiling, replacing bar stools, in one area, and the top floor has hammocks and a thatch roof. There's really nothing else like this three-story bar in Belize. For live music, your best bet is **Oceanside** (⊠ Front St. near public pier ☎ 226/0233). "Sunny place for shady people" is the slogan of the

CLOSE UP

National Symbols of Belize

National TREE: **Mahogany** (*Swietenia macrophilla*)

This prized tree has been heavily logged in Belize and large specimens are found in only a few areas. The "big leaf" mahogany tree can grow more than 150 feet high and takes 80 years to reach maturity. The wood has a coppery red sheen, a tight, knot-free grain, and a single mature tree can be worth US$100,000 or more.

National FLOWER: **Black Orchid** (*Encyclia cochleatum*)

The name is deceiving. Only the lip of the flower is black and the long, slender sepals and petals are yellow-green. These fragrant little flowers bloom year-round and can be found growing on trees in damp areas.

National BIRD: **Keel-Billed Toucan** (*Ramphastos solfurantus*)

Every cereal lover is familiar with this bird. The toucan, with its huge canoe-shape beak and bright yellow cheeks, can be found in open areas all over the country and loves to eat fruit.

National ANIMAL: **Baird's Tapir** (*Tapirello bairdii*)

Called the mountain cow by most Belizeans, the tapir is actually related to the primitive horse and rhinoceros. A beefy vegetarian, it can weigh up to 600 pounds and is often found in heavy bush, near rivers and streams.

National MOTTO: *Sub Umbra Florero*

"Under the Shade I Flourish" refers to the shade of the mahogany tree, which is on Belize's coat of arms and flag.

National DRINK: **Orange Fanta** and **Belikin Beer**

Unofficially, of course.

Lazy Lizard (⊠ At Split ☎ 226/0368), but after dark there's a spotlight pointed into the water, so you can see fish, small sharks, and occasionally even a crocodile swimming around. **Herbal Tribe** (⊠ Front St. ☎ 226/0110) is an open-air bar, heavy on the reggae. It also serves meals, including pizza, and there's a small art gallery.

Shopping

You won't find as many shops here as in San Pedro, but there are a few stand-out stores to poke around for some interesting souvenirs.

Caribbean Colors (⊠ Front St. ☎ 226/2206) has colorful watercolors and silk screenings by the owner, Lee Vanderwalker-Kroll, along with handmade jewelry, scarfs, and art by other artists. Also in the shop is the Coco Loco Café. **Annie's Boutique** (⊠ North end of island near Split at Chocolate's ☎ 226/0151) has some of Belize's best clothing for women and children. Here you'll find dresses and sarongs made with fabrics from Bali, unique silver jewelry, and Guatemalan bags.

Coco Plum Gardens Gift Shop (⊠ Back St. ☎ 226/0226) has Belizean arts and crafts.

Chan's (⊠ Middle St. at corner of street coming from public pier ☎ 226/0165) is the largest grocery in the village. Look for Marie Sharp's here.

UP-AND-COMING CAYES

Caye Chapel

❸ *½ mi (2 km) south of Caye Caulker, 6 mi (10 km) south of Amber-gris Caye.*

Not since the days of British colonialism has Belize had a real 18-hole golf course. But for traveling golfers, a course opened in 1999 on Caye Chapel, a privately owned 265-acre island. It's a beautiful par-72 course, playing to more than 7,000 yards, flat but long, with four par-5 holes. Challenges include brisk prevailing winds and an occasional crocodile. This is Belize's best course (a smaller 9-hole public course is near Bel-mopan at Roaring River Golf Club). If you're not staying at the Caye Chapel Island Resort, which grants guests full access, you can still play for BZ$400 per person, including lunch, club, and cart rental.

$$$$ **Caye Chapel Island Resort.** Designed as a corporate retreat, this resort
Fodor's Choice accommodates anyone who's got the cash. The expansive villas, which
★ stand at imperial attention along the seafront, are similar to what you might see in exclusive gated communities in Boca Raton, Florida. In-side you'll find every luxury—whirlpool baths, expansive wet bars, and kitchens with the latest German appliances. A dozen "budget" casitas, though anything but, have a price tag that's significantly less than the villas. Rates include all meals and unlimited golf. The golf course's clubhouse has a restaurant with indoor and open-air dining and stun-ning views of the sea. ⊠ *Caye Chapel* ☎ *226/8250* 📠 *226–8201* ⊕ *www.belizegolf.cc* 🛏 *8 villas, 12 casitas* ⚬ *Restaurant, fans, some in-room hot tubs, kitchens, cable TV, 18-hole golf course, tennis courts, pool, gym, beach, dive shop, dock, boating, marina, fishing, basketball, bar, laundry service, Internet, airstrip, travel services; no smoking* 🟰 *AE, D, MC, V* ⧇ *All meals included.*

Cayo Espanto

❹ *3 mi (5 km) west of San Pedro.*

Espanto means fright in Spanish, but there's nothing to be frightened of on this tiny island 5 km (3 mi) west of Ambergris Caye. Cayo Es-panto is all there is on this four-acre island. You can walk the caye in less time than it takes to drink a cold mojito.

$$$$ **Cayo Espanto.** On a tiny private island west of Ambergris Caye, this
Fodor's Choice super-luxury resort has a staff-to-guest ratio of two to one. Each villa
★ comes complete with a splash pool, Egyptian cotton linens, and a per-sonal butler. Several villas have walls that literally fold back to let in the Caribbean sun. As a guest, you meet with the chef to plan your day's meals, which are delivered to your own waterside table. For all this per-sonal care you'll pay a small fortune, up to BZ$5,000 a night, double, plus 25% service charge and tax. ⊠ *3 mi (5 km) west of Ambergris Caye* 📫 *Box 90, San Pedro* ☎ *888/666–4282 in U.S.* 📠 *221/3001* ⊕ *www. aprivateisland.com* 🛏 *5 villas* ⚬ *Dining room, room service, fans,*

cable TV, 4 pools, beach, dock, snorkeling, boating, fishing, laundry service, Wi-Fi, travel services ▭ *AE, MC, V* ⊗ *All meals included.*

St. George's Caye

❺ *9 mi (15 km) northeast of Belize City.*

Just a stone's throw from Belize City, this small caye is steeped in history. The state of Belize had its origins here, as St. George's Caye held the original British settlement's first capital. In 1798 the island was the site of a decisive battle with the Spanish. Islanders had only one sloop, while the Spanish had 31 ships. Their knowledge of the sea, however, helped them to defeat the invaders in two hours.

Getting to St. George's Caye couldn't be easier, as the boat trip from Belize City takes little more than 20 minutes. Affluent Belize City residents weekend in their private cottages here. Although St. George's Caye has great places to dive, many serious scuba enthusiasts choose to head out to the more pristine atolls.

$$$$ ▣ **St. George's Lodge.** In colonial days this long-established resort was a British favorite because of its proximity to Belize City. Today divers favor St. George's Caye, undoubtedly because of the diving program led by Fred Good. You have a choice of basic rooms in the main building or thatch cottages partly over the water. Electricity comes from the lodge's own windmills, and the shower water is heated by the sun. The restaurant serves homemade bread and soups and grilled snapper or grouper, and coffee is delivered to your door in the morning. Weekly dive packages start at around BZ$3,350 per person, including meals, with discounts for cash. ⊠ *St. George's Caye* ⌂ *1604 Maple St., Nokomis, FL 34275* ☎ *220/4444, 800/678–6871 in U.S.* ☏ *941/488–3953* ⊕ *www.gooddiving.com* ⤷ *8 rooms, 6 cabanas* ⚭ *Restaurant, fans, beach, dive shop, snorkeling, travel services; no a/c, no room phones, no room TVs* ▭ *AE, MC, V* ⊗ *All meals included.*

Tobacco Caye

❽ *11 mi (18 km) southeast of Dangriga.*

If you don't want to pay a lot for your place in the sun, Tobacco Caye may be for you. It's a tiny island—barely 4 acres, and a walk around the entire caye takes 10 minutes—but it's right on the reef, so you can wade in and snorkel all you want. Though the snorkeling off the caye is not as good as in some other areas of Belize (much of the coral is dead and most of the fish are small), you can see spotted eagle rays, moray eels, octopuses, and other sealife. All the accommodations here are budget places, basically simple wood cabins, some not much larger than sheds. A half-dozen hotels vie for space, making the islet seem even smaller than it is. Periodically they get blown away by storms but are rebuilt, usually a little better than they were before.

Though some places are increasing rates, most prices remain affordably low, around BZ$60–BZ$145 a day per person, including meals. A word of caution: hotels can be very casual about reservations. After making reservations months in advance, you may arrive to find that your reservation has been lost and the hotel is fully occupied. Fortunately, it's usually easy to find a room in another hotel. Lana's on the Reef and Tobacco Caye Paradise are the cheapest hotels, with rates starting around BZ$55 per person, including meals, but with tiny rooms with shared baths. The island has no shops, bars, or restaurants, except those at the hotels, but there is one dive shop. Boats leave from the Riverside Restaurant in Dangriga for the 30-minute, BZ$35 trip to Tobacco Caye. Get to the Riverside by 9 AM; most boats leave around 9:30 (though at busy times such as Easter they come and go all day long). You can get information on the boats, as well as breakfast, at the Riverside Café.

Tobacco Caye is at the northern tip of the South Water Caye Marine Reserve, a 62-square-mile reserve that's popular for diving and fishing and which has some of the most beautiful islands in Belize. As of November 2005, visitors to the South Water Caye Marine Reserve pay BZ$10 a day, for up to three days, or BZ$30 a week, park fee. Rangers come around and collect it from guests at the Tobacco Caye hotels.

$$ ▦ **Tobacco Caye Lodge.** This cluster of pastel blue cabins is a mere few feet from the turquoise sea. There's a bit more room here for stretching out than at the island's other lodges, as the property extends from the sea on the east to the back side of the caye. A thatch-roof bar is set away from the cabins, and three simple but filling meals are included in the rate. ⊠ *Tobacco Caye* ☎ *520/5033* ⊕ *www.tclodgebelize.com* ⇲ *6 cabins* ⚭ *Fans, beach, snorkeling, fishing, bar; no a/c, no room phones, no room TVs* ⊟ *MC, V* ⚭ *All meals included.*

$ ▦ **Gaviota's Coral Reef Resort.** On this island, you're locked into a meal plan at your hotel, so the quality of food matters. Here, the food, served family-style at fixed times, is very good. You'll enjoy fresh fish, beans and rice, and even salads. The clapboard rooms and cabins are tiny, but the location on the east side of the caye provides cooling breezes. At BZ$60 per person including all meals, it's a good value. ⊠ *Tobacco Caye* ☎ *509/5032* ⇲ *4 rooms, 5 cabins, all with shared baths* ⚭ *Some fans, beach, snorkeling, fishing; no a/c, no room phones, no room TVs* ⊟ *MC, V* ⚭ *All meals included.*

$ ▦ **Ocean's Edge Lodge.** Nestled beneath coconut palms on the southeast end of the island are these seven rustic two-story cabins. The young staff is amiable, and the dining room-cum-lounge has a bar, pool table, board games, small library, and karaoke system. ⊠ *Tobacco Caye* ☎ *601/8537* ⊕ *www2.symet.net/beltex* ⇲ *7 rooms* ⚭ *Fans, beach, dive shop, snorkeling, fishing, bar; no a/c, no room phones, no room TVs* ⊟ *MC, V* ⚭ *All meals included.*

South Water Caye

❾ *14 mi (23 km) southeast of Dangriga.*

Fodor'sChoice
★

This is one of our favorite underrated spots in Belize. The 15-acre South Water Caye has good off-the-beaten-reef diving and snorkeling in a stunning tropical setting, and the beach at the southern end of the island is one of Belize's sandy beauties. The reef is only a short swim from shore.

The downside of the small caye? The sand flies here can be a nuisance, and there aren't any facilities other than those at the island's two resorts and the International Zoological Expeditions' student dorm.

The nearby **Smithsonian Institution's Marine Research Laboratory** (⊠ Carrie Bow Caye) welcomes visitors by appointment; contact the Blue Marlin Lodge (see review below) for more information.

$$$$ ⊡ **Blue Marlin Lodge.** An excellent, though pricey, base for fishing, snorkeling, and diving trips, this Belizean-owned resort at the north end of the island is only 50 yards from the reef. Accommodations, which spread out over half the caye, range from rooms with plywood walls to cozy wood cabins to a trio of aquamarine-color concrete dome buildings. Rooms are so close to the sea that wave sounds may lull you to sleep. The resort has its own dive shop and two boats for diving and fishing. The restaurant and bar are great places to swap stories with other travelers. The minimum stay is four days. ⊠ *South Water Caye* ☎ *522/ 2243, 800/798–1558 in U.S.* 🖷 *522/2296* ⊕ *www.bluemarinlodge. com* ⤳ *8 rooms, 8 cottages* ⌂ *Restaurant, beach, dive shop, snorkeling, fishing, billiards, bar, babysitting, travel services; no a/c in some rooms, no room phones, no room TVs* ⊟ *MC, V* ⦿ *All meals included.*

★ $$$ ⊡ **Pelican Beach South Water Caye.** Steps from one of Belize's best beaches, where you can swim, snorkel, and fish to your heart's content and dive from shore, is this former convent–turned–peaceful island retreat. The colonial-era main house has a dining room serving fresh seafood and Belizean-style dishes on the ground floor, and five large rooms on the second floor. You can also stay in one of three cottages: Egret's Escape, a honeymoon cottage; Osprey's Nest, which sleeps six; and Heron's Hideaway, which has a porch over the water. Power here is solar, showers are rainwater, and toilets are the composting kind. ⊠ *South Water Caye* ☎ *522/2044* 🖷 *522/2570* ⊕ *www.pelicanbeachbelize.com* ⤳ *5 rooms, 3 cottages, 1 student dorm* ⌂ *Restaurant, beach, dive shop, snorkeling, boating, fishing, travel services; no a/c, no room phones, no room TVs* ⊟ *AE, MC, V* ⦿ *All meals included.*

THE ATOLLS

There are only four atolls in the Western Hemisphere, and three of them are off Belize (the fourth is Chinchorro Reef, off Mexico's Yucatán). The atolls—Turneffe, Lighthouse, and Glover's—are oval-shape masses of coral. A few small islands, some sandy and others mostly mangrove, rise up along the atolls' encircling coral arms. Within the coral walls are central lagoons, with shallow water 10 to 30 feet deep. Outside the walls, the ocean falls off sharply to 1,000 feet or more, deeper than any diver can go.

Unlike the more common Pacific atolls, which were formed from underwater volcanoes, the Caribbean atolls began forming millions of years ago, atop giant tectonic faults. As giant limestone blocks slowly settled, they provided platforms for coral growth.

Because of their remoteness (they're 25 mi to 50 mi from the mainland) and because most of the islands at the atolls are small, the atolls have remained nearly pristine. Only a few small dive and fishing resorts are here, and the serious divers and anglers who favor the area know that they have some of the best diving and fishing in the Caribbean, if not the world. The atolls are also wonderful for beachcombing, relaxing, and snorkeling—just bring plenty of books, as there are no shops or restaurants other than at the hotels.

Of course, paradise has its price: most of the atoll resorts are expensive and have minimum-stay requirements. Getting here also usually requires a long boat ride, sometimes rough enough to bring on *mal de mer*. Try to take one of the scheduled boats to the lodges or ride out on a dive or snorkel boat with a group; otherwise, you'll likely pay BZ$600 or more to charter a boat.

Turneffe Atoll

❻ *25 mi (40 km) east of Belize City.*

The largest of the three atolls, Turneffe, is the closest to Belize City. It's one of the best spots for diving, thanks to several steep drop-offs. Only an hour from Lighthouse Reef and 45 minutes from the northern edge of Glover's Reef, Turneffe is a good base for exploring all of the atolls.

The best-known attraction, and probably Belize's most exciting wall dive, is the **Elbow,** at Turneffe's southernmost tip. You may encounter eagle rays swimming nearby. As many as 50 might flutter together, forming a rippling herd. Elbow is generally considered an advanced dive because of the strong currents, which sweep you toward the deep water beyond the reef.

Though it's most famous for its spectacular wall dives, the atoll has dives for every level. The leeward side, where the reef is wide and gently sloping, is good for shallower dives and snorkeling; you'll see large concentrations of tube sponges, soft corals such as forked sea feathers and sea fans, and plenty of fish. Also on the atoll's western side is the wreck of the *Sayonara*. No doubloons to scoop up here—it was a small passenger and cargo boat that sank in 1985—but it's good for wreck dive practice.

Fishing here, as at all of the atolls, is world-class. You can fly-fish for bonefish and permit in the grassy flats, or go after migratory tarpon from May to September in the channels and lagoons of the atoll. Jack, barracuda, and snappers lurk in the mangrove-lined bays and shorelines. Billfish, sailfish, and other big creatures are in the blue water around the atoll.

Where to Stay & Eat

$$$$ 🏨 **Blackbird Caye Resort.** Deluxe cabanas at this gorgeous 166-acre resort have private bedrooms with king beds and separate living areas. Dine in style with new friends you'll make at the resort in a palapa with

2

hardwood floors, matching tables, and soaring thatch ceiling. Unlike some other atoll resorts, Blackbird Caye caters to snorkelers as well as to divers and anglers, with two boat trips daily for snorkelers. ⊠ *Turneffe Atoll* ℭ *Caye Resorts, Box 13099, Burton, WA 98013* ☎ *206/463–0833 or 888/271–3483* ⊟ *206/463–4081* ⊕ *www.blackbirdresort.com* ✑ *16 cabanas* ⵁ *Dining room, fans, some refrigerators, dive shop, snorkeling, fishing, bar, travel services; no room phones, no room TVs* ▭ *MC, V* ℗ *All meals included.*

$$$$ ⊡ **Turneffe Flats.** The sound of the surf is the only thing you'll hear at these smart blue-and-white beachfront cabins. The rooms, fitted with elegant hardwoods, are a far cry from the barebones fishing camp that occupied this site in the early '80s. You can dive here—a Pro 48 dive boat is on standby and the reef is only 200 yards from shore—but the ubiquitous fishing-pole racks suggest that snook, bonefish, and permit are still the dominant lure. You pay a pretty penny to indulge your passion, however—a weekly fishing package for two is around BZ$13,700. ⊠ *Northern Bogue Caye* ℭ *Box 36, Deadwood, SD 57732* ☎ *888/ 512–8812* ⊟ *623/298–5008* ⊕ *www.tflats.com* ✑ *10 rooms* ⵁ *Dining room, dive shop, snorkeling, fishing; no room phones, no room TVs, no kids under 12* ▭ *D, MC, V* ℗ *All meals included.*

★ $$$$ ⊡ **Turneffe Island Lodge.** White dive tanks serving as fence posts and a rusty anchor from an 18th-century British warship set the tone at this south end resort. This was Turneffe Atoll's first dive lodge, and it bagged the best spot a few hundred yards from the legendary Elbow. If you came to Belize for the diving, this is an ideal base. The rooms, in palm-shaded cottages with sea views, have been refurbished without spoiling the cozy feeling created by the varnished hardwood fittings. Seven beachfront cabanas are solid mahogany inside. The two-story colonial-style house holds the bar and the dining room. The resort isn't for penny-pinchers: a three-night beachcombing package is BZ$4,560 double, and dive and fishing rates are higher. ⊠ *Coco Tree Caye* ☎ *713/313–4670 or 800/874– 0118* ⊟ *713/313–4671* ⊕ *www.turneffelodge.com* ✑ *12 rooms, 7 cabanas* ⵁ *Dining room, fans, dive shop, snorkeling, fishing, bar, travel services; no room phones, no room TVs* ▭ *AE, MC, V* ☾ *Closed Sept. and Oct.* ℗ *All meals included.*

Lighthouse Reef Atoll, the Blue Hole & Half Moon Caye

❼ *50 mi (80 km) east of Belize City.*

If Robinson Crusoe had been a man of means, he would have repaired here for a break from his desert island.

Lighthouse Reef is about 18 mi (29 km) long and less than 1 mi (2 km) wide and is surrounded by a seemingly endless stretch of coral. Here you'll find two of the country's best dives.

Blue Hole. From the air, the Blue Hole, a breathtaking vertical chute that drops several hundred feet through the reef, looks like a dark blue eye in the center of the shallow lagoon. The Blue Hole was first dived by Jacques Cousteau in 1970 and has since become a diver's pilgrimage site. Just over 1,000 feet wide at the surface and dropping almost vertically to a depth of 412 feet, the Blue Hole is like swimming down a mineshaft. This excitement is reflected in the thousands of stickers reading, "I Dived the Blue Hole."

Half Moon Caye. The best diving on Lighthouse Reef is at this classic wall dive. Half Moon Caye begins at 35 feet and drops almost vertically to blue infinity. Floating out over the edge is a bit like free-fall parachuting. Magnificent spurs of coral jut out to the seaward side, looking like small tunnels; they're fascinating to explore and invariably full of fish. An exceptionally varied marine life hovers around this caye. On the gently sloping sand flats behind the coral spurs, a vast colony of garden eels stirs, their heads protruding from the sand like periscopes. Spotted eagle rays, sea turtles, and other underwater wonders frequent the drop-off.

Half Moon Caye National Monument. Belize's easternmost island offers one of Belize's greatest wildlife encounters, although it's difficult to reach and lacks accommodations other than camping. Part of the Lighthouse Reef system, Half Moon Caye owes its protected status to the presence of the red-footed booby. The bird is here in such numbers that it's hard to believe it has only one other nesting ground in the entire Caribbean (on Tobago Island, off the coast of Venezuela). Some 4,000 of these birds hang their hats on Half Moon Caye, along with iguanas, lizards, and loggerhead turtles. The entire 40-acre island is a nature reserve, so you can explore the beaches or head into the bush on the narrow nature trail. Above the trees at the island's center is a small viewing platform—at the top you're suddenly in a sea of birds that will doubtless remind you of a certain Alfred Hitchcock movie. Several dive operators and resorts arrange day trips and overnight camping trips to Half Moon Caye. The park fee here is a steep BZ$80 per person.

At this writing, visiting Lighthouse Reef is best done as a side trip from Ambergris Caye, Caye Caulker, or another location in northern Belize. Lighthouse Reef Resort on Northern Caye, a long-established dive lodge, is closed for rebuilding until 2008. Planned lodges and restaurants, which were announced in connection with the sale of lots on Long Caye, a 650-acre island, are in a state of limbo, as is the development of Long Caye itself. You may be able to stay at **Calypso Beach Retreat** (✉ Long Caye, Lighthouse Atoll ☎ 303/523–8165 ⊕ www.calypsobeachretreat.com), which is open occasionally, when there is demand from dive groups.

Glover's Reef Atoll

⑩   *70 mi (113 km) southeast of Belize City.*

Fodor'sChoice
★   Named after the pirate John Glover, this coral necklace strung around a 80-square-mi (208-square-km) lagoon is the southernmost of Belize's three atolls. There are five islands at the atoll. Visitors to Glover's Reef are charged a BZ$20 park fee (BZ$25 for fly-fishing).

Emerald Forest Reef. Although most of the best dive sites are along the atoll's southeastern side, this is the exception. It's named for its masses of huge green elkhorn coral. Because the reef's most exciting part is only 25 feet down, it's excellent for novice divers.

2

Long Caye Wall. This is an exciting wall with a dramatic drop-off hundreds of feet down. It's a good place to spot turtles, rays, and barracuda.

Southwest Caye Wall is an underwater cliff that falls quickly to 130 feet. It's briefly interrupted by a narrow shelf, then continues its near-vertical descent to 350 feet. This dive gives you the exhilaration of flying in blue space, so it's easy to lose track of how deep you are going. Both ascent and descent require careful monitoring.

Kayaking is another popular sport here; you can paddle out to the atoll's many patch reefs for snorkeling. Most hotels rent kayaks.

Where to Stay & Eat

$$$$ ⬚ **Isla Marisol.** At Isla Marisol you can sip a cold Belikin in a bar perched at the end of a pier, a hundred feet out in the Caribbean. After a breakfast of mango and johnnycake, you can dive "The Pinnacles," where coral heads rise 40 feet from the ocean floor. After a lobster dinner, wander back to your cabin, a breezy retreat built of tropical hardwoods. Beachcomber packages including meals and transport to the island start at BZ$1,050 per person for three days, diving at BZ$1,600, and fishing at BZ$1,850. ⊠ *Southwest Caye* ☎ *520/2056* ⊕ *www.islamarisolresort. com* ➮ *10 cabins* ⌂ *Fans, beach, dive shop, snorkeling, fishing, bar; no a/c, no room phones, no room TVs* ⊟ *AE, MC, V* ⦿ *All meals included.*

$$$$ ⬚ **Off the Wall Dive Center and Resort.** Though this resort focuses on diving, snorkelers, and anglers, there's excellent snorkeling and fishing as well. Depending on your point of view, you'll find the small wood cabins, composting toilets, and outdoor rainwater showers, either rustic or basic. The resort focuses on diving, but snorkelers and anglers have excellent options as well. Meals are served in a beachfront thatch palapa with sand floor. ⊠ *Long Caye* ☎ *614/6348* ⊕ *www.offthewallbelize.com* ➮ *4 cabanas* ⌂ *Fans, beach, dive shop, snorkeling, fishing, bar; no a/c, no room phones, no room TVs* ⊟ *MC, V* ⦿ *All meals included.*

$$$$ ⬚ **Manta Resort.** Even though the surroundings here aren't as pleasant as those at some of the other resorts with access to Glover's Reef (the island still looks bare from storm damage, although some palm trees have been planted), Manta itself is a relaxing divers' haven. A 50-foot dive boat with twin 850 HP diesels, along with several smaller boats, take divers, snorkelers, and anglers to the reef. Stay in one of two kinds of cabins: small cottages made of mahogany, or newer, larger, octagonal cottages with tile floors. Both are air-conditioned. Credit cards are accepted for the deposit only; you must pay the balance with a check. ⊠ *Glover's Reef Atoll* ⌂ *Caye Resorts, Box 13099, Burton, WA 98013* ☎ *800/326–1724 or 206/463–0833* ⎙ *206/463–4081* ⊕ *www.mantaresortbelize. com* ➮ *11 cottages, 1 2-bedroom cottage* ⌂ *Fans, beach, dive shop, snorkeling, fishing, bar; no room phones, no room TVs* ⊟ *MC, V* ⦿ *FAP.*

¢–$ ⬚ **Glover's Atoll Resort.** This little group of cabanas, including several built over the water, is a lesson in laid-back living. Forget about electricity, running water, and indoor bathrooms and surrender to a life of fishing, diving, snorkeling, and swimming. You bring your tackle for boat or shore fishing and your own food supplies, though simple meals and a few basics such as bottled water are sold, at fairly steep prices (a loaf of French bread is BZ$8), at the 9-acre island. Coconuts are free.

This is as close as they come to a *Gilligan's Island*–style vacation spot. Unless you come out on the weekly boat from Sittee River on Sunday, you'll pay BZ$600 or more for transportation. ✉ *Northeast Caye ⌂ Box 2215, Belize City ☎ 520/5016 🖶 223/5424 ⊕ www.glovers. com.bz ↪ 12 cabins with shared bath, 1 dorm, campground ⚑ Dining room, beach, dive shop, snorkeling, fishing; no a/c, no room phones, no room TVs ▤ MC, V ☉ Closed Sept. and Oct. most years.*

THE CAYES & ATOLLS ESSENTIALS

Transportation

BY AIR

Maya Island Airways and Tropic Air operate flights to Ambergris Caye and Caye Caulker from both the municipal and international airports in Belize City. Each has hourly service every day to Ambergris Caye between about 7:30 AM and 5:30 PM. In high season, additional flights are added to accommodate demand. Round-trip fares for the 20-minute flight are about BZ$104 (municipal) and BZ$186 (international).

The airstrip on Ambergris Caye is at San Pedro's southern edge. You'll always find taxis waiting at the airstrip, and most hotels run shuttles. If you're proceeding on foot, it's about five minutes to the hotels in town. The airstrip on Caye Caulker is at the island's south end. Hotels may send a golf cart to pick you up. Otherwise, you'll find that golf-cart taxis are available. Whether you arrive in San Pedro by air or by ferry from Belize City, you'll be met by a small crowd of friendly, but pushy cab drivers touting cheap lodging deals. Note that hotels pay these drivers a commission, which is reflected in the hotel rate. For the best rates call the hotel directly upon your arrival.

There are no scheduled flights to the other cayes, although Caye Chapel and Blackbird Caye have airstrips where charter flights can land. 🗹 **Maya Island Airways** ⌂ Box 458, Municipal Airport, Belize City ☎ 223/1140, 800/ 225–6732 in U.S. ⊕ www.mayaislandair.com. **Tropic Air** ⌂ Box 20, San Pedro ☎ 226/ 2012, 800/422–3435 in U.S. ⊕ www.tropicair.com.

BY BOAT & FERRY

A variety of boats connect Belize City with Ambergris Caye and Caye Caulker. The cost to Ambergris Caye is BZ$30 one-way for the 75-minute trip. The most dependable, operated by the Caye Caulker Water Taxi Association, leave from the Belize Marine Terminal on North Front Street. The speedy open boats depart Belize City at 8, 9, 10:30 AM, noon, 1:30, 3, and 4:30 PM and return from San Pedro, from Shark's Pier, at 7, 8, 9:30, and 11:30 AM, and 1, 2:30, and 3:30 PM. Caye Caulker Water Taxi Association boats from Belize City take 45 minutes to reach Caye Caulker, and cost BZ$20 each way. Departures are 8, 9, 10:30 AM, noon, 1:30, 3, 4:30, and 5:30 PM, with return trips departing the public pier in Caye Caulker between 6:30, 7:30, 8:30 and 10 AM, noon, 1:30, 3, and 4 PM. There's an additional return boat at 5 PM on Friday, Saturday, Sunday, and holidays. Boats can drop you at Caye Chapel as well.

To reach the more remote cayes, you're left to your own devices. You can charter boats in either San Pedro or Belize City, but they're not cheap. The resorts on the atolls run their own flights or boats, but these aren't available to the general public. Ask your hotel if it provides transportation. For the southern cayes, inquire about boats departing from Dangriga. Dangriga's Pelican Beach Hotel sends a boat to its resort on South Water Caye. If transportation to South Water Caye isn't included in your hotel package, you'll pay around BZ$110 per person. Several boats make the run from Dangriga to Tobacco Caye for BZ$35 per person one-way. Most boats leave Dangriga around 9:30 AM and return from Tobacco Caye midmorning. Check at the Riverside Restaurant in Dangriga or ask at your hotel on Tobacco Caye. Captain Buck is a dependable operator. Charter boats from Belize City, Dangriga, and elsewhere charge from BZ$500 to BZ$600, or more, one-way to the atolls.

⚡ Caye Caulker Water Taxi Association ✉ Marine Terminal, N. Front St. at Swing Bridge, Belize City ☎ 223/5752 ⊕ www.cayecaulkerwatertaxi.com.

⚡ Riverside Café ✉ South Riverside Dr., Dangriga ☎ 501/502−3449

BY TAXI, GOLF CART & BIKE

Regular taxi cabs are available in San Pedro and in the developed area south of town on Ambergris Caye. For a taxi, you can call Island Taxi, have your hotel arrange for a cab, or hail one of the cabs cruising the downtown area. There aren't any cabs on North Ambergris; to get there from San Pedro, you can take a water taxi. Scheduled service is available roughly hourly on the Island Ferry during the day until 10 PM. Rates are BZ$10 to $40, depending on the destination. After 10, you can arrange a custom pick-up. Rates are BZ$40 to $100, depending on your destination, the time of night, and the number in your party. Call Island Ferry or San Pedro Water Taxi.

On Ambergris Caye and Caye Caulker, there are no car rentals, but you can rent a golf cart. If you have a choice, get a gas cart rather than an electric so you don't run out of juice at an inopportune time; gas carts have a much longer range. Golf-cart rentals cost about as much as a car rental in the U.S.—around BZ$100 to $120 a day, or BZ$500 a week. Compare prices and ask for discounts. To drive a cart, you'll need a valid driver's license from your home country. On Ambergris Caye, there are a half dozen cart rental companies; Moncho's, Castle Cars, and Cholo's are three of the largest. Your hotel can also arrange a cart rental. On Caye Chapel, golf carts are included in the daily rate. Bicycles are for rent on Ambergris Caye and Caye Caulker for around BZ$10 to $12 a day, or BZ$80 a week.

CONTACTS **⚡ Taxis Island Taxi** ✉ Pescador Dr., San Pedro ☎ 226/3125.

⚡ Water Taxis Island Ferry ✉ Barrier Reef Dr., San Pedro ☎ 226/3231. **San Pedro Water Taxi** ✉ Beachfront, San Pedro ☎ 226/2194.

⚡ Bicycle Rentals Joe's Bike Rentals ✉ Pescador Dr. and Caribeña St., San Pedro ☎ 226/5371.

⚡ Golf-Cart Rentals Castle Cars ✉ Barrier Reef Dr., San Pedro ☎ 226/2421. **Cholo's** ✉ San Pedro ☎ 226/2406 ⊕ www.choloscarts.com. **Moncho's** ✉ Sea Star St., San Pedro ☎ 226/3262 ⊕ www.monchosrentals.com.

Contacts & Resources

BANKS & RESOURCES

Atlantic Bank, on Barrier Reef Drive in San Pedro, is open weekdays 8–2. Belize Bank, on Barrier Reef Drive in San Pedro, is open Monday–Thursday 8–3 and Friday 8–4:30. Alliance Bank in San Pedro is open 8–3 weekdays. There's just one bank on Caye Caulker, Atlantic Bank on Back Street, south of Chan's Market. It's open weekdays 8–2. Only the Atlantic Bank and Belize Bank ATMs accept ATM cards issued outside Belize. Atlantic Bank accepts cards on the Visa Electron network, and Belize Bank on PLUS, CIRRUS, and Visa Electron networks. Cash advances on your Visa or MasterCard are also available at these banks. Caye Bank, an international bank, has an office in San Pedro, but it doesn't offer retail banking services to local residents or island visitors.

Atlantic Bank ⊠ Barrier Reef Dr., San Pedro ☎ 226/2195 ⊠ Back St., Caye Caulker ☎ 226/0207. **Alliance Bank** ⊠ 33 Barrier Reef Dr., San Pedro ☎ 226/2136. **Belize Bank** ⊠ 49 Barrier Reef Dr., San Pedro ☎ 226/2482.

EMERGENCIES

The San Pedro Lions Polyclinic, which opened in 2005 on Ambergris Caye, has two physicians, three nurses, a pharmacist, and a health officer. The clinic has services just short of a full-scale hospital and is open weekdays from 8 to 5. A doctor and nurse are on 24-hour call. Two other doctors, three pharmacies, a dentist, and a hyperbaric chamber are also on the island.

On Caye Caulker, the Caye Caulker Health Center, usually staffed by a volunteer doctor, is open weekdays 8–11:30 and 1–4:30. For dental care or serious ailments you need to go to Belize City. There are no medical facilities on any of the other cayes, but if you have an emergency, call your embassy or contact Karl Heusner Memorial Hospital, the nation's main referral hospital, in Belize City. If you're on an island with an airstrip, Wings of Hope provides emergency airlift services.

For police emergencies, call 911 or 90. On marine radios, channel 16 is the international distress channel.

Clinics San Pedro Lions Polyclinic ⊠ Near airstrip, San Pedro ☎ 226/4052. **Caye Caulker Health Center** ⊠ Front St. near Lena's Hotel, Caye Caulker ☎ 226/0166. **San Pedro Hyperbaric Chamber** ⊠ Near airstrip, San Pedro ☎ 226/2851.

Other Emergency Contacts Karl Heusner Memorial Hospital ⊠ Princess Margaret Dr., Belize City ☎ 223/1548. **United States Embassy** ⊠ 29 Gabourel La., Belize City ☎ 227/7161. **Wings of Hope** ⊠ 1675 Sunrise Ave., Belize City ☎ 223/0078.

MAIL & SHIPPING

On Ambergris Caye the post office in San Pedro is open weekdays 8–noon and 1–4. On Caye Caulker the post office is on Back Street on the south side of town. It's open 9–noon and 2–5 weekdays and 9–noon Saturday. There are no post offices on other islands. Your hotel or lodge can arrange to mail letters and postcards for you.

Post Offices Caye Caulker ⊠ Back St. ☎ 226/0325. **San Pedro** ⊠ Alijua Bldg., Barrier Reef Dr. ☎ 226/2250.

2

TOURS

From Ambergris and Caulker, and from smaller cayes with advance planning, you can do day trips to the mainland to see Mayan ruins, try cave tubing, visit the Belize Zoo, and do other activities. However, because you have to get from the islands to the mainland, and then to your destination, the cost will be higher than if you did the tour from a closer point. From Ambergris Caye, a full-day cave tubing trip, combined with lunch and a visit to the zoo, runs around BZ$300 per person. A trip to Lamanai, including lunch and drinks, costs about BZ$270. A visit to Altun Ha, combined with lunch and a stop at Maruba Spa, is around BZ$150 to BZ$200. Tours are somewhat less expensive from Caye Caulker. A Lamanai trip runs about BZ$220, and one to Altun Ha and Maruba about BZ$160, not including lunch at Maruba. You can also take a day or overnight tour to Tikal, by air, on either Maya Island or Tropic Air. Both have two or more flights daily to Flores, Guatemala, via the international airport in Belize City. Air fares are BZ$613 round-trip to Flores from San Pedro or Caye Caulker.

All tour guides in San Pedro and on Caye Caulker should be members of their respective associations—if in doubt, ask to see identification. Among San Pedro's top tour operators are Tanisha Tours, which offers excellent trips to Altun Ha and Lamanai, along with manatee spotting trips, cave tubing, and others. SEAduced by Belize is unrivaled for its nature and kayak tours. SEAduced and SEArious Adventures both do other trips, including manatee spotting, visits to Altun Ha, and others. On Caye Caulker, Chocolate is the best-known guide and tour operator, though he is semiretired. He and the people he has trained are known for their full-day manatee trips. Tsunami Adventures, Carlos Tours, and Anwar Tours also run trips to the mainland. *See Caye Caulker section.*

Anwar Tours ⊠ Front St., Caye Caulker ☎ 226/0327. **Carlos Tours** ⊠ Front St., Caye Caulker ☎ 226/0058. **Chocolate Tours** ⊠ Front St., Caye Caulker ☎ 226/0151. **SEAduced by Belize** ⊠ Tarpon St., San Pedro ☎ 226/2254. **SEArious Adventures** ⊠ Beachfront, San Pedro ☎ 226/4202. **Tanisha Tours** ⊠ Middle St., San Pedro ☎ 226/2314 ⊕ www.tanishatours.com. **Tsunami Adventures** ⊠ Front St. at Split, Caye Caulker ☎☎ 226/0462 ⊕ www.tsunamiadventures.com.

VISITOR INFORMATION

A visitor information office opened in San Pedro in 2004, and one was set to open in 2006 in Caye Caulker. The San Pedro center is open just three hours a day, 10–1, Monday through Saturday. The best source of information on the islands is online. Operated by Marty Casado, AmbergrisCaye.com (⊕ www.ambergriscaye.com) has more than 6,000 pages of facts and figures on San Pedro. Caye Caulker's official Belize Tourist Industry Association Web site is ⊕ www.gocayecaulker.com. The Toucan Trail Web site (⊕ www.toucantrail.com) is another excellent source of information, especially for those looking for information on the less-expensive end of the spectrum. The *San Pedro Sun* newspaper publishes a free weekly tabloid-size visitor newspaper, *The San Pedro Sun Visitor Guide.*

San Pedro Visitor Information Center ⊠ Barrier Reef Dr., near Town Hall, San Pedro ☎ 226/2903 is open three hours a day, 10–1, Monday–Saturday.

Northern Belize

WORD OF MOUTH

"This summer we went to Lamanai with Lamanai Eco-Adventures. Errol Cadle was our guide, and we had a terrific time! We went on Sunday and had the place virtually to ourselves (no cruise ship folks)."
—CaymanSue

"From Ambergris Caye, I would definitely recommend Lamanai . . . [it's] in the middle of the jungle, the scenery is awesome."

—JeanH

"Chan Chich is also oriented towards birders, which means that guests go to bed early and get up very early. Howler monkeys may keep you awake at night. But it is so romantic. What a great setting."

—Naom

By Lan Sluder   **RAZZAMATAZZ AND BLING ARE IN SHORT SUPPLY** in northern Belize. Here you'll find more orange groves than beach bars, more sugarcane than sugary sand, and more farms than restaurants. Yet, if you're willing to give in to the area's easy-going terms and slow down to explore back roads and poke around small towns and villages, this northern country will win a place in your traveler's heart. You'll discover some of Belize's most interesting Mayan sites, several outstanding jungle lodges, and a sprinkling of small, inexpensive inns with big personalities.

Northern Belize includes the northern part of Belize District and all of Orange Walk and Corozal districts. All together, this area covers about 2,800 sq mi (7,250 sq km) and has a population of around 80,000. The landscape is mostly flat, with mangrove swamps on the coast giving way to savannah inland. Scrub bush is much more common than broadleaf jungle, although to the northwest near the Guatemala border are large, wild tracts of land with some of the world's few remaining old-growth mahogany trees. The region has many cattle ranches, citrus groves, sugarcane fields, and, in a few areas, marijuana fields.

The only sizeable towns in the region are Orange Walk, about 53 mi (87 km) north of Belize City, with about 16,000 residents, and the slightly smaller Corozal, population around 9,000, 85 mi (139 km) north of Belize City. Both are on the Northern Highway, a paved two-lane road that runs 95 mi (156 km) from Belize City up the center of the region, ending at the Mexican border.

Northern Belize gets less rain than anywhere else in the country (roughly 50 inches in Corozal), a fact that's reflected in the sunny disposition of the local population, mostly Mayas and Mestizos. Both Orange Walk and Corozal towns have a Mexican ambience, with central plazas the focus of the downtown areas. Most locals speak Spanish as a first language, though many also know English. Offering little in the way of tourism facilities itself, Orange Walk Town is a jumping-off point for trips to Lamanai and other Mayan ruins, to Mennonite farmlands, and to several well-regarded jungle lodges in wild, remote areas. Corozal Town, next door to Chetumal, Mexico, is a place to slow down, relax, and enjoy the laid-back atmosphere of a charming small town on the beautiful Corozal Bay (or, as Mexico calls it, Chetumal Bay).

If you tire of small-town pleasures, the Belize side of the Mexican border has three casinos and a duty-free zone. Corozal has begun to draw foreign expats looking for inexpensive real estate and proximity to Chetumal, the Quintana Roo Mexican state capital, whose population is about the same as the entire country of Belize. Sarteneja Village, in the far northeastern part of Corozal District, about 35 mi (57 km) from Corozal Town, is a still undiscovered fishing village at the edge of the sea, near the Shipstern Wildlife Reserve. On the way are several pristine lagoons, including the lovely Progresso Lagoon.

Numbers in the margin correspond to points of interest on the Northern Belize map.

History

The Maya settled this area thousands of years before the time of Christ. Cuello, near Orange Walk Town, dates from 2500 BC, making it one of the earliest known Mayan sites in all of Mesoamerica (the region between central Mexico and northwest Costa Rica). In the Pre-Classic period (2500 BC–AD 300), the Maya expanded across northern Belize, establishing important communities and trading posts at Santa Rita, Cerros, Lamanai, and elsewhere.

During the Classic period (AD 300–AD 900), Santa Rita, Lamanai, Altun Ha and other cities flourished. To feed large populations perhaps totaling several hundred thousand, the Maya developed sophisticated agricultural systems, with raised, irrigated fields along the New River and other river bottoms. After the mysterious collapse of the Mayan civilization by the 10th century AD, the region's cities went into decline, but the Maya continued to live in smaller communities and rural areas around the many lagoons in northern Belize, trading with other settlements in Belize and in Mexico. Lamanai, perched at the edge of the New River Lagoon, was continuously occupied for almost three millennia, until late in the 17th century.

The Spanish first set foot in these parts in the early 1500s. Spanish missionaries made their way up the New River to establish churches in Mayan settlements in the 16th and 17th centuries. You can see the remains of a Spanish church at the entrance of Lamanai near Indian Church Village. About this same time, small groups of shipwrecked British sailors established settlements in Belize. The English and Spanish occasionally had run-ins in Belize, but the Battle of St. George's Caye in 1789 effectively put an end to Spanish control in Belize.

In the second half of the 19th century, the so-called Caste Wars (1847–1904), pitting Maya insurgents against Mestizo and European settlers in Mexico's Yucatán, had an important impact on northern Belize. Refugees from the bloody wars moved south from Mexico, settling in Corozal Town, Orange Walk Town, Sarteneja, and also on Ambergris Caye and Caye Caulker.

Today, more than 40,000 acres of sugarcane is harvested by 4,000 farmers in northern Belize. Mennonites, who came to the Blue Creek, Shipyard, and Little Belize areas in the late 1950s, have contributed greatly to agriculture in the region, producing rice, corn, chickens, milk, cheese, and beans. And tourism, foreign retirement communities, and casino gaming are becoming important, especially in northern Corozal District.

EXPLORING NORTHERN BELIZE

The Northern Highway, a paved two-lane road, is the transportation spine of the region, running about 95 mi (156 km) from Belize City to the Mexican border at Chetumal, passing the two main towns in northern Belize, Orange Walk and Corozal. Mile marker signs begin in Belize City at the traffic circle where Princess Margaret Drive, Freetown

TOP REASONS TO GO

MAYAN SITES. Several of the most interesting Mayan sites in the region are in northern Belize. These include Altun Ha, Lamanai, and Cerros. Altun Ha gets the most visitors of any Mayan site in Belize, and Lamanai and Cerros are notable in part because of their beautiful locations—Lamanai on the New River Lagoon and Cerros on Corozal Bay. Less accessible (two are on private land and the third is in a remote area) but also of interest to Mayan enthusiasts are sites at La Milpa, Cuello, and Nohmul. There's also a small site, Santa Rita, in Corozal Town.

WILD, OPEN SPACES. This part of Belize has some of the country's wildest and most remote tracts of land. The quarter-million acres of Rio Bravo Conservation and Management Area hosts only a few thousand visitors each year. Although people are scarce, Rio Bravo teems with wildlife, because hunting is banned. The area has 250 species of trees, including some of the largest mahogany trees in Belize, 70 species of mammals including jaguars, and more than 400 types of birds. Other large tracts of land rich with flora and fauna include the adjoining Gallon Jug lands, 130,000 privately owned acres around Chan Chich Lodge. The Shipstern Reserve is a 22,000-acre expanse of swamps, lagoons, and forests on the Sarteneja peninsula. Huge numbers of birds nest at the Crooked Tree Wildlife Sanctuary, a network of inland lagoons and swamps.

JUNGLE LODGES. Northern Belize is home to several first-rate lodges, including Chan Chich Lodge, a paradise for birders and the place where you're most likely to spot the reclusive jaguar in the wild. Lamanai Outpost, on the banks of the New River Lagoon, is a center for crocodile research. The exotic Maruba Resort Jungle Spa focuses on bringing Mother Earth to you in the form of natural spa treatments.

RETIREMENT & SECOND-HOME SCOUTING. Corozal District has become a hot spot for expats seeking property for retirement, and for snowbirds looking for a vacation home at prices considerably lower than at beach areas such as Ambergris Caye or Placencia. Several hundred foreign expats live in Corozal District, and the numbers are growing. They're attracted by home prices that sound as if they're from the 1970s—a two-bedroom, modern home in a nice area can go for less than US$100,000, though you can always pay more.

Road, and Central American Boulevard meet, and increase going north. However, the markers are not well maintained and many are missing.

In 2005 a bypass around Orange Walk Town opened, providing a way to avoid the congested downtown. Buses between Belize City and Chetumal, Mexico, run frequently, roughly hourly during daylight hours, in both directions.

Branching off the Northern Highway are a number of tertiary roads, mostly unpaved, including the road to Crooked Tree Wildlife Sanctu-

Northern Belize

KEY

Mayan Site

Caribbean Sea

MEXICO

GUATEMALA

QUINTANA ROO

Chetumal
Santa Elena
Santa Rita
Consejo
Corozal Town **9**
Cerros
Buena Vista
Orange Walk Town **4**
Noh Mul
Cuello
August Pine Ridge
Yo Creek Village
San Felipe
Río Hondo

Bahía de Chetumal

Sarteneja **11**
Shipstern Wildlife Reserve
Copper Bank & Progresso Lagoon **10**

COROZAL DISTRICT

Maruba Spa
Marco Gonzalez
Altun Ha **2 3**

Ambergris Caye
San Pedro
Caye Caulker
Caye Chapel
St. George's Caye

Belize City

Ladyville
Hattieville

BELIZE DISTRICT

Burrell Boom
Crooked Tree **1**
Crooked Tree Wildlife Sanctuary
Community Baboon Sanctuary
Belize Zoo

Shipyard
Lamanai **5**

New River

ORANGE WALK DISTRICT

Blue Creek Mennonite Community **6**
La Milpa
Río Bravo Conservation Area **7**
Gallon Jug **8** Chan Chich
Chan Chich

0   20 miles
0   20 kilometers

ary; the Old Northern Highway that leads to Altun Ha ruins and Maruba Spa; a road to Shipyard, a Mennonite settlement, which also connects with roads to Lamanai ruins and to La Milpa ruins and Gallon Jug; the San Estevan Road that is a route to Progresso, Copper Bank, and the Cerros Maya ruins, or, via a different branch, to Sarteneja.

Bus service to the villages and other sites off the Northern Highway is limited, so to reach them you're best off with a rental car or a guided tour. Air service to northern Belize is spotty. Corozal Town has flights only to and from San Pedro (Ambergris Caye). Airstrips at Lamanai, Gallon Jug, and Sarteneja have charter service.

Tour boats run from near Orange Walk, and less frequently from Corozal, on the New River to Lamanai. Boats from San Pedro and Caye Caulker bring visitors from those islands to Altun Ha and environs via Bomba, a small coastal village.

When to Go
Corozal Town gets as little rain as Atlanta, Georgia, and the rest of northern Belize gets similarly moderate amounts, so the "rainy season"—generally June to November—here is not to be feared. It's hot and humid for much of the year, except in waterfront areas where prevailing breezes mitigate the heat. December to April is usually the most pleasant time, with weather similar to that of south Florida.

About the Restaurants
Restaurants are almost invariably small, inexpensive, family-run places, serving simple meals such as stew chicken with rice and beans. You'll rarely pay more than BZ$20 for dinner, and frequently much less. If there's a predominant culinary influence, it's from Mexico, and many restaurants serve tacos, tamales, *garnaches* (small, fried corn tortillas with beans, cabbage, and cheese piled on them), and soups such as *escabeche* (onion soup with chicken). A few places, mostly in Corozal Town, cater to tourists and expats, with burgers and steaks.

The restaurants (all of which are indicated by a ✕) that we list are the cream of the crop in each price category. Properties indicated by a ✕▦ are lodging establishments whose restaurant warrants a special trip.

About the Hotels
As with restaurants, most hotels in northern Belize are small, family-run spots. In Corozal and Orange Walk towns, most hotels are modest affairs with room rates generally under BZ$150 for a double. Generally, the hotels are clean, well maintained, and offer a homey atmosphere. They have private baths and plenty of hot and cold water, and many also have air-conditioning. Hotels and lodges in Crooked Tree, Sarteneja, Copper Bank, and Progresso are also small and inexpensive; few have air-conditioning. The jungle lodges near Lamanai, Gallon Jug, and Altun Ha, however, are a different story. Several of these, including Chan Chich Lodge, Maruba Jungle Lodge and Spa, and Lamanai Outpost Lodge, are upscale accommodations, with gorgeous settings in the jungle or on a lagoon.

GREAT ITINERARIES

IF YOU HAVE 3 TO 5 DAYS IN NORTHERN BELIZE

If starting in Belize City, rent a car and drive to Crooked Tree Wildlife Sanctuary, which has great birding and offers the chance to see the jabiru stork, the largest flying bird in the Americas. Spend a few hours here, canoeing on the lagoon and hiking trails near Crooked Tree Village. If you have an interest in birding, you'll want to overnight here at one of the simple lagoon-side lodges. Otherwise, drive on to Maruba, an upscale jungle lodge and spa. The drive from Crooked Tree takes about 45 minutes. While you're at Maruba, visit the Altun Ha Mayan site, which you can see in a couple of hours. On the second day, drive to Corozal Town, about 1½ hours from Maruba or Crooked Tree. Base here in Corozal Town for two days, at one of the small hotels on Corozal Bay, making day trips by boat to Lamanai and Cerros ruins (or you can drive). If you have additional days in the north, you can add a visit to Sarteneja or cross the border into Chetumal, Mexico.

Alternatively, after the first night in Crooked Tree or at Maruba, drive to the Lamanai Mayan site, and spend the night there at one of the lodges on the New River Lagoon, or, for a different experience, proceed to Blue Creek Village, a Mennonite area, and spend the night at Hillside B&B. Then, continue on through Programme for Belize lands to Chan Chich Lodge, and spend the rest of your time in northern Belize at this classic jungle lodge.

IF YOU HAVE 1 DAY IN NORTHERN BELIZE

With only one day, head to Lamanai, which with Caracol in the Cayo District is the most interesting of Belize's Mayan sites. Although you can drive, the most enjoyable way to get to Lamanai is by a 1½-hour boat trip, up the New River. Tour boats (BZ$80 per person) leave around 9 AM from the Tower Hill bridge over the New River just south of Orange Walk Town. If you're staying overnight at Lamanai, your hotel can arrange boat transportation.

The lodgings (all indicated with a 🏨) that we list are the cream of the crop in each price category. We always list the facilities that are available—but we don't specify whether they cost extra: when pricing accommodations, always ask what's included. Properties indicated by a ✕🏨 are lodging establishments whose restaurant warrants a special trip.

	$$$$	**$$$**	**$$**	**$**	**¢**
WHAT IT COSTS In Belize Dollars					
RESTAURANTS	over $50	$30–$50	$15–$30	$8–$15	under $8
HOTELS	over $500	$300–$500	$200–$300	$100–$200	under $100

Restaurant prices are per person for a main course at dinner. Hotel prices are for two people in a standard double room, including tax and service, in high season.

CROOKED TREE WILDLIFE SANCTUARY

❶ *33 mi (54 km) north of Belize City.*

A paradise for birders and animal lovers, this wildlife sanctuary encompasses a chain of inland waterways around the Northern Lagoon covering about 3,000 acres. Traveling through by canoe, you're likely to see iguanas, crocodiles, coatis, and turtles. The sanctuary's most prestigious visitor, however, is the jabiru stork, several of which usually visit between November and May. With a wingspan up to 12 feet, the jabiru is the largest flying bird in the Americas. For birders the best time to come is in the dry season, roughly from February to early June, when lowered water levels cause birds to group together to find water and food, making them easy to spot. Birding is good year-round, however, and the area is more scenic when the lagoons are full. Snowy egrets, snail kites, ospreys, and black-collared hawks, as well as two types of duck—Muscovy and black-bellied whistling—and all five species of kingfisher native to Belize can be spotted. Even on a short, one- to three-hour tour, you're likely to see 20 to 40 species of birds.

At the Crooked Tree **visitor center,** at the end of the causeway where you pay your BZ$8 sanctuary admission fee, you can arrange a guided tour of the sanctuary or rent a canoe (around BZ$10 per person per hour) for a do-it-yourself trip. You can also walk through the village and hike birding trails around the area. The visitor center has a free village and trail map. If you're staying overnight, your hotel can arrange canoe or bike rentals and set up tours and trips. A typical tour takes about three hours and costs around BZ$160 for up to four persons. It starts at your hotel or the visitor center with a boat ride on the lagoon, then up Spanish Creek, where you are met by a car and returned to your hotel or visitor center. Although tours can run at any time, the best time is early in the morning, when birds are most active.

One of Belize's oldest inland villages, **Crooked Tree,** is at the reserve's center. With a population of about 900, most of Creole origin, the community has a church, school, and one of the surest signs of a former British territory: a cricket pitch. There are many large cashew and mango trees around the village.

WORD OF MOUTH
Do you like birds, nature, and the simple life? I would recommend Crooked Tree Sanctuary. It is so close to Belize City.   —rbo

An excellent village guide is **Sam Tillett** (✉ Crooked Tree Village ☎ 220/7026). Expect to pay about BZ$20 to BZ$30 an hour for guide services.

✛ *Turn west off Northern Hwy. at Mile 30.8, then drive 2 mi (3 km)* ☎ *223/4987 for Belize Audubon Society* ⊕ *www.belizeaudubon.org/html/parks/ctws.htm* 🔳 *BZ$8.*

Where to Stay & Eat

$ ▥ **Bird's Eye View Lodge.** This two-story concrete hotel, though covered with bougainvillea and other flowers, seems out of place at a lagoon's edge. You'll find, however, that the friendly and welcoming service is consistent with Belize's down-home reputation. Many of the 18 spic-and-span rooms have views of the lagoon. The hotel's small and appealing dining room serves filling Creole fare (BZ$8–BZ$18). ⊠ *Crooked Tree* ☎ *225/7027* ✎ *birdseye@btl.net* ↘ *18 rooms* ⚲ *Restaurant, fans, lake, boating, horseback riding, laundry service; no a/c in some rooms, no room phones, no room TVs* ▤ *MC, V.*

ALTUN HA

⛰ ☾ ❷ *45 km (28 mi) north of Belize City.*

If you've never experienced an ancient Mayan city, make a trip to Altun Ha, which is a modern translation in Mayan of the name "Rockstone Pond," a nearby village. It's not Belize's most dramatic site— Caracol and Lamanai vie for that award—but it's one of the most accessible and most thoroughly excavated. The first inhabitants settled before 300 BC, and their descendants finally abandoned the site after AD 1000. At its height during the Classic period the city was home to 10,000 people.

A team from the Royal Ontario Museum first excavated the site in the mid-1960s and found 250 structures spread over more than 1,000 square yards. At Plaza B, in the Temple of the Masonry Altars, archaeologists unearthed the grandest and most valuable piece of Mayan art ever discovered—the head of the sun god Kinich Ahau. Weighing nearly 10 pounds, it was carved from a solid block of green jade. The head is kept in a solid steel vault in the Central Bank of Belize. If this temple looks familiar to you, it's because an illustration of the Masonry Altars structure appears on Belikin beer bottles.

Altun Ha is easily visited on your own—if you have a car. From Belize City, drive north on the Northern Highway to Mile 18.9 and turn right on the *Old* Northern Highway and go 10 ½ mi (17 km). The Old Northern Highway was once paved, but it's now a mix of gravel areas and sections with broken pavement (a few sections are fully paved). The turnoff from the Old Northern Highway to Altun Ha, on the left, is well-marked and the 2 mi (3 km) of roadsite is paved. If coming from Corozal or Orange Walk, you can also enter the Old Northern Highway at Carmelita Village, Mile 49 of the Northern Highway. Because the site is small, it's not necessary to have a tour guide, but licensed guides may offer their services when you arrive.

Tours from Belize City also are an option. Altun Ha is a regular stop on cruise ship excursions, and on days when several ships are in port in Belize City, typically midweek, Altun Ha may be overrun with cruise passengers. Cruise Calendar Web site (www.cruisecal.com) provides information on days when cruise ships are in port. There's limited bus service from Belize City to Maskall Village on the Old Northern Highway, but buses are infrequent and only drop you at the entrance road, so it's a long hike to the ruins.

Several tour operators in San Pedro also offer day trips to Altun Ha, often combined with lunch at Maruba Jungle Resort Jungle Spa (*see below*). Most of these tours are by boat, landing at Bomba Village. From here, a van makes the short ride to Altun Ha. ☎ *609/3540* ✉ *BZ$10* Daily 9–5.

3

MARUBA RESORT JUNGLE SPA

❸ *33 mi (53 km) north of Belize City.*

Though essentially a jungle lodge, Maruba Resort Jungle Spa has nearly become a tourist destination in itself, thanks to its exotic and somewhat sensual atmosphere. Maruba's spa touts its "Mood Mud" therapy, using six different mud baths. One, the red Daji mood mud, is supposed to arouse sexual passion.

Day visitors can have lunch or another meal at Maruba, take a swim (a second pool is reserved for overnight guests only), go horseback riding (BZ$60 per person for a 1½ hour ride), and have spa treatments. A day-spa package, including lunch and two treatments, is BZ$370. Individual spa treatments are BZ$60–BZ$300. For something a little different, in the late afternoon the lodge puts out food for black vultures, and about 200 show up. If you want a more tangible souvenir of your visit, residents of Bomba Village, a small riverside village nearby, have made a modest trade out of carving bowls and other items from zericote, mahogany, rosewood, and other tropical hardwoods.

Where to Stay & Eat

★ **$$$–$$$$** ✕⬚ **Maruba Resort Jungle Spa.** "Neo-primitive tribal chic" is how Maruba describes its style. We don't know about that, but the resort definitely delivers an exotic and luxurious experience in a jungle setting, complete with 24-hour electricity, air-conditioned cabanas, fresh flowers in the rooms, hot tubs (in some suites), and high thread-count sheets. The decor is near, if not actually over, the top, with gold-painted stucco walls, mock stained-glass windows made from old bottles, and bold fabric prints. The restaurant boasts "nouveau jungle" cuisine, which means that it's not rice and beans, but rather a selection of fish, shrimp, and pork dishes, sometimes interestingly prepared, with salads and vegetables from local gardens. At night the restaurant and bar are bathed in black light. Managers Nicky and Melanie Nicholson, like some of the guests, are thin, hip, and youthful. ⊠ *Mile 40 ½ Old Northern Hwy., Maskall Village* ☎ *225/5555 or 800/627–8227 in U.S.* 🖷 *225/5506* ⊕ *www.maruba-spa.com* ⇥ *16 rooms and suites* ♿ *Restaurant, fans, hot tubs in some rooms, cable TV, in-room DVDs, 2 pools, gym, outdoor hot tub, horseback riding, bar, shop, laundry service, Wi-Fi,; no phones in rooms* ▱ *AE, MC, V.*

NORTHWEST ORANGE WALK DISTRICT

This district borders both Mexico and Guatemala and holds four areas well worth the time it takes to visit them: Lamanai Archeological Reserve, at the edge of the New River Lagoon; the Mennonite communities of Blue Creek, Shipyard, and Little Belize; the 260,000-plus acres of the Río Bravo Conservation Area; and Gallon Jug lands, 130,000 acres in which the Chan Chich Lodge nestles. Mennonites immigrated to Belize in the 1950s and the most accessible and interesting community for visitors is Blue Creek Village, which is on the way to Río Bravo and Gallon Jug.

These areas, especially Río Bravo and Gallon Jug, are best visited on an overnight or multinight stay. You can visit Lamanai on a day trip by boat or road from Orange Walk Town, or even from Corozal Town (and guided day tours are also available from Belize City and even San Pedro and Caye Caulker), though it's well worth at least an overnight stay. If you're staying in Blue Creek, you can go to Río Bravo, Lamanai, and even Gallon Jug and Chan Chich on a day trip, but the poor roads will slow you down, and you'll have little time to explore. Both the Gallon Jug and Programme for Belize (Río Bravo) lands are private, with gated entrances, so you'll need advance permission to visit.

Orange Walk Town

❹ *52 mi (85 km) north of Belize City.*

Orange Walk Town is barely on the radar of tourists, except as a jumping-off point for boat trips to Lamanai, road trips to Gallon Jug and Río Bravo, or as a place to gas up en route from Corozal to Belize City. Though its population of around 16,000, mostly Mestizos, makes it the third-largest urban center in Belize (after Belize City and San Ignacio), it's more like a "county seat" in an agricultural area than a city. In this case, it's the county seat of Belize's sugarcane region and you'll see big tractors and trucks hauling sugarcane through the middle of town to the Tower Hill refinery. Happily, the new bypass around Orange Walk Town has reduced through-traffic.

The town's atmosphere will remind you a little of Mexico, with signs in Spanish, a central plaza, and sunbaked stores set close to the streets. The plaza, near the Orange Walk Town Hall, has a small market (daily except Sunday and holidays) with fruits, vegetables, and inexpensive local foods for sale. This was once the site of Fort Cairns, which dates to the Caste Wars of the 19th century.

> **WORD OF MOUTH**
>
> "St. Christopher's hotel in Orange Walk Town was excellent and incredible bargain. [We] took a Lamani excursion right from their dock on the New river. From the hotel you can walk to almost everything you want to see in townÖ[there] is an open air produce market and an adjacent "food court" with several excellent stalls selling Belizean food. The chicken mole my wife had there was memorable."
>
> —psbroome

What's in a Name?

The name Belize is a conundrum. According to *Encyclopaedia Britannica*, it derives from *belix*, an ancient Maya word meaning "muddy water." Anyone who's seen the Belize River swollen by heavy rains can vouch for this description. Others trace the name's origin to the French word *balise* (beacon), but no one can explain why a French word would have caught on in a region once dominated by the English (Belize was known as British Honduras). Perhaps nothing more than a drinker's tale, another theory connects Belize to the Maya word *belikin* (road to the east), which also happens to be the name of the national beer. Some say Belize is a corruption of Wallace, the name of a Scottish buccaneer who founded a colony in 1620; still others say the pirate wasn't Wallace but Willis, that he wasn't Scottish but English, and that he founded a colony not in 1620, but in 1638.

There was indeed a pirate named Wallace, a onetime lieutenant of Sir Walter Raleigh who later served as Tortuga's governor. Perhaps it was liquor or lucre that turned him into a pirate, but at some point in the early to mid-1600s, he and 80 fellow renegades washed up near St. George's Caye. They settled in and lived for years off the illicit booty of cloak-and-dagger raids on passing ships. In 1798, a fleet of 31 Spanish ships came to exterminate what had now blossomed into a upstart little colony. Residents had a total of one sloop, some fishing boats, and seven rafts, but their maritime knowledge enabled them to defeat the invaders in two hours. That was the last Spanish attempt to forcibly dislodge the settlement, though bitter wrangles over British Honduras's right to exist continued for nearly a century.

We may never know if Wallace and Willis were one and the same, but what's in a name, anyway? Grab a Belikin and come up with a few theories of your own.

C Las Banquitas House of Culture is worth an hour or two of your time. This small museum presents changing exhibitions on Orange Walk District history and culture. It's one of three government-supported Houses of Culture in Belize; the other two are in Belize City and Benque Viejo del Carmen. ✉ *Main St. and Bautista St.* ☎ *322–0517* ⊠ *Free, some exhibits have small fee* ⊙ *Tues.–Fri. 9–4, Sat. 8–1.*

If you're interested in orchids and bromeliads, **Godoy's Orchid Gardens,** has more than 200 varieties, including Belize's national flower, the black orchid. Godoy's exports orchids to the United States and elsewhere and sells them to many of Belize's hotels and lodges. This is a primarily wholesale business, but you can stop by and look around, and also purchase orchids here. ✉ *4 Trial Farm Rd.* ☎ *322/2969* ⊠ *Free.*

Where to Stay & Eat

$–$$ ✕ **El Establo Bar & Grill.** This friendly, family-run eatery near the northern end of the Orange Walk bypass opened in mid-2005. Your hosts are Albino and Ada Vargas, and it's a great place to stop on a trip between

Belize City and Corozal Town. Enjoy local dishes such as cow foot soup, *escabeche,* and, of course, rice and beans. ⊠ *Indian Hill, Northern Hwy.* ☎ *322–0094* ▭ *No credit cards.*

¢–$$ ✕ **Victor's Inn.** Victor's Inn is a truly local dining spot well off the busy main road, about 2 mi (3 km) east of Orange Walk Town in Petville near the Tower Hill sugar factory. Victor Ayuso and Sonya Espat serve authentic Belizean and Yucatec fare, including excellent pork dishes and, occasionally, gibnut (a large rodent). Not on the menu is a tame ocelot, one of the restaurant's mascots. ⊠ *Honey Camp Rd., Petville* ☎ *322/ 0094 or 302/1083* ▭ *No credit cards.*

¢–$ 🏨 **D*Victoria.** This is the largest and pinkest hotel in northern Belize and the only one in Orange Walk Town with a swimming pool. Rooms are large, with big black-and-white square tiles. Other than that, it's not particularly notable, but it's adequate for an overnight stay. Because it's on a busy street, and has a locally popular bar, it can be noisy. Ask for a room on the back side. ⊠ *40 Belize-Corozal Rd., Orange Walk Town* ☎ *322/2518* 🖷 *322/2847* ⊕ *www.dvictoria.com* ⤴ *31 rooms* ⚐ *Restaurant, fans, some in-room safes, cable TV, pool, bar, shop, laundry service, travel services; no room phones* ▭ *MC, V.*

¢ 🏨 **Hotel de la Fuente.** Opened in late 2005, Orlando de la Fuente's place is a step up from the other hotels in Orange Walk Town, and the remarkably low room rates, starting at BZ$50 with air-conditioning, put it among the best values in northern Belize. All rooms have air-conditioning, DSL broadband Internet, coffeemakers, and comfortable new beds. Two suites (BZ$140) have separate bedrooms and kitchenettes. When we visited, the lobby doubled as a pawnshop, handy if you need a little extra cash. ⊠ *14 Main St., Orange Walk Town* ☎ *322/2290* 🖷 *322/ 3651* ⊕ *www.hoteldelafuente.com* ⤴ *8 rooms, 2 suites* ⚐ *Fans, some kitchenettes, cable TV, in-room broadband, laundry service, travel services; no phones in rooms* ▭ *MC, V.*

¢ 🏨 **St. Christopher's Hotel.** On a quiet street near the Banquitos House of Culture and backing up on the New River, this family-run hotel has simple but clean rooms, with tile floors and brightly colored bedspreads, at reasonable rates. It's owned by the Urbina family, one of the oldest and largest families in the area, with roots in Orange Walk dating back to the early 1800s. The back gardens are attractive, alive with tropical plants, and you can relax in a thatch palapa with picnic tables next to the river. ⊠ *10 Main St., Orange Walk Town* ☎ *322/2420 or 302/1064* ✉ *rowbze@btl.net* ⤴ *25 rooms* ⚐ *Restaurant, fans, cable TV, laundry service, travel services; no a/c in some rooms, no room phones* ▭ *MC, V.*

Lamanai

🔺 ❺   *About 2½ hours northwest of Belize City, or 24 mi (39 km) south of* **Fodor'sChoice**   *Orange Walk Town.*

★   Lamanai ("submerged crocodile") is Belize's longest-occupied Mayan site, inhabited until well after Christopher Columbus discovered the New World in 1492. In fact archaeologists have found signs of continuous occupation from 1500 BC until AD 1700.

Lamanai's residents carried on a lifestyle that was passed down for millennia, until the Spanish missionaries arrived. You can still see the ruins of the missionaries' church in the nearby village of Indian Church. The same village also has an abandoned 19th-century sugar mill. With its immense drive wheel and steam engine—on which you can still read the name of the manufacturer, Leeds Foundry of New Orleans—swathed in strangler vines and creepers, it's a haunting sight.

> **WORD OF MOUTH**
>
> "If you like birds you can't go wrong with Lamanai and Chan Chich."
>
> −naomi

In all, 50 to 60 Mayan structures are spread over this 950-acre archaeological reserve. The most impressive is the largest Pre-Classic structure in Belize—a massive, stepped temple built into the hillside overlooking the New River Lagoon. Many structures at Lamanai have only been superficially excavated. Trees and vines grow from the tops of temples, and the sides of one pyramid are covered with vegetation. On the grounds you'll find a new visitor center with educational displays on the site, and pottery, carvings, and small statues, some dating back 2,500 years. Local villagers from the Indian Church Village Artisans Center set up small stands on the grounds to sell handmade carvings, jewelry, and other crafts, along with T-shirts and snacks.

What makes Lamanai so appealing is its setting on the west bank of a beautiful 28-mi-long lagoon, one of only two waterside Mayan sites in Belize (the other is Cerros, near Corozal Town). Nearly 400 species of birds have been spotted in the area and a troop of howler monkeys visits the archaeological site regularly.

There are several ways to get here. One option is to drive on the well-maintained but mostly unpaved road from Orange Walk Town. Turn west at the Orange Walk fire station. From here go to Yo Creek, then southwest to San Felipe Village, a total of 24 mi (39 km). In San Felipe go straight (the road to Chan Chich turns to the right) for another 12 mi (19 km) to reach the ruins. Another route by road is via Shipyard—the unpaved road to Shipyard is just south of Orange Walk Town, so watch for a sign. The best way to approach the ruins, however, is by boat, which takes about an hour and a half from Orange Walk. Boats leave around 9 AM from the Tower Hill bridge over the New River on the Northern Highway, about 6 mi (10 km) south of Orange Walk. The cost is BZ$80 per person. You can also take a 15-minute long charter plane from Belize City. Charter flights are around BZ$400 for up to four persons. If staying overnight at Lamanai, your hotel or lodge can arrange transport by boat or plane.

Lamanai Outpost Lodge and other hotels offer guided tours of the ruins, but you can also explore the site on your own. ⊠ *Near Indian Church Village, Orange Walk District* ☎ *BZ$10* ☉ *Daily 9–5.*

Where to Stay & Eat

$$$$ ✕▦ **Lamanai Outpost Lodge.** Perched on a low hillside on the New River Lagoon, this lodge has a near all-inclusive plan with all meals and activities, such as boat trips to catch and tag crocodiles, included. A dock extends 130 feet into the lagoon and is a good (and safe) place for swimming. The well-designed thatch cabanas sit amid lovely gardens and have porches with lagoon views. The Lamanai ruins are within walking distance. A jarring recent addition are the lodge's airboats, which break the stillness of the lagoon with the loud roar of airplane props. ⊠ *Indian Church Village* ☎ *223/3578, 888/733–7864 in U.S.* ☎ *220/9061* ⊕ *www.lamanai. com* ➟ *20 cabins* ⚭ *Restaurant, fans, refrigerators, lake, boating, bar, library, laundry service, Internet room, Wi-Fi, travel services; no a/c in some rooms, no room phones, no room TVs* ⊟ *AE, MC, V* ❑ *FAP.*

$$ ▦ **Lamanai South Lodge.** Opened in 2004, Lamanai South is a less-expensive but appealing alternative for overnighting near the Lamanai ruins. On 52 acres adjoining the New River Lagoon, the lodge has four rooms in a coral-color building steps from the water. The rooms, with cream-color stucco walls, have furniture made of local hardwoods, screen windows front and back for ventilation, and verandas with views of the lagoon. Above the rooms are a 2,000 square-foot second level, thatched, with restaurant and bar. Meal packages are BZ$90 per person per day. ⊠ *Indian Church Village* ☎ *615/1892* ⊕ *www.lamanaisouth.com* ➟ *4 rooms* ⚭ *Restaurant, fans, lake, boating, bar; no a/c, no room phones, no room TVs* ⊟ *MC, V* ❑ *MAP.*

Mennonite Communities

❻ *2½ hrs northwest of Belize City.*

The Mennonite religion emerged in Holland during the Protestant Reformation in the 16th century. These Anabaptists (so called for the practice of baptizing adults) first moved to Germanic lands—many in Belize still speak Low German, which combines elements of German and Dutch—and then to Prussia, the United States (mainly Pennsylvania), and Manitoba, Canada. In the 1950s some 3,000 Mennonites emigrated to Belize, where they established communities in Orange Walk and Cayo districts.

The Blue Creek Mennonite community, about midway between Orange Walk Town and Chan Chich Lodge—it's 33 mi (54 km) from Orange Walk Town via Yo Creek, August Pine Ridge, and San Felipe, and 36 mi (59 km) from Chan Chich—is predominantly progressive, which means the Mennonites accept modern conveniences such as automobiles and electricity. Near the Linda Vista shopping center is a small bed-and-breakfast where you can stay and learn a little about Mennonite life in Belize. About 6 mi (10 km) beyond Blue Creek, you'll enter the Río Bravo reserve managed by Programme for Belize.

Most of the Mennonites in Shipyard, which you reach via an unpaved road that turns west off the Northern Highway just south of Orange Walk Town, and Little Belize, which you can visit by driving northeast from Orange Walk Town via San Estevan, are conservative; they shun the use of cars and motorized farm equipment. Both Little Belize and Shipyard are primarily farming areas and have no hotels or tourist facilities, but the unexpected sight, on dusty rural roads, of pale-skin folks in old-fashion dress—the women in long plaid dresses and the men with suspenders and straw hats—in horse-pulled buggies will remind you of how diverse Belizean culture really is.

Where to Stay

$ 🏠 **Hillside Bed and Breakfast.** After Mennonites John and Judy Klassen finished raising their 10 children, they opened this small B&B. It has clean motel-like rooms with 24-hour electricity on a hill overlooking Blue Creek Village, with two larger thatch cabanas nearby, down steep wood steps. Kitchen facilities are available. The breakfast (BZ$10) is huge and delicious, with homemade bread, fresh-squeezed orange juice, and locally produced milk and eggs. ⊠ *General Delivery, Blue Creek Village* ☎ *323/0155* 📠 *323/0158* 🛏 *5 rooms, 2 cabanas* 🍴 *Fans, kitchen, laundry services, car rental; no a/c, no room phones, no room TVs* 🚫 *No credit cards.*

Río Bravo Conservation & Management Area

❼ *2½ hrs northwest of Belize City.*

Created with the help of distinguished British naturalist Gerald Durrell, the Río Bravo Conservation & Management Area spans 260,000 acres near where Belize, Guatemala, and Mexico meet. The four-hour drive from Belize City takes you through wildlands where you may encounter a troupe of spider monkeys, wildcats, flocks of ocellated turkeys, a dense shower of butterflies—anything but another vehicle.

Managed by Belize City–based Programme for Belize, a not-for-profit organization whose mission is the wise use and conservation of Belize's natural resources, the Río Bravo Conservation Area contains some 400 species of birds, 70 species of mammals, and 200 types of trees. About one-half of Río Bravo is managed as a nature reserve, and the rest is managed to generate income, from forestry and other activities, including tourism.

Within the reserve's borders are more than 60 Mayan sites; many have yet to be explored. The most important is **La Milpa,** Belize's largest site beside Caracol and Lamanai. At its height between AD 400 and 830, La Milpa was home to almost 50,000 people. The suburbs of this city spread out some 3 mi (5 km) from the city center, and the entire city encompassed some 30 square mi (78 square km) in area. So far, archaeologists have discovered 20 large courtyards and 19 stelae.

Visiting Río Bravo, like the other areas of northwestern Orange Walk, is best done in a four-wheel-drive vehicle. You must make arrangements to visit in advance with **Programme for Belize** (☎ 227/5616 in Belize City 📠 227/5635 🌐 www.pfbelize.org), as the entire Río Bravo Conservation area is managed by this private, nonprofit organization and the main road through its lands is gated. You also need advance reservations to stay at La Milpa Field Station (*see below*). Staying overnight or longer at this field station is the best way to see Río Bravo, but you can visit it briefly on a day trip. From Belize City or Corozal Town, drive to Orange Walk Town, going into town rather than taking the bypass. Turn west at the crossroads near the Orange Walk fire station toward Yo Creek. Continue on through Yo Creek, following the road that turns sharply south and goes through San Lazaro, Trinidad, and August Pine Ridge villages. At San Felipe, 24 mi (40 km) from Orange Walk Town, the road turns sharply to the west (right) at a soccer field. Follow this road for about 7 mi (12 km) to the Río Bravo bridge and into Programme for Belize lands. If you don't have your own car, contact Programme for Belize and ask if they can arrange transportation for you from Orange Walk Town or elsewhere.

Guides and information are available at La Milpa Field Station. Chan Chich Lodge, Lamanai Outpost Lodge, and other hotels also can arrange visits with guides to La Milpa and the Rí Bravo Conservation & Management Area. *Emory King's Driver's Guide to Beautiful Belize,* updated annually and available at many gift shops and hotels in Belize, has helpful maps and directions to this and other destinations in Orange Walk and other parts of Belize. The Programme for Belize Web site (*see above*) also has driving directions to La Milpa Field Station.

Where to Stay & Eat

$-$$ 🏨 **La Milpa Field Station.** About 3 mi (5 km) from La Milpa Mayan site, this field station is a combination of hotel and summer camp. Stay in a rustic thatch cabana with private bath or in a dorm that sleeps 30. Since you're in a remote area, you'll take all your meals, generally simple Belizean-style dishes such as rice and beans with stew chicken or pork, at the field station. Nine hiking trails are maintained around the lodge, and guides are available to take you to La Milpa and other Mayan sites. In spring and summer you can visit archaeological teams working at La Milpa. ✉ *1 Eyre St., Belize City* 🕿 *227/5616* 🖷 *227/5635* ⊕ *www. pfbelize.org* 🛏 *8 rooms with bath, 1 dormitory* ⚒ *Fans; no a/c, no room phones, no room TVs* ▭ *MC, V* 🍴 *FAP.*

Gallon Jug & Chan Chich Lodge

❽ *3½ hrs northwest of Belize City.*

The 130,000 acres of Gallon Jug Estates is owned by Barry Bowen, one of Belize's wealthiest businessmen. Living among the old-growth mahogany trees and many other tropical hardwoods are more than 350 species of birds and many mammals and reptiles. Jaguar sightings are fairly common around the lodge Chan Chich, averaging around one a week. You're likely to see toucans, many different hummingbirds, and flocks of parrots.

This is a working farm that produces coffee, cacao and corn, and raises cattle. It's the only truly commercial coffee operation in Belize, producing Gallon Jug Estates coffee from coffee trees on more than 100 acres. Gallon Jug Estates also produces hot sauces and delicious mango jams and others, which are for sale in Belize and elsewhere. Tours of the coffee plantings and the production facility, along with other farm tours, can be arranged through Chan Chich Lodge.

Snorkeling above the Belize Barrier Reef.

(top) Lamanai, a Maya ruin on the banks of a lagoon. (bottom left) Toucan. (bottom right) Scuba diver with hawksbill turtle, Half Moon Caye.

(top) Fishing on the beach. (bottom) Comparsas dancers at the San Pedro Carnival, Ambergris Caye.

(top left) Horseback riding through the forest in Chaa Creek. (top right) Ice-cream street vendor. (bottom) Snorkeler off Half Moon Caye.

(top) Deep Sea Fishing Pier in San Pedro. (bottom) Canoeing on the Macal River, Cayo District.

Garifuna musician on turtle-shell drums.

(top) Conch shells on Ambergris Caye. (bottom) Jaguar perched in tree.

Snorkeling off the Cayes.

Chan Chich, also owned by Bowen, is one of the best jungle lodges in Central America, if not the world. This is the only place to stay in the area. It's possible to visit on a day trip from La Milpa Field Station, Blue Creek Village, or even Lamanai or Orange Walk Town, but you need your own transportation and advance permission to come on the private property.

The easiest and fastest way to get here is by charter airplane (about BZ$500, depending on the number of people, to Gallon Jug Estates' own 3,000-foot airstrip). With a four-wheel-drive vehicle you can also drive to Chan Chich, about 3½ hours from Belize City. Follow the route to Río Bravo (*see above*) and continue on through Programme for Belize lands to the Cedar Crossing gatehouse and into Gallon Jug lands. It's a long but beautiful drive, and you're almost certain to see a considerable amount of wildlife along the dirt road. An alternate route is from the Cayo District in western Belize. However, at present, Chan Chich only occasionally grants permission to come via Programme for Belize lands, as most of the route is through private lands, and the roads are not well marked. In any case, you need to ask the lodge in advance for permission to visit by car, and the lodge will provide detailed driving directions. Chan Chich Lodge also can provide transfers by vehicle or by a combination of vehicle and boat on the New River.

Where to Stay & Eat

$$$$ ✕🖾 **Chan Chich Lodge.** Coca-Cola and Belikin "Belizeanaire" Barry
Fodor'sChoice Bowen built these cabanas, which are at once rustic yet eminently com-
★ fortable with thatch roofs, rich hardwood floors and furnishings, and wraparound verandas. It's set smack dab in the middle of a Mayan archaeological site, and regardless of how you feel about that, Chan Chich is simply one of the best jungle lodges in Central America. Former president Jimmy Carter is counted among the lodge's many illustrious previous guests. Guides lead wildlife excursions into the thousands of acres of surrounding bush. Tour options include bird-watching treks and horseback rides to Mayan ruins that remain undisturbed. You're more likely to see an elusive jaguar here than anywhere else outside the Belize Zoo. A gorgeous pool is screened to keep out insects. 🕮 *Box 37, Belize City* 🕾*223/4419, 800/343–8009 in U.S.* 🖷*223–4419* ⊕*www.chanchich. com* 🛏 *12 cabanas, 1 2-bedroom villa* ⚒ *Restaurant, fans, pool, lake, canoeing, horseback riding, bar, library, shop, laundry service, travel services, airstrip; no a/c, no room phones, no room TVs* ⊟*AE, MC, V* ⭐*FAP.*

COROZAL BAY

Corozal Bay, or Chetumal Bay as it's called on most maps, has turquoise waters and good fishing. It provides a beautiful waterside setting for Corozal Town and a number of villages along the north side of Corozal District. Tarpon, bonefish, permit, and other game fish are not hard to find. The drawback is that there are few natural beaches in Corozal District, although some hotels have trucked in sand to build human-assisted beach areas. Also, there's no good snorkeling or diving locally, and the Belize barrier reef is several long hours away by boat. However, the Mexican border and the city of Chetumal is 9 mi away. Chetumal, capital of Quintana Roo state, with a modern mall, air-conditioned multiplex movie theaters, and even a brace of McDonald's restaurants, provides a bustling counterpoint to easy-going Corozal. Casinos have sprung up on the Belize side of the border, and the fast-growing Costa Maya area, with its booming resort enclaves of Tulum, Playa del Carmen, Cozumel, and Cancun, is four to six hours away by car or bus.

Corozal Town

❾ *95 mi (153 km) north of Belize City.*

Settled by refugees from the Yucatán during the 19th-century Caste Wars, Corozal is the last town before Río Hondo, the river separating Belize from Mexico. Though thoroughly ignored by today's travelers, this friendly town is great for a few days of easy living. It's hard not to fall into the laid-back lifestyle here—a sign at the entrance of Reyes Grocery advertises STRONG RUM, 55 BELIZE DOLLARS A GALLON.

English is the official language in Corozal, but Spanish is just as common here. The town was largely rebuilt after Hurricane Janet nearly destroyed it in 1955, so it's neat and modern. Many houses are clapboard, built on wooden piles, and other houses are simple concrete block structures, though the growing clan of expats are putting up new houses that wouldn't look out of place in Florida. One of the few remaining colonial-era buildings is a portion of the old fort in the center of town. The history of Corozal, including a graphic portrayal of the brutality of colonial rule on the indigenous people, is depicted in a strikingly beautiful mural by Manuel Villamar Reyes on the wall of the **Corozal Town Hall,** ⊠ *1st St. S* ☎ *422/2072* 🖘 *Free* ☉ *Mon.–Sat. 9–Noon and 1–5 PM.*

In a landmark 1886 building near the market, the **Corozal Cultural Center,** now a museum and Belize Tourist Industry Association tourist information center, once served as a lighthouse. You can still see the spiral staircase and parts of the original beacon. On display are handblown rum bottles and a traditional Mayan thatch hut. ⊠ *Off 1st Ave. at edge of Corozal Bay* ☎ *422–3176* 🖘 *BZ$10* ☉ *Daily 8–5.*

Not far from Corozal are several Mayan sites. The closest, **Santa Rita,** is a short walk from the town's center. It's on a low hill across from the Coca-Cola plant. Only a few of its structures have been excavated, and there's currently no visitor center open, so it takes some imagination to picture this settlement, founded in 1500 BC, as one of the district's major trading centers. ⊠ *Corozal* ☎ *No phone* ☉ *Daily 8–5.*

A daily water taxi service, the *Thunderbolt,* runs from Corozal Town to San Pedro, Ambergris Caye, with a stop on demand at Sarteneja.

Where to Stay & Eat

¢–$ ✕ **Cactus Plaza.** For a great bargain, grab a seat and order a plateful of tacos, tostadas, *salbutes* (stuffed tortillas), and other Mexican finger foods. You won't be stuck with a big check: most entrées are less than BZ$4. Everything is freshly made and tasty. On weekends, this becomes more of a nightclub. ⊠ *6 6th St. S, 2 blocks west of bay* ☎ *442/0394* 🖃 *No credit cards.*

Where to Stay & Eat in Corozal Town

¢–$ ✕ **Patti's Bistro.** Although Patti's is next door to an undertaker and the street address is the unlucky number 13, you don't have to worry—the food here is among the best in town, the service is sprightly and friendly, and prices are very low. A delicious fried-chicken dinner with salad and mashed potatoes is only BZ$6.50 and a T-bone steak dinner only BZ$12. Sit inside or at one of the handful of outdoor tables. ⊠ *13 4th Ave.* ☎ *402/ 0174* ▭ *MC, V.*

$–$$ ✕▦ **Tony's Inn.** One of the oldest hotels and restaurants in Corozal, Tony's Inn is still going strong, despite the passing of its founder, Tony Castillo. His family now runs the motel and its popular restaurant, Y Not Grill & Bar, in a breezy bayside thatch palapa. The rooms have been upgraded and now all have air-conditioning, phones, and mahogany furniture. Fajitas (chicken, beef, shrimp, or combo) are the way to go in the restaurant. ⊠ *South End, Corozal Town* ☎ *422/2055 or 800/447–2931 in U.S.* ⊟ *422/2829* ⊕ *www.tonysinn.com* ⥲ *24 rooms* ⌂ *Restaurant, fans, cable TV, dock, bar, laundry service, Internet, meeting rooms, travel services, no-smoking rooms* ▭ *AE, MC, V.*

★ $ ▦ **Casablanca by the Sea.** It's worth a short trip to Consejo just to see the hand-carved mahogany doors gracing each room's entrance at this inn. Beverly Temte, an expat from New England, created this appealing, small hotel. In a quiet village, with views of Chetumal across

Corozal Bay, this is a fine place to get away. The best rooms are the three second-floor suites facing the bay. Other rooms are all on the small side. The first-floor restaurant serves tasty Belizean and American food. An added plus: the waterside area with palapa. Besides guests, the young Eastern European women employed as dancers at the casinos in the Free Zone often sunbathe here, too. ⊠ *8 mi (18 km) northeast of Corozal Town, Consejo* 🕾 *423/1018* 🖷 *423/1003* ⊕ *www.casablanca-bythesea. com* ⇥ *7 rooms, 3 suites* ⚑ *Restaurant, fans, cable TV, dock, bar, meeting rooms, travel services; no room phones* � *AE, MC, V.*

$ 🏨 **Copa Banana Guesthouse.** Opened in 2004, this homelike hotel, painted bright yellow, has five sunny suites carved out of two houses across the street from Corozal Bay. Guests share a kitchen, dining room, and living room. A two-bedroom apartment also is available for longer-term rental. The owners, who run a real estate agency in Corozal, also rent cars. Bikes are complimentary. ⊠ *409 Bay Shore Dr.* 🕾 *422/0284* 🖷 *422/2710* ⊕ *www.copabanana.bz* ⇥ *5 rooms, 1 apartment* ⚑ *Fans, cable TV, bicycles, car rental; no room phones, no smoking* 🚗 *MC, V.*

★ **$** 🏨 **Corozal Bay Inn.** With more than an acre of beachfront on Corozal Bay, the inn's large beach is courtesy of its owners, Doug and Maria Podzun, who trucked in tons of sand. The serene bayside resort has nicely done thatch cabanas in pastel colors and a restaurant and bar. The outdoor palapa restaurant, adjacent to the pool, has views of the bay and an artificial waterfall on one wall. ⊠ *Almond Dr. off Northern Hwy. at south end of Corozal Town* 🕾 *422/2691* 🖷 *836/9188* ⊕ *www. corozalbayinn.com* ⇥ *10 cabanas* ⚑ *Restaurant, refrigerators, cable TV, pool, beach, dock, fishing, bar, Wi-Fi Internet, travel services; no room phones* 🚗 *MC, V.*

Copper Bank & Progresso Lagoon

❿ *12 mi (20 km) southeast of Corozal.*

Copper Bank is a tidy and small (population around 500) Mestizo fishing village on Corozal Bay. The village is something of a footnote to the nearby Mayan site, Cerros. Like the Tulum site in Mexico, the small site of **Cerros** is unusual as it is directly on the water. With a beautiful setting on Corozal bay, the late Pre-Classic center dates to 2000 BC and includes a ball court, several tombs, and a large temple. One way to get here is by boat from Corozal, which costs around BZ$120 to BZ$180 for up to four people. You can also drive from Corozal Town, crossing the New River on the hand-pulled ferry. To get to the ferry from Corozal, take the Northern Highway south toward Orange Walk Town to just south of Jal's Travel and Paula's Gift Shop. Turn left and follow this unpaved road for 2½ mi (4 km) to the ferry landing. After crossing the river, you'll come to a T-intersection. Turn left for Copper Bank; the right turn takes you to Progresso. The trip to Copper Bank takes about a half hour, but longer after heavy rains, as the dirt road can become very bad, even impassable. As you enter Copper Bank, watch for signs directing you to "Cerros Maya." ⊠ *2½ mi (4 km) north of Copper Bank* 🕾 *No phone* 🎟 *BZ$10, although at times there's no caretaker to collect* ⊙ *Daily 8–4.*

Where to Stay

$ ⌂ **Copper Bank Inn.** Open in 2004, Copper Bank Inn is housed in what is probably the largest building in the village, a white, two-story 10,000-square-foot house. There's a small bar and restaurant on the first floor. The guest rooms are pleasant, with tile floors, mahogany furniture, wooden shutters, and white plaster walls. ✉ *Copper Bank Village* ☏ *608/0838* ⊕ *www.copperbankinn.com* ⬎ *10 rooms* ⌣ *Restaurant, fans, cable TV, laundry service; no room phones* ▭ *MC, V.*

Sarteneja

⓫ *40 mi (67 km) from Corozal.*

This small Mestizo and Creole community enjoys a bay setting that makes it one of the most relaxed and appealing in all of Belize. Lobster fishing and pineapple farming are the town's two main industries, though Sarteneja is also a center for building wooden boats.

Driving to Sarteneja from Corozal Town takes about 1¼ to 1½ hours via the New River ferry, Progresso Village, Little Belize, and Chunox Village. The road is unpaved and can be very muddy after heavy rains. You can also drive to Sarteneja from Orange Walk Town, a trip of about 40 mi (67 km) and 1½ hours. The daily water taxi from Corozal Town to San Pedro will drop you at Sarteneja, on request (BZ$30, around 45 minutes). You also can hire a private boat in Corozal to take you and your party to Sarteneja; the cost is negotiable but likely will be BZ$200 or more. Sarteneja has a recently opened airstrip, but at present there is no regular scheduled air service.

⚠ About 3½ mi (6 km) southwest of Sarteneja on the road to Orange Walk or Corozal is the **Shipstern Wildlife Reserve.** You pass the entrance and visitor center as you drive into Sarteneja.The 31 square mi (81 square km) of tropical forest forming the reserve are, like the Crooked Tree Wildlife Sanctuary, a paradise for bird-watchers. More than 250 species of birds have been identified here. Look for egrets (there are 13 species), American coots, keel-billed toucans, flycatchers, warblers, and several species of parrots. Mammals are in healthy supply as well, including peccaries, pumas, jaguars, and raccoons. The butterfly farm next to the visitor center once exported pupae but is now a small education area with some staff left flitting about. For overnight stays, cabins on the reserve may be rented for BZ$20 a night per person. Camping is BZ$10. ✉ *Sarteneja* ☏ *223/4533* 🖷 *223/4985* ⊕ *www.belizeaudubon.org* ⬚ *BZ$10.*

Where to Stay & Eat

Sarteneja has only a couple of very small, simple guesthouses.

$ ⌂ **Krisamis Bayview Lodge.** This little hotel, the "fanciest" in Sarteneja, has three rooms, each with two double beds, and two small thatch cabanas. Meals are available if ordered in advance. ✉ *Sarteneja Village* ☏ *423/2283* ⊕ *www.krisamis.com* ⬎ *3 rooms, 2 cabanas* ⌣ *Fans, laundry service; no a/c, no room phones, no room TVs* ▭ *MC, V.*

¢ 🏠 **Fernando's Seaside Guesthouse.** This little guesthouse, chosen as the Belize Tourist Board's "Best Small Hotel in Belize" in 2004, provides the peace and quiet—and low prices (BZ$60 for a room, or BZ$80 for a thatch cabana)—that you may be looking for. Owner Fernando Alamilla is a licensed guide and can arrange trips to Bacalar Chico National Park & Marine Reserve at the north end of Ambergris Caye. ✉*Sarteneja Village* 🕾*423/2085* ⊕*www.cybercayecaulker.com/sarteneja. html* ⤴*3 rooms, 1 cabana* ⚴ *Fans, bar, laundry service; no room phones, no room TVs* 🖃 *MC, V.*

NORTHERN BELIZE ESSENTIALS

Transportation

BY AIR

Tropic Air and Maya Island Air each fly four or five times daily between Ambergris Caye and the airstrip at Corozal, about 2 mi (3 km) south of town off the Northern Highway. The journey takes 20 minutes and costs BZ$75–BZ$80 one way. There's no direct service to Belize City or other destinations in Belize. Charter service is available to Chan Chich Lodge and the Indian Church/Lamanai area. An airstrip has opened at Sarteneja, and one Tropic Air flight from San Pedro to Corozal stops on demand at Sarteneja, and, from San Pedro to Corozal, two flights stop at Sarteneja. The one-way fare is BZ$81.

🛪 **Tropic Air** 🕾 226/2012, 800/422–3435 in U.S. ⊕ www.tropicair.com. **Maya Island Air** 🕾 422/2333, 800/225–6732 in U.S. ⊕ www.mayaairways.com.

BY BOAT & FERRY

An old, hand-pulled sugar barge ferries passengers and cars across the 100-yard-wide New River from just south of Corozal Town to the road to Copper Bank, Cerros, and the Shipstern peninsula. The ferry is free from 6 AM to 9 PM daily. To get to the ferry from Corozal, take the Northern Highway toward Orange Walk Town to just south of Jal's Travel and Paula's Gift Shop. Turn left and follow the road for 2½ mi (4 km) to the ferry landing. A bridge over the New River has been promised, but there's no word on when it may be built.

A daily water taxi operates between Corozal Town and Ambergris Caye, with a stop on demand at Sarteneja. The *Thunderbolt* departs from Corozal at the pier near Reunion Park behind Corozal Cultural Center at 7 AM and returns from San Pedro at 3 PM, leaving from the *Thunderbolt* dock on the back side of the island. Fare is BZ$45 one way to San Pedro and BZ$30 one-way to Sarteneja. *Thunderbolt* has three 250-horsepower outboards, a canopy cover with sliding windows, and bus-style seats. The trip usually takes about two hours but may be longer if there's a stop at Sarteneja.

🛥 **Thunderbolt** ✉ San Pedro Town 🕾 226/2217.

BY BUS

Several small bus lines, successors to Novelo's, which closed in late 2005, make the 3 to 3½-hour journey between Belize City and Corozal approximately every hour. Any nonexpress bus will stop and pick up almost any-where along the highway. The cost is about BZ$12, more for express serv-ice. Most buses also continue on to Chetumal, Mexico. There's limited bus service on the Old Northern Highway and from Orange Walk to Sarteneja.

BY CAR

Corozal is the last stop on the Northern Highway before you hit Mex-ico. The 95-mi (153-km) journey from Belize City will probably take about two hours, unless you're slowed by sugarcane trucks. The North-ern Highway is a two-lane paved road in good condition. Other roads, including the Old Northern Highway, roads to Lamanai, Río Bravo, and Gallon Jug, and the road to Sarteneja are mostly unpaved. Because tour and long-distance taxi prices are high, especially if you're traveling with family or in a group, you likely will save money by renting a car, de-spite the relatively high cost of car rental and fuel in Belize.

Car rental agencies in Belize City will deliver vehicles to Corozal and Orange Walk for a small fee, around BZ$80 to BZ$100. Corozal Bay Inn in Corozal Town (*see above*) has a couple of cars to rent. Corozal police enthusiastically ticket cars from other parts of Belize for such minor violations as parking the wrong way on a one-way street, so be espe-cially cautious. A rental car is useful in northern Belize, and almost es-sential if you're going off the beaten path, such as to Copper Bank, Progresso, or Sarteneja.

BY TAXI

To get around Corozal, call the Taxi Association or ask your hotel to arrange for transportation. Likewise, in Orange Walk call the Taxi As-sociation or ask your hotel to arrange a taxi.

🛈 **Taxi Association** ✉ 1st St. S, Corozal ☎ 422/2035. **Taxi Association** ✉ Queen Victoria Ave., Orange Walk ☎ 322/2560.

Contacts & Resources

BANKS & EXCHANGE SERVICES

Although American dollars are accepted everywhere in Corozal and Or-ange Walk, money changers at the Mexico border and in Corozal Town exchange Belize dollars for U.S. and Mexican currency, usually for bet-ter rates than in banks. The three banks in Corozal—Atlantic Bank, Be-lize Bank, and ScotiaBank—have ATMs, but only Belize Bank and Atlantic Bank accept cards issued outside Belize. Belize Bank's ATMs are on the CIRRUS, PLUS, and Visa Electron networks. Atlantic Bank is on the Visa Electron network. Orange Walk Town also has a branch of Belize Bank with an ATM that accepts foreign ATM cards.

🛈 **Atlantic Bank** ✉ 1 Park St. S, Corozal ☎ 422/3473. **Belize Bank** ✉ 5th Ave. at 1st St. S, Corozal ☎ 422/2087 ✉ Main and Park Sts., Orange Walk ☎ 322/2019. **ScotiaBank** ✉ 4th Ave., Corozal ☎ 422/2046 ✉ Main and Park Sts., Orange Walk ☎ 322/2194.

EMERGENCIES

For dental and medical care, many of Corozal's residents go to Chetu-mal, Mexico. In Corozal call Trummer Clinic if you need medical care or Dr. Glenda Major if you require a dentist. The Corozal Hospital, with only limited facilities, is on the Northern Highway. In Orange Walk, the Northern Regional Hospital doesn't look very appealing, but it provides emergency and other services. Consider going to Belize City for medical and dental care, if possible.

🛈 Doctors & Dentists **Trummer Clinic** ⊠ Santa Rita Rd. ☎ 422/2129. **Glenda Major, D.D.S.** ⊠ 1st St. S Corozal ☎ 422/2837.

🛈 Hospitals **Corozal Hospital** ⊠ Northern Hwy. ☎ 422/2076. **Northern Regional Hospital** ⊠ Northern Hwy. ☎ 322/2752.

🛈 Pharmacies **V-Mart Pharmacy** ⊠ 4th Ave. and 1st St. N Corozal ☎ 422/2597. **de la Fuente Drugstore** ⊠ 16 Main St., Orange Walk ☎ 322/2035.

INTERNET, MAIL & SHIPPING

The Corozal post office, on the west side of the main town plaza, is open 8:30–noon and 1–4:30. The Orange Walk post office has the same hours and is at the north end of town on the main road through town, Queen Victoria Avenue (locally known as Belize-Corozal Road, which is the same as the Northern Highway).

🛈 Internet In northern Belize, Charlotte's Web is the best place to surf the Web. Rates are around BZ$6 an hour.

Charlotte's Web ⊠ 78 5th Ave., Corozal ☎ 422/0135.

🛈 Post Offices **Corozal** ⊠ 5th Ave. ☎ 422/2462. **Orange Walk** ⊠ Queen Victoria Ave. ☎ 322/2345.

TOURS

As Corozal Town gets relatively few tourists, except those en route from Mexico or looking for real estate, it doesn't have many tour operators or guides. One knowledgeable local guide is Francisco Puck. Your hotel can usually arrange tours to Lamanai, Cerros, and other sites. Henry Menzies arranges trips to Mexico as well as to sites around Corozal. He'll also meet you in Chetumal and bring you across the border. In Orange Walk, Jungle River Tours and J. Avila & Sons run boat trips up the New River and can help arrange other tours and trips.

🛈 **J. Avila & Sons River Tours** ⊠ 42 Riverside St., Orange Walk ☎ 322/3068. **Henry Menzies** ⊠ Caribbean Village, South End, Corozal ☎ 422/3415. **Jungle River Tours** ⊠ 20 Lovers La., Orange Walk ☎ 302/2293. **Francisco Puck** ⊠ Corozal ☎ 422/0054.

VISITOR INFORMATION

Brochures and visitor information are available in the Corozal Cultural Center, near the market. The service is provided by the local chapter of the Belize Tourism Industry Association. An excellent source of general information on northern Belize is the Web site Northern Belize, ⊕ www.northernbelize.com. A good source of online information about Corozal is ⊕ www.corozal.com, put together by students at a local community college. A site with some local information on Orange Walk is managed by the Orange Walk Town Council, ⊕ www.owtowncouncil.com. Other sites on northern Belize are Belize North, ⊕ www.belizenorth.com, and Local Gringos, ⊕ www.localgringos.com.

🛈 Tourist Information **Corozal Cultural Center** ⊠ 1st Ave. ☎ 422/3176.

The Cayo

4

WORD OF MOUTH

"We canoed the Macal River from the Jungle Camp to San Ignacio, floated the Mopan River from San José Succotz Village (west of San Ignacio) for an hour or two, and did the Black Hole Drop at Caves Branch—all recommended."

—hopefulist

"Blue Hole National Park . . .was one of the highlights of our trip. The cave is a short hike through the jungle and the entranceway is lush and beautiful. We headed into the cave with our funny flashlight headgear and explored. [It] was both thrilling and scary, no guide goes with you, and there are no handrails!"

—Brooklyn Girl

By Lan Sluder   **WHEN THE FIRST JUNGLE LODGES OPENED** in the Cayo, Belize's largest district, not many people thought this wild area would become a tourist magnet. The mountainous region on the country's western border was too remote. Today, more than half of those touring Belize visit the Cayo during their trip, making this the country's second most popular destination, after Ambergris Caye.

El Cayo is Spanish for "the caye" or key. Local residents still call San Ignacio Town "El Cayo," or just "Cayo," which can potentially create some confusion for outsiders. The name is thought to have originally referred to the small island of land formed where the Macal and Mopan rivers meet at San Ignacio.

You'll know when you've entered the Cayo a few miles west of Belmopan, Belize's capital. Running along the Belize River for miles, the road winds out of the valley and heads into a series of sharp bends. In a few minutes you'll see cattle grazing on steep hillsides and horses flicking their tails.

Other things change as you enter the Cayo. The Creole people who live along the coast give way to Maya; English is replaced by Spanish as the predominant language; and off the main roads four-wheel-drive vehicles become a necessity. The lost world of the Maya comes alive through majestic, haunting ruins. And the Indiana Jones in you can hike through the jungle, ride horseback, canoe down the Macal or Mopan rivers, and explore incredible caves.

History

The Maya began settling the Belize River Valley of the Cayo some four thousand years ago. At the height of the Maya civilization, AD 300 to AD 900, Caracol, El Pilar, Xunantunich, Cahal Pech, and other cities and ceremonial centers in what is now the Cayo were likely home to several hundred thousand people, several times the population of the district today.

Spanish missionaries first arrived in the area in the early 17th century, but they had a difficult time converting the independent-minded Maya, some of whom were forcibly removed to the Petén in Guatemala. The first significant Spanish and British settlements were logwood and mahogany logging camps. The towns of San Ignacio and its adjoining sister town, Santa Elena, were established later in the 1860s. Though only about 70 mi (115 km) from Belize City, San Ignacio remained fairly isolated until recent times, because getting to the coast by horseback through the bush could take three days or longer. The Western Highway was paved in the 1980s, making it easier to get here. The first jungle lodges began operation and tourism now vies with agriculture as the main industry.

EXPLORING THE CAYO

The Cayo's main connection to the coast is the Western Highway, a paved two-lane road running 78 mi (128 km) between Belize City and the

TOP REASONS TO GO

NATIONAL PARKS & RESERVES
About 60% of the land in the Cayo District is national parks and reserves, which is good news if you like hiking, birding, wildlife spotting, canoeing, and other outdoor activities. The Mountain Pine Ridge, at more than 127,000 acres, is the largest forest reserve in Belize. Other national parks and protected areas you can explore include the Elijio Panti National Park, Five Blues Lake National Park, St. Herman's Blue Hole National Park, and Guanacaste National Park (here you can spot plenty of birds on hourly tours).

CAVES Although there are caves in Toledo and elsewhere in Belize, the Cayo has the most, the biggest, and the most exciting caves. Explore huge and mysterious underground chambers on foot or float on subterranean rivers through the underworld of the ancient Maya. Regardless of your fitness level and experience, or lack of it, in the Cayo you'll find a cave that's right for you.

MAYAN SITES The Cayo is home to the largest and most important

Mayan site in Belize, Caracol, with more than 35,000 buildings over 30 square mi (78 square km). It also has the most easily accessible Mayan sites, in the country, Cahal Pech and Xunantunich, along with dozens of smaller and less well known sites.

JUNGLE LODGES With more than 30 jungle lodges, the Cayo has far more than all the other districts of Belize combined. There's a lodge for every budget, from bare bones cabins along the Mopan River to ultradeluxe villas on the Macal River and in the Mountain Pine Ridge.

MOUNTAINS The Cayo's mountains of 2,000 to 3,000 feet provide a welcome respite from the heat and humidity of lowland Belize. Though lacking the craggy, alpine heights of the volcanic mountains of Guatemala or Costa Rica, the Mountain Pine Ridge and the north end of the Maya Mountain range make up for it with a dramatic line up of natural wonders—waterfalls, caves, pristine rivers, and a newly formed lake created by dams on the Macal.

Guatemala border. The highway is in generally good condition, but shoulders are narrow, and parts of the highway can be slick after rains.

At Belmopan, the paved Hummingbird Highway is Belize's most scenic road, cutting southeast through the Maya Mountains to Dangriga, passing Five Blues Lake and Blue Hole national parks. Mile markers on the Hummingbird start in Dangriga.

Secondary roads, mostly unpaved and difficult to drive on, branch off the Western Highway, leading to small villages and to the Mountain Pine Ridge, the Spanish Lookout Mennonite area, and various jungle lodges. The Mountain Pine Ridge is crisscrossed by an extensive network of gravel and dirt roads, some formerly logging trails.

Numbers in the margin correspond to points of interest on the Cayo map.

The Cayo

Yalbac Hills

Balize River

El Pilar

Mennonite Settlements

Guancaste National Park

Roaring Creek

WESTERN   HIGHWAY

Cotton Tree

❶ Belmopan City

Baking Pot

Teakettle Village

Balize River

Floral Park

Ontario Village

Roaring Creek

HUMMINGBIRD HIGHWAY

Georgeville

Tree Falls

WESTERN HIGHWAY

Esperanza

Rio Mopan

San ❷ Ignacia

Santa Elena

Cristo Ray

Ba rto n Creek Cave

Actun Tunichil Muknal

Caves Branch

Blue Hole Natural Park

Garcia Museum

Buenavista del Cayo

Pacbitun

Xunantunich

Mai Gate

Hidden Valley Falls

❸ Mountain Pine Ridge

Bald Hills

Mt. Baldy

Sibun Gorge

East Branch

Rio on Pools

Douglas de Silva

Rio Frio Caves

Mountain Pine Ridge Forest Reserve

Macal River

San Luis

Macal River

Caracol Natural Monument Reservation

❹ Caracol

Chiquibul National Park

KEY

Major Roads	
Minor Roads	
Seasonal Roads	
Mayan Site	

0   5 miles

0   5 kilometers

When to Go

The best time to visit the Cayo is late fall and winter, when temperatures generally are moderate. During the dry season, late February or March to May or early June, at the lower elevations around San Ignacio and Belmopan, daytime temperatures can reach 100°F, though it does cool off at night. Seasonal rains usually reach the Cayo in June. In summer, after the rains begin, temperatures moderate a little, but humidity increases. Year-round the Mountain Pine Ridge is noticeably cooler and less humid than anywhere else in Belize.

Safety in the Cayo

Although most visitors report feeling completely safe in the Cayo, there have been a series of robberies by armed bandits. Ask locally about any recent incidents before starting road trips to remote areas. At this writing, the U.S. Embassy had issued a warning about highway banditry on unpaved roads near the Guatemalan border.

About the Restaurants

San Ignacio is the culinary center of the Cayo, with close to 20 restaurants. Most are small spots, with only a few tables. Restaurants offer Indian, French, and German, as well as burritos and beans. Prices, designed to appeal to the budget and midlevel travelers who stay in town, rarely rise above the moderate level. At the jungle lodges outside San Ignacio, prices are much higher.

The restaurants (all of which are indicated by a ✗) that we list are the cream of the crop in each price category. Properties indicated by a ✗🏠 are lodging establishments whose restaurant warrants a special trip.

About the Hotels

In the Cayo you have two very different choices in accommodations: jungle lodges and regular hotels. Jungle lodges, regardless of price or amenities, offer a close-to-nature experience, typically next to a river or in a remote mountain setting. Most lodges house their guests in thatch cabanas, patterned after traditional Mayan houses. At the top end, lodges such as Blancaneaux and Chaa Creek deliver a truly deluxe experience, with designer toiletries, thick imported mattresses, and decor that wouldn't be out of place in *Architectural Digest*. At the other end, some budget lodges have outdoor bathrooms and thin, foam mattresses. In between are a number of midlevel lodges providing an off-the-beaten path experience at moderate prices.

Whereas the district's lodges are back-a-bush (a Belizean expression for out in the jungle), the Cayo's hotels are in towns or along the Western Highway. The area's least expensive hotels are clustered in San Ignacio, one of the backpacker centers of Belize. Hotels in and around Belmopan are a little more expensive, since they cater to people in the capital on government business. Whether hotel or jungle lodge, most properties in the Cayo are small, typically run by the owner.

Generally, inexpensive hotels and lodges maintain the same rate year-round, though some may discount a little in the off-season (generally mid-April to early December). More expensive places have off-season rates 30% to 40% less than high season.

The lodgings (all indicated with a 🖼) that we list are the cream of the crop in each price category. We always list the facilities that are available—but we don't specify whether they cost extra: when pricing accommodations, always ask what's included. Properties indicated by a ✕🖼 are lodging establishments whose restaurant warrants a special trip.

WHAT IT COSTS In Belize Dollars				
$$$$	**$$$**	**$$**	**$**	**¢**
RESTAURANTS over $50)	$25–$50	$15–$25	$8–$15	under $8
HOTELS over $500	$300–$500	$200–$300	$100–$200	under $100

Restaurant prices are per person for a main course at dinner. Hotel prices are for two people in a standard double room, including tax and service.

BELMOPAN CITY

❶ *50 mi (80 km) southwest of Belize City.*

It used to be said that the best way to see Belize's capital was through the rearview mirror as you head toward San Ignacio or south down the Hummingbird. It's a dreary cluster of concrete office buildings plunked in the middle of nowhere, proving that cities can't be created overnight. However, with the opening of the main campus of the University of Belize in Belmopan in 2002, the current relocation of several embassies from Belize City to Belmopan, and new commercial activity around the capital, Belmopan—finally—is showing some signs of life. However, we recommend you spend your time at nearby sites rather than in the city itself.

The **Belize Zoo** (⇨ *See* Chapter 1), one of the country's top sights, is only a half hour east of Belmopan via the Western Highway.

Worth a quick visit on the way out of Belmopan is Belize's small nature reserve, **Guanacaste National Park,** named for the huge guanacaste trees that grow here. Also called monkey's ear trees because of their oddly shaped seedpods, the trees tower more than 100 feet. The 50-acre park has a rich population of tropical birds, including smoky brown woodpeckers, black-headed trogons, red-lored parrots, and white-breasted wood wrens. You can try one of the eight hourly tours offered every day, or you can wander around on your own. ✉ *Mile 47.7, Western Hwy.* ☎ *223/4434 Belize Audubon Society in Belize City* 💲 *BZ$5* 🕐 *Daily 8:30–4:30; tours every hr 8:30–3:30.*

Less than a half hour south of Belmopan, **St. Herman's Blue Hole Natural Park,** has a natural turquoise pool surrounded by mosses and lush vegetation, excellent for a cool dip. The Blue Hole is actually part of an underground river system. On the other side of the hill is St. Herman's Cave, once inhabited by the Maya. A path leads up from the highway,

GREAT ITINERARIES

IF YOU HAVE 3 DAYS IN THE CAYO

Upon arrival at the international airport, immediately head to the Cayo by rental car, bus, or shuttle van. If you have time, stop en route at the **Belize Zoo.** Stay at one of the jungle lodges around San Ignacio, if it's in your budget. On your first full day in the Cayo, explore the area around **San Ignacio,** visiting the **Xunantunich** Mayan ruins, the **Belize Botanic Gardens** on the grounds of duPlooy's Lodge, and **Green Hills Butterfly Farm.** Assuming you have the energy, walk the **Rainforest Medicine Trail** and spend a few minutes at the **Natural History Center,** both at the Lodge at Chaa Creek. On the second day, if you're not planning to move on to **Tikal** in Guatemala after your stay in the Cayo, at least take a day tour there. Guided tours from San Ignacio usually include van transportation to the Tikal park, a local guide at the site, and lunch. Alternatively, if you're heading to Tikal later, take a day trip to **Caracol** in the **Mountain Pine Ridge.** Bring a picnic lunch and make stops at **Rio On** pools, the **Rio Frio** cave, and a waterfall, such as **Five Sisters.** On your final day, take a full-day guided tour of **Actun Tunichil Muknal.** Have dinner at a restaurant in San Ignacio.

IF YOU HAVE 5 DAYS IN THE CAYO

Rent a car at the international airport and drive to a jungle lodge near Belmopan. If you have time, stop en route at the **Belize Zoo** and do a quick driving tour of the capital. On your first full day, go **cave tubing** and take a **zip-line canopy tour** at Jaguar Paw Lodge. Alternatively, for a more strenuous day, take a trip with Caves Branch Adventure Camp, or do their cave tubing trip. End your day with dinner at your lodge and a night wildlife-spotting tour. On your second day, drive down the Hummingbird Highway and take a dip in the inland **Blue Hole.** Also, visit **St. Herman's Cave** and either hike around **Five Blues Lake National Park,** or go **horseback riding** at Banana Bank Lodge. On the third day, move on to a jungle lodge near San Ignacio or in the Mountain Pine Ridge. Explore the area around San Ignacio, visiting the **Xunantunich** Mayan ruins, the **Belize Botanic Gardens** at duPlooy's Lodge, and **Green Hills Butterfly Farm.** Assuming you have the energy, walk the **Rainforest Medicine Trail** and spend a few minutes at the **Natural History Center,** both at the Lodge at Chaa Creek. On the fourth day, rise early for a birding hike around your lodge. If you're not moving on to **Tikal** after your stay in the Cayo, take a day tour there. Guided tours from San Ignacio usually include van transportation to the Tikal park, a local guide at the site, and lunch. If you are indeed heading to Tikal later, make a day trip instead to **Caracol** in the **Mountain Pine Ridge.** Pack a picnic lunch and stop at **Rio On** pools, the **Rio Frio** cave, and a waterfall, such as **Five Sisters.** On your final day, take a full-day guided tour of **Actun Tunichil Muknal.**

4

right near the Blue Hole, but it's quite steep and difficult to climb unless the ground is dry. To explore St. Herman's cave beyond the first 300 yards or so, you must be accompanied by a guide (available at the park), and no more than five people can enter the cave at one time. With a guide, you also can explore part of another cave system here, the Crystal Cave (sometimes called the Crystalline Cave), which stretches for miles; the additional cost is BZ$20 per person for a two-hour guided tour. The park visitor center is 12½ mi (20½ km) from Belmopan. ⊗ *Daily 8–4:30* ✉ *Mile 42.5, Hummingbird Hwy.* ☑ *BZ$8.*

At **Five Blues Lake National Park,** you can hike 3 mi (5 km) of trails, explore several caves, or canoe and swim in the lake. Try to pick out the five shades of blue in the lake that supposedly gave the park its name. The park entrance is about 3½ mi (5 ¾ km) from the Hummingbird Highway, via a narrow dirt road. Overnight camping is available for BZ$5 per person. Canoes and bikes can be rented in St. Margaret's Village, and home stays in the village also can be arranged. The park is closed following heavy rains, usually for a total of about two months of the year, mostly in summer. ✉ *At end of Lagoon Rd., off Mile 32, Hummingbird Hwy.* ☑ *BZ$8, leave in self-service fee box if no attendant* ⊗ *Daily 8–4.*

Where to Stay & Eat

$$$ 🏨 **Jaguar Paw.** Although this lodge is down a long dirt road, it's anything but rustic. Eye-popping Mayan murals, by American painter Pamela Braun, adorn the main lodge's inner walls, which also has a 25-foot indoor waterfall. Each room has air-conditioning and a theme—the Victorian Room has a country armoire and sheer curtains; the Pioneer Room has a pebble-lined shower and rough-hewn wooden bed. Surrounding all this are 215 acres of jungle containing 9 mi (15 km) of hiking trails, a butterfly farm, a zip-line canopy tour, and caves that you (and at times hundreds of day-trippers from cruise ships and Ambergris Caye) can float through on an inner tube. ✛ *Off*

> **WORD OF MOUTH**
>
> "We stumbled onto Jaguar Paw on one of our last nights in Belize some years ago. The few miles' drive in were fairly tough but I loved the resort, owners were incredibly courteous, and I highly recommend it."
>
> –2jacks

Western Hwy., turn south at Mile 37 and follow dirt road 7 mi (11 km) ☎ *820/2023, 888/775–8645 in U.S.* ⊕ *www.jaguarpaw.com* ➪ *16 rooms* ⌂ *Restaurant, fans, pool, fishing, hiking, bar, travel services; no room phones, no room TVs* ▭ *AE, DC, MC, V.*

★ **$$$** 🏨 **Pook's Hill.** When the lamps are lit each night on the polished rosewood veranda, this low-key jungle lodge, on 300 remote acres, adjoining the 6,700-acre Tapir Mountain Reserve (open only to researchers) is one of the most pleasant places in the Cayo. The stone-and-thatch cabanas are laid out on a grassy clearing around a small, partially excavated Mayan site. During the day you can swim, ride

To AI or Not to AI

MANY LODGES AND RESORTS in Belize offer a tweaked version of the sort of all-inclusive you often find in Mexico or Jamaica: optional packages that include nearly everything, such as all meals, guided tours, and sports (fishing, diving, or sometimes even golfing). So when is it worth your money to choose one of these over selecting room, meals, and activities a la carte?

The answer is, it depends. If you're going to a remote caye resort or jungle lodge, you may not have a choice. When you're an hour away from the nearest restaurant, you're pretty much stuck eating at your hotel. On the other hand, at a destination such as Ambergris Caye, Caye Caulker, or Placencia, there are several excellent restaurants to choose from. It would be a shame to lock yourself into a single dining experience. A few resorts on Ambergris Caye, mainly those located on the far north end of the island (a long boat ride away from San Pedro), do offer all-inclusive or near-all-inclusive packages; however, for most people, one of the main

reasons for coming to Ambergris Caye is the opportunity to sample the variety of restaurants.

The main advantage of an all-inclusive or mostly inclusive package is that you don't have to worry about the details of travel planning. Once you've paid your fixed price, all you have to do is show up at the airport with your bags packed. The resort or lodge picks you up at the Belize International Airport, takes you on guided tours, provides your meals, and practically holds your hand. It's almost like being on a cruise, with few decisions to make. If you're the type of person who likes a fairly rigid, organized travel experience, an AI package is probably a good bet for you.

Before you book, be sure to total up the value of what you expect to get at the all-inclusive, and compare that with what you probably would pay on an a la carte basis. If some of the included activities don't appeal to you, it might actually be more expensive to go with an AI.

horses, go birding, or boat up the Roaring River to a series of caves. You can hike from here to Actun Tunichil Muknal. ✛ *At Mile 52 of Western Hwy., head south for 5 mi (8 km)* ☎ *820/2017* 🖷 *822/3361* ⊕ *www.pookshillbelize.com* ↦ *9 cabanas* ⚲ *Dining room, fans, hiking, horseback riding, river swimming, bar; no a/c, no room phones, no room TVs* ▭ *MC, V.*

$–$$$ 🏨 **Banana Bank Lodge.** Along the banks of the Belize River, this jungle lodge is one of the best spots for families. Equestrians of all skill levels can choose from 80 horses. Owners John and Carolyn Carr (he's a cowboy from Montana, she's a noted artist) arrange canoe trips and hikes on the lodge's 4,000 acres. Among the residents are a ravishing jaguar named Tika and a spider monkey. Thatch cabanas with curving walls are modest but comfortable (no air-conditioning, though), and there are three new air-conditioned rooms in the three-story Chateau Brio, and three budget rooms in the Chalet. ⊹ *From Western Hwy, turn north at Mile 46.9 and cross bridge over Belize River. Follow gravel/dirt road 3 mi (5 km) to Banana Bank sign. Turn right and follow dirt road for 2 mi (3 km)* ☎ 820/2020 🖶 820/2026 ⊕ *www.bananabank.com* ☜ *6 rooms, 7 cabanas ☖ Restaurant, fans, hiking, horseback riding, bar, travel services; no a/c in some rooms, no room phones, no room TVs* ☰ *MC, V.*

★ ¢–$$$ 🖾 ⚠ **Caves Branch Adventure Co. & Jungle Camp.** Budget-minded guests at this jungle lodge on a 58,000-acre private reserve will head to the bunkhouse or campground, while those in search of creature comforts will appreciate the mahogany and bamboo bungalows and suites. Owner Ian Anderson and his highly trained jungle guides offer more than a dozen wilderness adventures. On the tubing expedition to Footprint Cave you spend hours floating around underground lakes and crawling past stalagmites into dry chambers. Perhaps you'll take lunch where Maya once performed bloodletting rituals. Cold Belikins await you when you return, followed by a delicious dinner. "Bad Ass" expeditions into the jungle last seven to nine days. ⊠ *12 mi (19½ km) south of Belmopan at Mile 41½ of Hummingbird Hwy.* ☎ *822/2800* 🖶 *888/265–4579 in U.S.* ⊕ *www.cavesbranch.com* 🖾 *BZ$30–BZ$256* ☜ *4 suites, 10 cabanas, 7 with shared bath, 8 beds in bunkhouse ☖ Restaurant, fans, hiking, bar, Internet room, travel services; no a/c, no room phones, no room TVs* ☰ *MC, V.*

$$ 🖾 **Belize Jungle Dome.** If you think Belize isn't hip, check out the Jungle Dome. Andy, a former pro soccer player with Newcastle, and Simone, Dutch, and formerly a veejay for MTV Europe, moved to Belize in 2001 and built this little inn in the bush, topped with a geodesic dome, next door to Banana Bank Lodge. The two suites and standard room here have tile floors, lots of windows, and an uncluttered look. The owners and their comanager, Karen, from Canada, all have blogs about Belize, and you can do your own blogging at the wireless hotspot by the pool, take a yoga or Pilates class (group classes, BZ$30 an hour), and eat an organic meal on the terrace. You have access to hiking trails and other facilities at Banana Bank. ⊹ *From Western Hwy., turn north at Mile 46.9 and cross bridge over Belize River. Follow gravel/dirt road 3 mi (5 km) until you see Banana Bank sign. Turn right and follow dirt road 2 mi (3 km)* ☎ *822/2124* 🖶 *822/2155* ⊕ *www.belizejungledome.com* ☜ *1 room, 2 suites ☖ Restaurant, fans, kitchen, cable TV, pool, hiking, horseback riding, Wi-Fi, travel services; no room phones* ☰ *MC, V.*

The Outdoors

Belmopan and San Ignacio offer a similar lineup of outdoor activities, and since they're only about 20 mi (33 km) apart, you can stay in one area and enjoy the activities around the other.

Birding

Although there's good birding in many areas around Belmopan, **Pook's Hill Lodge,** 5½ mi [9 km] off the Western Highway at Mile 52½ (☎ 822/2017) is in a league of its own. The birding list from Pook's Hill includes the Mealy Parrot, Spectacled Owl, Aztec Parakeet, and Keel-billed Toucan.

Canoeing & Kayaking

The Belize River, wide and mostly gentle (Class I-II) offers good canoeing and kayaking. It was once used by loggers to transport mahogany to Belize City and hosts the annual La Ruta Maya Mountains to the Sea Canoe Race. The multiday race is held in March during the Baron Bliss holiday. You can also canoe or kayak portions of the Caves Branch River (also Class I-II). Many hotels and lodges arrange canoe or kayak trips, including **Caves Branch Adventure Co. & Jungle Lodge,** off the Hummingbird Highway (☎ 822/2800) and **Crystal Paradise Resort** (☎ 824/2772), in Cristo Rey Village near San Ignacio. Full-day canoe or kayak trips start at around BZ$120 per person.

Canopy Tours

You may feel a little like Tarzan as you dangle 80 feet above the jungle floor, suspended by a harness, moving from one suspended platform to another. **Jaguar Paw Lodge,** off Mile 37 of the Western Highway, (☎ 820/2023) has eight platforms set 100 to 250 feet apart. At the last platform you have to rappel to the ground. The cost is BZ$110 to BZ$150, depending on whether lunch and transportation are included. There's a 240-pound weight limit.

Caving

The area around Belmopan, with its karst limestone topography, is a paradise for cavers. At **St. Herman's Blue Hole National Park,** at Mile 42 of the Hummingbird Highway, there are two large caves, St. Herman's and the Crystal Cave. Both require a guide to explore (guides are available at the national park visitor center).

★ The most rewarding caving experience, however, is **Actun Tunichil Muknal,** or "Cave of the Crystal Sepulchre," southwest of Teakettle Village. You hike about 45 minutes, crossing the Roaring River three times, swim a few yards in the river, and enter the cave's hourglass-shape opening. Once inside, you clamber over large boulders and squeeze through tight passageways (even a large person can get through). You spend about three hours or longer inside. This is a real caving experience, with no lighting except what your guide provides and no well-marked walkways or roped-off platforms. If you're physically active and can swim don't hesitate. You'll see amazing limestone formations, thousand-year-old human calcified skulls and skeletons, and many Mayan artifacts including well-preserved pottery. Only a few licensed guides are authorized to run tours of the cave, among them **Emilio Awe,** (✉ 22 Burns Ave., San Ignacio ☎ 824/2477) and **Maya Walk** (✉ 19 Burns Ave., San Ignacio ☎ 824/3070 ⊕ www.mayawalk.com). The Belize government is training additional guides for the ATM (Actun Tunichil Muknal) tour, and more options may be available when you're in Belize. The tour costs around BZ$180–BZ$190 per person. Your hotel or lodge can arrange an ATM or other caving trip.

Cave Tubing

The most popular outdoor activity around Belmopan is cave tubing. You float down the Caves Branch River in an inner tube, at points going through dark limestone caves in the subterranean sections of the river.

Caves Branch River has two main entry points: near **Jaguar Paw Lodge,** (✉ Off Mile 37 of Western Hwy. ☎ 820/2023) and near **Caves Branch Adventure Co. & Jungle Lodge** (✉ Off Hummingbird Hwy. ☎ 822/2800). The Jaguar Paw access attracts more people and when several cruise ships are in port at Belize City, the river here can be jammed. There's a parking area about ½ mi (1 km) from Jaguar Paw, BZ$4 parking fee, and here you'll find a number of tour guides for cave tubing tours, which vary in length, generally costing from BZ$80 to BZ$150. ⇨ *See* tour operators in Belize City A to Z and San Ignacio section of this chapter. Cave tubing trips from Caves Branch Lodge are longer, require more hiking, and cost more. For example, the "River of Caves" trip, through 7 mi (12 km) of underground caves, takes much of a day and costs BZ$190 per person.

Cave tubing is subject to changes in the river levels. In the dry season (February–May or June), the river levels are often too low for cave tubing. Also, after heavy rains, the water level in the river is too high to safely float through caves, so in the rainy season (June–November) cave tubing trips may occasionally be canceled. Always call ahead to check if tours are operating.

Horseback Riding
The best equestrian operator in this part of Belize is **Banana Bank Lodge & Jungle Equestrian Adventure** (☎ 820/2020), off the Western Highway near Belmopan. Run by John Carr, a former Montana cowboy and rodeo rider, Banana Bank has about 80 horses, mostly quarter horses, a large round-pen riding arena, stables, and miles of jungle trails on a 4,000-acre ranch. A two- to three-hour ride costs BZ$120.

SAN IGNACIO

❷ *23 mi (37 km) southwest of Belmopan.*

When you hear the incredible commotion made by black Grackles in the town square's trees, and see the Hawksworth Bridge, the only public suspension bridge in Belize, you'll know you've arrived at San Ignacio, the hub of the Cayo district. San Ignacio is an excellent base for exploring western Belize. Nearby are three Mayan ruins, as well as national parks and a cluster of butterfly farms.

With its well-preserved wooden structures, dusty little San Ignacio is a Belizean town where you might want to linger. Evenings are cool and mosquito-free, and the colonial-era streets are lined with funky bars and restaurants. It's worth coming at sunset to listen to the eerily beautiful sounds of these iridescent Grackles. On Saturday mornings, **San Ignacio Market,** in an open field across from the soccer stadium, comes alive with farmers selling local fruits and vegetables. Vendors also hawk crafts, clothing, and household goods. A much smaller vegetable and fruit market is open weekdays on Burns Avenue, closer to town. ☉ *Sat. 7 AM–noon, though some vendors stay later.*

Nearby Sites

You can ask to work the crank yourself as you ride a hand-pulled ferry across the Mopan River, near the village of San José Succotz, toward the archaeological site of **Xunantunich** (pronounced *zoo-nan-too-nitch*), which means "stone maiden." As you hike through the profusion of maidenhair ferns to the ruins, you'll encounter numerous butterflies flitting through the air. A magnificent avenue of cohune palms announces your arrival at an important ceremonial center from the Maya Classic Period. Drinks and snacks are available at a visitor center that provides the history of the site. El Castillo, the massive 120-foot-high main pyramid, was built on a leveled hilltop. The pyramid has a spectacular 360-degree panorama of the Mopan River valley into Guatemala. On the eastern wall is a reproduction of one of the finest Mayan sculptures in Belize, a frieze decorated with jaguar heads, human faces, and abstract geometric patterns telling the story of the Moon's affair with Morning Light. ⊠ *Near San José Succotz Village, 6½ mi (11 km) southwest of San Ignacio on Benque Rd., Western Hwy.* ✆ *BZ$10* ⊗ *Daily 8–4.*

El Pilar, a less frequented archaeological site, is still being excavated under the direction of Anabel Ford, a professor at the University of California. Excavations of Mayan ruins have traditionally concentrated on public buildings, but at El Pilar the emphasis has been on reconstructing domestic architecture—everything from houses to gardens with crops used by the Maya. El Pilar, occupied from AD 700 to AD 1000, shows evidence of sentry posts in some areas, suggesting that this was a community of high-ranking officials surrounded by a hostile population. Two well-marked trails take you around the site. Because the structures haven't been stripped of vegetation, you may feel like you're walking through a series of shady orchards. Don't forget binoculars: in the 5,000-acre nature reserve there's some terrific bird-watching. Behind the main plaza a lookout grants a spectacular view across the jungle to El Pilar's sister city, Pilar Poniente, on the Guatemalan border. Note that several incidents of robbery have occurred at or near this site. ⊠ *8 mi (13 km) west of Bullet Tree Falls, Western Hwy.* ✆ *BZ$10* ⊗ *Daily 8–5.*

On private land, **Actun Chechem Ha,** which means "Cave of the Poisonwood Water," is a Mayan burial cave with artifacts that date back two millennia. There are many pots and a stela used for ceremonial purposes. To examine some of the pottery, you'll have to climb ladders, and getting to the cave requires a 35-minute walk, mostly uphill. Unfortunately, a few years ago some of the artifacts were stolen from the cave. Tour companies visit here from San Ignacio. ⊠ *10 mi (17 km) south of Benque Viejo* ☎ *820/4063 to arrange a visit* ✆ *BZ$50 for guided tour for up to 3 people, if arranged with owner; tours including transportation from San Ignacio or your lodge and often including lunch and swimming at Vaca Falls are around BZ$100 per person* ⊗ *By appointment.*

One of the most unusual attractions in Belize, **Poustinia Land Art Park** is a collection of 30 original works of art by artists from about a dozen countries, including Belize, Norway, Guayana, Brazil, Guatemala, and

England, scattered about some 60 acres of a former cattle ranch. It's owned by Luis Alberto Ruiz, a Belmopan architect, who calls Poustinia an "environmental project." Poustinia is a Russian word for "desert of the soul." Among the works of outdoor art, which some would call funky and others fascinating, are "Downtown," by Venezuelan artist Manuel Piney, and "Returned Parquet," a visual reference in mahogany parquet flooring to Belize's colonial history by Tim Davies, a British artist. Getting around the park, which is open by appointment only, to see the art requires many hours of sometimes strenuous hiking. Be sure to bring insect repellent. Two simple cabins at the site are available for rent "to artists and short-term visitors" for BZ$80 double a night. Electricity is provided three hours a day, with extra hours of power available at additional cost. ⊠ *Hydro Rd., 2½ mi (5 km) south of Benque Viejo, 8 mi (13 km) southwest of San Ignacio* ☎ *822/3522 to arrange a visit* ⊠ *BZ$10* ☉ *By appointment.*

☾ The **Rainforest Medicine Trail,** gives you a quick introduction to traditional Mayan medicine. The trail takes you on a short, self-guided walk through the rain forest, giving you a chance to study the symbiotic nature of its plant life. Learn about the healing properties of such indigenous plants as red gumbo-limbo and man vine and see some of the endangered medicinal plants that Arvigo and her colleagues rescued. The shop here sells Mayan medicinal products like Belly Be Good and Flu Away. "Field Guide to Useful Plants of the Rainforest Medicine Trail" is sold at the gift shop for BZ$10. ⊠ *Next to Lodge at Chaa Creek* ☎ *824/ 2037* ⊠ *BZ$12 for Rainforest Medicine Trail, BZ$16 including Natural History Center and Blue Morpho Breeding Center; free to Chaa Creek guests* ☉ *Daily 9–5.*

☾ The **Chaa Creek Natural History Center** has a tiny library and lots of displays on everything from butterflies to snakes (pickled in jars). Outside is a screened-in blue morpho butterfly-breeding center. If you haven't encountered blue morphos in the wild, you can see them up close here and even peer at their slumbering pupae, which resemble jade earrings. Once you're inside the double doors, the blue beauties, which look boringly brown when their wings are closed, flit about or remain perfectly still, sometimes on your shoulder or head, and open and close their wings to a rhythm akin to inhaling and exhaling. Tours are led by a team of naturalists. ⊠ *The Lodge at Chaa Creek* ☎ *824/2037* ☎ *824/2501* ⊕ *www.chaacreek.com* ⊠ *BZ$10 or BZ$16 combined with Rainforest Medicine Trail; free to Chaa Creek guests* ☉ *Daily 9–4.*

The life's work of Ken duPlooy, an ornithologist who died in 2001, and
☾ the personable Judy duPlooy is the **Belize Botanical Gardens,** a collection of hundreds of trees, plants, and flowers from all over Central America. Enlightening tours of the gardens, set on a bank of the Macal River, are given by Heather, daughter of Ken and Judy, who is the director of the gardens, and by local Maya who can tell you the names of the plants in Maya, Spanish, and English as well as explain their varied medicinal uses. An orchid house holds the duPlooys' collection of more than 100 orchid species. ⊹ *duPlooy's Lodge; from San Ignacio, head 4¾ mi (7½ km) west on Benque Rd., turn left on Chial Rd., San Ignacio* ☎ *824/*

3101 ☎ 824/3301 ⊕ *www.belizebotanic.org* ✆ *BZ$10 self-guided tour, BZ$15 guided tour* ⊙ *Daily 9–5.*

The small hilltop community of **Spanish Lookout**, about 12 mi (19 km) north of the Western Highway, is one of the centers of the Mennonite community in Belize. The village's blond-haired, blue-eyed residents may seem out of place in this tropical country, but they're actually responsible for many of Belize's major projects. They built nearly all the area's resorts, and most of the eggs and milk you'll consume during your stay comes from their farms. The women dress in cotton frocks and head scarves, and the men don straw hats, suspenders, and dark trousers. Some still travel in horse-drawn buggies, though many Mennonites around Spanish Lookout have embraced pickup trucks and modern farming equipment. The cafés and small shops in Spanish Lookout offer a unique opportunity to mingle with these world-wary people, but they don't appreciate being gawked at or photographed any more than you do.

Where to Stay & Eat

The lodges along the Mopan River, a dark jade-color river that winds into Belize from Guatemala, tend to be in the moderate to budget range, the exception being the Mopan River Resort. Those lodges along the Macal River, with some exceptions, are typically more upmarket.

San Ignacio

$–$$ ✕ **Sanny's Grill.** Sanny's democratic motto proclaims: PRICES ANYONE CAN AFFORD. With a hot grill and sizzling spices, this restaurant transforms Belizean basics, like chicken or pork chops, beyond standard fare. Try the champagne shrimp or lime-thyme red snapper, along with the tastiest, spiciest rice and beans in the Cayo. Eat them in the casual dining room or out on the covered deck. In a residential area off Benque Road, the place can be hard to find after dark. ⊠ *23rd St., heading west of San Ignacio, look for sign just beyond Texaco station* ☎ *824/2988* ▭ *MC, V* ☉ *No lunch Sun.*

¢–$$ ✕ **Café Sol.** No need to wilt in the sun here, as you can sit in the shade of a large mango tree at this little downtown café and enjoy healthy vegetarian, vegan, and white-meat dishes. For breakfast, try the vegetarian sausages and rich banana pancakes. The fresh-made guava, mango, lime, and watermelon juices are refreshing. ⊠ *West St.* ☎ *824/2166* ▭ *MC, V.*

¢–$$ ✕ **Serendib.** What's a Sri Lankan restaurant doing on Burns Avenue? The Ceylonese owner came to Belize with the British Army, and like many other squadies, decided to stay on and open a business. Over the years, the menu here has migrated more to Belizean, Chinese, and American dishes than Sri Lankan, but you can still get authentic curries. The restaurant is a comfortable, cool escape from the crowds on the street outside. ⊠ *27 Burns Ave.* ☎ *824/2302* ▭ *MC, V* ☉ *Closed Sun.*

$ ✕ **Royal Indian Restaurant.** This is the best Northern Indian food in Belize outside of Belize City. It has a nice selection of vegetarian dishes, including *palak paneer* (spinach with cheese), *shai paneer* (cheese with vegetable gravy), and *prantha* (fried bread stuffed with vegetables), all about BZ$10, along with delicious chicken dishes such as *hara masala murgh* (chicken with yogurt and spinach), plus pizzas and sandwiches. ⊠ *Far West St. and Bullet Tree Rd., next to Martha's Guesthouse* ☎ *621/2200* ▭ *No credit cards.*

¢–$ ✕ **Eva's.** Not merely a bustling café-bar, this Cayo institution also acts as an Internet café, bulletin board, information center, trading post, tour center, and meeting place. In addition to the bacon, eggs, and sandwiches, Eva's serves authentic Belizean fare. The food may not always be as good as at some other restaurants in town, but the atmosphere makes up for it. Mugs of wickedly strong black tea are always available, along with copious quantities of Belikin. Presiding over the colorful chaos is Bob Jones, a garrulous British ex-serviceman, who can divulge information about anything from canoe rental to what to do if you get bitten by a fer de lance. ⊠ *22 Burns Ave.* ☎ *824/2267* ⊕ *www.evasonline.com* ▭ *No credit cards.*

¢–$ ✕ **Hode's Place Bar & Grill.** Bigger than it looks from the outside, with a large shaded patio and swings and slides for the kids at the back, Hode's is popular for cold beers, karaoke, and billiards. Oh yes, it also has good food in large portions and at modest prices. ⊠ *Savannah Rd., next to sports stadium* ☎ *824/2522* ▭ *MC, V.*

¢ ✕ **Old French Bakery.** All the tasty French temptations that you can't get elsewhere in Belize are available at this little bakery, run by Sean and Blanco Bachet. Pick up a baguette of crusty French bread and an authentic croissant for only a couple of Belize dollars. It's open from 7 AM to 8 PM every day. ⊠ *Main Sq., across from taxi stand* ☎ *604/4651* ⊟ *No credit cards.*

$-$$ ✕⊞ **San Ignacio Resort Hotel.** Queen Elizabeth visited here once, and this in-town hotel has been trading inon that event ever since. While far from deluxe, it does have spacious and comfortable rooms with verandas facing the jungle. In late 2005 the entrance and lobby were completely renovated. The Running W Restaurant specializes in steak, and the Stork Bar is one of the best places in town to get a drink. Birding and other excursions can be arranged by the staff. There's an iguana hatchery on the property and next door is a small casino, a branch of the Princess casinos in Belize City and Corozal, packed with video poker machines, one-armed bandits, and a few live tables. ⊠ *Buena Vista Rd.* ☎ *824/ 2034* 🖨 *824/2134* ⊕ *www.sanignaciobelize.com* ➾ *24 rooms* ⌂ *Restaurant, cable TV, pool, bar, casino, laundry service, Internet, meeting rooms, travel services* ⊟ *AE, MC, V.*

¢-$ ✕⊞ **Martha's Guesthouse and Restaurant.** With spic 'n' span rooms, a popular restaurant, handy laundry, and convenient tours, Martha's provides just about everything you need, in an affordable package right in the heart of downtown San Ignacio. The regular rooms, most with shared bath, have white walls and polished wood floors, but for a little more you can get a larger room with cable TV, fridge, and balcony. The First Lady Suite is worth the climb up to the fourth floor, as it's large enough for a family, has a kitchenette, and a huge veranda with views of the hills. Martha's Restaurant, with a sweet garden patio, is open 7 AM–10 PM every day, serving pizza, sirloin steak (BZ$20) and local dishes such as chaya tamales (chaya is a type of greens grown around Cayo). Martha's stays booked, even off-season. ⊠ *10 West St.* ☎ *804/ 3647* 🖨 *824/2917* ⊕ *www.marthasbelize.com* ➾ *10 rooms, 7 with shared baths, 1 suite* ⌂ *Restaurant, fans, kitchenette in suite, refrigerators in some rooms, cable TV in some rooms, bar, laundry services, travel services; no a/c in some rooms, no room phones, no TV in some rooms* ⊟ *AE, MC, V.*

$$$ ⊞ **Windy Hill Resort.** The cabanas at this lodge all have private verandas and are perched on a low hill across the landscaped grounds. Furnishings are custom-made from local hardwoods, and decorations include handwoven Guatemalan rugs. Each cabana is cooled by a ceiling fan. You can lounge around the swimming pool and enjoy the nice views across the valley. The resort is on 100 acres at the edge of San Ignacio, right beside the highway. It runs many tours to Tikal, Caracol, and other destinations. Windy Hill has many packages with tours and meals included, starting at around BZ$2,200 for a double for two nights. ⊠ *Benque Rd., Western Hwy., 1 mi (1½ km) west of San Ignacio* ☎ *824/2017* 🖨 *824/3080* ⊕ *www.windyhillresort.com* ➾ *25 cabanas* ⌂ *Restaurant, fans, cable TV, pool, horseback riding, Internet room, travel services; no a/c in some rooms, no room phones* ⊟ *AE, MC, V.*

4

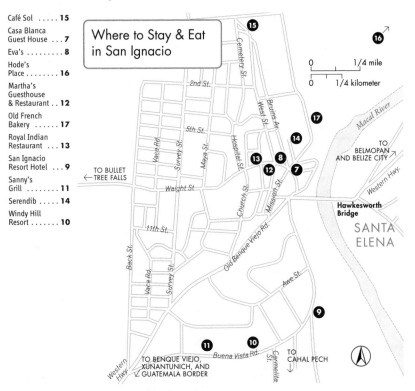

★ ¢–$ 🏨 **Casa Blanca Guest House.** Though it's in the center of San Ignacio, on bustling Burns Avenue, this small hotel, winner of the Belize Tourism Board's "best small hotel award" in 2003, is an oasis of quiet and one of Belize's top budget choices. The rooms, with cool white walls trimmed in mahogany and locally made wood furniture, are a big step above typical budget lodging. You can prepare yourself snacks or full meals in the shared kitchen. Casa Blanca is often fully booked, even off-season. ✉ *10 Burns Ave.* ☎ *824/2080* ⊕ *www.casablancaguesthouse.com* ⇗ *9 rooms* ⚲ *Fans, cable TV, travel services; no a/c in some rooms, no room phones* ⊟ *MC, V.*

$–$$ 🏨 **Maya Mountain Lodge.** Designed with the nature lover in mind, this hilltop lodge aspires toward comfort rather than luxury. Owners Bart and Suzi Mickler designed the nature trails. One passes 150 edible jungle plant species; the other focuses on ornamental plants. In summer they run workshops on ecology, birding, and other subjects. The white-washed cottages all have private patios. A large wooden building has rooms, recently renovated with air-conditioning added, for budget-conscious guests. The pleasant open-air dining room serves tempting, wholesome food. There's an above-ground pool, and the lodge runs a variety of tours and trips. ✉ *Cristo Rey Rd., 1 mi (2 km) outside San Ignacio* ☎ *824/2164* 🖷 *824/2029* ⊕ *www.mayamountain.com* ⇗ *8 cottages,*

6 rooms △ Restaurant, fans, pool, hiking, laundry service, Internet room, travel services; no room phones, no room TVs ▭ AE, MC, V.

¢ ⊞ **Aguada.** Budget travelers should jump at the opportunity to stay in this tidy, attractive, and cheap hotel in Santa Elena, a low-key town adjoining San Ignacio. Aguada is so popular that the owners, a Belizean-American couple, have added more rooms overlooking the pool. There's a friendly restaurant with Belizean dishes and American standards like burgers. In the large common room are a TV and games. The hotel is a short taxi or bus ride to San Ignacio. The hotel has a van that runs to and from the airports in Belize City for around BZ$70 a person. ⊠ *Santa Elena* ☎ *824/3609* ⊕ *www.aguadahotel. com* ⇨ *14 rooms △ Restaurant, pool, travel services; no room phones, no room TVs ▭ MC, V.*

Along the Mopan River

¢–$ ✕ **Benny's Kitchen.** This little open-air restaurant near Xunantunich has won many fans who come for hearty Mayan and Creole dishes at rock-bottom prices. Most items on the menu are BZ$8 or less, including *chilimole* (chicken with mole sauce), cow foot soup, *escabeche* (onion soup with chicken), and stewed pork with rice and beans and plantains. The classic Mayan Pibil (porked cooked in an underground oven), when available, is BZ$12. The banana *licuados* (milk shakes) are delicious. ⊠ *San José Succotz Village, across Benque Rd., Western Hwy., from ferry to Xunantunich, Turn south just west of ferry and follow signs about 3 blocks* ☎ *823/2541* ▭ *No credit cards.*

★ $$$$ ⊞ **Mopan River Resort.** Belize's first truly all-inclusive resort is one of the best values in the Cayo. Once you've taken the short ferry trip across the Mopan River to the resort's manicured palm-studded grounds, you're in your own private bit of paradise, and everything except border fees and site admission charges is included in the price, from meals and drinks to trips to Tikal and Barton Cave, transfers from Belize City, and even tips. The thatch cabanas have traditional façades, but have modern amenities like cable TVs, air-conditioning, and minibars with gratis soft drinks and beer. The swimming pool, lighted by constantly changing fiber-optic lights, provides a romantic setting for a late-night swim. Buffet meals are taken family-style, so you get to know the other guests. Co-owner Pamella Picon is an ordained minister who can marry you in the resort's wedding chapel. ⊠ *Benque Viejo del Carmen* ☎ *823/2047* ⊟ *823/3272* ⊕ *www.mopanriverresort.com* ⇨ *12 cabanas △ Dining room, some kitchens, minibars, refrigerators, cable TV, pool, laundry service, Wi-Fi, travel services; no room phones, no smoking ▭ D, MC, V* ⫙*All-inclusive* ⊘ *Closed July–Oct.*

○ $ △ ✕⊞ **Clarissa Falls Resort.** The rumbling low falls are the first and last sounds of the day at Clarissa Falls. It's a well-known place among

> **WORD OF MOUTH**
>
> "I took a trip to Belize the end of May and stayed for a week at the Mopan. I highly recommend this place—I traveled alone, so it was safe, everything was scheduled for me, and I shared great times with the other guests. The food was all wonderful; and the owners, Jay and Pamella, were awesome."
>
> –twizzler

Belizeans, who come for tasty enchiladas (BZ$3), tacos (two for BZ$1.50) and black bean soup served in an open-air palapa overlooking the Mopan River. Owner Chena Galvez and her sister Anna create the simple, savory food, which the friendly staff serves in copious quantities. This rolling 800-acre expanse of grassy pasture is the Galvez family cattle ranch. Chena has spent her life here and over the years has built a small colony of homey thatch cabanas. Prices are a little high considering the basic nature of the accommodations, but you're also paying for the idyllic setting. If you're on a tight budget, there's a bunkhouse (BZ$30 per person) and camping (BZ$15). ⊠ *Benque Rd., near Mile 70, Western Hwy., 5½ mi (9 km) west of San Ignacio* 🖀 *824/3916* ⊕ *www.clarissafalls.com* 🛏 *11 cabanas, 1 bunkhouse with 10 beds* ♨ *Restaurant, fans, 1-hole golf course, boating, hiking, horseback riding, bar, laundry services, travel services; no a/c, no room phones, no room TVs* ▭ *MC, V.*

★ ¢ 🏔 **The Trek Stop.** After a day out and about, a cold Belikin and filling Mexican and Belizean dishes await you at this cluster of neat-as-a-pin cabins. Tent camping (BZ$10 per person) is also available, as is a common kitchen for preparing your own grub. Michigan expats and their Belizean partners opened this spot on top of a hill near Xunantunich in 1998. It's an exceptional find, particularly for budget travelers, as cabins (with showers and composting toilets around the corner) start at just BZ$24 per person or BZ$40 double. A large new double cabin with private bath is BZ$70. Here you can also hike nature trails, visit the butterfly farm, and play Frisbee golf at the only disc golf course in Belize. ⊠ *San José Succotz Village, 6 mi (9 km) west of San Ignacio* 🖀 *823/ 2265* ⊕ *www.thetrekstop.com* 🛏 *8 cabins, 7 without private bath* ♨ *Restaurant, hiking, bar, travel services; no a/c, no room phones, no room TVs* ▭ *MC, V.*

¢ 🏠 **Parrot Nest.** Get a bird's-eye view from one of two cabins built on posts under a tall guanacaste tree. The lodge also has four earthbound cabins. All lodgings are comfy, and very good values. You can canoe in the Mopan River, which surrounds the lodge on three sides. Parrot Nest is often booked solid. For BZ$2 a *collectiva* (collective taxi) takes you here from downtown San Ignacio, and a regular taxi will cost about BZ$16. Yes, you'll definitely see parrots here. ⊠ *Bullet Tree Falls* ⊕ *www.parrot-nest.com* 🛏 *6 cabins, 5 with shared baths* ♨ *Restaurant, fans, bar, laundry services, travel services; no a/c, no room phones, no room TVs* ▭ *MC, V.*

Along the Macal River

$$–$$$$ 🏠 **The Lodge at Chaa Creek.** This was the first jungle lodge in the Cayo, FodorsChoice and owners Mick and Lucy Fleming have spent 30 years polishing Chaa ★   Creek to a fine, rich patina. To start, the gracefully landscaped grounds, surrounded by 330 acres of rolling hills above the Macal River, are magnificent. There's a friendly staff of 100. The whitewashed stone cottages with thatch roofs and custom-made furnishings are both simple and elegant. Ideal for honeymooners are the "tree top" suites (BZ$640) with whirlpools. For cost-conscious travelers there's the Macal River Camp, with small A-frame rooms on individual wooden platforms (BZ$220 double including meals). The resort's spa is the best in Belize. Dinner

(BZ$52) by lantern light is a special event. Additionally, Chaa Creek's tours are among the country's finest. ⊠ *Chial Rd., southwest of San Ignacio, From San Ignacio go 4¾ mi (7½ km) on Benque Rd., Western Hwy., turn left on Chial Rd.* ☎ *824/2037* 🖥 *824/2501* ⊕ *www. chaacreek.com* ↪ *18 rooms in duplex cottages, 4 suites, 3 villas, 10 casitas* ⚒ *Restaurant, fans, spa, hiking, horseback riding, river swimming, laundry service, Internet room, meeting rooms, travel services; no a/c, no room phones, no room TVs* ⊟ *AE, D, MC, V.*

★ ♻ **$$$** 🏠 **duPlooy's Lodge.** High above a bend in the Macal River called Big Eddy is this remarkable, relaxing lodge whose grounds include the 45-acre Belize Botanic Gardens. From your vantage point on the covered deck and 200 feet of canopied walkway, 30 feet above the forest floor, you'll see iguanas sunning in the trees and, perhaps while sipping a beer, you can do your bird-watching in comfort. You can swim and dive off the rocks from the sandy beach below. Bungalows are filled with hardwood furnishings. The two-story La Casita has wraparound porches, king-size beds, whirlpool bath, fridge, and great views. There are less expensive rooms in the jungle lodge, and the River House has family suites. The food is terrific (full meal plan is BZ$80 a person), and there's always a vegetarian option. ⊹ *Head 4¾ mi (7½ km) west on Benque Rd., turn left on Chial Rd., San Ignacio* ☎ *824/3101* 🖥 *824/3301* ⊕ *www.duplooys.com* ↪ *4 cabanas, 15 rooms* ⚒ *Dining room, fans, hiking, horseback riding, river swimming, laundry service, Internet room, travel services; no a/c, no room phones, no room TVs, no smoking* ⊟ *MC, V.*

★ **$$$** 🏠 **Ek 'Tun.** At Ek 'Tun sapphire blue water gushes from natural mineral springs into a rock-lined pool among towering palms. You're immersed in complete solitude here—you can even skinny-dip, if you like—with only the howler monkeys for company. Arrive by river skiff to the 200-acre grounds, which have giant ceiba trees and flowering shrubs. With only two rustic but lovely thatch-roof cottages, this is more of a bed-and-breakfast in the jungle than a traditional lodge. On the extensive network of trails you can spot orange-breasted falcons and toucans. Excellent meals (breakfast and dinner total BZ$56 per person) are served in a stucco-and-thatch dining room overlooking the Macal River. ⊠ *On Macal River 12 mi (20 km) upriver from San Ignacio* ☎ *820/3002* ⊕ *www.ektunbelize.com* ↪ *2 cabanas* ⚒ *Dining room, pool, hiking, bar, travel services; no a/c, no room phones, no room TVs, no kids under 18; no smoking in cabanas* ⊟ *MC, V.*

$–$$ 🏠 **Black Rock River Lodge.** Set some 800 feet above limestone cliffs and the Macal River gorge, Black Rock may have the most beautiful setting of any lodge in the country. The well-shaded cabins, which come in deluxe, river-view, and shared-bath versions, have stone floors and custom-made hardwood furniture and views across Black Rock canyon. The ecoconscious management runs the lodge on hydro and solar power. Since you're a 35-minute drive (about BZ$50 by taxi) from San Ignacio, partly on a narrow, single-lane dirt trail, by necessity you'll take all your meals here (the full meal plan is BZ$70 per person) and do most tours with the lodge. Black Rock is under the same ownership as Caesar's Place hotel and gift shop at Mile 60, Western Highway. ✉ *On Macal River 13 mi (22 km) upriver from San Ignacio, Box 48, San Ignacio* ☎ *824/2341* 🖶 *824/3449* ⊕ *www.blackrocklodge.com* ⤳ *13 cabins, 1 with shared bath* ⚘ *Dining room, fans, hiking, horseback riding, laundry service, travel services; no a/c, no room phones, no room TVs* ▤ *AE, MC, V.*

$–$$ ▣ **Crystal Paradise Resort.** This lodge is operated by the Tut (pronounced Toot) family—Mom and Dad Tut and 10, yes, 10, children. Mom and the daughters cook and run the lodge, and several of the sons are accomplished guides for birding, caving, and river expeditions. There's a range of lodging, from simple rooms to traditional thatch cabanas with views of the Macal River Valley. Rates, starting at BZ$150 double, are affordable, but are made even more so as delicious, fresh-made breakfasts and dinners are included in the price. ✉ *Cristo Rey Rd., Cristo Rey Village* ⊕ *www.crystalparadise.com* ⤳ *8 cabanas, 5 rooms,* ⚘ *Dining room, fans, hiking, horseback riding, river swimming, laundry service, travel services; no a/c, no room phones, no room TVs* ▤ *MC, V.*

The Outdoors

San Ignacio is the center for touring in western Belize. Just walk along busy Burns Avenue and you'll see signs for all kinds of tours and find the offices of several tour operators. Individual tour guides, who by law must be Belizean citizens and be licensed by the government, may work for tour operators, for a lodge or hotel, or they may freelance on their own. Many hang out at Eva's downtown, or at other restaurants in town. You can stop in and sign up for the next day's tours, usually at lower rates than from the larger operators. Obviously, the more layers of costs involved, the higher the price for you, but on the other hand larger operators have more resources, and they have their long-term reputations to protect, so they *may* be more reliable. Tours from lodges usually are more costly than if booked with an independent tour operator. Also, some lodges try to sell packages of tours rather than individual ones.

Most jungle lodges offer a full range of day trips, using either their own guides or working with independent guides and tour companies. The largest lodge-affiliated tour operations are Chaa Creek Expeditions and Windy Hill Tour Company, but Crystal Paradise, duPlooy's, Maya Mountain, Cahal Pech Village, San Ignacio Resort Hotel, and other hotels and lodges also do many tours and trips.

If you have a rental car, you can visit all of the Mayan sites in the Cayo on your own, along with other attractions such as the butterfly farms, the Belize Botanic Gardens, Rainforest Medicine Trail, and many of the attractions in the Mountain Pine Ridge. However, for most caving tours, you'll need a guide, and for canoe and kayak trips, you'll need drop-off and pick-up. Local guides also are critical for nature hikes and birding trips, as many of these guides have remarkable local knowledge and ability to spot things you probably wouldn't see otherwise.

Here are a range of rates you can expect to pay for selected trips. These charges are per person and usually include transportation, lunch (on full-day trips), and in the case of river trips, drop-off and pick-up. Admission to Mayan sites, border fees, and gratuities to guides are usually extra.

On some trips, such as to Tikal or Caracol, there's a flat fee for one to four persons, so the more going together, the cheaper.

Guided nature walk, at lodge: BZ$20 to BZ$40

Morning birding walk, at lodge: BZ$20 to BZ$30

Day trip to Tikal: BZ$120 to BZ$250 (cheaper for larger parties)

Overnight trip to Tikal: BZ$250 to BZ$500

Day trip to Caracol: BZ$80 to BZ$200 (cheaper for larger parties)

Half-day tour of Xunantunich: BZ$40 to BZ$100

Mountain Pine Ridge tour: BZ$70 to BZ$120

Actun Tunichil Muknal: BZ$150 to BZ$200

Barton Creek Cave with canoe: BZ$60 to BZ$100

Self-guided canoe or kayak trip on Macal or Mopan rivers: BZ$50 to BZ$70

Half-day horseback riding: BZ$60 to BZ$120

Mountain bike rental: BZ$25 to BZ$70 a day (complimentary at some lodges)

Birding

The area around San Ignacio is very good for birding because it contains such a variety of habitats—river valleys, foothills, lagoons, agricultural areas, and broadleaf jungle—each of which attracts different types of birds. For example, Aguacate Lagoon near Spanish Lookout attracts water birds such as Night Herons, Neotropic Cormorants, and Whistling Ducks. Open land and pastures are good for spotting Laughing Falcons, Vermillion Flycatchers, Eastern Meadowlarks, and White-tailed Kites.

There's good birding on the grounds of most of the lodges along the Mopan and Macal rivers, including **Chaa Creek, Ek 'Tun, duPlooy's, Crystal Paradise,** and **Clarissa Falls.** In addition, local guides and tour companies run birding trips. One of the best known is **Paradise Expeditions** (☎ 824/2772).

Canoeing & Kayaking

The Cayo's rivers, especially the Mopan and Macal, make it an excellent place for canoeing and kayaking. Most of the larger resorts, like **Chaa Creek** and **duPlooy's,** have canoes or inflatable kayaks. Generally you put in the Macal around Chaa Creek and paddle and float down to the Hawksworth Bridge at San Ignacio, a trip that takes about two hours. You'll pay about BZ$50 a person for canoe rental and pick-up. You'll see iguanas and bird life on the banks, and if you dip in for a swim, don't be surprised if tiny (teethless) fish school around you to figure out if you're food. In San Ignacio you can rent canoes from **Toni Canoes** (☎ 824/3292), which also organizes guided trips and overnight camping trips. If you'd rather float down the Mopan on an inner tube, **The Trek Stop** (☎ 823/2265) rents them for BZ$20, a rate that includes drop-off and pick-up.

Do exercise caution. You won't believe how fast the rivers, especially the Macal, can rise after a heavy rain. Following rains in the Mountain Pine Ridge, it can reach a dangerous flood stage in just a few minutes. Also, there have been some incidents of visitors in canoes being stopped and robbed on the Macal. Watch weather forecasts, and ask locally about safety on the rivers.

Caving

Fodor'sChoice
★
Over the millennia, as dozens of swift-flowing rivers bored through the soft limestone, the Maya Mountains became pitted with miles of caves. The Maya used them as burial sites and, according to one theory, as subterranean waterways that linked the Cayo with communities as far north as the Yucatán. Previously, the caves fell into a 1,000-year slumber, disturbed only by the nightly flutter of bats. In recent years the caves have been rediscovered by spelunkers. First on the scene was Ian Anderson, owner of **Caves Branch Adventure Co. & Jungle Camp** (⊠ 12 mi [19½ km] south of Belmopan ☎☎ 822/2800 ⊕ www.cavesbranch. com). He and his friendly staff of trained guides run exhilarating adventure-theme caving, tubing, and hiking trips from a tiki-torchlighted jungle camp just south of Belmopan. (⇨ *See* Belmopan lodging, *above*.) **Emilio Awe** (⊠ 22 Burns Ave., San Ignacio ☎ 824/2477) is considered one of the top caving guides in the country. **Pacz Tours** (⊠ Cahal Pech, San Ignacio ☎ 824/2477) and **Maya Walk** (⊠ 19 Burns Ave., San Ignacio ☎ 824/3070 ⊕ www.mayawalk.com) specialize in tours to the spooky, wonderful Actun Tunichil Muknal near Belmopan. David Simson, of **David's Adventure Tours** (⊠ San Ignacio ☎ 824/3674), was the first to do tours of the now-popular Barton Creek Cave. You can canoe through Barton Creek, 8 mi (13 km) southeast of San Ignacio.

Hiking

Most of the lodges have hiking trails. Black Rock River Lodge, Ek'Tun, Chaa Creek, Maya Mountain, and duPlooy's all have especially good areas for hiking. If you want even more wide-open spaces, head to the Mountain Pine Ridge, which offers hundreds of miles of hiking trails, mostly old logging roads. ⇨ *See* Mountain Pine Ridge, *below.*

Horseback Riding

When it comes to horseback riding adventures, whether on the old logging roads of the Mountain Pine Ridge or on trails in the Slate Creek Preserve, the undisputed local experts are found at the lodges of **Mountain Equestrian Trails** (⊠ Pine Ridge Rd. ☎ 820/4041 ⊕ www.metbelize. com) and **Lodge at Chaa Creek** (⊠ Chial Rd. ☎ 824/2037 ⊕ www. chaacreek.com). **Easy Rider** (⊠ Collins Ave., San Ignacio ☎ 824/3734) also runs equestrian tours of the Mayan ruins and other points of interest in the region.

Shopping

Caesar's Place (⊠ Mile 60, Western Hwy., east of San Ignacio ☎ 824/2341) has one of the best selections of Belizean and Guatemalan crafts in Belize.

In town, **Arts & Crafts of Central America** (⌧ 24 Burns Ave. ☎ 824/ 2253) has a small selection of crafts, at competitive prices.

MOUNTAIN PINE RIDGE

★ ❸ *17 mi (27 km) south of San Ignacio.*

The Mountain Pine Ridge Forest Reserve is a highlight of any journey to Belize and an adventure to reach.

The Mountain Pine Ridge is the high country of Belize—low mountains and rolling hills are covered in part by vast pine forests and crisscrossed with old logging roads. The higher elevations provide cooler temperatures and, of course, outstanding views.

Aside from pines, you'll see lilac-color mimosa, St. John's wort, and occasionally a garish red flower known as hotlips. Look out for the craboo, a wild tree whose berries are used in a brandylike liqueur believed to have aphrodisiac properties. Birds love this fruit, so any craboo is a good place to spot orioles and woodpeckers.

The best way to see this area is on a mountain bike, a horse, or your own feet, not bouncing around in an Isuzu Trooper.

Sights to See

Inside the Mountain Pine Ridge Forest Reserve is **Hidden Valley Falls.** Also known as the Thousand Foot Falls (it actually drops nearly 1,600 feet), it's the highest in Central America. A thin plume of spray plummets over the edge of a rock face into an ostensibly bottomless gorge below. The catch is that the viewing area (admission BZ$3), where there is a shelter, some benches, and a public rest room, is some distance from the falls. Many visitors find the narrow falls unimpressive from this vantage point. To climb closer requires a major commitment: a steep climb down the side of the mountain is several hours. At the nearby **Río On** you can sunbathe on flat granite boulders or dunk yourself into crystal-clear pools and waterfalls.

☙ Just outside the reserve are the **Río Frio Caves.** They're only a few miles by car down a steep track, but ecologically speaking, these caves are in a different world. In the course of a few hundred yards, you drop from pine savanna to tropical forest. Nothing in Belize illustrates its extraordinary geological diversity as clearly as this startling transition. A river runs right through the center and over the centuries has carved the rock into fantastic shapes. Swallows fill the place, and at night ocelots and margays pad silently across the cold floor in search of slumbering prey. Seen from the dark interior, the light-filled world outside seems more intense and beautiful than ever. Rising vertically through the cave's mouth is a giant hardwood tree, *Pterocarpus officialis*. Its massive paddle-shape roots are anchored in the sandy soil of the riverbank and its green crown strains toward the blue sky.

☙ More than 30,000 pupae are raised annually at the **Green Hills Butterfly Ranch and Botanical Collections,** the largest and best of Belize's butterfly farms. For a closer look at the creatures, the facility, located outside the Mountain Pine Ridge reserve, has about 30 species in huge flight area. Jan Meerman, who's published a book on Belize's butterflies, runs the place with Dutch partner Tineke Boomsma. On the grounds also are many flowers, including passionflowers, bromeliads, heliconias, and orchids. ⊠ *Mile 8, Pine Ridge Rd. (also called Chiquibul Rd.)* 🖼 *820/ 4017* 🖭 *BZ$8 for guided tour* ⊙ *Daily 8–4.*

The **Chalillo Dam Lake** was created in late 2005 by the controversial damming of the Macal River for a power plant. The 150-foot-high dam with a span width of 420 feet destroyed a habitat for endangered species such as the Scarlet Macaw and was opposed by environmentalists in Belize and around the world. It is unknown how many Mayan sites were flooded. However, the dam may eventually have an upside: providing a new lake ecosystem for birds (Scarlet Macaws are still present in the area around the dam) and wildlife, not to mention recreational activities on the reservoir. The lake, which initially flooded some 2,500 acres, will eventually extend some 12 mi (20 km) along the Macal and Raspacula river valleys, in some places over a half-mile wide. As of this writing, however, some of the area looks like a campaign ad against clear-cutting. Submerged logs and debris in the still-filling reservoir and continuing construction on dams mean that the lake and dams are not yet open to the public.

Where to Stay & Eat

$$$–$$$$ ✕🖼 **Blancaneaux Lodge.** As you sweep down this upscale resort's hibiscus- and palm-lined drive, past the croquet lawn, you may get a whiff of Beverly Hills. Indeed, the lodge is owned by director Francis Ford Coppola. Spread on a hillside above the Privassion River, the villas with their soaring thatch ceilings, Japanese-style tile baths, and screened porches overlooking the river have appeared in *Architectural Digest*. The filmmaker's own villa is available (BZ$900 double) when he isn't in residence. A fleet of Land Rovers takes you to remote Mayan ruins or on shopping trips to Guatemala. Those with their own planes can fly into the resort's landing strip, or you can come on a charter flight from Belize City. The restaurant is one of the best in the Cayo, specializing in Italian dishes and serving wines from Coppola's wineries. ⊠ *Mountain Pine Ridge, Turn right at Blancaneaux sign 4½ mi (7½ km) from Mountain Pine Ridge entrance gate* 🖼 *824/3878, 800/746–3743 in U.S.* 🖼 *824/3919* ⊕ *www.blancaneaux.com* 🖭 *7 cabanas, 5 villas* ⚍ *Restaurant, fans, in-room safes, mountain biking, croquet, hiking, horseback riding, river swimming, spa, bar, shop, laundry service, Internet room, airstrip, travel services; no a/c, no room phones, no room TVs* ⊟ *AE, MC, V* ⥠*| CP.*

FodorśChoice
★

$$ ✕🖼 **Five Sisters Falls & Lodge.** With a laid-back and romantic style, this Belizean-owned lodge is perched on a steep hill above the five small waterfalls that give the place its name. A small, open-air hydraulic lift will take you down to the river if you're eager to avoid the 286 steps. After your swim, the thatch-roof bar is a great place to unwind. Accommodations are in attractive suites or thatch cabanas with screened porches. A privately owned villa, managed by the lodge, with stunning riverside setting below the falls (BZ$500), is the top choice here. Its driveway allows you to avoid the steep steps. The lodge's restaurant, with a beautiful view of the falls, prepares savory Belizean food. ⊠ *Mountain Pine Ridge, Turn right at Blancaneaux and Five Sisters signs 4½ mi (7 ½ km) from Mountain Pine Ridge entrance gate. Continue past airstrip about 1 mi (1½ km)* ☎ *820/4005, 800/447–2931 in U.S.* 🖷 *820/4024* ⊕ *www. fivesisterslodge.com* 🛏 *10 cabanas, 4 suites, 1 2-bedroom villa* ♧ *Restaurant, fans, hiking, bar, shop, laundry services, meeting room, travel services; no a/c, no room phones, no room TVs* ☐ *MC, V* ⦿ *CP.*

> ### WORD OF MOUTH
>
> "[W]hen we finally arrived at Five Sisters Lodge, it felt like we'd died and gone to heaven. A very spacious cabana with a screened-in porch, hammock, and mosquito-netted beds—really felt luxurious after our time in Tikal. After lunch, we spent the afternoon swimming in the refreshing waterfalls. Just lovely. It's like nature's Jacuzzi."
> —msteacher

★ $$$ 🏨 **Hidden Valley Inn.** Owned by a prominent Belize City family, Hidden Valley Inn sits on more than 7,000 acres and has more than a dozen waterfalls and 90 mi (150 km) of hiking and mountain biking trails. The estate grounds, including the waterfalls, are for the exclusive use of guests and not open to the public. For romantics, a catered champagne lunch can be enjoyed at your own private waterfall. The cottages have mahogany furnishings, tile floors, and fireplaces. Dinner (BZ$52) is served in the Main House, which has vaulted ceilings and four fireplaces. After dinner, sip on coffee grown on the premises. There are excellent birding opportunities here. ⊠ *Mountain Pine Ridge, Turn left at Hidden Valley Inn sign 3¾ mi (6¼ km) from Mountain Pine Ridge entrance gate* ☎ *822/3320* 🖷 *822/3334* ⊕ *www.hiddenvalleyinn.com* 🛏 *12 cottages* ♧ *Restaurant, fans, mountain bikes, hiking, horseback riding, bar, laundry service, travel services; no a/c, no room phones, no room TVs* ☐ *AE, MC, V.*

The Outdoors

Birding
Birding is great in the Mountain Pine Ridge, and, surprisingly, it's even better now that many of the pines were felled by the southern pine beetle. Without the tall pines, it's much easier to spot Orange-breasted Falcons, Blue Crown Motmots, White King Vultures, Stygian Owls, and other rare birds. Some of the best birding is at **Hidden Valley Inn**, a destination for numerous birding tours, and open only to guests.

Caving
Easily accessible in the Cayo is the Río Frio Cave (⇨ *see above*). You can also do trips to Barton Creek Cave, about 8 mi (13 km) northwest of Mountain Pine Ridge entrance gate, off Mountain Pine Ridge Road, and to Actun Tunichil Muknal from Mountain Pine Ridge. Hidden Valley Inn has two caves open only to guests of the inn.

A Crime of Flowers

A RATHER PLAIN LOOKING PALM LEAF has become a big-money target for poachers in Belize—and a huge problem for the Forestry Department. The leaves in question, Xate (pronounced Sha-tay), are widely used in the floral industry because they stay fresh looking for for 45 to 60 days after harvest. They come from three *Chamaedorea* palm species: *C. elegans*, known as parlor palm; *C. oblongata*, called Xate macho; and *C. ernesti-augustii*, or fishtail. The latter is most sought after, fetching up to one U.S. dollar at its final destination, though poachers get only a fraction of that.

Xate grows wild in Belize, and also in parts of Guatemala and Mexico. Guatemalan Xate collectors, called *xateros*, have stripped much of their own El Petén jungles and have now moved on to Belize, crossing the border into the Chiquibul and other remote areas. *Xateros* earn more collecting Xate than working at regular jobs, if they can even find work in the economically depressed rural areas of El Petén. Not surprisingly, Belizeans are increasingly joining the ranks of Xate poachers. The harvesters sweep through the jungle, removing the palm leaves with a pocket knife or machete. Each palm plant produces two to five useable leaves.

Unfortunately, the poachers do more than just collect Xate. They sometimes stumble across Mayan sites and loot them for priceless artifacts. Some trap toucans, parrots, and the endangered Scarlet Macaw for sale on the black market, and they hunt wild animals, including protected tapirs, for food. The Belize Forestry Department has reported significant depletion of native wildlife in areas with large numbers of Xate collectors. In a few cases, *xeteros* have been implicated in robberies or in attacks on researchers and on Belize Defence Forces soldiers.

In early 2006 Belize Forestry Department officers came across 13 men close to the Hummingbird Highway near Belmopan loading Xate leaves onto a tractor. They arrested three of the men, two Belizeans and a Guatemalan, and confiscated more than 80,000 Xate leaves, with a street value of US$84,000. Two of the men were convicted of illegal harvesting but were fined only US$425 total. With little chance of getting caught and only modest fines if they are, Xate poachers are working at minimal risk.

What can you do to reduce the damage done by illegal Xate collectors? First, avoid buying flower arrangements that contain Xate, unless you're sure that the Xate was harvested legally. You can also support an effort by the Natural History Museum in London, in cooperation with the Belize Ministry of Natural Resources and the Belize Botanic Gardens at duPlooy's Lodge near San Ignacio, to encourage sustainable, organic growing of Xate by Belizean farmers.

—Lan Sluder

Hiking

With its karst limestone terrain, extensive network of old logging trails and roads, and cooler temperatures, the Mountain Pine Ridge is ideal for hiking. All of the lodges here have miles of marked trails. You can also hike along the roads (mostly gravel or dirt), as there are very few cars in the Pine Ridge. Most people find this more pleasant than trying to fight their way through the bush. The mountain area around Baldy Beacon is especially beautiful; it may remind you of part of the Highlands of Scotland.

All of the Mountain Pine Ridge and Chichibul Wildnerness is lightly populated, and some of the residents, such as unemployed squatters who have moved into this remote area, may not always have your best interests at heart. Cell phones don't usually work here, although there has been talk of installing some cell phone towers as a security measure. Lodges such as Hidden Valley Inn provide radio phones to guests who are hiking. Always leave word with a responsible party about your hiking plans and time of expected return. Carry plenty of water, food, a compass, and basic medical supplies, especially on long hikes to remote areas. You may want to hire a guide.

Horseback Riding

In this remote area with virtually no vehicular traffic and many old logging roads, horseback riding is excellent. **Blancaneaux Lodge** and **Hidden Valley Inn** offer horseback riding, and **Mountain Equestrian Trails** (⊠ Pine Ridge Rd. ☎ 820/4041 ⊕ www.metbelize.com) runs riding trips into the Pine Ridge. A full-day trip costs around BZ$160.

Mountain Biking

Mountain Pine Ridge has the best mountain biking in Belize on hundreds of miles of remote logging roads. Blancaneaux and Hidden Valley Inn provide complimentary mountain bikes to guests. Mountain Bikes can also be rented in San Ignacio at **The Trek Stop** (⊠ San José Succotz ☎ 823/2265 ⊕ www.thetrekstop.com) for BZ$24 a day.

If you want your biking motorized, **ATV Adventure Tours** (⊠ San Ignacio ☎ 610/2728 or 604/2563) offers Honda Recon 250 All Terrain Vehicles for trips in the Mountain Pine Ridge, at BZ$260 a day.

Shopping

The village of San Antonio, on the way to the Mountain Pine Ridge reserve, is home to the **Tanah Art Museum** (⊠ San Antonio ☎ 824/3310), run by four sisters with clever hands and great business acumen. Look for their eye-catching slate carvings. At the other end of the village is the Magana family's arts-and-crafts shop, **Magana Zaac-tunich Art Gallery** (⊠ San Antonio ☎ No phone), which specializes in wood carvings.

CARACOL

40 mi (65 km) south of San Ignacio, a 3-hr journey by road.

FodorsChoice
★

Caracol (Spanish for "snail") is the most spectacular Mayan site in Belize, as well as one of the most impressive in Central America. It was once home to as many as 200,000 people (nearly the population of modern-day Belize). It was a metropolis with five plazas and 32 large structures covering almost a square mile. Altogether there are some 35,000 buildings at the site, though only a handful has been excavated. Once Caracol has been fully excavated it may dwarf even the great city of Tikal, which is a few dozen miles away in Guatemala. The latest evidence suggests that Caracol won a crushing victory over Tikal in the mid-6th century, a theory that Guatemalan scholars haven't quite accepted. Until a group of *chicleros* (collectors of gum base) stumbled on the site in 1936, Caracol was buried under the jungle of the remote Vaca Plateau. It's hard to believe it could have been lost for centuries, as the great pyramid of Caana, at 140 feet, is Belize's tallest structure.

⊹ *From Mountain Pine Forest Ridge reserve entrance, head south 14 mi (23 km) to village of Douglas DiSilva; turn left and go 36 mi (58 km)* 🖼 *BZ$15* ☉ *Daily 8–4.*

The Ruins

The main excavated sections are in four groups, denoted on archaeological maps as A, B, C, and D groups. The most impressive structures are the B Group at the northeast end of the excavated plaza. This includes Caana, or "Sky Palace," listed as Structure B19-2nd, along with a ball court, water reservoir, and several large courtyards. The A Group, on the west side of the plaza, contains a temple, ball court, and a residential area for the elite. The Temple of the Wooden Lintel (Structure A6) is one of the oldest and longest-used buildings at Caracol, dating back to 300 BC. It was still in use in AD 1100. To the northwest of the A Group is the Northwest Acropolis, primarily a residential area. The third major plaza forming the core of the site is at the point where a causeway enters the "downtown" part of Caracol. The D Group is a group of structures at the South Acropolis.

Near the entrance to Caracol is a small but interesting visitor center. If you've arrived on your own, a guide usually can be hired at the site, but you can also walk around on your own. A brochure on the site is sold for BZ$4. Seeing all of the excavated area involves several hours of hiking around the site. Be sure to wear comfortable shoes and bring insect repellent, as occasionally mosquitoes and other bugs are a nuisance. Also, watch for anthill mounds and, rarely, snakes. This part of the Chiquibul Forest Reserve is a good place for birding and wildlife spotting. Around the ruins are troops of howler monkeys and flocks of oscellated turkeys, and you may also see deer, coatimundis, foxes, and other wildlife at the site or on the way.

Tips

Advance permission to visit Caracol is no longer required, and you can drive there on your own. The road to Caracol through the Mountain Pine Ridge is in generally good shape, as it was improved in 2004 and 2005, partly in connection with construction of the Chalillo Dam (⇨ *see above*). Only a short section is paved, however. If you want to drive on your own, be sure to inquire from the guard at the Mountain Pine Ridge entrance gate or, if you're already in the Pine Ridge, at your lodge, about road conditions before attempting it, especially after heavy rains. In 2005 there were several incidents of robberies by armed bandits, who stopped private cars and tour vans on the road to Caracol— ask locally about safety tips.

Tours

Most visitors to Caracol come as part of a tour group from San Ignacio, or from one of the lodges in the Mountain Pine Ridge. Full-day tours, which often include a picnic lunch and stops at Río Frio Cave, Río On, and other sights in the Mountain Pine Ridge, cost from about BZ$100 to BZ$175 per person, depending on what is included and the number of people going. Tours from independent operators generally cost less than those from lodges. Because of its remote location, Caracol gets only about 12,000 visitors a year. That's about one-tenth the number who visit Altun Ha, one-fifth the number who visit Xunantunich, and a small fraction of the number who see Tikal. Thus, you're in a small, exclusive company, and on some slow days you may be one of only a handful of people at the site. Excavations usually are carried out in the winter, typically January through March.

THE CAYO ESSENTIALS

Transportation

BY AIR

Most people bound for the Cayo fly into Belize City, but there are no longer any scheduled flights on to San Ignacio. Many Cayo hotels and lodges have van transportation from both airports in Belize City for about BZ$250–BZ$300 for up to four people, one-way. Several hotels run shuttle vans, both for their own guests and for other visitors coming to the Cayo, between Belize City and San Ignacio, for around BZ$60–BZ$70 a person. Among them: **Aguada** (✉ Santa Elena ☎ 804/3609 ⊕ www.aguadahotel.com); **Cahal Pech Village** (✉ San Ignacio ☎ 824/3740 ⊕ www.cahalpechvillageresort.com); and **The Trek Stop's San Ignacio Shuttle** (✉ San José Succotz ☎ 823/2265 ⊕ www.thetrekstop.com or www.sanignacioshuttle.com), which uses a new 15-passenger Kia van and at BZ$60 is priced a little lower than some other shuttles. The San Ignacio Shuttle leaves Café Sol in San Ignacio around 8:30 AM and departs the international airport around 1 PM, getting to San Ignacio about 3 PM. Schedule is subject to change. You must call or e-mail ahead for reservations for the San Ignacio Shuttle and all the other shuttles. The San Ignacio Shuttle guarantees the shuttle will run, even if only one person has made a reservation.

A taxi from the international airport near Belize City to San Ignacio will cost around BZ$200–BZ$250 (for the cab, not per person), depending on your bargaining ability.

BY BUS

Novelo's has frequent service between Belize City and San Ignacio. The journey on the Western Highway takes about three hours and costs BZ$8–BZ$12, depending on whether the bus is local or express.

BY CAR

There are several small auto rental companies in San Ignacio, but none in the Mountain Pine Ridge. They rent four-wheel-drive vehicles for around BZ$160 a day. Most hotels can also arrange a rental car for you.

Other than the well-maintained two-lane Western Highway, most roads in the Cayo are unpaved and dusty in the dry season, muddy in the rainy season. To get to the Cayo, simply follow the Western Highway from Belize City. Watch out for "sleeping policemen" (speed bumps) near villages along the route.

Coming into San Ignacio is a little confusing. As you go through the "twin town" of Santa Elena and head into San Ignacio, you'll see the Hawksworth Bridge straight ahead. The bridge is one-way coming from the west but this is not well marked and those unfamiliar with the area always try to drive across the bridge the wrong way. Locals flap their arms and jump up and down, trying to direct the cars to the right. Though this has been going on for years, no one has taken the time to put up a big diversion sign, even though the police station is just across the bridge. It's a typical Belize situation.

From the Western Highway, there are two routes into the Mountain Pine Ridge, both just east of San Ignacio: the Mountain Pine Ridge Road (also sometimes called the Chiquibul Road or the Georgeville Road), at Georgeville at Mile 61.6 of the Western Highway, and the Cristo Rey Road, with the turnoff at Mile 66.5 of the Western Highway. From the Western Highway, the entrance to the Mountain Pine Ridge is 10.2 mi (17 km) via the Mountain Pine Ridge Road and 14.8 mi (25 km) via the Cristo Rey Road. Both roads, cut through limestone, are equally rough, except the first mile of the Cristo Rey Road is paved, as well as a few short sections farther on. If coming from Belmopan you'll save a little time by taking the first road you see, at Georgeville, but if coming from San Ignacio or points west, take the Cristo Rey Road. Large green road signs clearly mark both turns.

Heading southeast from San Ignacio on the Cristo Rey Road, a little beyond San Antonio, the Cristo Rey Road meets the Mountain Pine Ridge Road coming from Georgeville. Turn right to go into the Mountain Pine Ridge. After 2½ mi, a guard at a gatehouse will record your name and license plate number. The main road through the Mountain Pine Ridge to Caracol is being improved, partly to provide better access to Caracol and also due to the construction of the Challilo Dam and other dams on the Macal River ⇨ *see below.* Some of the roads in the Pine Ridge have names, but most have numerical monikers, like A10. The main road through the Mountain Pine Ridge that passes the four area lodges and Douglas DiSilva Village is mostly a dirt road that can become almost impassable after heavy rains.

To not run afoul of traffic rules, turn right before the Hawksworth Bridge, following the detour to what is called the "lower bridge." Cross this and follow Savanah Road around the sports stadium and, if you're lucky, you'll soon end up back on Western Highway just to the west of San Ignacio, or after you cross the river, you can turn left and go through to Burns Avenue, the main street in town. From San Ignacio, the Western Highway continues on about 9 mi (15 km) to the Guatemala border. This stretch is locally known as the Benque Road.

To get to Spanish Lookout, the Mennonite area, turn north off the Western Highway at about Mile 63.

Taxis are plentiful in and around San Ignacio, but they're expensive if you're going to a remote lodge. For example, a taxi from San Ignacio to one of the Mountain Pine Ridge lodges is likely to be around BZ$80 to BZ$100, and to one of the lodges west of San Ignacio, about BZ$40 to BZ$50 (rates are negotiable). Taxis within San Ignacio shouldn't be more than BZ$6 to most points. Collective taxis (they pick up as many passengers as possible) run to the Guatemala border for around BZ$5. You can find taxis at Market Square, around Burns Avenue, or call **Cayo Taxi Association** at 824/2196 or **San Ignacio Taxi** at 824/2155, or have your hotel call one.

🚗 **Cayo Auto Rentals** ✉ 81 Benque Rd., San Ignacio ☎ 824/2222 ⊕ www. cayoautorentals.com. **Safe Tours Belize** ✉ Western Hwy., Santa Elena ☎ 824/3731.

Contacts & Resources

BANKS & EXCHANGE SERVICES
Although American dollars are accepted everywhere, you can exchange money at the border crossing in Benque Viejo del Carmen. Banks in San Ignacio include Atlantic, Belize Bank, and ScotiaBank. They are all downtown on Burns Avenue. All have ATMs, but currently only Belize Bank and Atlantic Bank accept ATM cards issued outside the country.

🏦 **Banks Atlantic Bank** ✉ 17 Burns Ave., San Ignacio ☎ 824/2596. **Belize Bank** ✉ 16 Burns Ave., San Ignacio ☎ 824/2031. **ScotiaBank** ✉ Burns Ave. at Riverside St., San Ignacio ☎ 824/4190.

EMERGENCIES
In case of emergency, there's the private La Loma Luz Hospital, in Santa Elena, east of San Ignacio, as well as the public hospital, San Ignacio Hospital.

🏥 **Hospitals La Loma Luz Hospital** ✉ Western Hwy., Santa Elena ☎ 824/3253. **San Ignacio Hospital** ✉ Western Hwy., San Ignacio ☎ 824/2066.

🚨 **Hot Lines Police** ☎ 911 or 824/2111.

💊 **Pharmacies The Pharmacy** ✉ 24 West St., San Ignacio ☎ 824/2510.

INTERNET, MAIL & SHIPPING
The San Ignacio post office is on Hudson Street near the vegetable market. It's open weekdays 8–noon and 1–4:30 and Saturday 8–noon.

📮 **San Ignacio Post Offices** ✉ Hudson St., San Ignacio ☎ 824/2049. **Eva's** is a busy café with internet. ✉ 22 Burns Ave. ☎ 824/2267Visitor Information

VISITOR INFORMATION
There is no official tourism information office in Cayo. The best way to find out what's going on in the San Ignacio area is to stop by **Eva's** in San Ignacio, a café that doubles as an unofficial visitor center. Owner Bob Jones, a British ex-soldier, knows the Cayo like the back of his hand. You can also contact local tour operators. The Belize Tourism Board Web site, ⊕ www. travelbelize.org, has some information on visiting Cayo. Another Web site, Toucan Trail, ⊕ www.toucantrail.com, supported by the Belize Tourism

Board, has excellent information on budget travel in Belize, including Cayo. Belize Explorer, ⊕ www.belizeex.com, formerly operated by BTIA but now a private Web site affiliated with Cahal Pech Village hotel in San Ignacio and a few other hotels, still has some useful information on tours, attractions, and travel services in Cayo.

🏠 **Eva's** ✉ 22 Burns Ave., San Ignacio ☎ 824/2267.

The Southern Coast

WORD OF MOUTH

"Just got back from Jaguar Reef . . . it is AWE-SOME!! It sits on the Caribbean, and the rainforest (including the Mayan ruins) is at the back door. There is excellent snorkeling (as good as the north side of the Caymans), hiking, kayaking, tubing in caves, and much more. On some of the tours, you get to see the 'real' country and animals. We even had a puma run across the road in front of us!"
—Cvechko

"If you want long beautiful beaches, go to low-key Placencia, where you'll find a 7-mile-long beach."
—Ronaldo

By Lan Sluder

AS ALWAYS IN BELIZE, the transition from one landscape to another is swift and startling. As you approach the Hummingbird Highway's end in coastal Dangriga, the lush, mountainous terrain of the north gives way to flat plains bristling with orange trees. Farther south the Stann Creek Valley is Belize's San Fernando Valley, where most of its fruit is grown. Bananas were the original bumper crop here and though banana plantations are still an important industry, the railroad built to transport the fruit no longer exists. Equally startling to the change in scenery is the cultural segue: whereas San Ignacio has a Spanish air, the southern coast is strongly Afro-Caribbean.

Tourist dollars, the staple of contemporary Belize, have largely bypassed Dangriga to land 35 mi (56 km) south in Placencia, the region's most striking destination. Several years ago there were only three small resorts north of town. Now there are about 20, stretching up to the village of Seine Bight and beyond. Plans are in the works for hundreds of new condos and a number of hotels. The paving of the Southern Highway from Dangriga all the way to Punta Gorda (except for a short stretch near Golden Stream) has made the region much more accessible. Off the main highway, however, most roads consist of red dirt and potholes.

Real estate sales are a driving force in Placencia, Hopkins, and elsewhere along the coast. The lure is the beaches. The Southern Coast has the best beaches on the mainland, although as elsewhere inside the protecting barrier reef, the low wave action means the beaches are narrow and there's usually sea grass in the water close to shore. (Sea grass—not seaweed, which is an algae—may be a nuisance for swimmers, but it's a vital part of the coastal ecosystem, acting as a nursery for sea life.) Much of the seafront land north of Placencia has been divided into lots awaiting development; if things continue at this pace, the area will one day rival Ambergris Caye as Belize's top beach destination.

History

As elsewhere in Belize, the Maya were here first. They had settlements in what is now Stann Creek District at least from the Early Classic period (around AD 300) until the Post-Classic period (about AD 1200). However, for reasons we don't yet know, this part of Belize did not have the large Mayan cities that existed to the north, west, and south. Or, at least, archaeologists haven't discovered such city remains yet. None of the few known Mayan sites in the area, including the Mayflower complex south of Dangriga, have been extensively excavated, but they appear to have been small ceremonial centers.

In the 1600s small numbers of English, some of whom were pirates, settled on the Placencia peninsula, though most eventually left the area. In the next century English traders and farmers, some from Nova Scotia, arrived in what is now Dangriga. They called their coastal trading posts "stands," which was corrupted to "stann." Hence, the name Stann Creek. On November 19, 1823, a group of Garinagu from the Bay Islands of Honduras, former African slaves who had intermarried with Carib Indians in the southern Caribbean, arrived at the mouth of the Stann Creek River, at what was then called Stann Creek Town. This date

TOP REASONS TO GO

BEACHES

First and foremost, the sandy shore is the draw here. The mainland's best beaches are on the Placencia peninsula and around Hopkins. Although they're not the wide beaches with white, talcum-powder sand that made Cancun famous—most of the beaches here are narrow ribbons of khaki—they're ideal for lazing in a hammock under a cocopalm, as the tropical breeze from the sea lulls you to dreamland. And you don't have to fight the crowds for a spot on the beach, either. In fact, you may have a whole stretch to yourself.

JAGUARS

The world's first and only jaguar preserve is the Cockscomb Basin Wildlife Sanctuary. Chances are you won't actually see one of these big, beautiful cats in the wild, as they roam the high bush mainly at night, but you may see tracks or hear a low growl in the darkness. Hiking the trails of the Maya Mountains is a great experience in itself.

WATER SPORTS

One of the world's best permit fisheries is off the Southern Coast, and anglers won't be disappointed in the bonefish, tarpon, and other sports fishing, either. Placencia makes an excellent base for anglers, as there are many good local fishing guides, and a range of accommodations from budget to deluxe. The barrier reef here is 15 mi (25 km) or more off the coast, so it's a long trip out, even with the fast boats the dive shops use, but there are patch reefs around closer islands, with excellent snorkeling. Serious divers will find two of Belize's three atolls, Turneffe and Glover's, within reach. This part of Belize also is beginning to attract sailing fans. In a charter sailboat you can hop from island to island in the protected waters inside the reef.

A PLACE BETWEEN TWO WORLDS

The beach resorts on the Southern Coast boast that they're midway between the reef and the jungle, so you have the best of both worlds. That's true enough, as this is one area of Belize where you can snorkel or swim in the sea in the morning and then see a Mayan site or do a jungle hike in the afternoon. But the drive to the ruin or trailhead may be a little longer than it appears on the map, due to some of the unpaved roads you'll travel, and the boat ride out to the barrier reef may take an hour or more. So enjoy the two worlds, but, remember, you're on Belize time.

CULTURAL EXPERIENCES

The Southern Coast is a patchwork quilt of cultures. A Garífuna village may remind you of a seaside village in Senegal, while just down the road is a Creole village with a distinctive Caribbean air. Inland, Maya live much as they have for thousands of years next door to mestizos from Guatemala and Honduras who have come here to work the banana plantations or citrus groves. Sprinkled around are gringos from the United States, Canada, and Europe, looking for a retirement home or trying to make a buck in tourism. It's not so much a melting pot as a tropical stew, full of different flavors, a cultural experience to savor.

5

is still celebrated in Belize as Garífuna Settlement Day. Later, the name of Stann Creek Town (but not the district) was changed to Dangriga, which means "sweet water" in the Garífuna language.

Creoles from Jamaica came to Stann Creek in the 1700s, mainly to work in logging, and, later, in fishing. In the late 1800s, several families, originally from Scotland, Portugal, Honduras, and elsewhere, arrived in Placencia. The names of these families—Garbutt, Leslie, Westby, and Cabral—are still common on the peninsula.

In the 19th and early 20th century, the fertile soils of the coastal plain were found to be ideal for growing bananas and citrus, and soon agriculture became the most important industry in the region. The first railroad in Belize, the Stann Creek Railway, built by the United Fruit Company to transport bananas, started operation around World War I. The railroad closed in the 1950s and several of the old railroad bridges can be seen from the Hummingbird Highway.

The first small tourist resorts were developed on the Placencia peninsula as well as at Maya Beach in the 1960s and 1970s, but the bad roads and lack of infrastructure meant that few visitors got this far south. Until it was resurfaced 1999, the Hummingbird Highway was a potholed nightmare, and the paving of the Southern Highway wasn't completed until 2003 (a short 9-mi [15-km] section is still unpaved). Placencia Village was connected to the electrical grid in 1993, and Hopkins Village got its first telephone in the mid-1990s.

The first fishing cooperative was established in Placencia in 1962. Although fishing is still a way of life for a few people on the coast, the big money now is in shrimp farming, and there are several large aquaculture operations on the Placencia Lagoon.

Hurricane Iris in October 2001 devastated much of the Southern Coast south of Maya Beach, but the area has bounced back stronger than ever. Most of the beachfront land on the coast has been sold to foreigners, and several large real estate development projects have been announced for the Hopkins area, the coast between Hopkins and the Placencia peninsula, and for Placencia. Some of these may actually come to fruition. Today, tourism and real estate development are supplanting agriculture as the leading industries on the coast.

EXPLORING THE SOUTHERN COAST

Coming from the north, two roads lead to the Southern Coast: the Hummingbird Highway from Belmopan, and the Coastal Road (also sometimes, misleadingly, called the Coastal Highway) from La Democracia on the Western Highway. The Hummingbird Highway is paved and is the most scenic drive in all of Belize. The Coastal Road is unpaved, dusty, or muddy depending on the amount of rain. Despite the name, it does not hug the coast, and in fact you never glimpse the sea from it. Also, the loose gravel roadway is an accident waiting to happen. Due to the large number of car wrecks on it, some car rental agencies in Belize City specifically prohibit drivers from taking this road, and others boost the

GREAT ITINERARIES

5

IF YOU HAVE 3 DAYS ON THE SOUTHERN COAST

Base yourself in Placencia. On your first full day, walk the sidewalk in Placencia Village, hear the latest gossip, and get to know a little of village life. Hang out on the beach at your hotel and get on Belize time, then have drinks and dinner in the village. On your second day, take a snorkel trip to Laughing Gull Caye or another snorkel area, or, if you dive, do a full-day dive trip to Turneffe or Glover's atoll. On your final day, drive, or take a guided tour, to Cockscomb Basin Wildlife Sanctuary. Be sure to stop at the Maya Centre craft cooperative for gift shopping. If there's time, also visit the Mayflower Mayan site and waterfall. End the day with dinner at the Bistro at Maya Beach Hotel.

IF YOU HAVE 5 DAYS ON THE SOUTHERN COAST

Drive or fly to Dangriga (the closest airport to Hopkins).While in Dangriga, stop by the Garifuna museum, then proceed by taxi or rental car to Hopkins to stay at one of its beach resorts. On your first full day, relax on the beach in the morning, then tour Cockscomb Basin Wildlife Sanctuary and hike the jungle trails. Be sure to stop at the Maya Centre craft cooperative. Have dinner at one of the local restaurants in Hopkins Village. On your second full day, visit the Mayflower Mayan site and waterfall in the morning, and spend the rest of the day on the beach. On your third day, rise early and drive (or go by taxi) to Placencia. If the weather's good, take a snorkel trip. Have dinner in Placencia Village. On your fourth day, if you dive, do a day dive trip to Turneffe or Glover's atoll, or go fishing for permit or tarpon. If you catch anything edible, have one of the local restaurants prepare it for you for dinner. Or, simply spend a lazy day in a hammock at the beach and around the pool. On your final day, if you're interested in Mayan sites, do a day trip to Lubaantun and Nim Li Punit near Punta Gorda, or else go on a tour of Monkey River.

deductible you have to pay if you have an accident on this road. In short, if you're driving, take the Hummingbird.

The Hummingbird runs 54.5 mi (89 km) from Belmopan to Dangriga. As it approaches Dangriga, it technically becomes the Stann Creek District Highway, but most people simply refer to the entire road as the Hummingbird Highway. About 6 mi (10 km) from Dangriga is the junction with the Southern Highway, another good, mostly paved road running 100 mi (164 km) to Punta Gorda. The Southern Highway is not as scenic as the Hummingbird, although for much of its length the low Maya Mountains are visible to the west.

Off the spine of the Southern Highway, various shorter, mostly unpaved, roads lead to villages on the coast and inland: from the highway, it's about 4 mi (7 km) to Hopkins and also to Sittee Village; 25 mi (42 km) to Placencia Village; 5 mi (8 km) to Big Creek; 13 mi (21 km) to Monkey River.

The road everyone loves to hate is the road to Placencia from the Southern Highway. Only short sections at Seine Bight and Placencia villages are paved, and after heavy rains the road can be mucky and muddy. Even in the best conditions, it's a 45-minute drive from Placencia Village back to the junction with the Southern Highway. A few years back, the Belize government announced plans to pave the road, but the money went to other things.

There are no scheduled water taxis or ferries from Belize City to Placencia or anywhere on the Southern Coast. Buses run frequently from Belmopan to Dangriga and then on south to Punta Gorda. Some, not all, stop at Hopkins and Placencia. Going south by bus is a long haul. With connections, figure six to eight hours from Belize City or San Ignacio to Placencia, less to Dangriga or Hopkins.

You'll arrive fresher if you fly. From Belize City (both international and municipal airports) there are frequent flights to Dangriga and Placencia.

Numbers in the margin correspond to bullets on the Southern Coast map.

When to Go

The weather on the Southern Coast is similar to that in central and northern Belize, only a little wetter. On average, for example, Cayo District has rain, or at least a shower, on 125 days a year, while in Stann Creek District there's some rain on 183 days. Of course, most of these days the rain is followed by sunshine. About 60% of the rain in this area comes during the approximately 30 days of the year when fronts cross the region—cold fronts from the north in the late fall and winter, and tropical fronts in summer.

In summer, daytime temperatures along the coast reach the high 80s °F, occasionally the 90s, usually falling at night to the mid-70s. In winter, expect temperatures in the low to mid-80s by day, falling to the mid- or high 60s most nights. On or near the sea, it feels cooler due to the prevailing breezes from the sea, which go calm only occasionally, usually for a few days at a time in summer. Humidity is high most of the year, typically 80% or more. Water temperatures from November to March are usually in the mid- to high 70s °F. For the rest of the year they are in the low 80s.

About the Restaurants

Broiled, grilled, fried, sautéed, cooked in lime juice as ceviche, or barbecued on the beach: anyway you eat it, seafood is the lifestuff on the Southern Coast. Restaurants here serve fish, lobster, conch, and shrimp, often fresh from the boat, or, in the case of shrimp, straight from the shrimp farms near Placencia.

The restaurant scene, however, is still developing. You'll find mostly small, locally owned spots; some are breezy beachside joints with sand floors, and others wood shacks. Placencia has by far the largest number of eateries, with Hopkins a distant second. Most of the more upscale restaurants are in beach resorts. One, the Bistro at Maya Beach Hotel, is among the best restaurants in the country.

The restaurants (all of which are indicated by a ✕) that we list are the cream of the crop in each price category. Properties indicated by a ✕🏠 are lodging establishments whose restaurant warrants a special trip.

About the Hotels

There are two different kinds of lodging to choose from on the Southern Coast: small, basic hotels, often Belizean-owned, and upmarket beach resorts, usually owned and operated by Americans or Canadians. The small hotels are clustered in Placencia Village, Hopkins Village, and in Dangriga town. The beach resorts are on the Placencia peninsula north of Placencia Village and also near Hopkins. Several of these resorts, including Francis Ford Coppola's Turtle Inn and the Inn at Robert's Grove on the Placencia peninsula, Kanantik between Hopkins and Placencia, and Hamanasi in Hopkins, are among the best hotels in Belize.

A recent phenomenon on the Placencia peninsula and near Hopkins is the development of condominiums. Four new condo developments opened in 2005–2006. Several other large condo developments have been announced for Placencia, including Ara Macaw, a gated community, which is supposed to eventually have 1,000 units. Another is Cocoplum, a 78-acre development on the peninsula, with a proposed "condotel" (a condominium hotel) and private homes and condos. Only time will tell whether these and other plans will actually materialize, but it's clear that this area has reached a tipping point where development by large international companies is inevitable.

There also are a small number of vacation rental houses near Hopkins and on the Placencia peninsula.

The lodgings (all indicated with a 🏠) that we list are the cream of the crop in each price category. We always list the facilities that are available—but we don't specify whether they cost extra: when pricing accommodations, always ask what's included. Properties indicated by a ✕🏠 are lodging establishments whose restaurant warrants a special trip.

WHAT IT COSTS In Belize Dollars				
$$$$	**$$$**	**$$**	**$**	**¢**
RESTAURANTS over $50	$25–$$50	$15–$25	$8–$15	under $8
HOTELS over $500	$300–$500	$200–$300	$100–$200	under $100

Restaurant prices are per person for a main course at dinner. Hotel prices are for two people in a standard double room, including tax and service.

DANGRIGA

❶ *99 mi (160 km) southeast of Belmopan.*

With a population of around 9,000, Dangriga is the largest town in the south and the home of the Garífuna or Black Caribs, as they're also known. The plural is Garinagu.

For the traveler, there's not much to keep you in Dangriga. Though the town is on the coast, there are no good beaches, no first-class hotels, few restaurants, and, except for a small museum on Garífuna culture in the outskirts of town, not much to see. Rickety clapboard houses on stilts and small shops line the downtown streets, and the town has a kind of end-of-the-road feel. Dangriga isn't really dangerous, though it has a rough vibe, a little like Belize City, that's off-putting for many visitors.

Each year, on November 19 and the days around it, the town cuts loose with a week of Carnival-style celebrations. Garífuna drumming, costumed Jonkunu dancers, punta music, and a good bit of drinking make up the festivities of Garífuna Settlement Day, when these proud people celebrate their arrival in Belize and remember their roots.

Sights to See

Named after a Garífuna heroine who came to Belize with her 13 children, founding the village of Punta Negra in Toledo District, the **Gulisi Garífuna Museum,** opened in late 2004, has a number of displays on Garífuna history and life. Three exhibits are on Garífuna migration from Africa to St. Vincent, then to Roatan and Belize. Another exhibit is on Thomas Vincent Ramos, a visionary Garífuna leader who, in 1941, established the first Garífuna Settlement Day. Other displays are on Garífuna food, clothing, and music and dance. On exhibit are a number paintings by Garífuna artists including Benjamin Nicholas. ⊠ *Mile 2, Hummingbird Hwy.* ☎ *502/0639* ✉ *BZ$10* ☉ *Weekdays 10–5, Sat. 8–noon.*

Declared a national park in 2001, **Mayflower Bocawina National Park** has three minor Mayan ceremonial sites: Mayflower, T'au Witz, and Maintzunum, near Silk Grass Creek. Nearby are the three waterfalls Bocawina Falls, Three Sisters Falls, and Antelope Falls. To get to Bocawina and Three Sisters Falls, which are close together, it's an easy hike of about 1¼ mi (2 km) on the marked Bocawina Falls trail. The trail to Antelope Falls, about 1¾ mi (3 km), is somewhat more difficult due to some steep sections that can be slick after rains. Maps of the trails are available at the small visitor center. So far, little excavation has been conducted at the Mayan sites, but the parklike setting at the base of the Maya Mountains is beautiful. ⊠ *Off Mile 6, From Southern Hwy. go 4½ mi (7 ½ km) west on dirt road to park visitor center* ✉ *BZ$10* ☉ *Daily 8–4.*

One of the most beautiful lagoons in Belize, **Southern Lagoon,** is about 25 mi (41 km) north of Dangriga—a 45-minute car ride. This lagoon is home to many West Indian manatees, and on beaches nearby, Hawksbill turtles nest May to October. The Northern and Western lagoons also are in this area. The small Creole village of **Gales Point** (☎ 209/8031 community phone for village), population about 500, set beside the lagoon, is home to several drum makers, including Boombay Andrewin and Emmeth Young. They both give Creole-style drumming lessons (about BZ$15 an hour) at the Maroon Creole Drum School. You can find Young at his snack and gift shop, the **Sugar Shack** (⊠ Gales Point Village ☎ 603/6051 ☉ hrs vary but generally Mon.–Sat. 9–5). Handmade

The Garífuna Struggle

PERHAPS THE MOST UNUSUAL of the ethnic groups calling Belize home, the Garífuna's story is both bizarre and moving, an odyssey of exile and dispossession in the wake of the confusion wrought in the New World by the Old. The Garífuna are descended from a group of Nigerian slaves who were shipwrecked on the island of St. Vincent in 1635. The Caribs, St. Vincent's indigenous population, fiercely resisted the outsiders at first, but they eventually overcame their distrust.

In the eyes of the British colonial authorities, the new ethnic group that developed after years of intermarriage was an illegitimate and troublesome presence. Worse still, the Garífuna sided with, and were succored by, the French. After nearly two centuries of guerrilla warfare, the British decided that the best way to solve the problem was to deport them en masse. After a circuitous and tragic journey across the Caribbean, during which thousands perished of disease and hunger, the exiles arrived in Belize.

That the Garífuna have preserved their cultural identity testifies to Belize's extraordinary ability to encourage diversity. They have their own religion, a potent mix of ancestor worship and Catholicism; their own language, which, like Carib, has separate male and female dialects; their own music, a percussion-oriented sound known as punta rock; and their own social structure, which dissuades young people from marrying outside their community. In writer Marcella Lewis, universally known as Auntie Madé, the Garífuna also had their own poet laureate. In 2002 the United Nations designated the Garífuna as a World Heritage culture.

drums of coconut wood, cashew wood, or mahogany cost BZ$100 to $800. ✦ *To Gales Point: from Dangriga, go northwest on Hummingbird Hwy. 8 ½ mi (14 km) to village of Melinda; turn right on Manatee Hwy. (Coastal Rd) and follow 13 mi (21 km) to turnoff, a sharp right turn. This dirt road to Gales Point Village runs about 2½ mi (4 km) until it ends at lagoon and Manatee Lodge.*

Where to Stay & Eat

Unless you have a special interest in Garífuna culture or are heading out to Tobacco, Southwater, or other offshore cayes, you'll probably not spend much time in Dangriga. Several sights of interest are near Dangriga, though these can also be easily visited from Hopkins, another Garífuna settlement.

Near Dangriga

$ ▦ **Mama Noots Jaguar Lodge.** Being environmentally conscious doesn't have to come at the expense of comfort. A combination solar, wind, and hydro system generates this resort's electricity. Most of the produce served in the open-air dining room is grown on the grounds. Rooms, in thatch cabanas or a modern concrete building, have views of the rugged Maya Mountains. Because the resort is *back-a-bush* (in the jungle), owners Kevin and Nanette Denny advise guests to bring lightweight "jungle clothing," plus plenty of insect repellent and an adventuresome spirit. Nearby are the Mayflower archaeological site and miles of jungle trails and waterfalls. ⊠ *Near Mayflower archaeological site, off Mile 6, Southern Hwy., 6 mi (10 km) south of junction of Hummingbird and Southern Hwys.* ☎ *422/3666* ⊕ *www.mamanoots.com* ⌂ *6 rooms, 1 duplex cabana* ⟨ *Dining room, fans, hiking, bar, travel services; no a/c, no room phones, no room TVs, no smoking* ⊟ *AE, MC, V.*

$ ⊞ **Manatee Lodge.** This colonial-era lodge, just feet from the Southern Lagoon and surrounded by tropical flowers, has one of the most stunning settings on the Southern Coast. With its fading white façade like something out of a Graham Greene novel, and sometimes lackadaisical service, the lodge may not quite live up to its setting, but in minutes you can be on a boat looking for manatees (BZ$110 for a tour from the hotel) or on a deserted beach. Rooms on the second floor are simple but have polished wood floors and views of the lagoon. ⊠ *Gales Point Village* ☎ *220/8040* ⊕ *www.manateelodge.com* ⌂ *8 rooms* ⟨ *Dining room, fans, boating, bar, travel services; no a/c, no room phones, no room TVs, no smoking* ⊟ *AE, MC, V.*

Dangriga

¢–$ ✕ **Riverside Café.** Information, rather than the food or atmosphere, is what you come here for. Fishermen and the guys who run boats out to Tobacco Caye and other offshore cayes hang out here, and if you're going to the islands you can arrange transportation while you're sipping a beer or having a plate of rice and beans. ⊠ *S Riverside Dr., Dangriga* ☎ *523/9908* ⊟ *No credit cards* ⊙ *Daily 6 AM–10 PM.*

$–$$ ⊞ **Pelican Beach Resort.** Despite linoleum on some of the floors and thin wood walls, this waterfront hotel on the north end of Dangriga, near the airstrip, is the best the town has to offer. Most rooms are in a two-story colonial-style building with a veranda. Some have porches with sea views. The restaurant has dependable food and service and the staff is knowledgeable and friendly. Though there's a dock and small beach area, the water's not very appealing for swimming. It's about a half hour stroll to the center of town. The resort has an annex on Southwater Caye, an hour away by boat. ⅅ *Box 2, Dangriga* ☎ *522/2044* 🖷 *522/2570* ⊕ *www.pelicanbeachbelize.com* ⌂ *20 rooms* ⟨ *Restaurant, fans, cable TV, dock, boating, bar, laundry service, Internet, meeting rooms, travel services; no a/c in some rooms* ⊟ *AE, MC, V.*

$ ⊞ **Bonefish Hotel.** If you're overnighting in Dangriga before heading out to Tobacco Caye or another offshore caye, this little hotel, painted aquamarine and white, is an acceptable option. It's near the sea and the riverside area where the boats go out and under the same management as Blue Marlin Lodge on Southwater Caye. Rooms are carpeted and clean. ⊠ *15 Mahogany St., Dangriga* ☎ *522/2243* 🖷 *522/2296* ⊕ *www. bluemarlinlodge.com* ⌂ *7 rooms* ⟨ *Restaurant, fans, refrigerators in some rooms, cable TV, laundry service, travel services; no room phones* ⊟ *AE, MC, V.*

¢   ⊞ **Ruthie's Cabanas.** This is the closest you can come to staying in a Garífuna home in Dangriga. Owners Ruthie and Meeto Flores built

Development, Belize-Style

"People are building $500,000 houses on $5,000 roads!" This is the sentiment of many who watch in amazement as huge condos and luxury houses sprout up along narrow, muddy golf cart trails. In some areas, huge 5,000-square-foot homes are being built where there is no municipal water or sewerage system, and in more remote parts of the country, no electricity or telephone. One 25-mile stretch of almost entirely unpaved road is now sprinkled with massive gated communities and condo projects. One developer has announced plans for a 400-housing-unit project that includes a golf course, but not everyone believes the project will actually be built. Another, Coco Plum II, has plans for condos, a condotel, and private homes on man made lagoons near Seine Bight Village.

Belize's lack of infrastructure is nothing new. As late as the 1980s, open sewers were common all over Belize City. Even today, in some rural villages, especially in Toledo District, telephone service is a rare commodity and drinking water comes from a community well. With the unemployment rate in Belize in the low double digits, and with good, high-paying jobs scarce, many hope that the new housing boom will provide a needed economic boost and sustainable job growth. But environmentalists are taking a darker view.

In the Hopkins area, on the south side of Sittee Point, environmentalists worry that some of the tallest mangroves in the Western Hemisphere will fall prey to developers. It is illegal to remove endangered mangroves in Belize without a government permit, but this rule, and many other environmental protections, are largely ignored. It isn't unusual for homeowners and developers with waterfront property to simply tear out these precious trees and deal with possible fines later.

Belize effectively has no zoning or comprehensive land-use planning. Environmental regulations, while strict in theory—every development is required to have a formal Environmental Impact Plan approved by the national government—often fail in practice. Protective regulations and permit procedures are circumvented, flaunted, or just plain ignored. Government officials, whose resources are stretched thin, often can't provide oversight on development projects. According to environmentalists, government officials are corrupt; they believe that developers can do what they like, if the price is right.

Economic growth, the environment, and the housing boom in Belize is complex, with parties facing off on a multitude of issues. Who knows if everyone will ever see eye-to-eye.

–Lan Sluder

the thatch cabanas themselves, live in a two-story building next door, and go out of their way to make you feel at home. The small rooms all have private baths and are steps from the sea, so you get a nice breeze, though the swimming is not good here. Ruthie is a good cook and prepares traditional Garífuna dishes such as *hudut* (fish cooked in coconut milk) and, for breakfast, delicious coconut bread. ✉ *31 Southern Foreshore, Dangriga* ☎ *502/3184* ⬐ *5 rooms* ⚭ *Dining room, fans, cable TV, travel services; no a/c in rooms, no room phones* ▭ *No credit cards.*

HOPKINS VILLAGE

❷ *10 mi (17 km) south of Dangriga on the Southern Hwy., then 2 mi (3⅓ km) east on a partially paved road.*

Hopkins is an intriguing Garífuna coastal village of about 1,000 people, halfway between Dangriga and Placencia. Garífuna culture is more accessible here than in Dangriga. Hopkins has the same toast-color beaches as those in Placencia, and a number of new resorts have opened to take advantage of them. Americans, Canadians, and Europeans are snapping up beachfront land here at prices somewhat lower than in Placencia or on Ambergris Caye, but so far only a few vacation homes and condos have been built. If there's a downside to the area, it's the biting sand flies, which can be vicious.

In the center of town you can watch local Garífuna boys hone their drumming skills at the **Lebeha Drumming Center** (☎ 608/3143). *Lebeha* means "the end" in the Garífuna language, a reference to the school's location at a small guesthouse and bar near the north end of the village. Visitors are welcome. The drums, mostly made by a noted drum maker in Dangriga, Austin Rodriquez, are of mahogany or mayflower wood, with deerskin on the drumhead. Other instruments include *shakas,* or shakers, calabash gourds filled with fruit seeds, and turtle shells. The boys, mostly in their early teens, usually play punta rock, first made famous by Andy Palacio, a Garífuna from Barranco village in Toledo, rather than the more traditional Garífuna music. The drumming goes on nightly, though the most activity is on weekends. Donations are accepted, and you can purchase a CD of Lebeha drumming.

Where to Stay & Eat

In addition to the resorts and hotels listed below, Hopkins has about 20 small guesthouses, mostly run by local villagers but also by some expats who have found the easygoing Hopkins life suits them. Typically just two or three rooms are built next to the home of the owner, who has an eye to tapping the growing tourism market in Hopkins. Most don't look like much from the outside but have the necessities including electricity and, usually, private baths. Among the better ones are **Wabien Guest House** (☎ 523/7010), **Yugadah Inn** (☎ 503/7089), **Seagull's Nest Guest House** (☎ 522/0600), **Whistling Seas Vacation Inn** (☎ 608/0016), **Ransoms Seaside Gardens** (☎ No phone), and **Laruni Cabins** (☎ 523/7026). Rates in almost all cases are less than BZ$100 for a double, with the least expensive ones, usually a block or two back from the water, costing less than BZ$50 for a double. At these guesthouses, it's usually not necessary to make reservations. When you arrive in the village, just walk around until you find one that suits you.

¢–$$ ✕ **Innies Restaurant.** At Innies, as at most of the other local restaurants in Hopkins, you're eating in a spot that was once somebody's house or back porch. In this pink dining room with linoleum floor, you dine on picnic tables with oilcloths, and the inexpensive food is well prepared. Fried chicken with rice and beans or french fries is around BZ$5, and fish dinners are a little more. Traditional Garífuna dishes such as *hudut* (fish cooked in coconut milk and served with mashed plantains) are also available. ✉ *Hopkins, south end of village* ☎ *523/7026* ▭ *No credit cards.*

¢–$$ ✕ **Iris's Place Restaurant.** Iris's little dining room in a small, blue concrete building has only four tables. Don't let the appearance or hand-lettered sign put you off. Inside it's clean, and the food is tasty. Besides the ubiquitous stew chicken with rice and beans, you can get seafood, including lobster and conch in season. For breakfast, bacon and eggs and fry jacks cost around BZ$4. ✉ *Hopkins, south end of village* ☎ *523/7019* ▭ *No credit cards.*

¢ ✕ **Whistling Seas Vacation Inn.** Run by a former Seine Bight resident who moved to Hopkins after Hurricane Iris, this inn provides a wonderful time and you won't pay more than BZ$20 per meal. Try authentic Garífuna cuisine like *sere* (fish in coconut milk) or *bundiga* (green bananas, fish, and spices in coconut milk); they also offer french fries and burgers, along with Creole dishes. Usually there's a Garífuna special of the day. ✉ *Hopkins* ☎ *503/7203.*

¢ ✕ **Yugadah Inn.** A family of sisters, all good cooks, run this small hotel and restaurant on the sea (*Yugadah* means "coastal village" in the Garífuna language). They prepare food in a traditional, freestanding kitchen. ✉ *Hopkins* ☎ *502/7089.*

★ $$$$ ▦ **Hamanasi.** From the dirt road the hotel looks inconspicuous, but with beautifully landscaped grounds, top-notch accommodations, and an excellent dive program, Hamanasi (Garífuna for "almond") is actually among Belize's superior beach and dive resorts. Upon your arrival, you'll notice that the manicured grounds and lobby are all lined with artwork. The "zero effect" pool seems to stretch to infinity, and the lobby and other public areas have artwork and pottery. Choose from regular rooms, gorgeous suites with king-size four-poster beds of barba jolote wood, and "tree houses" on stilts. Most people come here for the diving opportunities, but you won't feel out of place if you want to snorkel or just laze around the pool. The restaurant, which has a romantic outdoor dining area, serves delicious seafood. ✉ *Hopkins* ✎ *Box 265, Dangriga* ☎ *520/7073, 877/552–3483 in U.S.* 🖷 *520/7090 or 954/351–9740* ⊕ *www.hamanasi.com* ➥ *8 rooms, 10 suites* ⚴ *Restaurant, fans, refrigerators, pool, beach, dive shop, dock, boating, fishing, bar, shop, Internet room, travel services; no room phones, no room TVs, no smoking in rooms* ¶⊙¶ *CP* ▭ *MC, V.*

★ $$$$ ▦ **Kanantik Reef & Jungle Resort.** At this all-inclusive luxury resort, you can experience the barrier reef without having to make decisions more complicated than whether to have fish or steak for dinner. You can frolic on a palm-lined private beach and snorkel, sail, or kayak at your leisure. Kanantik—a Mopan Maya word meaning "to take care"—has air-conditioned cabanas tucked onto 300 acres south of Hopkins. Echoing African themes, the large and luxuriously outfitted cabanas are striking round structures with conical roofs. Everything except motorized fishing and imported liquors is included in the daily rate. ⊠ *Off Southern Hwy., between Hopkins and Placencia peninsula* ⓓ *Box 1482, Belize City; Box 150, Dangriga* ☎ *520/8048 or 800/965–9689, 877/759–8834 in U.S.* 🖨 *520/8089* ⊕ *www.kanantik.com* ⇆ *25 cabanas* ⚘ *Dining room, fans, refrigerators, pool, beach, dive shop, dock, snorkeling, boating, fishing, horseback riding, bar, laundry service, Internet room, airstrip, travel services; no room TVs, no kids under 14* ⊟ *MC, V* ⦿ *All-inclusive.*

$$$–$$$$ 🏨 **Belizean Dreams.** This collection of three-bedroom, three-bath condos is among the most upmarket accommodation choices on the Southern Coast. All villas have exactly the same floor plans and furnishings, but units 1 and 9 are directly on the beach, and the others have sea views. The units, with hardwood and natural stone floors and custom-made cedar and mahogany furniture, can be reserved as a complete villa, or choose a single bedroom or two-bedroom suite. The bedrooms have vaulted ceilings with exposed beams and four-poster king beds. You can dine at nearby resorts or have a chef prepare a private meal for you at the condo. Some units have a five-day minimum stay. ⊠ *Hopkins* ☎ *523/7272, 800/456–7150 in U.S. and Canada:* ⊕ *www.belizeandreams.com* ⇆ *9 3-bedroom villas* ⚘ *Room service, fans, some kitchens, some rooms with refrigerators, cable TV, pool, Wi-Fi, travel services* ⊟ *MC, V.*

$$–$$$$ 🏨 **Jaguar Reef Lodge.** At night, with a row of torches burning on the beach and the waterside thatch-covered dining room glowing in lamplight, this lodge has an East African feel. Nestled on the coast, it has views over the water in one direction and of the Maya Mountains' green slopes in the other. The whitewashed duplex cabanas with thatch roofs have soaring pitched ceilings with exposed wooden beams. The newer Colonial suites and rooms have local artwork, salt-tile floors, and custom-made hardwood furnishings. For those who aren't excited about swimming in the sea, there's a seaside pool. The dining room's meals

> ### WORD OF MOUTH
>
> "Jaguar Reef is very very nice (not plush but excellent) and the people are wonderful. Everyone we spoke with there raved about the value—you got sooo much for your money!"
> –Cvechko

(dinner is BZ$48) can be taken inside or outside. You'll find the staff here polite and easygoing. ⊠ *Hopkins* ⓓ *Box 297, Dangriga* ☎ *520/7040, 800/289–5756 in U.S. and Canada* 🖨 *520/7091* ⊕ *www.jaguarreef.com* ⇆ *8 rooms, 9 suites, 1 2-bedroom suite, 7 duplex cabanas* ⚘ *Restaurant, fans, in-room safes, some kitchenettes, refrigerators, cable TV in some rooms, pool, gym, beach, dive shop, dock, snorkeling, fishing, bar, shop, laundry service, Wi-Fi, travel services; no room phones, no room TVs, no smoking in rooms* ⊟ *MC, V.*

$$ 🏨 **Pleasure Cove Lodge.** This small beachfront resort, with rooms in earth tones arranged around a courtyard with a pool, is an option if you don't need all the amenities of the larger resorts but want more than a guesthouse offers. Pleasure Cove also has a one-bedroom villa with kitchen (BZ$500). ⊠ *Sittee Point, 1 mi (1½ km) south of Hopkins* ☎ *520/7089,*

Med School in Belize

Want to get your medical degree with a little snorkeling, diving, and fishing on the side? You may be able to do that in Belize. Belize is home to four offshore medical schools which target students who, although they may be motivated and talented, cannot get admission to med school in the U.S., Canada, or Western Europe. Curricula parallels that of med schools in the United States, though equipment and resources are much more limited. The basic sciences program is five semesters, or the equivalent, and can be completed in as little as 20 months. The clinical medicine program involves about 72 weeks of clinical rotations at hospitals in the U.S. or elsewhere. Most graduates are able to find positions in their fields, according to the schools, although an M.D. degree from a tiny offshore med school may not be quite as prestigious as one from Harvard Medical School.

Interested? Contact one of these schools for more information:

Medical School of the Americas (Belize), Ambergris Caye 1000 Coconut Dr. (Box 127), San Pedro ☎ 226/3744 ⊕ www.mua.edu.bz

St. Luke's University School of Medicine Box 557, Belmopan City ☎ 877-545-8537 in the U.S. and Canada ⊕ www.stluke.edu.bz

Central America Health Sciences University Belize Medical College Box 989, Belize City ☎ 225/4288 ⊕ www.cahsu.edu

InterAmerican School of Medical Science U.S. Information Office: 10 N. Post. St., Ste. 642, Spokane, WA 99201 ☎ 509/838-0592 ⊕ www.interamericanschool.com

–Lan Sluder

612/221-0603 in U.S. ⊕ www.pleasurecovelodge.com ⤴ 5 rooms, 1 suite, 1 villa ⚭ Restaurant, fans, kitchen, Internet room, travel services; no room phones, no room TVs ☰ MC, V.

$ ✕▦ **Beaches and Dreams Seafront Inn and Restaurant.** New hotels are popping up all around the region, but Beaches and Dreams managed to secure one of the area's nicest tan-color stretches of shoreline. This tiny inn, which changed hands in late 2005, has two octagonal cottages, each with vaulted ceilings, rattan furniture, and a small veranda just a few feet from the sea. The new co-owner, who formerly ran a restaurant in Alaska, says he plans a lot of changes at the restaurant and wants to add "lots of live music, happy hours, and fun, fun, fun." Bikes and kayaks are complimentary. ⊠ *Sittee Point* ☎ 523/7259 ⊕ *www.beachesanddreams.com* ⤴ 4 rooms ⚭ Restaurant, fans, beach, bar, travel services; no a/c, no room phones, no room TVs ☰ MC, V ⊠ BP.

$ ▦ **Hopkins Inn.** Greg and Rita Duke are helpful hosts at their little beachfront cottage colony in Hopkins. The four cozy cabins have tile floors, ceilings paneled in local hardwoods, and porches with sea views. A continental breakfast with fruit and locally baked bread is brought to your cabin each morning. German is spoken. ⊠ *Hopkins* ☎ 523/7283 ☎ 523/7013 ⊕ *www.hopkinsinn.com* ⤴ 4 cottages ⚭ Fans, refrigerators, travel services; no room phones, no room TVs ⊠ CP ☰ No credit cards.

¢–$ 🏨 **Tipple Tree Beya Hotel.** This tiny beachfront hotel provides a comfortable alternative to the coast's upmarket resorts. Run by friendly Patricia Sturman, the inn has rooms that are simple but immaculately clean, as well as a separate private cabin with a kitchenette. You can even pitch a tent on the beach (or just pretend you're roughing it by kicking back in a hammock). Bicycles and kayaks are available for rent. ⊠ *Hopkins* 🕿 *520/7006* ⊕ *www.tippletree.com* ⥍ *4 rooms, 1 with shared bath, 1 cabin* ⚓ *Beach, snorkeling, travel services; no a/c, no room phones, no room TVs* ▤ *MC, V.*

¢–$ 🏨 **Toucan Sittee.** Neville Collins ran a store in San Ignacio before he retired to this 20-acre farm on the Sittee River, where he grows 60 different kinds of fruit trees including 10 mango varieties. This peaceful retreat has wood cottages on stilts with apartments and shared rooms. When not relaxing among the ginger plants, take advantage of the activities that Collins can arrange, such as canoeing, hiking, and bird-watching. Meals (dinners BZ$20) use organic ingredients grown on the farm. There are delicious wood and vegetarian options. Like all lodges in these parts, this one can get a bit buggy, so bring repellent. ⊠ *Sittee River* 🕿 *523/7039* ⊕ *www.toucansittee.info* ⥍ *2 rooms with shared bath, 2 apartments, 1 bunk house with 5 beds* ⚓ *Fans, refrigerators, fishing; no a/c, no room phones, no room TVs* ▤ *MC, V.*

¢ 🏨 **All Seasons Guest House.** The three small but immaculate guest rooms here each are designed around a theme. The Jungle Room has a zebra motif and mosquito net on the bed; the Butterfly Room has accents in the deep blue of the Blue Morpho; the Bamboo Room has, well, bamboo and a ceiling fan. There's a sunny patio and garden, and you can rent a motor scooter here (BZ$75 a day). Owner Ingrid Stahl also speaks German. ⊠ *Hopkins* ✉ *Box 251, Dangriga* 🕿 *523/7209* ⊕ *www.allseasonsbelize.com* ⥍ *3 rooms* ⚓ *Fans, refrigerators, travel services; no a/c in some rooms, no room phones, no room TVs* ▤ *No credit cards.*

¢ 🏨 **Jungle Jeanies.** Although not actually in the jungle, this group of wood cabanas on stilts is on about 2 acres of beachfront nicely shaded by coconut palms. You can rent kayaks and windsurfers here, or just relax in a hammock. You can also pitch your tent for BZ$14 per person. "Jungle Jeannie" Barkman and husband "Jungle John" are actually Canadians who have lived in Belize for years. The owners usually spend summers in Canada, but the hotel stays open. ⊠ *Hopkins* 🕿 *523/7047* ⊕ *www.junglejeanie.com* ⥍ *5 cottages* ⚓ *Fans, refrigerators, travel services; no room phones, no room TVs* ▤ *No credit cards.*

The Outdoors

Hopkins is less than 10 minutes by road from the paved Southern Highway and is ideally situated for a variety of outdoor adventures, both land and sea. Here's the distance from Hopkins to selected points of interest:

Belize Barrier Reef: 10 mi (17 km)

Cockscomb Basin Wildlife Sanctuary: 10 mi (17 km)

Glover's and Turneffe Atolls: 25 mi (42 km)

Mayflower Bocawina National Park: 15 mi (25 km)

Bird-Watching

Cockscomb Basin Wildlife Sanctuary has excellent birding, with some 300 species identified in the reserve. You can also sometimes see the Jabiru Stork, the largest flying bird in the Western Hemisphere, in the marsh areas just to the west of Hopkins Village. Keep an eye out as you drive into the village from the Southern Highway. North of Hopkins is Fresh Water Creek Lagoon and south of the village is Anderson Lagoon. These lagoons and mangrove swamps are home to many water birds, including herons and egrets. A kayak trip on the Sittee River should reward you with kingfishers, toucans, and various flycatchers. About 30 minutes by boat off Hopkins is Man-o-War Caye, a bird sanctuary that has one of the largest colonies of frigate birds in the Caribbean, more than 300 nesting birds. **Hamanasi, Jaguar Reef,** and other hotels arrange bird-watching trips. Costs for guided birding tours run from BZ$50 to $200 per person, depending on where you go and the length of time.

Canoeing & Kayaking

When kayaking or canoeing on the Sittee River you can see many birds and, possibly, manatees and crocodiles. If you go on a tour with a licensed guide from a local lodge, expect to pay BZ$100 to BZ$150 per person. Several hotels in Hopkins, including **Tipple Tree Beya Hotel, Hopkins Inn, Jungle Jeannies,** and **All Seasons Guest House** rent kayaks, canoes, and other water equipment by the hour or day. Although it's possible to do sea kayaking from Hopkins, often the water is choppy. Long sea-kayaking trips should only be tried by experienced kayakers, preferably with a guide.

Caving

Caving tours from Hopkins typically go to St. Herman's Cave and the Crystal Cave at Blue Hole National Park on the Hummingbird Highway. Cost is around BZ$120 per person.

Diving

Diving off Hopkins is very good to terrific. The barrier reef is closer here–about 10 mi (17 km) from shore–than it is at Placencia. Diving also is fairly costly here. Half-day, two-tank dive trips to the reef or the South Water Caye Marine Reserve are around BZ$200, not including regulator, BCD, wet suit, and other equipment rental, which can add BZ$50. Dive shops with fast boats can also take you all the way to the atolls—Turneffe, Glover's, and even Lighthouse. These atoll trips generally start early in the morning, at 6 or 7 AM and last all day. Costs for three-tank atoll dives are around BZ$280 to BZ$340 for Glover's and Turneffe, and BZ$500 for Lighthouse. In late spring, when whale sharks typically show up, local dive shops offer dives to see the Belizean behemoths for around BZ$350 to BZ$400.

One of the best diving operations in Southern Belize is at **Hamanasi** (☎ 520/7073 ⊕ www.hamanasi.com). Here you'll find the newest equipment and the biggest boats. **Second Nature Divers** (⊠ At Jaguar Reef Lodge ☎ 520/7040 ⊕ www.secondnaturedivers.com) has a good reputation as well.

Helicopter Tours

The owner of **Jaguar Reef Lodge** once was a helicopter pilot, and the lodge offers helicopter tours. You can see the barrier reef, Glover's Atoll, Cockscomb Basin, and even Caracol from the air. Prices range from BZ$250 to BZ$800 per person.

Horseback Riding

Local lodges arrange horseback-riding trips, working with ranches near Belmopan and Dangriga. A full-day horseback trip, including transportation to the ranch and lunch, is around BZ$150 per person.

Hiking

Most hiking trips go to Cockscomb Basin Wildlife Sanctuary, where there are a dozen short hiking trails near the visitor center. Full-day trips to Cockscomb generally cost about BZ$120 to BZ$150 per person from Hopkins and can be booked through your hotel. If you're a glutton for punishment, you can go on a guided hike to Victoria Peak, the second-highest mountain peak in Belize. The 40-mi (67-km) hike from the visitor center at Cockscomb Basin Wildlife Sanctuary to the top entails inclines of 45 to 60 degrees. Most of these trips require three to five days up and back and cost in the range of BZ$1,000 per person. One guide who will take you is **Marcos Cucul** (⊕ www.mayaguide.bz). He is a jungle survival guide who is a member of the Belize National Cave and Wilderness Rescue Team.

Manatee-Watching Tours

Local lodges offer trips to Gales Point and the Southern Lagoon to try to spot Antillean manatees, a subspecies of West Indian manatees. These large aquatic mammals—adults weigh 800 to 1,200 pounds—are related to elephants. They're found in shallow waters in lagoons, rivers, estuaries, and coastal areas in much of Belize, and are especially common in the lagoons around Gales Point. These gentle herbivores can live 60 years or longer. The cost of manatee-spotting trips varies but is around BZ$150 per person. Under Belize government guidelines, you're not permitted to feed manatees, to swim with them, or to approach a manatee with a calf.

Snorkeling

Snorkeling off Hopkins is excellent, though expensive compared with the Northern Cayes. Half-day snorkeling trips from Hopkins to the Belize Barrier Reef, usually a pristine section of it in the South Water Caye Marine Reserve, cost from BZ$100 to BZ$150 per person, depending on whether you're snorkeling from an island on the reef or from a boat (the boat costs more). These snorkel trips are about twice as pricey as those to Hol Chan from Ambergris Caye or Caye Caulker, partly because the trip out and back to snorkel sites here is much longer, and also because there's less competition to hold prices down. Full-day snorkel trips to Glover's Atoll, which has some of the best snorkeling in the Caribbean, are around BZ$150 to BZ$200.

Windsurfing

Windsurfing is a growing sport in Hopkins, as the wind is a fairly consistent 10 to 15 knots, except in August and September when it sometimes goes calm. The best winds are in April and May. **Windschief**

(☏ 523/7249 ⊕ www.windschief.com) rents well-maintained equipment for BZ$10 for the first hour, then BZ$5 for additional hours, or BZ$60 a day. Private lessons are BZ$60 an hour. Several hotels also rent windsurfing equipment.

Shopping

Shopping is limited in Hopkins, where the local "shopping center" is a small clapboard house with a few dozen items for sale. Locals traditionally make much of what they use in daily life, from cassava graters to fishing canoes and paddles, and drums and *shakas* (shakers made from a calabash gourd filled with seeds). Around the village, you'll see individuals selling carvings and other local handicrafts made from shells and coconuts. Also, several small shops or stands, including **JoyJah's Gift Shop, Kulcha Gift Shop,** and **Tribal Arts,** none of which have phones, sell locally made crafts. You can bargain for the best price, but remember that there are few jobs around Hopkins and that these craftspeople are trying to earn money to help feed their families. **Jaguar Reef Resort** (☏ 520/7040) has a fine little gift shop filled with pottery and embroidery as well as Garífuna crafts. The store also carries Marie Sharp's superb hot sauces, New Age music, and drugstore items like sunscreen and the crucial no-see-um bug repellent. **Hamanasi** (☏ 520/7073) also has a well-stocked gift shop.

COCKSCOMB BASIN WILDLIFE SANCTUARY

★ ☾ ❸ *10 mi (17 km) southwest of Hopkins.*

The mighty jaguar, once the undisputed king of the Central and South American jungles, is now endangered. But it has a haven in the Cockscomb Basin Wildlife Sanctuary, which covers 102,000 acres of lush rain forest in the Cockscomb Range of the Maya Mountains. Thanks to this reserve, as well as other protected areas around the country, Belize has the highest concentration of jaguars in the world.

Some visitors to Cockscomb are disappointed that they don't see jaguars and that wildlife doesn't jump out from behind trees to astound them as they hike the trails. The experience at Cockscomb is indeed a low-key one, and seeing wildlife usually requires patience and luck. You'll have the best chance of seeing wild animals, perhaps even a jaguar or one of the other large cats, if you stay overnight, preferably for several nights, in the sanctuary. You may also have better luck if you go for an extended hike with a guide. Several nearby lodges, such as **Hamanasi,** offer night hikes to Cockscomb, departing around dusk and returning around 9 PM.

Cockscomb Basin also has native wildlife aside from the jaguars. You might see other cats—pumas, margays, and ocelots—plus coatis, kinkajous, deer, peccaries, and, last but not least, tapirs. Also known as the mountain cow, this shy, curious creature appears to be half horse, half hippo, with a bit of cow and elephant thrown in. Nearly 300 species of birds have been identified in the Cockscomb Basin, including the

On Jaguars

Jaguars are shy, nocturnal animals that prefer to keep their distance from humans, so the possibility of viewing one in the wild is small. The jaguar, or *el tigre*, as it's known in Spanish, is nature's great loner, a supremely independent creature that shuns even the company of its own kind. Except during a brief mating period and the six short months the female spends with her cubs before turning them loose, jaguars live alone, roaming the rain forest in splendid isolation. At certain times of year, however, jaguars are routinely spotted here. In some months, visitors at Cockscomb see jaguars almost every day, especially early in the morning before sunrise.

Keel-Billed Toucan, the King Vulture, several hawk species, and the Scarlet Macaw.

Within the reserve is Belize's best-maintained system of jungle and mountain trails, most of which lead to at least one outstanding swimming hole. The sanctuary also has spectacular views of Victoria Peak and the Cockscomb Range. Bring serious bug spray with you—the reserve swarms with mosquitoes and tiny biting flies called no-see-ums—and wear long-sleeve shirts and long pants. The best times to hike anywhere in Belize are early morning, late afternoon, and early evening, when temperatures are lower and more animals are on the prowl.

You have to register in a thatch building at Maya Centre on the Southern Highway before proceeding several miles to the visitor center. In the same building is a gift shop selling baskets and slate carvings by local Maya craftspeople, at good prices. The road winds through dense vegetation—splendid cahune palms, purple mimosas, orchids, and big-leaf plantains—and as you go higher the marvelous sound of tropical birds, often resembling strange windup toys, grows stronger and stronger. This is definitely four-wheel-drive terrain. You may have to ford several small rivers as well as negotiate deep, muddy ruts. At the end, in a clearing with hibiscus and bougainvillea bushes, you'll find a little office where you can buy maps of the nature trails, along with rest rooms, several picnic tables, cabins, and a campground.

Walking along these 12 well-marked nature trails is a good way to get to know the region. Most are loops of ½–1½ mi (1–2 km), so you can do several in a day. The most strenuous trail takes you up a steep hill; from the top is a magnificent view of the entire Cockscomb Basin. ⊠ *Outside Maya Centre* ☎ *227/7369* ✑ *BZ$10* ☉ *Daily 8–5.*

Where to Stay & Eat

Although most visitors come to Cockscomb on day trips and stay in Hopkins, Placencia, or Dangriga, you can camp in the reserve for BZ$10 a night per person, or for a little more money, you can stay in pleasant new rooms in a dormitory with solar-generated electricity for BZ$37 per person. Also, a small house and two cabins, each with private bath, can accommodate up to four or six people (BZ$107 per house/cabin). An old, primitive cabin with 10 bunk beds is BZ$16 per person. There's a communal kitchen for cooking. No fishing or hunting is allowed in the reserve, and pets are prohibited. Book in Belize City through the **Belize Audubon Society** (☎ 223/5004 ⊕ www.belizeaudubon.org).

¢ ▣ **Tutzil Nah Cottages.** Gregorio Chun and his family, Mopan Maya people who've lived in this area for generations, provide accommodations in simple thatch cabanas. Meals also are available, for BZ$12–BZ$24, and the Chuns provide a range of tours to Cockscomb and Mayan sites. ⊠ *Near Maya Centre, Mile 13½, Southern Hwy.* ☎ *520/3044* ⊕ *www. mayacenter.com* ⇨ *2 cabanas* ⌂ *No a/c, no room phones, no room TVs* ▭ *No credit cards.*

MAYA BEACH & THE NORTHERN PENINSULA

❹ *36 mi (61 km) south of Dangriga by road.*

Dusty in dry weather and a muddy slop after rains, the largely dirt road that runs 25 mi (41 km) from the Southern Highway to Placencia Village is called the Peninsula Road or the Placencia Road, or just "the road," but whatever it's called, it's the only artery down the peninsula. Beginning at Riversdale—about 8½ mi (14 km) from the Southern Highway, at the elbow where the peninsula joins the mainland—you'll get a quick glimpse through mangroves of the startlingly blue Caribbean. As you go south, the Placencia Lagoon is on your right, and behind it in the distance rise the low Maya Mountains. On your left, a few hundred feet away, beyond the remaining mangroves and a narrow band of beach, is the sea.

The northern peninsula from Riversdale south to Maya Beach, which is about 7 mi (12 km) south of Riversdale, once had just a few small seaside houses, and Maya Beach was a sleepy beach community. Now, "For Sale" signs dot the roadside and several new condominium communities and resorts are open or are being planned. These new resorts and condo developments join a small group of laid-back seaside hotels and cabins.

Traveling from Riversdale to Maya Beach to Seine Bight and Placencia, you'll find no clear delineation between one area and another. Even local residents may not be entirely sure exactly where one community ends and another begins.

If you stay at the northern end of the peninsula, you may want a rental car because public transportation is limited to an on-again, off-again shuttle and a few buses bound to or from Dangriga. Taxis are expensive (about BZ$40 to Placencia village from Riversdale, and BZ$30 from Maya Beach).

Where to Stay & Eat

$$–$$$$ ✕ **Mango's.** About as tropical as you can get, Mango's is a laid-back bar and restaurant on the beach that makes its home in a thatch cabana on stilts. Ever popular are the burgers with banana chips or fries, but you

Placencia
Peninsula

*Placencia
Lagoon*

Maya Point
Market ◆

CARIBBEAN SEA

Barefoot
Auto Rental ◆

Lola's
Arts ◆

Seine Bight
Police Station ◆

Airstrip ✛

can also get spicy burritos, grilled snapper, and even lobster. Or, join the local crowd that gathers to drink beer and munch chips and salsa. ⊠ *Maya Beach, 1 mi (2 km) north of Seine Bight, on main Rd.* ☎ *520/ 4056* ▤ *MC, V.*

¢–$$ ✕ **Hungry Gecko.** Above the Maya Beach grocery store, the Hungry Gecko is a café serving inexpensive Belizean and Honduran food. Owner Doris Herrera cooks to please local tastes, with plenty of coconut milk and red *recado* (achiote with other spices). ⊠ *Maya Beach, 1 mi (2 km) north of Seine Bight, on main road, across from Mango's* ▤ *No credit cards* ⊗ *Closed Wed.*

$$$ ✕▣ **The Placencia.** Transplant an upscale Texas condo community to Belize, and you might end up with something like the Placencia, formerly called Zeboz. The resort opened in 2003 and has luxurious amenities: tennis courts, an upscale restaurant with a 9,000-bottle wine cellar, the largest swimming pool in Belize, and 1,000 feet of sandy beachfront, with a dock that goes out some 200 feet. The one-bedroom apartments are spacious and have a whirlpool bath and tile floors. The Capriccio restaurant serves Italian and some Belizean dishes. If you don't want to leave, you can buy a condo here, starting at about US$150,000. The owners are building additional condos in a gated community. ⊠ *Maya Beach, 4 mi (6½ km) north of Seine Bight* ☎ *520/4110* 🖶 *520/4112* ⊕ *www.theplacencia.com* ⊅ *32 condo apartments* ⌂ *Restaurant, fans, kitchenettes, cable TV, tennis court, pool, beach, dive shop, dock, snorkeling, fishing, small spa, bar, laundry services, Internet room, travel services* ▤ *AE, MC, V.*

$–$$ ✕▣ **Maya Beach Hotel and Bistro.** Before ending up here, owners John
Fodor'sChoice and Ellen Lee (he's Australian, she's American) traveled the world and
★ worked in 20 countries. They obviously figured out what travelers love, because their bistro by the beach is one of our favorite restaurants in all of Belize, and the hotel is a small oasis of easygoing charm. The Bistro menu changes frequently, but among the standards you'll go gaga over are the gazpacho with grilled shrimp, ultrafresh ceviche, delicious snapper stack, and cocoa-dusted pork chop on a risotto cake. In addition to the simple but pleasant hotel rooms with views of False Caye and the sea, the hotel rents several apartments nearby with access to a pool. Some have minimum-stay requirements. ⊠ *Maya Beach* ☎🖶 *520/8040, 800/ 503–5124 in U.S.* ⊕ *www.mayabeachhotel.com* ⊅ *6 rooms, 4 apartments* ⌂ *Restaurant, fans, some kitchens, beach, snorkeling, fishing, bar, Internet, travel services; no a/c in some rooms, no room phones, no TV in some rooms* ▤ *MC, V* ⊗ *Bistro closed in July.*

$$$–$$$$ ▣ **Bella Maya.** Developed by a company in London that specializes in "emerging market" real estate and that has other projects in Latvia, Bulgaria, and Brazil, the first phase of Bella Maya opened in mid-2006. Bella Maya is expected to eventually have a total of 60 condominium apartments, most available for nightly rental. The 1,100-square-foot apartments, all with two bedrooms and two baths, have travertine marble floors, fully equipped kitchens with granite countertops, and private verandas. The 4-acre grounds stretch across the peninsula from lagoon to sea, with piers on each side, a long seaside pool, and a tennis court. ⊠ *5 mi (8 km) north of Seine Bight* ☎ *0207 731 2200 in England* 🖶 *0207*

A Creole Primer

The Creole language is associated with the Creole or black people of Belize, especially those around Belize City. But people all over Belize know the Creole language and speak it daily. You'll hear Creole spoken by Mennonite farmers, Chinese shopkeepers, and Hispanic tour guides. Creole was brought to Belize by African slaves and former slaves from Jamaica and elsewhere in the Caribbean. Creole words are primarily of English origin, with some words from several West African tongues, Spanish, Miskito (an indigenous language of Central America, spoken by some 200,000 people in Honduras, Nicaragua, and Belize), and other languages.

Spoken in a lilting Caribbean accent and combined with a grammar and syntax with West African roots, the language, despite English word usage, is difficult for foreigners to understand. Plurals aren't used often in Creole. For some, knowing how to speak Creole is a test you have to pass before you can become a "real" Belizean. However, with the increasing number of Hispanic immigrants in Belize, it's heard less and less, while Spanish is heard more and more.

Here are a few Creole words and phrases:

Ah mi gat wahn gud guf taim: I had a really good time

Bwah: Boy

Bashment: Party

Chaaly prise: A large rat, after Sir Charles Price, an 18th-century Jamaican planter

Chinchi: A little bit

Dis da fi wi chikin: This is our chicken (well-known slogan of Mennonite chicken company)

Dollah: A Belize dollar

Fowl caca white and tink eh lay egg: A chicken sees its white droppings and thinks it laid an egg (said of a self-important person)

Grind mean: Ground meat

Gyal: Girl

Humoch dis kaas?: How much is this?

Ih noh mata: It doesn't matter

Madda rass: Foolishness (literally, mother's ass)

Tiga maga but eh no sic: Tiger's skinny but he's not sick (that is, don't judge a book by its cover)

Waawa: Foolish

Wangla: Sesame seed or candy made from sesame seeds

Weh di beach deh?: Where's the beach?

Yerrisso: Gossip, from "Ah her so" (so I hear)

5

736 1512 ⊕ *www.bellamayaresort.com* ⊅ *60 units* ♻ *Restaurant, fans, cable TV, tennis, pool, beach, docks, snorkeling, fishing, bar, laundry services, Wi-Fi, travel services* ▭ *AE, MC, V* ⦿❙ *CP.*

$$–$$$ ▦ **Calico Jack's Village.** Co-owner Chester Williams developed a new hurricane-resistant technique, employing foam-filled concrete blocks, to build this small beachfront resort at the peninsula's far north end. Nine rustic, cohune-palm thatched cabanas, some of which have air-conditioning, are set about 60 feet from the sea. On recent visits, the grounds were in need of a little TLC and an old vehicle was rusting near the entrance drive. Service, however, is eager, and the beach is pretty, though as elsewhere on the peninsula sand flies can be irksome and there's sea grass in the water. Jutting from the shore are two tempting private piers with thatch palapas and hammocks. ⊠ *Maya Beach, 4 mi (6½ km) north of Seine Bight* ☎ *523/8009* 🖶 *520/8103* ⊕ *www.calicojacksvillage.com* ⊅ *9 cabanas* ♻ *Restaurant, fans, pool, beach, docks, snorkeling, fishing, bicycles, badminton, bar, Internet, travel services; no a/c in some rooms, no room phones, no room TVs* ▭ *AE, MC, V* ⦿❙ *CP.*

$$ ▦ **Green Parrot Beach Houses.** This resort has Mennonite-built cottages, now showing a little wear, along a nice stretch of beach, each with a kitchenette and dining area. The sleeping quarters are upstairs in a loft-like space with a pitched wooden roof. One nifty feature is an octagonal wall panel, operated by pulleys, which can be opened for a bedside view of the ocean. Two of the thatch cabanas have outdoor showers. The beachfront restaurant has a limited menu. ⊠ *No. 1 Maya Beach, 4 mi (6½ km) north of Seine Bight* ☎ *523/2488* ⊕ *www.greenparrot-belize.com* ⊅ *6 cabins, 2 cabanas* ♻ *Restaurant, fans, beach, dock, snorkeling, bar, airport shuttle; no a/c, no room phones, no room TVs* ▭ *MC, V* ⦿❙ *CP.*

$$ ▦ **Ocean's Edge Beach Houses.** The two beach houses at this seaside hideaway each have a loft bedroom on the second level, with views of the water from the jalousie windows, and a living area and kitchen on the first floor. Constructed in 2001, the houses have rustic exteriors of local woods. You can sit on your deck and see False Caye, a nice snorkeling area about 30 minutes by kayak (complimentary) from the beach. The property is managed by the owners of Barnacle Bill's (*see below*). Five-day minimum stay. ⊠ *49 Maya Beach Way, north end of Maya Beach, 3 mi (5 km) north of Seine Bight* ☎ *866/367–7679 in U.S. and Canada* 🖶 *514/697–9435* ⊕ *www.oceansedge-belize.com* ⊅ *2 houses* ♻ *Fans, kitchens, refrigerators, cable TV, beach, snorkeling; no a/c, no room phones, no room TVs* ▭ *MC, V.*

$$ ▦ **Singing Sands.** The six wood-and-thatch cabanas here are small and simply decorated with Guatemalan needlecrafts. They were relocated after Hurricane Iris (2001) and now have better views. Singing Sands has a dock with a nice area for swimming, and a pool for those who'd rather take a dip in fresh water. ⊠ *Maya Beach* 🖶🖶 *520/8022* ⊕ *www.singingsands.com* ⊅ *6 cabanas* ♻ *Restaurant, fans, pool, beach, dock, bar, laundry service, Internet, travel services; no a/c, no room phones, no room TVs* ▭ *MC, V* ⦿❙ *CP.*

$–$$ ▦ **Maya Breeze Inn.** Choice is what it's about at this resort. You can choose from three cabins and two apartments on the sea side of the road, or take a room in the lagoon-side hotel. The cabins are older, wood units, while the hotel rooms are in a modern concrete building with terra-cotta floors and private balconies. One of the apartments has a cathedral ceiling and a third-floor loft with a terrific view of the sea. ⊠ *Maya Beach, 2 mi (3 km) north of Seine Bight* 🖼 *523/8012* ☎ *888/458–8581 in U.S.* ⊕ *www.mayabreezeinn.com* 🛏 *3 cabins, 2 apartments, 4 rooms* ⚄ *Fans, some in-room safes, some kitchens, refrigerators, cable TV, beach, snorkeling, laundry services, travel services; no room phones* 🖭 *MC, V.*

$ 🏠 **Barnacle Bill's Beach Bungalows.** "Barnacle Bill" Taylor, known as the wit of Maya Beach, and wife Adriane rent a pair of wooden Mennonite bungalows set among palm trees about 60 feet from the surf. Each cottage is on stilts and has a private bath and a kitchen where you can prepare your own meals. Bill and Adriane can arrange to stock your fridge and pantry in advance, if you like. There are complimentary bikes and kayaks. All in all, this is a laid-back and delightful little place. ⊠ *23 Maya Beach Way* 🖼 *523/8010* ⊕ *www.gotobelize.com/barnacle* 🛏 *2 cottages* ⚄ *Fans, beach, snorkeling, fishing, bicycles, airport shuttle; no a/c, no room phones, no room TVs* 🖭 *MC, V.*

$ 🏠 **Beachfront Suites.** Think small, act independently: there are only two self-catering suites at this private home, painted a tropical pink and blue. Both suites are on the second floor, and each have full kitchens, ice-cold air-conditioning, double doors opening to a veranda with views of the water, custom-made hardwood furnishings, and broadband Internet for BZ$150 and BZ$170 which make the suites an excellent value. ⊠ *253 Plantation, 1½ mi (3 km) south of Riversdale in the Plantation development* 🖼 *606/1521* 🖼 *520/4112* ⊕ *www.beachfrontinbelize.com* 🛏 *2 suites* ⚄ *Fans, kitchens, beach, snorkeling, laundry services* 🖭 *No credit cards.*

SEINE BIGHT

⑤ *47 mi (77 km) south of Dangriga.*

Like Placencia, its Creole neighbor to the south, Seine Bight is a small coastal fishing village. It may not be for long, though, as Placencia's resorts are stretching north to and through this Garífuna community, one of six predominantly Garífuna villages in Belize. The beach is among the best in Belize, though garbage sometimes mars the view. Hotels do rake and clean their beachfronts, and several community cleanups have been organized in an effort to solve this problem. All the businesses catering to tourists are along the main road (actually, it's the only road) that leads south to Placencia Village. The name Seine Bight derives from a type of net, called a seine, used by local fishermen. Bight means an indentation or inward bend in the coastline.

Like Placencia Village, Seine Bight was devastated by Hurricane Iris in October 2001, and many of the village's simple wooden homes were destroyed. However, any traces of the storm have been erased by expanding resorts and new residential construction.

Where to Stay & Eat

$$$-$$$$ ✕⊞ **The Inn at Robert's Grove.** Energetic New Yorkers Bob and Risa
Fodor'sChoice Frackman invite you to stay at their place on a palm-lined stretch of
★ beach, recently expanded and upgraded. You can play tennis and
swim in the sea or one of the three beachside pools. Their chef packs
lunches for boat rides to deserted cayes and serves dinner in the sea-
side dining room. Such personal attention makes this one of Belize's
top beach resorts. Although the regular rooms and junior suites have
been beautifully refurbished, opt for the deluxe suites, most with ve-
randas overlooking the ocean and kitchens. The hotel has a dive cen-
ter and two private cayes for picnics or overnight trips. ⊠ ½ mi (1
km) south of Seine Bight ☎ 523/3565, 800/565–9757 in U.S. 🖷 523/
3567 ⊕ www.robertsgrove.com ➟ 20 rooms, 32 suites ♻ 2 restau-
rants, fans, some kitchens, some refrigerators, cable TV, 2 tennis
courts, 3 pools, gym, spa, beach, dive shop, dock, snorkeling, wind-
surfing, boating, fishing, bars, shop, laundry service, Internet room,
airport shuttle, travel services ⊟ AE, MC, V.

$$-$$$$ ⊞ **Laru Beya Villas.** A condo colony that opened its first buildings in late
2005, Laru Beya sits on seven beachfront acres. Rooms are bright and
sunny, with tile floors and bamboo furniture. The larger villa units, with
up to three bedrooms, have full kitchens, and some have rooftop Jacuzzis
and verandas with sea views. ⊠ ½ mi (1 km) south of Seine Bight, south
of Robert's Grove ☎ 523/3476, 800/813–7762 in U.S. and Canada
⊕ www.larubeya.com ➟ 14 units ♻ Fans, some kitchens, cable TV, pool,
beach, volleyball, bar, Internet ⊟ MC, V.

$$-$$$ ⊞ **Nautical Inn.** The rooms at this inn are in two-tier octagonal buildings,
shipped from North Carolina. They've got American-style fixtures, firm
mattresses, and glass-wall showers. The pool is one of the nicest on the
peninsula. There are canoes as well as a dive boat to transport you to the
reef. On Wednesday evening the hotel hosts Garífuna drummers and coconut bowling. ⊠ Seine Bight ☎ 523/3595, 800/688–0377 in U.S. 🖷 523/
3594 ⊕ www.nauticalinnbelize.com ➟ 12 rooms ♻ Restaurant, fans, some
refrigerators, cable TV, pool, beach, dive shop, dock, fishing, shop, Internet room, airport shuttle, travel services ⊟ AE, MC, V.

Shopping

Painter and writer Lola Delgado moved to Seine Bight from Belize City
in the late 1980s. Her workshop, **Lola's Art** (☎ 601/1913 ⊙ 8 AM–9 PM),
displays her cheerful acrylic paintings of local scenes (BZ$100 and up).
She also sells hand-painted cards and some of her husband's wood carvings. Espresso and pastries are available. The workshop is up a flight of
steps in a tiny wooden house off the main street, behind the football field.

PLACENCIA

❻ 5 mi (8 km) south of Seine Bight, 52 mi (85 km) south of Dangriga.

Set in a sheltered half-moon bay with crystal-clear water and almost 3
mi (5 km) of palm-dotted white sand, this fishing village is straight out

Placencia Village

Placencia Lagoon

Placencia Community Center

Wallen's Market & Hardware

Placencia Pharmacy

School

Art N Soul Gallery

Ocean Motion Dive Shop

Soccer Field

Post Office

Placencia Tourism Center

Seahorse Dive Shop

Placencia Fisherman's Coop

The Moorings Belize

CARIBBEAN SEA

of a Robert Louis Stevenson novel. Founded by pirates, the community is now inhabited by an extraordinary mélange of people. To the west, the Cockscomb Range ruffles the tropical sky with its jagged peaks; to the east, a line of uninhabited cayes grazes the horizon. From here you can dive along the reef, hike into the jungle, look for Scarlet Macaws in Red Bank Village to the southwest (between December and February), explore the Mayan ruins at Lubantuun, or treat yourself to some of the best sportfishing in the country. Once you arrive you'll probably just want to lie in a hammock with a good book, perhaps getting up long enough to cool off in the waves.

Placencia is so small that it doesn't even have a main street—it has a concrete path just wide enough for two people. Setting off purposefully

WORD OF MOUTH

"Just came back from Belize on Tuesday. What an amazing time! A great place to eat in Placencia is De Tatch—you won't believe the size of the shrimp they serve and the huge portions. Delicious."

–cindyandrick

from the southern end of town, the path meanders through everyone's backyard, passes wooden cottages on stilts overrun with bougainvillea and festooned with laundry, then, as if it had forgotten where it was headed in the first place, peters out abruptly in a little clearing filled with lovely white morning glories. Stroll along the sidewalk, and you've seen the town. If you don't mind it being a little rough around the edges, you'll be utterly enchanted by this rustic village, where the palm trees rustle, the waves lap the shore, and no one is in a hurry.

Along the path are most of the village's quaint guesthouses and palapa-covered cafés, which serve mainly burgers, rice and beans, and a bit of seafood. With the opening of more and more small resorts up the peninsula, Placencia's restaurants are beginning to compete with those in Ambergris Caye.

In 2001 the eye of Hurricane Iris came ashore right at Placencia. Few homes or hotels were spared, and many of the old frame structures, especially on the sea side, were blown down or washed away forever. Today, however, except for a few vacant lots and some gaps in lines of coconut palms, you wouldn't know that a storm had blown through.

Where to Stay & Eat

$-$$$ ✕ **De Tatch Café.** This open-air bar and restaurant with a "tatch" roof long has been one of the most popular hangouts in the village. Try the huge shrimp burrito and wash it down with a few cold Belikins. If you go fishing and catch something, the restaurant will prepare it for you. Breakfasts are good here, too. ⊠ *In village near Seaspray Hotel* ☎ *523/ 3148* ▭ *MC, V.*

$-$$$ ✕ **The Galley.** Listen to recorded jazz and enjoy perfectly broiled lobster, or delicious grilled fish, at this pleasant and peaceful restaurant (peaceful as long as there's not a big soccer game going on at the field nearby). You can dine in the moonlight on the veranda, or inside. ⊠ *Across from soccer field in Placencia Village* ☎ *523/3133* ▭ *MC, V.*

$-$$ ✕ **Trattoria Placencia.** You can parla Italiano, Americano, or Creole at this Italian and seafood place on the beach. Owner Cris is from Rome and "Greg da Barman" is from New York, though he's lived in Belize for many years. The pastas are freshly made—try the seafood fettucine or ravioli. They even have espresso. Capisce? ⊠ *In village, near Seaspray Hotel and De Tatch Café* ☎ *609/3143* ▭ *MC, V* ☼ *Closed Sun. No lunch.*

$-$$ ✕ **Wendy's.** No, not that Wendy's. This Wendy's is a little local restaurant, operated by Wendy Lemus, that's often packed for lunch and

> ## WORD OF MOUTH
>
> "Loved Placencia . . . did snorkle trips, sailing trips, and a Monkey River trip. We had a car, so we went to the Zoo one day. Love the place!"
>
> –CaymanSue

Where to Stay & Eat in
Placencia Village

Airstrip

Placencia
Lagoon

CARIBBEAN SEA

dinner. The grilled fish is fresh and delicious, and there also are Creole dishes (like stew chicken with rice and beans) and mestizo dishes (like escabeche). In late 2005 the interior was completely redone in a Mexican pueblo style. ⊠ *Main road near dock in Placencia Village* ☎ *523/ 3335* ⊟ *MC, V.*

$–$$ ✕ **Pickled Parrot Bar & Grill.** This popular feet-in-the-sand restaurant and bar is in the heart of Placencia. Fresh seafood is the main draw, but owner Wende Bryan also offers pizza, fajitas, and burgers. ⊠ *Off main road, behind Wallen's Market* ☎ *604/0278* ⊟ *V* ☾ *Closed Sun.*

¢–$ ✕ **Garden Brew.** Placencia's first and only coffeehouse, the Garden Brew brews rich Guatemalan coffees. In warm weather (and when isn't it warm in Placencia?) the iced coffee is refreshing. Teas, baked goods, soups, and sandwiches are also available. ⊠ *In village, behind Wallen's store* ☎ *523/3617* ⊟ *MC, V.*

¢ ✕ **Tutti-Frutti.** Authentic, Italian-style gelati is the thing here. Try the fruit flavors, made from natural ingredients. ⊠ *In village on main road, across from Wendy's* ☎ *No phone* ⊟ *No credit cards.*

$$$$ ✕⊡ **Turtle Inn.** Francis Ford Coppola's second hotel in Belize is among the country's most exotic resorts, and it's on one of Placencia's best beaches. Furnishings, art, and most of the construction materials were selected in Bali by Coppola and his wife. The two-bedroom villas have not one or two, but three bathrooms (two Japanese-style ones indoors and one in a walled outdoor garden). You'll be assigned a walkie-talkie–carrying "houseman" who will see to any requests, including a massage from a resident Thai masseuse. The open-air restaurant is great for pizza (baked in a wood-burning oven), seafood, and Neibaum-Coppola wines, and a second restaurant is planned. Try to get a seafront cabana to catch the breeze, as there's no air-conditioning. ⊠ *Placencia Village* ☎ *800/746–3743 in U.S. and Canada* ⊕ *www.blancaneauxlodge. com* ➪ *14 cabanas* ⚖ *Restaurant, fans, 2 pools, beach, dive shop, boating, spa, shop, travel services; no a/c, no room phones, no room TVs* ⊟ *AE, MC, V* ◯ *CP.*

Fodor'sChoice
★

★ **$$$$** ⊡ **Chabil Mar Villas.** Chabil Mar means "beautiful sea" in Ketchi Mayan, and the sea and almost 400 feet of beach here are indeed gorgeous at this new gated condo development. The villas are tastefully designed and luxuriously furnished, down to wine corkscrews and service for eight. Although each unit is different, they're all upscale, with features such as marble floors, original art, and four-poster king beds. Every comfort and convenience is at hand, from broadband Internet to DVD players to washers and dryers. There's no restaurant, but you can have meals prepared and brought to your condo. ⊠ *Peninsula Rd. north of Placencia Village* ☎ *523/3606* 🖷 *523/3213* ⊕ *www.chabilmarvillas.com* ➪ *3 1- and 18 2-bedroom condos* ⚖ *Fans, kitchens, cable TV, DVDs, pool, beach, broadband Internet, travel services; no smoking* ⊟ *AE, MC, V* ◯ *CP.*

$–$$$ ⊡ **Saks at Placencia.** Formerly an iconic barefoot paradise called Kitty's Place, in 2005 this resort was taken over by new owners without any hotel experience. Although the grounds still look great, and the beach remains one of the peninsula's best, it's not quite what it once was. Saks offers a mixed bag of accommodations, from single rooms to studios and three seafront cottages, all now with air-conditioning. A two-bedroom suite, rented on a weekly basis (BZ$3360 in season) is an addition for 2006. The resort also rents several nearby houses by the week. ☒ *1½ mi (2½ km) north of Placencia* ☎ *523/3227* 🖷 *523/3226* ⊕ *sak-satplacencia.com* ⇱ *3 cottages, 1 suite, 4 rooms, 8 rental houses* ♤ *Restaurant, some kitchens, refrigerators, pool, beach, boating, bar, shop, laundry service, Internet room, travel services; no room phones, no TV in some rooms* ⊟ *AE, D, MC, V.*

$–$$$ 🏨 **South Waters Resort.** This new beachside resort has three condo units with full kitchens, air-conditioning, cable TV, DVD players, and walk-in closets. There are also four less-expensive rooms. The hotel's restaurant and bar, the Crow's Nest, is under a big thatch palapa with views of the sea. It has live entertainment at times and, with its ship's hull-shape bar, has become a popular drinking spot. Even the local Rotary Club meets here. ☒ *Near middle of Placencia Village, on beach* ☎ *523/3308* 🖷 *523/3208* ⊕ *www.southwatersresort.com* ⇱ *4 rooms, 3 suites* ♤ *Restaurant, fans, some kitchens, some refrigerators, beach, bar, travel services; no a/c in some rooms, no room phones, no TVs in some rooms* ⊟ *MC, V.*

$$ 🏨 **Mariposa Beach Suites.** Wings painted on posts in the gardenlike grounds signal that you've arrived at Mariposa (Spanish for "butterfly"). Owners Peter and Marcia Fox have converted the ground floor of their beachfront home into a brace of suites, each with a queen bed and kitchen. Pamela Braun, a Belize-based American artist, painted the Mayan decorations on the walls. Out back is a small cottage, and on the 175-foot beach are thatch palapas with hammocks for lounging. If you like, the Foxes will stock your kitchen with groceries. This is the opposite of a big resort, an appealing spot if you're searching for a home away from home. ☒ *1½ mi (2½ km) north of Placencia* ☎ *523/4069* 🖷 *523/4076* ⊕ *www.mariposabelize.com* ⇱ *2 suites, 1 cottage* ♤ *Fans, kitchens, beach, travel services; no a/c, no room phones, no room TVs* ⊟ *MC, V.*

$ 🏨 **Harry's Cozy Cabanas.** Harry Eiley's three varnished-wood cabanas in the "Bakader" area with screened porches are as nice as Harry is, though they don't have quite as much character. Each has a kitchenette with a refrigerator. The hotel is in a quiet area away from the main part of the village. ☒ *Placencia Harbor* ☎ *523/3155* ✎ *harbaks@yahoo.com* ♤ *Fans, kitchenettes; no a/c, no room phones, no room TVs* ⊟ *MC, V.*

★ $ 🏨 **Tradewinds.** If you're yearning for a cottage right on the beach but don't want to spend a lot of money, then this little cottage colony is for you. Five cabins, painted in Caribbean pastels, are small but pleasant. They have the best spot in the village, secluded about 20 feet from the sea at the peninsula's south point. ☒ *South Point, Placencia* ☎ *523/3122* ⇱ *5 cabins* ♤ *Fans, refrigerators, beach, snorkeling; no a/c, no room phones, no room TVs* ⊟ *MC, V.*

¢–$ 🏨 **Seaspray Hotel.** There's no whirlpools or room service at this blue-and-white, wooden hotel. You just get a clean room, not far from the water, at a fair price. Your choice of rooms includes budget ones in the back to rooms with a porch and sea views. There's one cabin with a porch and kitchenette, about 30 feet from the sea. ☒ *Near middle of*

Placencia Village ☎ *523/3148* 🖷 *523/3364* ⊕ *www.seasprayhotel.com* 🛏 *19 rooms, 1 cabin* ♻ *Restaurant, fans, some kitchenettes, some re-frigerators; no a/c, no room phones, no room TVs* 🖃 *AE, D, MC, V.*

¢ 🖽 **Lydia's Guest House.** For cheap and cheerful, plus friendly and clean, stay at this budget guesthouse in Placencia Village. Many guests become regulars, coming back again and again. You can use the refrigerator and basic shared kitchen to prepare your meals. Owner Lydia Villanueva also manages several nearby rental houses and apartments, if you need more space. ⊠ *North end of Placencia Village* ☎ *523/3117* 🖷 *523/3354* ⊕ *www.placencia.com/members/lydias.html* 🛏 *8 rooms, all with shared bath* ♻ *Fans; no a/c, no room phones, no room TVs* 🖃 *MC, V.*

¢ 🖽 **Manatee Inn.** Run by a friendly young Czech couple, the Manatee Inn is good value for your money. The rooms on the second floor of this wood-frame, two-story lodge are simply furnished, extremely clean, and have hardwood floors and private baths. Larger apartments, perfect for families, are on the first floor. The beach is a couple hundred feet away. ⊠ *At north end of Placencia Village* 🖷🖷 *523/4083* ⊕ *www.manateeinn. com* 🛏 *6 rooms, 2 apartments* ♻ *Fans; no a/c, no room phones, no TV in some rooms* 🖃 *AE, MC, V.*

Vacation Rental Houses

In addition to hotels and beach resorts, Placencia has a growing number of vacation rentals, private homes, and apartments that are available on a weekly, sometimes daily, basis. Among these are **Colibri Beach Villa** (☎ 523/3125 ⊕ www.colibribelize.com), a lovely efficiency apartment at the north end of Placencia Village, with furniture and fixtures from Italy, BZ$340 a night; **Captain's House** (☎ 523/4018 ⊕ www.destinationsbelize.com), a three-bedroom house on the beach on the north end of Placencia village, constructed almost entirely of mahogany (BZ$400 a night or BZ$2,500 weekly); **Las Amigas** (☎ No phone ⊕ www.lasamigasbelize.com), two cabanas near the water in the village, which has kitchenettes, bedroom, and veranda (BZ$800 weekly); and **Casa del Sol** (☎ No phone ⊕ www.casadelsolbelize.com), one of the most luxurious houses on the peninsula, with swimming pool, beach, and four bedrooms and four baths, renting for BZ$1,400 a night (one- and two-bedroom sections of it are also available, starting at BZ$500 a night).

Nightlife

Nightlife in Placencia is generally limited to drinking at a handful of local bars, although you may hear live music on weekends at the Tipsy Tuna or J-Byrds.

Crows Nest (⊠ At South Waters Resort, Placencia Village ☎ 523/3412) is in an open-air thatch palapa with a nautical theme. The bar, made to look like part of a ship's hull, is a pleasant spot to sip a cold one with a view of the water.

J-Byrds Bar (⊠ At docks, Placencia Village ☎ 523/3412) attracts a fairly hard-drinking crowd, and there's a dance party on Friday nights and karaoke on Saturday.

At **Sugar Reef** (⊠ Placencia Village, on west side on canal ☎ 523/ 3289) local expats congregate for drinks and a bite to eat. Wednesday is karaoke night, and Saturday afternoon you can play in a horseshoe tournament.

The popular **Tipsy Tuna Sports Bar** (⊠ Placencia Village, on beach ☎ No phone) has live music some weekend nights, and you can always shoot pool or watch sports on a big-screen TV.

The Outdoors

Fishing

The fly-fishing on the flats off the cayes east of Placencia is some of Belize's best. This is one of the top areas in the world for permit. The area from Dangriga south to Gladden Caye is called "Permit Alley," and the mangrove lagoons off Punta Ycacos and other points south of Placencia are also terrific permit fisheries. You'll encounter plentiful tarpon— they flurry 10 deep in the water at times—as well as snook. You can also catch king mackerel, barracuda, wahoo, and cubera snapper. However, a lingering impact of Hurricane Iris in 2001 is that there are no longer any good bonefish flats close to shore at Placencia. Bonefish are still around, but they're now several miles away, off the cayes.

Fishing guides in Placencia are down-to-earth, self-taught guys who have fished these waters for years. They use small skiffs called pangas. The many excellent guides in Placencia include Wyatt Cabral, Julian Cabral, Egbert Cabral, Bruce Leslie, Eworth Garbutt, Daniel Cabral, Dermin Shivers, and Arthur Vernon. For more information and help matching a local guide to your specific needs, get in touch with **Mary Toy at Destinations Belize** (☎ 523/4018 ⊕ www.destinationsbelize.com). You may also want to talk with **Wyatt Cabral** (☎ 523/3534 ⊕ www.wyattsfishing. com). He's a native of Placencia who is considered one of the best fly-fishing guides. Another well-known fly-fishing guide is **Julian Cabral** (☎ 610/1068). Or contact **Bill Kiene at Kiene's Fly Shop** (☎ 916/486–9958, 800/400–0359 in U.S. ⊕ www.kiene.com), who has been to Placencia many times and is very familiar with fishing conditions here.

Most of the better hotels also can arrange guides, many of whom pair with specific hotels. For example, Arthur Vernon works almost exclusively for Turtle Inn.

Expect to pay around BZ$500 to BZ$750 for a full day of fly-fishing, spincasting, or trolling. That includes your guide, boat, and lunch. If you're on a budget, you can rent a canoe and try fishing the Placencia lagoon on your own, where you may catch snook, barracuda, and possibly other fish.

The guides usually provide trolling gear for free, but they charge about BZ$40 a day for light spincasting tackle gear, and you may be happier with your own spinning gear. If you're serious about fly-fishing, of course you'll want to bring your own gear. For fly-fishing for snook, permit, and tarpon, the experts recommend you bring a 9/10 weight rod, 9-foot, 20-pound leader (80-pound shock leader for tarpon), clear slowsinking line, and extra spool weight-forward floating line. Bring Clouser Half and Half, Berke's Juvineel, Cockroach, Black Death, Bluewater Mullet, Bauer's Fur Crab, Palometa Crab, Del's Merkin, Mangrove Critter, and other flies. For bonefish, you'll want a 7- to 9-weight rod, 7- to 9-weight floating line, and Boggle Head, Bonefish Bitters, and Flash Shrimp flies.

If you fish with live bait, the primary baitfish are silversides, shrimp, and crab. Lures and plastic baits should mimic these baitfish.

For reef and tarpon spin fishing, you'll need some fairly heavy reels, such as a Penn Spinfisher 5500 or 6500 Saltwater Spinning Reel with 25-pound test line. For tarpon, bring gummy minnows, in all colors. For bones, bring a Penn 4500 SS or similar with 6- to 10-pound test line. Leave your surf rod at home, as it will be of little use in Placencia. Don't forget to bring polarized sunglasses, a good fishing hat, insect repellent, lots of sunscreen and lip salve, and, if you're wading, thick-soled flats boots.

Sailing

The Moorings (⊠ Placencia Harbor, Placencia ☎ 888/952–8420 in U.S. ⊕ www.moorings.com) offers bareboat catamaran charters, with a week's sailing going for around BZ$8,000 to BZ$14,000. **Next Wave Sailing** (⊠ Placencia Harbor, Placencia ☎ 523/3391 ⊕ www. nextwavesailing.com) offers day and sunset cruises, with snorkeling, along with private charters, on a 50-foot catamaran. Day sails are BZ$160 per person and include drinks, lunch, and snacks. Sunset cruise is BZ$90. **Talisman** (⊠ Placencia Harbor, Placencia) is a 52-foot ketch offering day sailing trips for BZ$240 per person or longer trips from BZ$540 to BZ$650 including meals and drinks. **TMM Placencia** (⊠ Placencia Harbor, Placencia ☎ 800/633–0155 in U.S. ⊕ www.sailtmm.com), also in San Pedro, expanded into Placencia in 2003. Rates vary, depending on boat type and time of year, but range from BZ$5,400 to more than BZ$18,000 a week, not including provisions, cruising fee (BZ$30 per person), and incidentals. Skippers and cooks are each an additional BZ$200 per day.

Scuba Diving

This far south, the reef is as much as 20 mi (33 km) offshore, necessitating boat rides of at least 45 minutes to reach dive sites. Because this part of the reef has fewer cuts and channels, it's also more difficult to get out to the seaward side, where you'll find the best diving. As a result, most of the diving in this region is done from offshore cayes, which are surrounded by small reefs, usually with gently sloping drop-offs of about 80–100 feet. This isn't the place for spectacular wall dives—you're better off staying in the north or heading out to the atolls. Near Moho Caye, southeast of Placencia, you'll find brilliant red-and-yellow corals and sponges that rarely appear elsewhere in Belize. Whale sharks, gentle giants of the sea, appear off Placencia, in the Gladden Spit area, in late spring and early summer. You can snorkel or dive with them on day trips (around BZ$160–BZ$300) from Placencia. The best time to see whale sharks is three or four days before and after a full moon, April through early June.

Diving costs a little more in Placencia than elsewhere. All-day trips, including two-tank dive, all gear, and lunch, run BZ$150–BZ$210. Snorkeling is about BZ$100–BZ$120 for a trip that lasts almost all day.

Most of the larger resorts, like the Inn at Robert's Grove and Turtle Inn, have good dive shops and also offer snorkel trips at competitive prices. Brian Young runs the respected **Seahorse Dive Shop** (☎ 523/3166). For snorkeling trips and gear there's **Ocean Motion** (☎ 523/3363), on the sidewalk in the heart of Placencia Village (by the grocery store).

In any event, keep an ear out for weather warnings. In 2005 a party of Americans didn't heed small-craft warnings and managed to find a dive shop that would take them out. The boat had problems, and the divers spent long hours in the water. One young woman died, and the dive operator lost his license for life.

THE SOUTHERN COAST ESSENTIALS

Transportation

BY AIR

There are more than 20 flights daily between Belize City and Placencia. Both Tropic Air and Maya Island Air fly from Belize City (BZ$140 one-way from the municipal airport, BZ$160 from the international airport). The airstrip is about 2 mi(3 km) north of Placencia's center, so you'll probably want to take a taxi (BZ$10 from the center of town) if your hotel doesn't provide a shuttle.

The same airlines also fly from Belize City to Dangriga (around BZ$70 from the municipal airport, BZ$100 from the international airport). Maya Island Air also has flights to Savannah airstrip across the Placencia Lagoon in Big Creek (about BZ$150 from municipal airport) and will stop at the airstrip near Kanantik on demand. There's no airstrip at Hopkins. If going there, fly to Dangriga.

You'll generally fly in small turbine or prop aircraft, such as the 13-passenger Cessna Caravan C208. Some flights from Belize City make multiple stops—at Dangriga, Placencia, and sometimes Big Creek—as they fly south to Punta Gorda, while others are nonstop. In any event, the total time you'll spend in the airplane is short, less than an hour to Placencia.
Maya Island Air ✉ Placencia airstrip ☎ 523/3475 ⊕ www.mayaairways.com. **Tropic Air** ✉ Placencia airstrip ☎ 523/3410 ⊕ www.tropicair.com.

BY BOAT & FERRY

There are no scheduled boat or ferry services from Belize City to points along the Southern Coast, nor are there any scheduled water taxis or ferries between those points or to offshore cayes. However, there's a scheduled water taxi, a small boat named the *Hokey Pokey,* between Placencia Village and Mango Creek and Independence, two adjacent villages on the west side of Placencia Lagoon. With a combined population of about 3,000, the villages of Mango Creek and Independence are home to residents who work at Big Creek, a nearby deep-water port that ships bananas, citrus, and, now, oil from Belize's new wells in Spanish Lookout, Cayo. There's little of interest to most tourists here. Currently the boat departs the fuel dock in Placencia Village at 10 AM and 4 PM and 5 PM. From the Kingfisher dock in Mango Creek it departs at 6:30 AM, 7:30 AM, 8 AM, 2:30 PM, and 4:30 PM. One-way fare is BZ$5. The schedule changes frequently, so ask locally.

From Placencia, a weekly boat, the Gulf Cruza, runs to Puerto Cortes, Honduras, with a stop in Big Creek across the lagoon to clear immigration and customs. The boat departs Placencia at 9:30 AM Friday, arriving in Honduras at 2 PM. It returns the next day from Puerto Cortes at 10 AM, arriving in Placencia at 2 PM. Fare is BZ$100 per person one-way. You can purchase tickets and make reservations at the BTIA Placencia Tourism Center.

From Dangriga, another boat charter runs twice weekly to Puerto Cortes. The *Nesymein Neydy,* a 47-foot cabin cruiser that can accommodate 60 people, and *Nesymein Neydy II,* a 32-foot cruiser that can carry up to 30, depart from the North Riverside in Dangriga at 11 AM Wednesday and Saturday, returning from Puerto Cortes from the fish market at 9 AM on Monday and Friday. The trip takes about three hours and costs BZ$100 per person one-way.

The boat trips to Puerto Cortes can be very rough and wet. If you're prone to seasickness, take antinausea medications and avoid the trip entirely in stormy weather.

Also from Dangriga, boats go out daily to Tobacco Caye. There are no fixed schedules, but the boats generally leave around 9 to 9:30 AM, and the fare is BZ$35 per person one-way. Ask at the Riverside Café.

🚩 **Hokey Pokey** ⊠ Placencia ☎ 523/2376. **Gulf Cruza** ⊠ Placencia ☎ 523/4045. **Nesymein Neydy Charter Boats** ⊠ North Riverside, Dangriga ☎ 522/3227 ⊕ www. belizenet.com/boatcharters/index.html#schedules.

BY BUS

As of this writing, the Belizean bus system is in transition. The largest Belize bus company, Novelo's, closed in 2005. Smaller bus companies are scrambling to replace Novelo's and its subsidiaries, Southern Transport and Northern Transport. In the south, James Bus Line continues to run from Belize City via Belmopan to Dangriga and Independence and then Punta Gorda. Schedules are subject to change, but James Bus Line has about five to six buses daily, with departures starting at 5:30 AM and ending at 5:30 PM. Two of the buses stop in Placencia, while the other buses stop in Independence across the lagoon. *(See*Hokey Pokey *ferry schedule above, in the Boat & Ferry Travel section.)*

With connections, the trip from Belize City to Dangriga and Hopkis is three to four hours; Placencia is around five to six hours or more, depending on the number of stops. Buses are usually old U.S. school buses or ancient Greyhound buses, are often crowded, and don't have air-conditioning or rest rooms. You'll arrive much more refreshed if you arrive by air—the flight's less than an hour.

The main bus stop in Placencia is in the village near the Shell station. Some buses also stop at Hopkins, near the T-intersection from the Southern Highway. The bus station in Dangriga is seven blocks south of town on the main road, near the Texaco and Shell stations.

🚌 **James Bus Line** ✉ 7 King St., Punta Gorda ☎ 702/2049.

BY CAR

To get to Placencia, head southeast from Belmopan on the Hummingbird Highway. The highway is one of Belize's best roads, as well as its most scenic. On your right rise the jungle-covered Maya Mountains, largely free of signs of human habitation except for the occasional field of corn or beans. As you approach Dangriga you'll see large citrus groves.

Although the so-called Manatee Highway or Coastal Road (it actually runs several miles from the coast), which begins at Mile 30 of the Western Highway, is a shortcut to Dangriga and points south, the road is unpaved. It's dusty in dry weather and muddy after rains. Occasionally the wood bridges on the road wash out. The road is so accident-prone that some car rental companies prohibit renters from driving the road, and others increase the deductible you pay if you have a wreck on the road. Our advice: take the Hummingbird Highway.

The Southern Highway is now beautifully paved from Dangriga south, except for a short section near Golden Stream. The turnoff to Hopkins is at Mile 10 of the Southern Highway, and the turn to Placencia is at Mile 22.2. From the Southern Highway to Placencia most of the 25-mi (42-km) road is unpaved and can be treacherous after rains, even for four-wheel-drive vehicles.

There are now two gas stations in Placencia Village, and one at Riversdale. Dangriga has several gas stations.

One small local outfit, Barefoot Rentals, rents cars in Placencia. Rates are around BZ$160 a day for a Geo Tracker or Isuzu Trooper. Barefoot will drop the car to you at your hotel or the Placencia airstrip. Budget and other rental agencies in Belize City will deliver a car to Placencia, Hopkins, or Dangriga for a fee of around BZ$100–BZ$140.

🚗 **Barefoot Rentals** ✉ Placencia ☎ 607/5125 🖷 523/3594 ⊕ www.barefootrentals.net.

BY TAXI

If you need a ride to the airport in Dangriga, call Neal's Taxi. Fare from downtown to the airstrip at the town's north end costs about BZ$6. Taxis are more expensive in Placencia, given the relatively short distances involved. It's BZ$40 one-way for one or two persons and BZ$20 per person for three or more from Placencia Village to the north end of the peninsula (where Calico Jack's and the Placencia are); BZ$30 one-way from Placencia Village to Maya Beach for one or two persons and BZ$15 per person for three or more; BZ$10 for one or two persons and BZ$5 per person for three or more from Placencia Village to the airstrip. Your hotel can arrange a taxi for you, or call Percy Neal or Samuel Burgess.

A shuttle van service runs from time to time up and down the peninsula. When the van operates, fare is around BZ$4 per person. Ask at your hotel if it's running, but don't count on it.

🚩 **Neal's Taxi** ⊠ 1 St. Vincent St., Dangriga ☎ 522/3309. **Percy Neal** ⊠ Placencia ☎ 523/3202. **Samuel Burgess** ⊠ Placencia ☎ 523/5125.

Contacts & Resources

BANKS & EXCHANGE SERVICES

There are now two banks in Placencia. Atlantic Bank has a new office on the Peninsula Road just north of Placencia Village, and Scotia Bank is in the village. The Atlantic Bank office has an ATM that accepts foreign ATM cards on the Visa Electron network.

Belize Bank in Dangriga accepts foreign-issued ATM cards on the PLUS, CIRRUS and Visa Electron networks. First Caribbean International Bank in Dangriga has an ATM that accepts foreign cards on the Visa Electron network. There are no banks in Hopkins.

ATMs in Belize frequently are off-line or out of money, so don't depend completely on your ATM card.

🚩 **Banks Atlantic Bank** ⊠ Peninsula Rd., Placencia ☎ 523/3386. **Belize Bank** ⊠ 24 St. Vincent St., Dangriga ☎ 522/2903. **First Caribbean International Bank** ⊠ Commerce St., Dangriga ☎ 522/2015. **Scotia Bank** ⊠ Main St., Placencia ☎ 523/3277.

EMERGENCIES

Although Placencia has a small medical clinic with a nurse, plus an acupuncturist, a part-time chiropractor, and a natural healer, and Hopkins has a medical clinic, for serious medical attention you should go to Dangriga or Belize City. A pharmacy with very limited supplies is at Wallen's store in Placencia.

🚩 **Hospitals Dangriga Regional Hospital** ⊠ Stann Creek District Hwy., Dangriga ☎ 522/2078. **Placencia Medical Clinic** ⊠ In center of village near primary school, Placencia ☎ 523/3326.

INTERNET, MAIL & SHIPPING

The Placencia post office is on the second floor of a wooden building at the south end of the sidewalk. It's usually open 8:30–noon and 1–4 weekdays. The Dangriga post office is near the Bonefish Hotel, at the south end of town. Currently there's no post office in Hopkins.

🚩 **Dangriga** ⊠ Near Bonefish Hotel ☎ 522/2035. **Placencia** ⊠ South end of sidewalk ☎ 523/3104. **De Tatch** ⊠ In center of village, Placencia ☎ 503/3385. **Purple Space Monkey** ⊠ Peninsula Road, across from soccer village, Placencia ☎ 523/4094. **Sittee River Internet** ⊠ Sittee River Village ☎ 603/8358. **Val's Laundry** ⊠ Mahogany and Sharp Sts., Dangriga ☎ 502/3324.

Many resorts on the Southern Coast now offer Internet access, either wireless or in Internet rooms. In addition, there are several Internet cafés in Placencia Village, and in Dangriga and near Hopkins. You'll pay around BZ$10 an hour for access.

TOURS

Altogether, Placencia has about 75 licensed tour guides. Most of the guides, except the fishing guides, work on a contract basis for resorts or tour operators. These tour guides and operators offer dive and snorkel trips to Laughing Bird or other cayes and to the barrier reef, wildlife tours to Monkey River, birding tours to Red Bank, hiking trips to Cockscomb Basin Wildlife Sanctuary, and excursions to Mayan ruins such as Mayflower, Nim Li Punit, or Lubaantun.

The larger resorts on the peninsula, including Inn at Robert's Grove, Turtle Inn, Nautical Inn, Rum Point Inn, and others, offer a variety of tours and trips, using tour guides they have come to trust. ⇨ *See* Where to Stay & Eat sections, *above,* for contact information.

Mary Toy's Destinations Belize is a full-service tour and travel operation, offering fishing, boating, sailing, and other trips with some of the best guides in the region, along with hotel reservations. Mary is a former attorney from St. Louis who left the practice of law to practice her fishing and beachcombing skills in Belize. Other tour operators include Caribbean Tours and Joy Tours.

For first-time visitors, taking a couple of sea and land tours is a good way to become familiar with what the area offers. If you have a rental car, you can do some of the trips, such as to Cockscomb, Mayflower, and the ruins near Punta Gorda, on your own. To book tours and trips, check with your hotel or walk along the sidewalk in Placencia Village, where several of the tour operators have small shops. You can also check with the Belize Tourism Industry Association (BTIA) visitor information office. You'll probably pay a little less by booking in the village instead of at your hotel, but the savings may not be worth the effort.

For the more adventurous traveler, Toadal Adventures, one of the top operators on the Southern Coast, has excellent biking, hiking, and kayaking tours. Aahsum Adventures recently split off from Toadal Adventures and also offers adventure tours.

Day trips to Nim Li Punit and Lubaantun Mayan sites near Punta Gorda cost around BZ$150–BZ$160 per person, while day trips to the Mayflower ruins and waterfalls run about BZ$120. Half-day snorkeling trips inside the reef, to Laughing Bird Caye and other snorkel spots, are around BZ$100 to BZ$110. A full day of snorkeling on the reef is around BZ$120–BZ$130. Boat trips to Monkey River are around BZ$90, while a boat excursion on the Placencia Lagoon to look for manatees is around BZ$80. Cockscomb trips run about BZ$60. Most full-day trips include a picnic lunch. If you're going to an area with an admission fee, such as Cockscomb, the fee is additional.

Aahsum Adventures ✉ Placencia ☎ 523/3159 ⊕ www.aahsumbelize.com. **Caribbean Tours** ✉ Placencia ☎ 253/3481 ⊕ www.ctbelize.com. **Destinations Belize** ✉ Placencia ☎ 253/4018 ⊕ www.destinationsbelize.com. **Joy Tours** ✉ Placencia ☎ 253/3325

⊕ www.belizewithjoy.com. **Toadal Adventures Belize** ⊠ Point Placencia, Placencia ☎ 253/3207 ⊕ www.toadaladventure.com.

VISITOR INFORMATION

The Placencia office of the Belize Tourism Industry Association is in a building near the Shell gas station at the village's south end. The BTIA publishes the *Placencia Breeze,* an informative monthly newspaper and has a very helpful Web site listing all accommodations, restaurants, and bars, ⊕ www.placencia.com. Another extremely helpful site on Placencia is put together by local resident Mary Toy, ⊕ www.destinationsbelize.com. Hopkins has several interesting Web sites put together by local residents, including ⊕ www.hopkinsbelize.com and ⊕ www.cometohopkins.com. 🚩 **Belize Tourism Industry Association** ⊠ Point Placencia, Placencia ☎ 523/4045.

Toledo & the Deep South

WORD OF MOUTH

"There are trips daily from Placencia to Lubaantun and Nim Li Punit, both in the Maya villages of the Toledo district. I think both are impressive. Lubaantun for its beauty and Nim Li Punit for its extraordinary stelae."

—Katie Valk

By Lan Sluder **FOR MANY YEARS ILL-MAINTAINED ROADS,** spotty communications, and the country's highest annual rainfall—as much as 180 to 200 inches—kept Belize's southernmost region off-limits to all but the most adventurous of travelers. The precipitation hasn't changed (you'll need boots and an umbrella in the rainy season), but with improvements to the Southern Highway—all of the highway has been beautifully paved, except for a short stretch near Golden Stream—and the opening of new lodges and hotels, the riches of Toledo District (pronounced with a short "e," Tow-leh-doh, by the locals) are finally becoming accessible.

Toledo is the only part of Belize that has a genuine rain forest, and its canopy of trees conceals a plethora of wildlife, including jaguars, margays, and tapirs, and an assortment of tropical birds. The area's rich Mayan heritage is just being unearthed, with archaeologists at work at Pusilha, Nim Li Punit, Uxbenká, and elsewhere. Contemporary Maya—mainly Mopan and Ketchi—still live in villages around the district, as they have for centuries, along with the Garífuna, Creoles, East Indians, and others who constitute the Toledo population of 25,000.

Don't expect to come to Toledo and lounge on the sand. The area doesn't have good beaches: the waters of the Gulf of Honduras are almost invariably muddy from silt deposited by numerous rivers flowing from the Maya Mountains. What *can* you expect? Exceptional fishing (Toledo has one of the world's best permit fisheries) and cayes off the coast that are well worth exploring. The closest are the Snake Cayes; farther out are the Sapodilla Cayes, the largest of which is Hunting Caye. A horseshoe-shape bay at the caye's eastern end has beaches of white coral where turtles nest in late summer.

History

The Maya, mostly a group called the Manche Chol Maya, established sizeable ceremonial centers and midsize cities in Toledo beginning almost 2,000 years ago. Uxbenká is one of the oldest centers, dating to AD 200. In the Classic period, Lubaantun, which flourished in the 8th and 9th centuries, is thought to have been the administrative center of the region, but for reasons still unclear it was abandoned not long after this. In Southern Belize as elsewhere in Mesoamerica, the Mayan civilization went into a long, slow decline beginning a little more than 1,000 years ago.

Spanish conquistadores, including Hernándo Cortés himself in 1525, came through Southern Belize in the early 16th century, but the Maya resisted the Spanish and, later, Britain's attempts to control and tax them. The British, who arrived as loggers, tried put the Maya in "reservations" and eventually, in the 18th and 19th centuries, moved nearly the entire Manche Chol population to the highlands of Guatemala.

In the late 19th century, groups of Mopan and Ketchi Maya began moving into Southern Belize from Guatemala, establishing more than 50 villages around Toledo. Around the same time, Garífuna from Honduras settled in Punta Gorda, Barranco, and Punta Negra.

TOP REASONS TO GO

RAIN FORESTS

The greenest, lushest jungles in Belize are in Toledo, fed by heavy rains and temperatures that stay mostly above 70°F. Bright yellow-and-orange Lobster Claw, Red Ginger, masses of pink on Mayflower trees, and orchids of all colors splash the emerald green landscape of the Deep South in wild profusion. Waterfalls and caves add mystery, while Scarlet-rumped Tanagers, Black-headed Trogans, Green Kingfishers, and Roseate Spoonbill (only a few colorful examples of the hundreds of species of birds here) add their trills to the rain forest cacophony.

OUTPOST ATMOSPHERE

Punta Gorda has that end-of-the-road feel, that sense that this is the last outpost on Earth. Yes, the Southern Highway does end here—but it's more than that. Here you get the feeling that even in today's world of 6 billion people, there are still places where you could, if you needed to, hide out for awhile and not be found. Be sure to bring a Graham Greene novel, or something by Conrad.

FISHING

Among serious anglers, Southern Belize has a reputation for having one of the world's great permit fisheries, and for its large populations of tarpon and bonefish. The flats off Punta Ycacos are prime permit and bonefish grounds, and freshwater lagoons near Punta Negra hold snook, small tarpon, and other fish.

MAYA & GARÍFUNA CULTURE

Other areas of Belize (not to mention Guatemala and Honduras) may have more spectacular ruins than Toledo, although several of the sites here, including Nim Li Punit and Lubaantun, have unusual architecture not seen anywhere else in the region. But where the Deep South shines is in its contemporary Mayan culture. Dozens of Mopan and Ketchi villages exist much as they have for centuries, even millennia. You can visit the villages and even stay awhile in guesthouses or homestay programs. There are also the Garífuna villages of Punta Negra and Barranco and the town of Punta Gorda (PG). Settlement Day (November 19) celebrations in PG are beginning to rival those in Dangriga.

6

Southern Belize, with its rainy conditions and remoteness from Belize City, has languished economically for most of the 20th century. The paved Southern Highway may help boost tourism in the region in coming years.

EXPLORING TOLEDO & THE DEEP SOUTH

The main road to the Deep South is the newly paved Southern Highway, which runs 100 mi (164 km) from the intersection of the Hummingbird Highway to Punta Gorda town. Only a 9-mi (15-km) section, from Golden Stream at Mile 68.6 to Big Falls at Mile 77.6, is unpaved and rough going.

As you travel south on the Southern Highway, the Great Southern Pine Ridge is on your right, starting at about Mile 55. Farther in the distance are the Maya Mountains. On your left is the Caribbean Sea, and farther south, below Punta Negra, the Gulf of Honduras.

Branching off the Southern Highway are mostly unpaved roads, some barely more than muddy trails, that go to small villages. On the Southern Highway about 33 km (20 mi) north of Punta Gorda, at about Mile 83, you'll come to an intersection. If you turn left you'll stay on the Southern Highway to PG; if you turn right on the San Antonio Road, you'll go to San Antonio Village and other Mayan villages. To reach PG from the land side, continue on to Mile 95, turn right on Saddleback Road, and go 5 mi (8 km). To enter from the Bay of Honduras side, turn left and go the same distance.

Requena's Charter Service & Water Taxi (☎ 722/2070) runs scheduled water taxis from PG to Puerto Barrios, Guatemala. The hour to hour-and-a-half trips begin daily at 9 AM; they return at 2 PM. Fares are BZ$35 one-way, plus a BZ$7.50 government conservation fee.

Numbers in the text correspond to numbers in the margin & on the Toledo & Deep South Map.

Safety

Punta Gorda is generally a safe, friendly town. With normal precautions, you should have no problem walking around, even after dark. The nearby Mayan villages are also relatively free of crime. Guatemala's Caribbean coast, just a short boat ride away, has a reputation for lawlessness, which can occasionally spill over into Toledo.

When to Go

June through September is the peak of the rainy season in Toledo. Unless you love a good thunderstorm come sometime from December to April.

About the Hotels

The entire Toledo District has only about 30 hotels, most of them in and around Punta Gorda. Most are small and owner-run. You can usually show up without reservations and look for a place that suits you. Clean rooms are under BZ$100, and for BZ$150 to BZ$200 you can stay at a charming small inn.

About the Restaurants

With relatively few tourists coming to the region, and most local residents unable to afford to eat out regularly, restaurants in Toledo often are here today and gone tomorrow. Restaurants that do make it are usually simple affairs, mostly basic spots serving local fish and staples like stew chicken with beans and rice. Prices are low—you'll rarely pay more than BZ$20 for dinner. Nearly all the restaurants in Toledo are in PG.

PUNTA GORDA

❶ *102 mi (164 km) south of Placencia.*

Most journeys south begin in the region's administrative center, Punta Gorda. PG (as it's affectionately known) isn't your typical tourist destination. Though it has a wonderful setting on the Gulf of Honduras, it has no real beaches. There are few shops of interest to visitors, only one tiny museum, and little nightlife. Don't expect many tourist services.

So why, you ask, come to PG? First, simply because it isn't on the main tourist track. The accoutrements of mass tourism are still, refreshingly, missing here. Schoolchildren may wave at you, and residents on the street may strike up a conversation with you. Also, with several new hotels to choose from, it's a comfortable base from which to visit the surrounding Mayan villages, the offshore cayes, and the high bush of the Deep South.

Founded in 1867 by Confederate immigrants from the United States and later settled by missionaries, Punta Gorda once had 12 sugar estates, each with its own mill. After World War II, Great Britain built an important military base here, but when that closed in 1994, the linchpin of the local economy was yanked out. With some increase in tourist dollars, and a growing interest by foreigners in real estate here, PG is starting to pick up again, but the town maintains a frontier atmosphere.

In keeping with its evangelical origins, many PG visitors are missionaries who vie for the souls of the Maya by offering them free dentistry or medicine. But on market days—Monday, Wednesday, Friday, and Saturday, with Wednesday and Saturday usually being the largest—the town comes to life with vendors from nearby Mayan villages and even from Guatemala. They pack the downtown market area with colorful fruit and vegetable stands. Fresh fish also are sold in a building at the market, daily except Sunday, and for a small fee you can have your fish cleaned.

☪ If you're interested in learning more about the Creole culture, stop by the **Kriol Museum.** It's just a room in the house of singer Lila Vernon, but it has some interesting displays about Creole history and music, along with some items typical of Creole households. FYI: Kriol is the spelling of Creole used by the National Kriol Council of Belize. ⊠ *6 Front St., Punta Gorda* ☎ *702/2140* ✉ *Donations accepted.*

The Outdoors

Punta Gorda and Toledo offer great opportunities for outdoor activities—fishing, diving, snorkeling, sea and river kayaking, and caving. The problem has been that due to the small number of visitors to the Deep South, and the limited number of tour operators, visitors often arrived to find that few tours were actually available, or if they were running, tended to cost much more than in other parts of the country. In late 2005 and early 2006, a group of hotels and tour operators, Toledo Tourism Partners, moved to remedy this by joining together to offer a regular series of fixed tours at a moderate cost, with specific tours and trips always running on specific days of the week (as long as there are a minimum of two persons booked on the trip). So now, on a stay of several days (assuming this works as it's expected to), you can be assured of getting specific tours. You can always add custom tours or trips, based on your own interests.

Hotels and tour operators involved in this program include TIDE Tours, TASTEE Tours, Sun Creek Lodge, Sea Front Inn, the Lodge at Big Falls, and others. The full-day trips usually involve a mix of activities, such as snorkeling and fishing. The specific tours are as follows, although the days, rates and tour descriptions may change:

Monday: Port Honduras Marine Reserve, with manatee and dolphin spotting, snorkeling, swimming, and fishing; BZ$186 per person

Tuesday: Blue Creek, with cave swimming and hiking; BZ$152 per person

Wednesday: Same as Monday

Thursday: Pueblo Viejo Mayan village, hiking, visiting a waterfall, and Dem Dats Doin' botanical gardens; BZ$168 per person

> **WORD OF MOUTH**
>
> "Belize has some of the best diving to be found anywhere, along with numerous Maya sites, caving, horses, birding, hiking, kayaking and canoeing and is it English-speaking."
>
> —Katie Valk

Friday: Canoe trip on Moho River, with visit to the Garífuna village of Barranco; BZ$160 per person

Saturday: Visit to Lubaantun Mayan site and Rio Blanco Park; BZ$168 per person

Sunday: Sapodilla Cayes, with snorkeling, fishing, and beach swimming; BZ$194 per person.

All Things Green

Hot springs, fresh-water lagoons, caves, and hiking trails dot the **Agua Caliente Wildlife Sanctuary,** a good-size nature preserve. You can fish here as well. ⊠ *About 13 mi west of Punta Gorda, From Punta Gorda, take Southern Hwy. 10 mi (16 km) north. Turn left on Laguna Rd. and go 3 mi (5 km). The trail to wildlife sanctuary begins in village. Ask a local resident to show you where it begins.*

Ever been fresh-water snorkeling? Check out the Bladen River in the **Bladen Forest Reserve.** The river snakes through the reserve, allowing for excellent kayaking, canoeing, swimming, and, yes, freshwater snorkeling. Tours are given by interns from the Belize Foundation for Research and Environmental Education (BFREE), which is on the reserve's grounds. To visit Bladen Forest Reserve, contact BFREE. ⊠ *Off Mile 59, Southern Hwy.* ☎ *614/3896* ⊕ *www.bfreebelize.net.*

One of the largest undisturbed tropical rain forest areas in Central America is the **Columbia Forest Reserve.** It's in a remote area north of San José Village, and the karst terrain—an area of irregular limestone in which erosion has produced sinkholes, fissures, and underground streams and caves—is difficult to navigate, so the only way to see this area is with a guide and with advance permission from the Belize Forestry Department. It has extremely diverse ecosystems because the elevation ranges from about 1,000 to over 3,000 feet, with sinkholes as deep as 800 feet. You'll find areas of true "high bush" here (old-growth tropical forest and parts that have never been logged at all). Much of the rich flora and fauna of this area has yet to be documented. For example, one brief 12-day expedition turned up 15 species of ferns never found before in Belize, along with several new species of palms, vines, and orchids. ⊠ *North of San José Village* ☎ *722/2765.*

Rio Blanco National Park is a tiny national park (105 acres) with a big waterfall. The Rio Blanco waterfall splashes over rough limestone boulders into a deep pool, which you can jump into for a refreshing swim. You reach the waterfall after hiking a well-marked trail. Upstream a short distance from the falls is a nice area for a picnic, shaded by trees and flowering bushes. ⊠ *30 mi (49 km) west of Punta Gorda between Santa Cruz and Santa Elena villages, on road to Jalacte.*

One of the wildest and most remote areas of Belize is the **Sarstoon-Temash National Park,** between the Temash and Sarstoon rivers in the far south of Toledo District on the border of Guatemala. Red mangroves grow along the river banks; animals and birds rarely seen in other parts of Belize, including white-faced capuchin monkeys, can be spotted here, along with jaguars (if you're lucky), ocelots, and tapirs. The only way to see this area is with a guide by boat. ⊠ *About 13 mi south of Punta Gorda by boat.*

Toledo Botanical Arboretum is an organic farm with a growing collection of fruit trees (now more than 50 varieties) and other local plants and trees. The farm and gardens are part of the Dem Dats Doin' organization run by Yvonne and Alfredo Villoria. For a tour, call in advance, or go with one of the Thursday tours (*see above*) that include a visit to the farm. ⊠ *1¼ mi (2 km) from turnoff to Lubaantun* ☎ *772/2470* 🖙 *BZ$10.*

Fishing

For bonefish and tarpon, head to the estuary flats in the Port Honduras marine reserve at the end of the Río Grande, or go northward to Punta Ycacos. In the Marine Reserve, anglers pay a day-park fee of BZ$20, or BZ$60 for three to seven days. There is no fee for the Punta Ycacos, unless you fish in the Port Honduras reserve. **El Pescador PG Resort** (☎ 722/0050, 800/242–2017 in U.S. ⊕ www.elpescadorpg.com) is the leading fishing lodge in Toledo and can provide good local guides. **Fish & Fun** (⊠ 7 Front St., Punta Gorda ☎ 702/0180), operated by Ovel Leonardo, runs snorkeling and fly-fishing trips to nearby rivers and the cayes. **John "Jackie" Young** (⊠ Front St., Punta Gorda ☎ 702/0061 ⊕ www.puntagordabelize.com/jackieyoung) runs fly-fishing and spin-casting trips in the Port Honduras Marine Reserve and also on Toledo rivers and lagoons. **TIDE Tours** (⊠ Prince and Main Sts., Punta Gorda ☎ 722/2129 ⊕ www.tidetours.com) offers six-night fishing and camping packages, including meals, camping gear, and air transfers from Belize City, for around BZ$3,400 per person.

Scuba Diving

This far south the reef has pretty much broken up, but individual cayes have their own small reef systems. The best of the bunch is at the Sapodilla cayes, seven cayes with great wall dives. Lime Caye in the Sapodillas has camping, and Hunting Caye has a lighthouse. The only drawback is that because they're 40 mi (64 km) off the coast, a day's dive trip costs around BZ$300 per person or more, depending on how many people go. The Snakes Cayes are closer in, about 30 km (18 mi) northwest of Punta Gorda. The four Snakes—East, West, South, and Middle—are so named because of boa constrictors that once inhabited the islands. They have several notable dive sites. **TIDE Tours** (⊠ Prince and Main Sts., Punta Gorda ☎ 722/2129 ⊕ www.tidetours.com) can arrange diving, snorkeling, and other trips to the Sapodilla and Snakes Cayes.

Snorkeling

The turquoise waters lapping up the shores of the usually deserted white-sand beach on Snake Caye are good for snorkeling. **TASTEE Tours** (⊠ Front St., Punta Gorda ☎ 722/2070) runs eight-day trips to the Port Honduras Marine Reserve that include manatee watching at Frenchman Lagoon, an island picnic, snorkeling around the Snake Cayes and Abalone Caye, and trolling for fish (either catch-and-release or for your dinner). Tours run Monday and Wednesday; cost is BZ$186 per person.

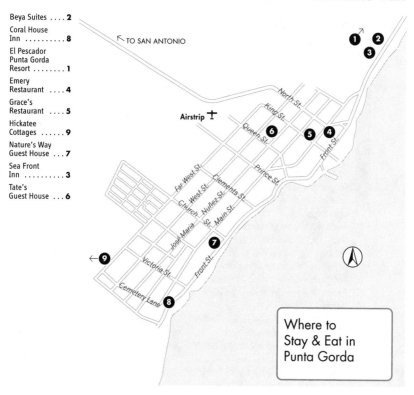

← TO SAN ANTONIO

Airstrip ✝

Where to
Stay & Eat in
Punta Gorda

TIDE Tours (✉ Prince and Main Sts., Punta Gorda ☎ 722/2129 ⊕ www.tidetours.com) runs full-day snorkeling trips to Snake Caye. For two people, it's BZ$250 per person; for four, it's BZ$142.

Where to Stay & Eat

$–$$ ✕ **Emery Restaurant.** When it's open (the proprietor sometimes closes it for weeks or months at a time), this is the best restaurant in town. The grilled fish is always fresh and delicious, and the expansive open-air section (but with a roof to keep out the rain) is pleasant. ✉ *North St.* ☎ *No phone* 🖃 *No credit cards.*

¢–$$ ✕ **Grace's.** An established spot, Grace's has genuine value and serves a hearty plate of beans and rice and other Belizean staples. Get a seat near the entrance and eye the town's street life. This is PG's best place for a full breakfast of eggs, bacon, fry jacks (a Belizean version of a sopaipilla) and, of course, beans. For dinner you can always get chicken, but you can usually get fresh fish, too. ✉ *19 Main St.* ☎ *702/2414* 🖃 *No credit cards.*

$$$ 🏨 **El Pescador Punta Gorda Resort.** El Pescador PG (associated with Am-
Fodor'sChoice bergris Caye's El Pescador) opened in 2002 to capitalize on the area's
★ fishing opportunities, but it's also trying to attract guests interested in

Belize's Multicultural Gumbo

The celebration of Belize's historic multiculturalism begins on its flag: the two strapping young men—one black and the other white—are woodcutters standing beneath a logwood tree. Under them is a Latin inscription: *sub umbra floreat*—"In the shade of this tree we flourish."

Belize is a rich gumbo of colors and languages. Creoles, once the majority, now make up only about one-fourth of the population. Creoles in Belize are descendants of slaves brought from Jamaica to work in the logging industry. By the early 18th century, people of African descent came to outnumber those of British origin in Belize. The two groups united early in the country's history to defeat a common enemy, the Spanish. Most of the Creole population today is concentrated in Belize City and Belize District, although there are predominantly Creole villages elsewhere, including the villages of Gales Point and Placencia. English is the country's official language and taught in school, although, an English dialect, Creole, is widely spoken.

Mestizos are the fastest growing group in Belize and make up almost one-half of the population. These are persons of mixed European and Maya heritage, typically speaking Spanish as a first language and English as a second. Some migrated to Belize from Mexico during the Yucatán Caste Wars of the mid-19th century. More recently, many "Spanish" (as they're often called in Belize) have moved from Guatemala or elsewhere in Central America. Mestizos are concentrated in northern and western Belize.

Numbering close to a million at the height of the Mayan kingdoms, the Maya today constitute only about one-tenth of the Belize 280,000 population. There are concentrations of Yucatec Maya in Corozal and Orange Walk districts, Mopan Maya in Toledo and Cayo districts, and also Ketchi Maya in about 30 villages in Toledo. Most speak their Mayan dialect, and either English or Spanish, or both.

About 1 in 20 Belizeans is a Garífuna. The Garinagu (the plural of Garífuna) are of mixed African and Carib Indian heritage. Most originally came to Belize from Honduras in the 1820s and 1830s. Dangriga and Punta Gorda are towns with large Garífuna populations, as are the villages of Seine Bight, Hopkins, and Barranco. Besides their own tongue—an Arawakan-based language with smatterings of West African words—many Garinagu speak English and Creole.

Other groups include several thousand Mennonites, sizable communities of East Indians, and Chinese, mostly from Taiwan and Hong Kong. Belize's original white populations were English, but today's "gringos" are mostly expats from the United States and Canada, with some from the United Kingdom. All these groups find in this tiny country a tolerant and amiable home.

Whatever the background of its citizens, Belize's population is young. More than two out of five Belizeans are under 15 years of age, and the median average age is around 19 years, more than 16 years younger than the median age in the United States.

other adventures. On 470 acres above the Rio Grande River (you can ride a small tram car to the bottom), the lodge has awesome views of the sea and jungle. Howler monkeys troop by regularly. After a day on a fishing skiff or exploring the Toledo rain forest, dive into the pool, then sup on fish and fresh vegetables from the lodge's farm. The spacious cottages have vaulted ceilings, tile floors, and ice-cold air-conditioning. All-inclusive fishing packages start at BZ$2600 per person for three days. ⊠ *5 mi (8 km) north of Punta Gorda* 🕭 *Box 135, Punta Gorda* ☎ *722/0050, 800/242–2017 in U.S.* 🖷 *722/0051* ⊕ *www.elpescadorpg.com* 🗘 *12 cottages* ⌂ *Dining room, fans, pool, fishing, billiards, bar, shops, travel services; no room phones, no room TVs* ▭ *MC, V.*

$ 🖭 **Beya Suites.** From the verandas on the second floor of this bright pink, waterfront hotel, you have expansive views of the Gulf of Honduras. Despite the name, the hotel has rooms rather than true suites, but they're modern, with tile floors, plaster walls, and air-conditioning. The Belizean-owned hotel has a restaurant and bar. ⊠ *Front St., #6 Hopeville, Punta Gorda* ☎ *722/2188* 🖷 *722/2509* ⊕ *www.beyasuites. com* 🗘 *6 rooms* ⌂ *Restaurant, fans, cable TV, bar, laundry service Internet, travel services; no room phones* ▭ *AE, MC, V.*

★ $ 🖭 **Coral House Inn.** Americans Rick and Darla Mallory renovated this 1938 British colonial-era house and turned it into one of the most pleasant small guesthouses in the country. It's near the sea at the end of Front Street, about as far south as you can go on paved roads in Belize. You'll recognize the house by coral-color paint and the vintage VW van parked in front. The four guest rooms have tile floors, new beds, a/c, and wireless high-speed Internet. There's a small pool and complimentary bikes. ⊠ *151 Front St., Punta Gorda* ☎ *722/2878* ⊕ *www.coralhouseinn.net* 🗘 *4 rooms* ⌂ *Fans, pool, Wi-Fi, travel services; no room TVs, no room phones* ▭ *MC, V.*

★ $ 🖭 **Hickatee Cottages.** A young British couple, Ian and Kate Morton, built this new lodge at the edge of PG, opened in 2005. Three Caribbean-style cottages have zinc roofs and private verandas and are nestled in lush foliage. They're outfitted with locally made furniture and hardwood floors. Bikes are complimentary, and meals made with fruits and vegetables from the owners' organic nurseries next door are available (dinner is BZ$30). ⊠ *Ex-Servicemen Rd., Punta Gorda., From Front St. turn right at Texaco station and follow Main St. through town. At PG Hospital, turn right on Cemetery La. After 2 blocks, turn half-left on Ex-Servicemen Rd. Follow road for 1 mi (1 ½ km); Hickatee Cottages is on left.* ☎ *662/4475* ⊕ *www.hickatee.com* 🗘 *3 cottages* ⌂ *Dining room, fans, travel services; no a/c, no TV, no room phones* ▭ *MC, V.*

$ 🖭 **Sea Front Inn.** With its pitched roofs and stone-and-wood façade, this four-story hotel may remind you of a ski lodge in the Swiss Alps. Directly overlooking the Gulf of Honduras, with the green humps of the Saddle Back Mountains as a backdrop, its top floors command especially spectacular views. There are a dozen single and double rooms and two suites with kitchenettes. Each is unique, fitted with Belizean hardwoods. A third-floor restaurant (open only for breakfast) has a roof supported by rosewood tree trunks etched with Mayan carvings. If you're staying longer, there are three apartments in the back, renting for BZ$1,400 to $1,700 a month. ⊠ *Front St., Punta Gorda*

☎ 722/2300 🖨 722/2682 ⊕ *www.seafrontinn.com* 🖅 *12 rooms, 3 apartments* ♧ *Dining room, fans, cable TV, travel services; no room phones* ▭ *MC, V.*

¢ 🖬 **Nature's Way Guest House.** In this ramshackle house near the water are an assortment of rooms for travelers on a budget. It feels a bit like a hostel, as it serves as a sort of meeting place for travelers exploring the frontier or heading on to Guatemala or Honduras. Choose from one of the spartan rooms or a bunk in one of the dorm-style rooms. On the breakfast-only menu are tofu, yogurt, and granola. The owner is glad to share with you his strong opinions on Toledo and just about anything else. ⊠ *83 Front St., Punta Gorda* ☎ *722/2119* 🖅 *17 rooms with shared bath* ♧ *Restaurant, travel services; no a/c, no room phones, no room TVs* ▭ *No credit cards.*

¢ 🖬 **Tate's Guest House.** If you don't demand luxury, you couldn't find a nicer spot in PG. Run by William Tate, a long-time post office worker in PG, and his family, this guesthouse on a quiet residential street is an excellent value. The rooms are immaculate, and the atmosphere is friendly and cheerful. One room has a kitchenette, and there's also a small common kitchen with refrigerator and microwave for guest use. ⊠ *34 José Maria Nuñez St., Punta Gorda* ☎ *722/0147* 🖅 *5 rooms* ♧ *Fans, kitchenette, cable TV, travel services; no a/c, no room phones* ▭ *No credit cards.*

THE MAYA HEARTLAND

❷ Drive a few miles out of town, and you find yourself in the heartland of the Maya people. Half the population of Toledo is Maya, a far higher proportion than any other region. The people here are more cohesive and more political than anywhere else in Belize. The Toledo Maya Cultural Council has created an ambitious network of Maya-run guesthouses, and in 1995 it initiated the Mayan Mapping Project. By collating oral history and evidence of ancient Mayan settlements, the project hopes to secure rights to land that the Maya have occupied for centuries, but that the Belizean government have ceded to multinational logging companies. There's also a separate, privately run Mayan homestay program, where you stay in local homes rather than in guesthouses. *See* Where to Stay and Eat *below* for information on these two programs.

The Maya divide into two groups: Mopan Maya–and Ketchi-speaking peoples from the Guatemalan highlands. Most of the latter are recent arrivals, refugees from repression and overpopulation. Each group tends to keep to itself, living in separate villages and preserving unique traditions. Among the Ketchi villages in Toledo are Crique Sarco, San Vincente, San Miquel, Laguna, San Pedro Columbia, Santa Teresa, Sunday Wood, Mabelha, and Corazon. Mopan Maya villages include San Antonio, Pueblo Viejo, and San José.

Sights to See

Maya Villages

The Mopan Maya village of **San Antonio,** a market town 35 mi (56 km) west of Punta Gorda, is Toledo's second-largest town, with a population of more than 2,000. It was settled by people from the Guatemalan village of San Luis, who revere their former patron saint. The village church, built of stones carted from surrounding Mayan ruins, has a stained-glass window donated by another city with a connection to the saint: St. Louis, Missouri. The people of San Antonio haven't forgotten their ancient heritage, though, and each June 13 they take to the streets for a festival that dates back to pre-Columbian times.

A little farther west is the Ketchi village of **San Pedro Columbia,** a cheerful cluster of brightly painted buildings and thatch houses. One of the most eye-catching is a raspberry-red grocery called the People Little Store. On the way to San Pedro Columbia, don't miss **Blue Creek,** a beautiful stretch of river dotted with turquoise swimming holes. A path up the riverbank leads to a series of dramatic caves. The Hokeb Ha Cave is fairly easy to explore on your own, but others should be visited only with a local guide or on a tour. International Zoological Expeditions, a Connecticut-based student travel organization, has established a **jungle lodge** at Blue Creek, with seven rustic cabanas and a restaurant. To visit Blue Creek, you have to get permission from the IZE jungle lodge (☎ 508/655–1461, 800/548–5843 in U.S. ☎ 508/655–4445). Don't swim in the river at night—a poisonous snake called the fer-de-lance likes to take nocturnal dips.

Maya Ruins

Three of Toledo's major Mayan sites have already been excavated: Nim Li Punit, Uxbenká, and Lubaantun.

Nim Li Punit, a Late Classic site discovered in 1976, has 26 unearthed stelae, including one, Stela 14, that is 30 feet tall—the largest ever found in Belize and the second largest found anywhere in the Mayan world. Nim Li Punit, which means "Big Hat" in the Ketchi Mayan language, is named for the elaborate head gear of a ruler pictured on Stela 14. Shady trees cool you off as you walk around the fairly small site (you can see it all in an hour or so). Stop by the informative visitor center on the premises to learn more about the site. Nim Li Punit is near the Ketchi village of Indian Creek, and children (and some adults) from the village usually come over and offer jewelry and crafts for sale. ⊠ *27 mi (44 km) northwest of Punta Gorda off Mile 72½, Western Hwy.* ☎ *BZ$10.*

Lubaantun, which lies beyond the village of San Pedro Columbia, is a Late Classic site discovered in 1924 by German archaeologist Thomas Gann, who gave it a name meaning "place of fallen stones." Lubaantun must have been an awe-inspiring sight: on top of a conical hill, with views to the sea in one direction and the Maya Mountains in the other, its stepped layers of white-plaster stone would have towered above the jungle like a wedding cake. No one knows exactly what function the structures served, but the wealth of miniature masks and whistles found suggests it was a center of ceramic production. The trio of ball courts and the central plaza with tiered seating for 10,000 spectators seems like a Maya Madison Square Garden. There's a small visitor center at the site.

In the last century Lubaantun became the scene of the biggest hoax in modern archaeology. After it was excavated in the 1920s, a British adventurer named F. A. Mitchell-Hedges claimed to have stumbled on what became known as the Crystal Skull. Mitchell-Hedges described the incident in a potboiler, *Danger, My Ally,* in 1951. According to the book, the Crystal Skull was found under an altar at Lubaantun by his daughter Anna. Mitchell-Hedges portrayed himself as a serious archaeologist and explorer: in truth, he was a magazine hack who was later exposed in England as a fraud and a grave robber. The Crystal Skull made good copy. Also known as the Skull of Doom, it was supposedly used by Mayan high priests to zap anyone they didn't care for. Mitchell-Hedges claimed it was 3,600 years old and had taken 150 years to fashion by rubbing a block of pure rock crystal with sand. A similar skull, in the possession of the British Museum, shows signs of having been manufactured with a dentist's drill. Anna Mitchell-Hedges, who today lives in Ontario, has promised to one day reveal the secret. So far, she has adamantly refused to allow the Crystal Skull to be tested and has denied all requests by the Belizean government to return it. ⊠ *20 mi (33 km) northwest of Punta Gorda, about 1 mi (1½ km) from village of San Pedro Columbia* ⊠ *BZ$5.*

✪ **Pusilha,** a Classic-period ceremonial site with a plaza and several stelae on the banks of the Moho River, about 1 mi (1½ km) from the Guatemala border, is currently under excavation by Dr. Geoffrey Braswell of the University of California at San Diego. The site is not open to the public, but you may be able to visit by asking permission of the *alcalde* (mayor) of San Benito village or of the archaeologists, if they're on-site. The Pusilha remains are at the back of the village along the Moho River. By road from Punta Gorda, go 21 km (13 mi) north on the Southern Highway to the San Antonio junction. Turn left on the San Antonio Rd. and go 6 ¼ km (3 ¾ mi). Turn left on the road to Blue Creek village and go past Blue Creek and Jordan village to Santa Teresa village, about 22 km (13 mi). Take a right on San Benito Poité Rd. for 11 ⅔ km (7 mi) to San Benito Poité village. It's easier to reach by boat up the Moho River, and most visitors will want to arrange a guided trip from PG. Except for the Southern Highway and a section of the San Antonio Road, these roads are unpaved and may be impassable after heavy rains. ⊠ *About 2 hours by back roads from Punta Gorda, near village of San Benito Poite on banks of Moho River.* ☎ *772/2470.*

✪ **Uxbenká,** or "ancient place," is near Santa Cruz Village, about 3 mi (5 km) west of San Antonio. This small ceremonial site has a main plaza with six structures, and a series of smaller plazas. More than 20 stelae have been found here, six of them carved. This site is not officially open to visitors, but if you ask a villager in Santa Cruz, you can probably get an informal guided tour.

Where to Stay & Eat

$$$$ 🏨 **Indian Creek Lodge.** One of the most unexpected sites on the Southern Highway is the Indian Creek Lodge, which rises out of nowhere beside the road as a high-walled compound with cabanas lined up a hillside. Nearby is a private airstrip. The thatch cabanas have delightful views of two freshwater lagoons; some also have views the rest of the property, a sprawling private preserve. On our visits we've never seen any guests here. This is one of four properties in southern Belize being developed by Ken Karas and his company, Belize Lodge & Excursions. All the properties operate as all-inclusives, with a three-night minimum. ⊠ *Southern Hwy., 25 mi north of Punta Gorda* ☎ *720/2004* 🖶 *223/ 6324* ⊕ *www.belizelodge.com* ⇨ *12 cabins* ♤ *Dining room, fans, canoeing, hiking, bar, shop, laundry services, travel services; no a/c, no room phones, no room TVs* ⊟ *MC, V* ⎮◯⎮ *All-inclusive.*

★ 🖾 **The Lodge at Big Falls.** Relax beside a meandering jungle river, listen
☾ **$$–$$$** to otters splash, and admire colorful butterflies at this small lodge on 30 placid acres beside the Rio Grande River. This is a birder's paradise: 350 species have been recorded within 5 mi of the lodge. American owners Marta and Rob Hirons built the six thatch cabanas with tile floors and private baths. After dinner (BZ$48), you can read up on naturalist lore in the lodge's Resource Center, where you can use satellite Internet by the light of kerosene lamps. ⊠ *Off Mile 79, Southern Hwy.* 🖃 *Box 103, Punta Gorda* ☎ *888/865–3369 in U.S. and Canada* ⊕ *www.thelodgeatbigfalls.com* ⇨ *6 cabañas* ♤ *Restaurant, pool, bicycles, hiking, bar, library, shop, Internet room, travel services; no a/c, no room phones, no room TVs* ⊟ *MC, V.*

☾ ¢ 🖾 **Sun Creek Lodge.** This little lodge, open since 2004, is run by Bruno and Melissa Kuppinger. He's German; she's Belizean. Bruno runs tours and Melissa focuses on the lodge and does the cooking. The thatch cabañas are simple but comfortable, with outdoor showers surrounded by plants. The grounds are nicely landscaped with flowering shrubs. Car rentals are available. ⊠ *About 14 mi (23 km) northwest of Punta Gorda, off Mile 86, Southern Hwy.* ☎ *604/2124* 🖶 *722/0179* ⊕ *www. belizenet.de* ⇨ *4 cabañas with shared baths* ♤ *Dining room, hiking, Internet, car rentals, travel services; no room phones, no room TVs* ⊟ *MC, V* ⎮◯⎮ *CP.*

¢ 🖾 **T.E.A.** The Toledo Ecotourism Association arranges stays in one of 10 participating Mayan and Ketchi villages. You stay in a simple but clean guesthouse, typically with thatch roof, bunk beds, and outside bathroom, then visit Mayan homes for breakfast, lunch, and dinner. The English-speaking staff arrange vegetarian or special meals. During the day there are walks to the nearby ruins or to waterfalls that empty into shimmering pools. Before you book this kind of stay, though, know that the point of it is to get an authentic feel for the region—this can be a rare opportunity to learn about the culture, but if the thought of chickens running in and out of your digs isn't your idea of a nice vacation, this isn't the stay for you. ⊠ *Front St., Punta Gorda* ☎ *722/2096* 🖶 *722/ 2199* 🖂 *ttea@btl.net* ♤ *Hiking; no a/c, no room phones, no room TVs* ⊟ *No credit cards* ⎮◯⎮ *FAP.*

☾ ¢ 🖾 **Tranquility Lodge.** Swim in pristine Jacinto Creek or just relax in the gardens at this small and serene lodge on 20 acres near the town of Jacintoville. There aren't even any phones to disturb you. The ground-floor rooms are attractively furnished, and the price (BZ$100) makes peace and quiet affordable. ⊠ *1st driveway on right on San Felipe Rd., off Southern Hwy. near Jacintoville, Toledo, 7 mi (11 ½ km) north of Punta Gorda* ☎ *No phone* ⊕ *www.tranquility-lodge.com* ⇨ *4 rooms* ♤ *Din-*

6

HELPING OUT IN BELIZE

Want to help others less fortunate than you? Want to make the world a better place? Then you may want to investigate volunteer opportunities in Belize. There are basically three kinds of volunteer opportunities available:

Church and mission trips. This typically involves a week to several weeks of volunteer work in a medical or dental clinic, or building churches or homes, or other hands-on assistance. Usually these volunteer groups are based outside of Belize, often at a church or school or as a part of a local medical society. In most cases, volunteers pay for their own transportation to Belize, along with personal expenses in the country, but food and lodging sometimes are provided by the mission. Your best bet is to contact your church, college, or local medical society and ask if they know of upcoming mission trips to Belize.

Independent volunteering. Find a worthwhile organization and volunteer your services. Conservation organizations, churches, libraries, medical clinics, humane societies, and schools are among those that may welcome volunteers. You usually won't receive any lodging or food in return for your volunteer activities. To arrange this kind of independent volunteer work, you usually need to be in Belize and make personal contact with the organization you are seeking to help.

Organized volunteer programs. These volunteer programs often revolve around conservation, such as working with wildlife or reef preservation. A few programs offer volunteer opportunities in education, animal care, or social work. Some programs require volunteers to pay a placement fee, which can be several hundred dollars or more, plus pay for room, board, and transportation to Belize. In other programs volunteers do not pay a fee and they may receive food and lodging in exchange for their volunteer work, but they usually have to pay transportation and incidental expenses out of pocket. For longer-term volunteering, consider the U.S. Peace Corps, which has a significant presence here.

Some organizations that accept volunteers in Belize:Belize Zoo and Tropical Education Center. The Belize Zoo, one of the great conservation organizations in Central America, and the adjoining Tropical Education Center have a wide range of education and outreach programs. A few motivated volunteers are accepted to assist Belize Zoo and TEC programs. ✆ Box 1787, Belize City ☎ 220/8003 ⊕ www.belizezoo.org.

Cornerstone Foundation. This nonprofit's programs include cultural, community service, and peace-related volunteer programs in Cayo District. Volunteers commit for a minimum of three weeks to three months. For longer-term programs, individuals pay US$300 to US$400 a month for housing; couples and families, US$600. There is a US$100 application fee, a weekly meal fee of around US$15, and other fees. Those involved in three-week programs such as the AIDS Education or Natural Healing programs pay a fee of around US$550 to US$650. At any one time, the foundation may have from 1 to 18 volunteers in Belize, plus local staff. ⊠ *90 Burns Ave., San Ignacio* ☎ *824/2373* ⊕ *www.peacecorner. org.*

Green Reef. Green Reef is a private, nonprofit group based in San Pedro, devoted to protecting the marine and coastal resources. Green Reef currently doesn't have a volunteer coordinator, but it says it is interested in hearing from prospective volunteers, especially those with skills in photography, fund-raising, community involvement, and education. ⊠ *100 Coconut Dr., San Pedro* ☎ *226/3254* ⊕ *www.greenreefbelize.com.*

Monkey Bay Wildlife Sanctuary. Monkey Bay is a private wildlife sanctuary and environmental education center on 1,070 acres near the Belize Zoo. It has some volunteer opportunities in conservation and community service. Monkey Bay also offers homestay programs, as well as 12- to 21-day education and adventure programs for students (middle school to university). The education programs are at rates of about US$75 a day. ⊕ *Box 187, Belmopan City* ☎ *820/3032* ⊕ *www.monkeybaybelize.org.*

Mount Carmel High School. Many of the faculty members at this high school are volunteers. Volunteers, who must be four-year university graduates and be "willing to teach in a Catholic environment," commit to teach for a period of one to two years. In return, they receive room, board, and US$12.50/week in spending money. ⊠ *Benque Viejo del Carmen* ☎ *823/2024* ⊕ *www. mchsbenque.org.*

Plenty International. Plenty, founded in 1974, places 8 to 10 volunteers annually in Toledo District and elsewhere. Volunteers should have medical, midwifery, marketing, and other skills. The minimum commitment is three months, and a nominal (US$30) placement fee is charged. There are no stipends or other payments to volunteers, but in some cases volunteers may receive food and housing. ⊕ *Box 394, Summertown, TN 38483* ☎ *913/964-4323* ⊕ *www. plenty.org.*

–Lan Sluder

6

ing room, hiking, bar, Internet, travel services; no room phones, no room
TVs ⊟ No credit cards ⦿| CP.

¢ 🖼 **Village Homestay Network.** Run by Dem Dats Doin' ecofarm, the Village Homestay Network arranges for visitors to stay with Mayan families in one of three Toledo villages: Aguacate, a Ketchi village; San José, a Mopan village; and Na Luum Ca, also Mopan. You sleep in a hammock in a traditional thatch hut with dirt floor, help with daily activities such as making tortillas, and eat meals with the host family. Bathrooms are outhouses, and you bathe in a river. ⊠ *Punta Gorda* ☎ *722/2470* ✍ *demdatsdoin@btl.net* ⛰ *Hiking; no a/c, no room phones, no room TVs* ⊟ *No credit cards* ⦿| *FAP.*

TOLEDO & THE DEEP SOUTH ESSENTIALS

Transportation

BY AIR

Maya Island Air and Tropic Air fly south to Punta Gorda from both the municipal (BZ$178 one-way) and international (BZ$207 one-way) airports. There are about five flights daily on each airline. The Punta Gorda airstrip is on the town's west side from the town square, walk four blocks west on Prince Street.

🛪 **Maya Island Air** ⊠ Punta Gorda airstrip ☎ 722/2856 ⊕ www.mayaairways.com.
Tropic Air ⊠ Prince St. ☎ 722/2008 ⊕ www.tropicair.com.

BY BOAT

Requena's provides daily boats, departing around 9 AM from the docks on Front Street, Punta Gorda, to Puerto Barrios, Guatemala. Fares are BZ$35 one-way. You must pay a BZ$7.50 conservation fee when departing PG, and a US$10 exit fee when departing Guatemala for Belize. To make a reservation, you need to provide your full name, date of birth, nationality, and passport number. If you're flying to PG just to catch the water taxi to Puerto Barrios, take the 8 AM Maya Island flight from the municipal airstrip in Belize City. Requena's will pick you up at the airstrip.

🛪 **Requena's Charter Service** ⊠ 12 Front St., Punta Gorda ☎☎ 722/2070 ⊕ www. puntagordabelize.com/requena/.

BY BUS

For routes south to Dangriga, Placencia, and Punta Gorda, try James Bus Line. From Belize City to Punta Gorda it's a six- to eight-hour trip via Belmopan and Dangriga, depending on connections and whether it's an express or local bus. It costs around BZ$24–BZ$28. Most buses are old U.S. school buses—they're usually crowded and have no air-conditioning. If you have the budget, you're better off flying.

Buses run frequently—generally about every two hours during daylight hours—on the Southern Highway between Dangriga and PG, but public transportation is very limited off the highway. On market days (generally Monday, Wednesday, Friday, and Saturday) buses leave the main plaza in PG around noon. Different buses, mostly old American school buses operated by local entrepreneurs, go to different villages, returning on market days very early in the morning. There's no published schedule—you have to ask locally. Fares are modest, BZ$2–BZ$4. As of this writing, buses served the villages of Barranco, Big Falls, Crique Jute, Crique Sarco, Golden Stream, Indian Creek, Jalacte, Laguna, San Antonio, San Marcos, San Miquel, San Pedro Columbia, Pueblo Viejo, and Silver Creek.

James Bus Line ⊠ 7 King St., Punta Gorda ☎ 702/2049.

BY CAR

The journey to Punta Gorda via the Hummingbird and Southern highways used to be a chiropractor's nightmare: a bone-shuddering marathon via Belmopan, Dangriga, and Big Creek across some of Belize's worst roads. The paving of the Hummingbird and Southern highways has made the trip much shorter and more pleasant. At this writing, only a short section of the Southern Highway near Golden Stream was unpaved. It's now one of Central America's best roads.

Off the Southern Highway, most roads are unpaved. In dry weather they're bumpy but passable. However, after heavy rains, the dirt roads can turn into quagmires, even for four-wheel-drive vehicles. Most tertiary roads are not well marked, so you may have to stop frequently for directions. Despite this, the high cost of taxis and the infrequent bus service to and from the Mayan villages are arguments for having a rental car.

BY TAXI

Taxis in the Deep South are available mostly in PG. You can find taxis at Central Park in PG, or your hotel can call one for you. Any trip within PG should cost around BZ$6, with additional charges for extra stops. You can also hire a taxi to take you to nearby villages, but negotiate the rate in advance; it could be anywhere from BZ$20 to BZ$150, or more, depending on the destination. If you want a car and driver, a taxi likely will charge you around BZ$300 a day.

There are no major car rental companies in Punta Gorda, but Sun Creek Lodge has a few rental cars. They cost around BZ$140 per day.

Sun Creek Lodge ⊠ About 14 mi (23 km) northwest of Punta Gorda, off Mile 86, Southern Hwy. ☎ 604/2124 📠 722/0179.

Contacts & Resources

BANKS & EXCHANGE SERVICES

The only bank in Punta Gorda is Belize Bank. Happily, it does have an ATM that accepts foreign-issued ATM cards (on the PLUS, CIRRUS, and Visa Electron systems).

Banks & ATMs Belize Bank ⊠ 30 Main St. at Hospital St. ☎ 722/2324.

EMERGENCIES

Hospitals Punta Gorda Hospital ⊠ Main St. at south end of town ☎ 722/2026.

MAIL & SHIPPING

The Punta Gorda post office is on Front Street across from the ferry dock. Hours are 8:30–noon and 1–4:30 weekdays.

Post Offices Punta Gorda post office ⊠ Front St. ☎ 722/2087.

TOURS

TIDE Tours, a subsidiary of the Toledo Institute for Development and Environment, a nonprofit organization promoting ecotourism in Toledo, is the largest operator of tours in southern Belize. It offers fishing, kayaking, snorkeling, trips to Mayan ruins, and cultural tours. Another sizeable tour operator is TASTEE Tours, associated with Requena's Water Taxi Service.

The Toledo Tour Guide Association has about 16 members. All are licensed by the Belize government. Some of these tour guides work for the larger tour operators, and others work independently.

A group of hotels and tour operators (*see The Outdoors, above*) have banded together to offer a variety of tours on a fixed daily schedule. ⚐ **TASTEE Tours** ✉ 12 Front St., Punta Gorda ☎ 722/2795 🖷 722/2070 ⊕ www. puntagordabelize.com. **TIDE Tours** ✉ Prince and Main Sts., Box 150, Punta Gorda ☎ 722/2129 🖷 722/2655 ⊕ www.tidetours.org. **Toldeo Tour Guide Association** ⬦ Box 147, Punta Gorda ⊕ www.puntagordabelize.com/ttga/index.htm.

VISITOR INFORMATION

The office of the Belize Tourism Industry Association (BTIA), on Front Street near the water taxi dock, is open Tuesday–Saturday 9–noon and 1–4:30, Sunday 9–noon. It has brochures and information on local hotels, tours, and bus schedules.
⚐ **Belize Tourism Information Center** ✉ Front St. ☎ 722/2531.

Tikal & Environs

WORD OF MOUTH

"Tikal is fabulous. We hired a guide who gave us a great overview and the confidence to explore on our own the following day. We climbed to the top of all the pyramids (sore legs!), including the one in El Mundo Perdido to watch the sunset. Beautiful."
—msteacher

"Do the overnight in Tikal. So worth it! Spending the night gives you the advantage of being in the park first thing in the morning and late in afternoon without day trippers. A sunset and sunrise on the temples is breathtaking."
—Fry69

By Lan Sluder   **THE JUNGLES OF EL PETÉN** were once the heartland of the Mayan civilization. The sprawling empire—including parts of present-day Mexico, Belize, Honduras, and El Salvador—was once made up of a network of cities that held hundreds of thousands of people, but a millennium ago this fascinating civilization went into a mysterious decline and soon virtually disappeared. The temples that dominated the horizon were swallowed up by the jungle.

Today, ancient ruins seem to just crop up from El Petén's landscape. In comparison with the rest of Guatemala, which has 15 million people in an area the size of Tennessee, El Petén is sparsely populated. Fifty years ago, El Petén had fewer than 20,000 residents. Due to massive immigration from other areas of Guatemala, El Petén now has more than half a million people (almost twice the population of the entire country of Belize). Still, nature reigns supreme, with vines and other plants quickly covering everything that stands still a little too long. Whatever your primary interest—archaeology, history, birding, biking—you'll find plenty to do and see in this remote region.

Four-wheel-drive vehicles are required to get to many of the archaeological sites, while others, such as those in the Mirador Basin, are reachable only by boat or on foot. The difficulty doesn't just enhance the adventure, it gives you time to take in the exotic scenery and rare tropical flora and fauna that's with you all the way.

If you drive instead of fly from Belize, you'll notice the difference in Guatemala almost the instant you cross the border. Spanish replaces English, and except in some hotels and other tourist businesses, very little English is spoken. Prices for everything from beer to meals to lodging are considerably lower. Starting at the border, where you may be asked for a small fee to enter Guatemala (there is no such entry fee), bribes and petty corruption are a way of life. Extreme poverty is much more evident, and by comparison with this part of Guatemala, Belize looks middle-class.

History

When the Mayan civilization was at its peak, they developed one of the earliest forms of writing, the very first mathematical system to use zero, complex astronomical calculations, advanced agricultural systems, and an inscrutable belief system. It was during this zenith that spectacular cities such as Tikal were built. By the time the Europeans arrived, the Mayan civilization had already mysteriously collapsed.

Until the 1960s the ElPetén region was a desolate place. This all changed when the Guatemalan government began offering small tracts of land in El Petén for US$25 to anyone willing to settle it. The landless moved in droves and today, the population is more than 500,000—a 25-fold increase in around 50 years.

Unemployment in El Petén is high and tourism—mostly associated with Tikal and other Mayan sites—is the main industry. Many make ends meet through subsistence farming, logging, and marijuana cultivation.

TOP REASONS TO GO

TIKAL

Tikal is usually ranked as the most impressive of all Mayan sites, and many put it—along with Angkor Wat in Cambodia, the pyramids of Egypt, the Great Wall of China, the Petra temples in Jordan, the Greek and Roman ruins, and the Machu Picchu Inca site in Peru—among the wonders of the ancient world. Although Caracol and other Mayan sites in Belize are magnificent, none truly rivals Tikal in visual impact. Its much more excavated than any large site in Belize, and its setting in the jungle, rich with wildlife and birds, will never be forgotten.

OTHER MAYAN RUINS

Tikal is the best known, but hardly the only important, Mayan site in El Petén. El Mirador, close to the Mexican border, was a giant city-state, perhaps larger than Tikal, and in the Mirador Basin are the remains of at least four other centers, including Nakbé, El Tintal, Xulnal, and Wakná; most are still covered in jungle.

LOW PRICES

Although prices in El Petén are a little higher than in some other areas of Guatemala, in comparison with Belize, the area is rife with travel bargains. Overall, price levels in Guatemala for hotels, meals, and tours are one-third to one-half less than in Belize. Except at Tikal Park, where the three on-site hotels are overpriced, you can get a decent hotel room with private bath for US$20 to US$25, and even the better hotels with a lovely setting and charm are rarely more than US$100. Simple meals are a couple of dollars, and bus travel costs about US$1 an hour. Craft items, including beautiful woven fabrics, handmade hats, and carved slate and wood, are inexpensive.

FLORES & PETÉN ITZÁ

Unlike its larger, less atmospheric neighbors, the island town of Flores has a charming European feel, with red-roof houses and cobblestone streets. You can dine in little bistros with lakeside views or stay in simple, inexpensive inns. Lago de Petén Itza is the second-largest lake in Guatemala. You can kayak around the lake or take a *lancha* (small boat) to explore its distant corners.

SHOPPING FOR HANDICRAFTS

The most famous of Guatemala's handicrafts are handwoven fabrics—women in nearly every village weave traditional patterns. But Guatemala's indigenous population creates countless other kinds of handicrafts, such as ceramics, wood carvings, baskets, toys, statues, bags, or hats. Guatemala's markets are a wonderful way to witness the everyday lives of the population. Vendors line a jumble of narrow passages and hawk everything from fruits and vegetables to toiletries. Although other areas of Guatemala, especially the highlands where many of the crafts are created, have better shopping and more markets than you'll find in El Petén, there's an open-air market in Santa Elena, and a number of little shops in Flores. The village of El Remate near Tikal is known for its unique wood carvings, and the border town of Melchor de Mencos also has *tiendas* (small booths or stores) catering to crafts-hungry tourists.

7

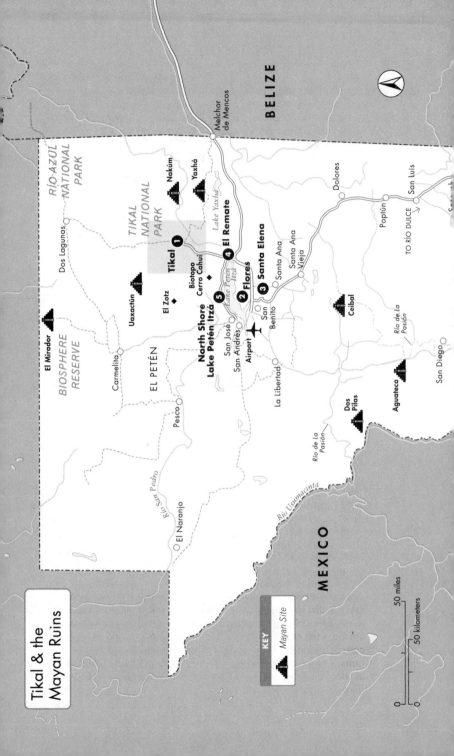

Tikal & the Mayan Ruins

KEY

▟ Mayan Site

BELIZE

Melchor de Mencos

RÍO-AZUL NATIONAL PARK

Nakúm

Yaxhá

TIKAL NATIONAL PARK

Lake Yaxhá

Dos Lagunas

① Tikal

④ El Remate

③ Santa Elena

Biotopo Cerro Cahuí

Santa Ana

Uaxactún

El Zotz

⑤

② Flores

San Benito

North Shore Lake Petén Itzá

Lake Petén Itzá

Santa Ana Vieja

Dolores

San Luis

Poptún

TO RIO DULCE

San José

San Andrés

Airport

Ceibal

Río de la Pasión

El Mirador

EL PETÉN

La Libertad

San Diego

BIOSPHERE RESERVE

Carmelita

Dos Pilas

Pesco

Aguateca

Río San Pedro

Río de la Pasión

El Naranjo

Río Usumacinta

MEXICO

0   50 miles

0   50 kilometers

EXPLORING TIKAL & ENVIRONS

Guatemala is a rugged country where major roads are few and far between and highways are all but nonexistent. But because there are only two airports—one in Guatemala City, the other in Flores—you're forced to do most of your travel by land. All but the hardiest travelers will want to stay in the larger towns and explore the more isolated regions on day trips. Most of the roads in El Petén are still unpaved, the exceptions being the road from Santa Elena–Flores to Tikal, the road from Río Dulce in the south to Santa Elena–Flores, and a few others.

From the Belize border, it's about 62 mi (100 km) by road to Tikal, and from the Belize border to Flores it's slightly longer (70 mi [112 km]). This road, from the scruffy Guatemalan border town of Melchor de Mencos, is unpaved for the first 15 mi (25 km) or so. Paving work is ongoing and may be completed by the time you visit. At El Cruce, also known as Ixlu, the road splits, turning north to Tikal and southwest to Santa Elena and Flores. If, instead of going on to Tikal, you turn west near the village of El Remate, the road (unpaved here) takes you around the north end of Lake Petén Itzá, passing the villages of San José and San Andrés, and ending up at the town of San Benito, adjoining Santa Elena. Driving, by car or van, the trip to Tikal from the Belize border is roughly 1½ hours, depending on road conditions.

When to Go

The weather around Tikal is similar to that in the Cayo—very hot in spring, with some rain; hot and always humid in summer and fall; and a little cooler and more pleasant but still often hot and a bit muggy in winter. Most people visit Tikal from June to August and from Christmas to April. The busiest time of year in all of Guatemala is *Semana Santa*, the week from Palm Sunday to Easter Sunday, though it's not as busy in El Petén as elsewhere.

About the Restaurants

In El Petén, you have a couple of choices for dining: *comedores*, which are small eateries along the lines of a U.S. café or diner, with simple and inexpensive local food; and restaurants, that, in general, are a little nicer and serve a wider selection of food, often with an international or American flavor. Restaurants are mostly in Flores and other towns. You can also eat at street stalls (if you don't have a sensitive tummy), and buy cheap and wonderful fruits, breads, cheeses, and other items for picnics at markets and groceries.

The basis of Guatemalan, especially Mayan, food is corn, usually eaten as a tortilla, as a tamale, or on the cob. Black beans accompany most meals, either whole beans cooked in a broth or mashed and refried. Meats are often served in *caldos* (stews) or cooked in a spicy chili sauce. Thin and tender *lomito*, a popular cut of beef, is on the menu in most restaurants. The most popular fish is the delicious *robálo*, known elsewhere as snook. The *queso fundido* (melted cheese with condiments and tortillas), which is sometimes served as an appetizer, is a good choice for light eaters.

Breakfast is usually tortillas, eggs, and beans. Lunch is the biggest meal of the day, and you can save money by ordering *comidas corridas,* two- or three-course specials. Dinner is usually a little more expensive than lunch, even for the same items.

In El Petén, many restaurants serve wild game, or *comida silvestre.* Although often delicious, the game has usually been taken illegally. You might see *venado* (venison), *coche del monte* (mountain cow or peccary), and *tepezcuintle* (paca, a large rodent) on the menu.

A tip of about 10% is standard at most Guatemalan restaurants.

About the Hotels

El Petén now has a wide range of lodging options, from suites at luxurious lakeside resorts to stark rooms in budget hotels. Flores has many lodging choices, and the number of hotels there keeps prices competitive. The hotels in the much larger Santa Elena, the gateway to the island town of Flores, are generally larger and more upscale than the places in Flores, but with less atmosphere. El Remate, about 22 mi (35 km) from Flores on the road to Tikal, is a pleasant alternative, with several excellent small, mostly inexpensive hotels. At Tikal itself are three lodges, all somewhat overpriced (by Guatemalan, but not Belizean, standards) and often catering to groups. They have the great advantage of being right at the park. On the north side of Lago de Petén Itzá are several hotels, including a couple of the most upscale in the region: Francis Ford Coppola's La Lancha and the largest resort hotel in the area, Hotel Camino Real Tikal. Bellhops and maids expect tips only in the more expensive hotels.

	WHAT IT COSTS In Guatemalan Quetzales				
	$$$$	$$$	$$	$	¢
RESTAURANTS	over 130	100–130	70–100	40–70	under 40
HOTELS	over 760	560–760	360–560	160–360	under 160

Restaurant prices are per person for a main course at dinner. Hotel prices are for two people in a standard double room, including tax and service. Remember that most hotels in El Petén charge a total of 22% tax on top of the room rate.

TIKAL

Fodor'sChoice ★

① *22 mi (35 km) north of El Remate, 42 mi (68 km) northeast of Flores.*

You rise shortly before dawn. It isn't long before you hear the muffled roars of howler monkeys in the distance. After a quick cup of coffee you and your fellow adventurers follow your guide through the deserted plazas toward the pyramid that towers over everything else. The climb up the side is difficult in the dark, but after scrambling up rickety ladders and over roots and vines you find yourself at the top. You glance to the east, past the endless expanse of jungle, just as the sun starts to rise.

Tikal is one of the most popular tourist attractions in Central America—and with good reason. Smack in the middle of the 222-square-mi

(575-square-km) Parque Nacional Tikal, the towering temples are ringed on all sides by miles of virgin forest. The area around the ruins is great for checking out creatures that spend their entire lives hundreds of feet above the forest floor in the dense canopy of trees. Colorful birds like yellow toucans and Scarlet Macaws are common sights.

Although the region was home to Maya communities as early as 600 BC, Tikal itself wasn't established until sometime around 200 BC. One of the first structures to be built here was a version of the North Acropolis. Others were added at a dizzying pace for the next three centuries. By AD 100 impressive structures like the Great Plaza had already been built. But even though it was a powerful city in its own right, Tikal was still ruled by the northern city of El Mirador. It wasn't until the arrival of a powerful dynasty around AD 300 that Tikal arrogated itself to full power. King Great Jaguar Paw sired a lineage that would build Tikal into a city rivaling any of its time. By AD 500 it's estimated that the city covered more than 18 square mi (47 square km) and had a population of close to 100,000.

The great temples that still tower above the jungle were at that time covered with stucco and painted with bright reds and greens, and the priests used them for elaborate ceremonies meant to please the gods and assure prosperity for the city. What makes these structures even more impressive is that the Maya possessed no metal tools to aid in construction, had no beasts of burden to carry heavy loads, and never used wheels for anything except children's toys. Of course, as a hierarchical culture they had a slave class, and the land was rich in obsidian, a volcanic glass that could be fashioned into razor-sharp tools.

By the 6th century Tikal governed a large part of the Mayan world, thanks to a leader called Caan Chac (Stormy Sky), who took the throne around AD 426. Under Caan Chac, Tikal became an aggressive military and commercial center that dominated the surrounding communities with a power never before seen in Mesoamerica. The swamps protected the city from attack and allowed troops to spot any approaching enemy. Intensive agriculture in the *bajos* (lowlands) provided food for the huge population. A valuable obsidian trade sprang up, aided by the city's strategic position near two rivers.

Tikal thrived for more than a millennium, forming strong ties with two powerful centers: Kaminal Juyu, in the Guatemalan highlands, and Teotihuacán, in Mexico City. The city entered a golden age when Ah-Cacao (Lord Chocolate) ascended the throne in AD 682. It was Ah-Cacao and his successors who commissioned the construction of most of the city's most important temples. Continuing the tradition of great structures, Ah-Cacao's son commissioned Temple I, which he dedicated to his father, who is buried beneath it. He also ordered the construction of Temple IV, the tallest temple at Tikal. By the time of his death in 768, Tikal was at the peak of its power. It would remain so until its mysterious abandonment around AD 900.

For almost 1,000 years Tikal remained engulfed by the jungle. The conquistadors who came here searching for gold and silver must have passed

GREAT ITINERARIES

IF YOU HAVE 1 DAY

You can visit **Tikal** on a day trip, and get a good sense of its grandeur, although if you have the time it's better to spend at least one or two nights. If you're in Belize City or on Ambergris Caye or Caye Caulker, fly from the international airport at Belize City to the airport at Santa Elena and **Flores,** a pastel-painted town in El Petén. If you're in the San Ignacio area, cross the border on your own. Take a bus or taxi to the border and walk across, and then go by Guatemalan taxi or minibus to Tikal; if you don't want to worry about the logistics, take one of the many Tikal day tours offered by tour operators and hotels in the Cayo. You'll have several hours to explore Tikal before returning to Belize. Hire a guide at the park to show you around.

IF YOU HAVE 2 DAYS

Fly or bus from Belize City to **Flores,** the red-roof town in El Petén, or from the San Ignacio area cross the border (take a bus or taxi to the border and walk across) and then go by minibus or taxi to Tikal. Head straight to the **Tikal** ruins. Depending on your schedule, you may choose to spend the night either at Tikal park so you can see the ruins in the morning (a must for birders), or in Flores, El Remate, or elsewhere along the shores of **Lake Petén Itzá.** If you arrive at the park after 3 PM, your ticket will be good for admission the next day as well. You can easily spend two days, or longer, exploring the ruins. You may want to hire a guide for your first day, then wander about on your own on the second. If you have additional time, consider an extension in El Petén. The town of Flores, with its lakeside bistros and cobblestone streets, merits at least a half-day stroll. With scores of other ruins in the region, you could spend weeks traveling off the beaten track.

right by the overgrown ruins, mistaking them for rocky hills. The native Peténeros certainly knew of the ancient city's existence, but no one else ventured near until 1848, when the Guatemalan government dispatched archaeologists to the region. Tikal started to receive international attention in 1877, when Dr. Gustav Bernoulli commissioned locals to remove the carved wooden lintels from across the doorways of Temples I and IV. These items were sent to a museum in Basel, Switzerland.

In 1881 and 1882 English archaeologist Alfred Percival Maudslay made the first map showing the architectural features of this vast city. As he began to unearth the major temples, he recorded his work in dramatic photographs—you can see copies in the museum at Tikal. His work was continued by Teobert Maler, who came in 1895 and 1904. Both Maler and Maudsley have causeways named in their honor. In 1951 the Guatemalan air force cleared an airstrip near the ruins to improve access for large-scale archaeological work. Today, after more than 150 years of digging, researchers say that Tikal includes some 3,000 buildings.

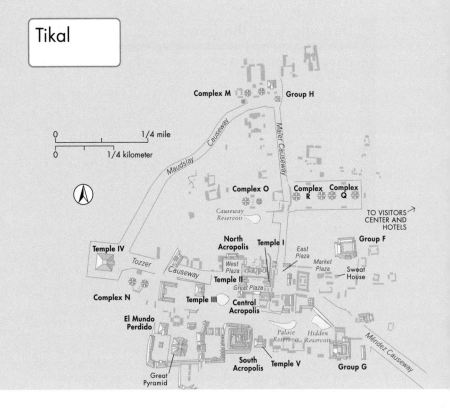

Tikal

Complex M

Group H

Maudslay Causeway

Maler Causeway

0 — 1/4 mile
0 — 1/4 kilometer

Complex O

Causeway Reservoir

Complex R Complex Q

TO VISITORS CENTER AND HOTELS

Temple IV

Tozzer Causeway

North Acropolis

Temple I

East Plaza

Market Plaza

Group F

Sweat House

West Plaza

Temple II

Great Plaza

Complex N

Temple III

Central Acropolis

El Mundo Perdido

Palace Reservoir

Hidden Reservoir

Méndez Causeway

South Acropolis

Temple V

Group G

Great Pyramid

Countless more are still covered by the jungle. ✉ *Parque Nacional Tikal* ☎ *No phone* ⊕ *www.tikalpark.com* 💵 *Q50* 🕐 *Daily 6–6.*

The Tikal Ruins

You can tour Tikal on your own or with local guides. The guides, which can be booked at the guide-booking desk near the visitor center, make the visit more interesting, though don't believe everything they tell you. Tours are US$50 for up to five people. Wear comfortable shoes and bring water—to see the entire site, you walk about 6 mi (10 km).

As you enter Tikal, keep to the middle trail. You'll soon arrive at the ancient city's center, filled with awe-inspiring temples and intricate acropolises. The pyramid that you approach from behind is **Temple I,** known as the Temple of the Great Jaguar because of the feline represented on one of its carved lintels. It's in what is referred to as the **Great Plaza,** one of the most beautiful and dramatic in Tikal. The Great Plaza was built around AD 700 by Ah-Cacao, one of the wealthiest rulers of his time. His tomb, comparable in magnitude to that of Pa Cal at the ruins of Palenque in southern Mexico, was discovered beneath the Temple of the Great Jaguar in the 1960s. The theory is that his queen is buried beneath **Temple II,** called the Temple of the Masks for the decorations on its façade. It's a twin of the Temple of the Great Jaguar.

Dancing with the Dead

COLORFUL CEMETERIES, WITH THEIR turquoises and pinks, mauves and sky blues, play an integral part in the living fabric of contemporary Guatemalan society. It's not uncommon to see entire families visiting their deceased relatives on Sunday. But a visit to the cemetery need not be mournful, and they often bring a bottle of alcohol to share among themselves, occasionally tipping the bottle to the earth, so that their dead relatives also get their share. Incense is burned and shamans perform ancient rites alongside Catholic and evangelical priests. Day of the Dead gives family members their greatest chance to celebrate and honor their deceased relatives with music, dance, song, festivals and, yes, much drinking and merriment.

Celebrating the dead rather than mourning their passing is a Mayan tradition that reaches back to pre-Columbian times. The *Popol Vuh* or Mayan Bible as it's sometimes referred to looks toward an active relationship with deceased friends and relatives. "Remember us after we have gone. Don't forget us," reads the *Popul Vuh*. "Conjure up our faces and our words. Our image will be as dew in the hearts of those who want to remember us."

It is unknown who authored the *Popol Vuh*, which was translated into Spanish in the early 18th century by Father Francisco Ximénez, but the practices and myths of the sacred book of the Maya still make their way into the Day of the Dead celebrations across Guatemala. The book has also been integral in understanding the traditions, cosmology, and mythology of the Quiché. According to scholars,

it's one of the finest surviving aboriginal American manuscripts.

The country's two most fascinating Day of the Dead celebrations take place in Santiago Sacatepéquez and Todos Santos Chuchumatán on November 1. In Santiago Sacatepéquez, a Cakchiquel pueblo located 19 mi (30 km) from Antigua, the villagers gather in the early morning hours and have a procession through the narrow streets to the cemetery. Once there, they take part in what is one of Guatemala's most resplendent ceremonies, flying giant kites of up to 2 meters in diameter to communicate with those who have passed away. The villagers tie messages to the kite tails to let the dead know how they are doing and to ask God for special favors. The colorful celebration is finished with a lunch feast of *fiambre*, a traditional dish of cold cuts, boiled eggs, vegetables, olives, and other delicacies.

The color scheme of the cemeteries is more than just decorative: turquoise and green tombs signify an adult member of the family was recently interred in the above-ground crypts, whites and yellows indicate the passing of an elderly family member, and pinks and blues are reserved for deceased children.

Whether you're lucky enough to see Guatemala's cemeteries during the Day of the Dead celebrations, they are still worth a visit. Although foreigners are welcome in the cemeteries, it's important to respect the traditions and dignity of those visiting deceased relatives—tread softly and leave your camera behind.

—Gregory Benchwick

In fact, construction of matching pyramids distinguishes Tikal from other Mayan sites.

The **North Acropolis,** to the west of Ah-Cacao's temple, is a mind-boggling conglomeration of temples built over layers and layers of previous construction. Excavations have revealed that the base of this structure is more than 2,000 years old. Be sure to see the stone mask of the rain god at Temple 33. The **Central Acropolis,** south of the Great Plaza, is an immense series of structures assumed to have served as administrative centers.

If you climb to the top of one of the pyramids, you'll see the gray roof combs of others rising above the rain forest's canopy but still trapped within it. **Temple V,** to the south, underwent a $3 million restoration project and is now open to the public. **Temple IV,** to the west, is the tallest-known structure built by the Maya. Although the climb to the top is difficult, the view is unforgettable.

To the southwest of the plaza lies the **South Acropolis,** which hasn't been reconstructed, and a 105-foot-high pyramid, similar in construction to those at Teotihuacán. A few jungle trails, including the marked Interpretative Benil-ha Trail, offer a chance to see spider monkeys and other wildlife. Outside the park, a somewhat overgrown trail halfway down the old airplane runway on the left leads to the remnants of old rubber-tappers' camps and is a good spot for bird-watching.

At park headquarters are two small archaeological museums that display Mayan artifacts. They are a good resource for information on the enigmatic rise and fall of the Maya people, though little information is in English. **Museo Lítico or Stelae Museum** has stelae found at Tikal and interesting photos from early archaeological excavations. ⊠ *Near visitor center* ☷ *US$1.50* ☉ *Daily 9–noon, 1–4:30.*

Museo Tikal, also known as the Tikal Sylvannus G. Morley Museum has a replica of Ha Sawa Chaan K'awil's burial chamber and some ceramics and bones from the actual tomb (the jade, however, is replica) ⊠ *Near visitor center* ☷ *Free with ticket from Museo Lítico* ☉ *Weekdays 9–5, weekends 9–4.*

Where to Stay & Eat

There are three hotels on the park grounds: Tikal Inn, Jungle Lodge, and Jaguar Inn. At all of these you pay for the park location rather than good amenities and great service. Electric power is from generators, which usually run from around 6 AM to 9 or 10 PM. Camping is also available, at the park campsite (US$4) or at the Jaguar Inn. Three *comedores* (similar to a bodega) are at the entrance to the park, and you can also get food in the park, at the hotels, and at little comedores.

★ $$$–$$$$ ✕⌂ **Tikal Inn.** This cluster of comfortable bungalows wraps around a well-manicured garden and a pool. It's set apart from the other lodgings, affording a bit of privacy. The rooms have a modern feel, yet they have thatch roofs and stucco walls decorated with traditional fabrics.

A small restaurant has a menu that changes daily. ✉ *Parque Nacional Tikal* ☎ *7926–1917* 🖶 *7926–0065* ✐ *hoteltikalinn@itelgua.com* ☞ *27 rooms* ⚄ *Restaurant, fans, pool; no a/c, no room phones, no room TVs* ▤ *AE, DC, MC, V* ⑩ *CP.*

$$$$ 🔲 **Jungle Lodge.** Built to house archaeologists working at Tikal, this hotel has cute duplexes, with a noticeable lack of privacy—the dividing wall between the rooms does not meet the ceiling. The rooms are clean, and the older section was renovated in 2005. ✉ *Parque Nacional Tikal* ☎ *2477–0570* 🖶 *2476–0294* ⊕ *www.junglelodge.guate.com* ☞ *46 rooms, 34 with bath* ⚄ *Restaurant, fans, pool; no a/c, no room phones, no room TVs* ▤ *No credit cards* ⑩ *Breakfast and lunch included.*

$$ 🔲 ⚠ **Jaguar Inn.** Although this small hotel won't win any travel awards and has the feel of a backpacker's place, it's considerably less expensive than the other two hotels in the park and has a good restaurant. The small rooms have tile floors and wooden furnishings, with Guatemalan fabrics. Reservations are sometimes "lost," even if you have confirming e-mail. ✉ *Parque Nacional Tikal* ☎ *No phone* ⊕ *www.jaguartikal.com* ☞ *9 rooms in cabins, 1 dorm* ⚄ *Restaurant, fans, Internet room; no a/c, no room phones, no room TVs* ▤ *V* ⑩ *Breakfast and lunch included.*

TIKAL ENVIRONS

Flores

★ ❷ *133 mi (206 km) north of Río Dulce, 38 mi (61 km) northeast of Sayaxché.*

The red-roof town of Flores, on an island surrounded by the waters of Lago Petén Itzá, is on the site of the ancient city of Tatyasal. This was the region's last unconquered outpost of Mayan civilization, until finally falling to the Spanish in 1697. The conquerors destroyed the city's huge pyramids.

Today the provincial capital is a pleasant place to explore, with its narrow streets lined with thick-walled buildings painted pink, blue, and purple. Flowering plants droop over balconies, giving the town a tropical flavor. There's a central square presided over by a colonial church. Connected to the mainland by a bridge and causeway, Flores serves as a base for travelers to El Petén. It's also the center of many nongovernmental organizations working for the preservation of the Mayan Biosphere, an endangered area covering nearly all of northern Petén. Flores is also one of the last remaining vestiges of the Itzá, the people who built Mexico's monumental Chichén Itzá.

In the 1800s, before it was a departure point for travelers headed for the ruins, Flores was called Devil's Island because of the prison on top of the hill (a church stands there now). Since 1994 the building has been home to the **Centro de Información sobre la Naturaleza, Cultura, y Artesanía de Petén** (✉ North side of Parque Central ☎ 7926–0718). This center has a small museum with photographs of the region and information about local resources, such as allspice, chicle (a chewing-gum

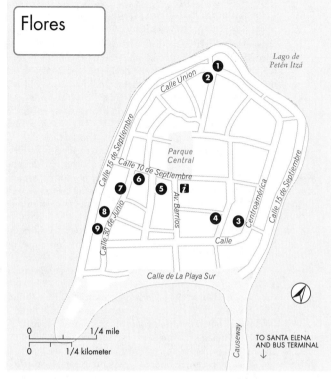

Flores

base made from tree sap), and *Xate* (a shade palm used in floral decorations). A gift shop sells wood carvings, woven baskets, cornhusk
dolls, and even locally made peanut butter.

Where to Stay & Eat

¢–$$$ ✕ **Capitán Tortuga.** The large, cartoonlike Capitán Tortuga sign may fool
you into thinking this restaurant is just for kids, but the excellent grilled
steak and seafood options make this one of Flores' best restaurants. The
pinchos (grilled kebabs) are cooked on an open barbecue, sending en-
ticing aromas throughout the restaurant. There's a nice patio out back,
which offers tremendous sunset views of the lake. ⊠ *Calle 30 de Junio
and Callejón San Pedrito* ☎ 7926–0247 ☰ MC, V.

¢–$$ ✕ **La Luna.** With its homemade paper lamp shades illuminating lovely
blue walls, La Luna inspires romance on any moonlit night. But you can
just as easily fall in love with what we think is the best restaurant in
town when you stop in for a delicious lunch. Choose from inventive dishes,
including wonderful vegetarian options like the stuffed squash in white
sauce. Many people drop by for a drink at the bar. ⊠ *Calle 30 de Junio*
☎ 7926–3346 ☰ AE, DC, MC, V ◷ *Closed Sun.*

¢–$ ✕ **Maya Princess Café.** An interesting, eclectic variety of Mexican, Thai,
and local dishes will fill you up without breaking the bank at this pink-

walled backpacker hangout. Movies are shown at night. ⊠ *Av. Reforma at 10 de Noviembre* ☎ 7926–3797 ☰ *MC, V.*

¢–$ ✕ **Las Puertas.** On a quiet side street, Las Puertas was named for its six screened doors. It's a favorite hangout for locals and travelers alike. The friendly couple who run the place take great pride in serving only the freshest foods. Notable are the delicious sandwiches made with home-made bread and mozzarella cheese and the giant goblets of incredible iced coffee. In the afternoon you can relax with a fruit drink as you play one of the many board games. Don't forget to stop back at night for a hearty dinner and live music. ⊠ *Calle Central at Av. Santa Ana* ☎ 7926–1061 ☰ *AE, DC, MC, V* ⊘ *Closed Sun.*

¢ ✕ **Pizzeria Picasso.** If you find yourself returning to Pizzeria Picasso, it's because the brick-oven pizza is incomparably hot and delicious. The decor, featuring a print of Picasso's *Guernica,* is another draw. If you're not in the mood for pizza, there are a variety of pastas as well. Save room for cheesecake or tiramisu and a cup of steaming cappuccino. ⊠ *Calle Centroamérica* ☎ 7926–0673 ☰ *AE, DC, MC, V* ⊘ *Closed Mon.*

$ ✕▥ **Hotel Sabana.** This small hotel, with four floors in one section and five in another, offers simple rooms that open onto a terrace overlooking the pool. A sundeck has nice views of the lake. This is a reliable choice if you need some creature comforts such as air-conditioning and a room TV. ⊠ *Calle Union and Av. Libertad* ☎☎ 7926–1248 ⊕ *www.hotelsabana.com* ⊅ *28 rooms* ⚲ *Restaurant, cable TV, pool, bar* ☰ *AE, DC, MC, V.*

$ ✕▥ **Hotel Santana.** Sitting right on the water, this bright pink hotel is the best lodging on the island. All the rooms open up onto wide balconies with wicker chairs where you can enjoy the view. The sunny central courtyard surrounds a pleasant pool. ⊠ *Calle 30 de Junio* ☎☎ 7926–0662 ⊕ *www.santanapeten.com* ⊅ *32 rooms* ⚲ *Restaurant, in-room safes, cable TV, pool, Internet* ☰ *AE, DC, MC, V.*

$ ▥ **Hotel Petén.** Take a dip in this lovely hotel's arabesque plunge pool to escape the midday heat. Rooms are simply furnished, but if you ask for one facing the lake, you'll have an incredible view of Lake Petén Itza. ⊠ *Off Calle 30 de Junio* ☎☎ 7926–0593 ⊕ *www.corpetur.com* ⊅ *21 rooms* ⚲ *Restaurant, fans, cable TV, pool, bar, Internet, travel services* ☰ *AE, DC, MC, V* ⏋⏍ *BP.*

¢ ✕▥ **Hospedaje Doña Goya.** A rooftop terrace with hammocks swinging in the breeze is the best part of this budget lodging. If you prefer, grab a good book and sink into one of the comfortable lounge chairs. The hotel is clean and well run, which explains why it is so popular. Arrive early in the day to secure a room. A bed in the dorm is Q25. ⊠ *Calle Union* ☎ 7926–3538 ⊅ *6 rooms, 3 with bath, dormitory* ⚲ *Fans; no a/c, no room TVs* ☰ *No credit cards.*

Nightlife

Discoteca Raices (⊠ Av. Periferico) is the island's only true disco. The bar at the **Maya Princess** (⊠ Av. La Reforma and Av. 14 de Noviembre) shows nightly movies on a big-screen TV.

Las Puertas (⊠ Calle Central at Av. Santa Ana ☎ 7926–1061) has live music every night. The artsy **La Luna** (⊠ Calle 30 de Junio ☎ 7926–3346) has a pleasant atmosphere.

Sports & the Outdoors

BOATING   Boat trips on Lake Petén Itzá can be arranged through most hotels in Flores or by haggling with boat owners who congregate behind the Hotel Santana. Tours often include a stop at Paraíso Escondido, a small mainland park northwest of Flores.

Santa Elena

❸ *¼ mi (½ km) south of Flores.*

Although it lacks the charms of neighboring Flores, gritty Santa Elena is pretty much unavoidable. Most services that you'll need for your trip to El Petén, from currency exchange to travel planning, are usually offered here. There are also nicer hotels here than in Flores.

Where to Stay & Eat

★ $$$$ ✕🏨 **Villa Maya.** You could lie in bed and count the birds flying by your window at these modern villas on beautiful Lago Petén Itzá. Some 50 species have been spotted in the area. If you're more interested in wildlife, ask an attendant where to find the troop of spider monkeys that roams the grounds and the adjacent rain forest. All the rooms, tastefully decorated with colorful weavings and mahogany accents, have terrific views. Vans shuttle you to and from Tikal. ✉ *7 mi (12 km) east of Santa Elena* 🕿 *5415–1592, 2334–8136 in Guatemala City* 🖨 *5514–0226, 2334–8134 in Guatemala City* ⊕ *www.villasdeguatemala.com* 🛏 *56 rooms* ⅀ *Restaurant, room service, pool, boating, bicycles, horseback riding, shop, laundry service, Internet, travel services, free parking; no room TVs* ▤ *AE, DC, MC, V.*

> **WORD OF MOUTH**
>
> "We really enjoyed a couple of nights at the Villa Maya and will stay there again. They have their own private lagoon and the pools were very nice. They also have a hot tub. It is only a 20 minute cab ride into Flores if you want to go there to eat. The food at Maya was very good we thought."
>
> —Suzie2

$$$ ✕🏨 **Maya International.** This string of thatch bungalows built over Lago Petén Itzá has lost a bit of its former grandeur. The simple accommodations are surrounded by water speckled with water lilies, which were sacred to the Maya. From the private balconies you can watch the waterfowl who forage here for their dinner. For your own meals there's the moderately priced restaurant, housed in a round building set out over the water. The set menu changes daily. ✉ *3 blocks east of bridge to Flores* 🕿 *7926–1276, 2334–8136 in Guatemala City* 🖨 *7926–0087 or 2334–8134* ⊕ *www.villasdeguatemala.com* 🛏 *24 rooms* ⅀ *Restaurant, cable TV, laundry service, free parking* ▤ *AE, DC, MC, V.*

$$$ ✕🏨 **Petén Espléndido.** You're not on Flores, but the views of that pretty island from your private balcony are the next best thing. The pool, surrounded by palm trees, is a great place to spend an afternoon sunbathing. Sit at one of the shaded tables on the terrace or in the pretty dining room and enjoy the *especial del día* (daily special). The hotel is popular among business travelers, who appreciate the fully equipped con-

vention center. Families enjoy the paddleboats on the lake. ⊠ *At foot of bridge leading to Flores* ☎ *7926–0880* 🖷 *7926–0866* ⊕ *www. petenesplendido.com* ⇘ *62 rooms* ♿ *Restaurant, in-room safes, cable TV, pool, bar, convention center, airport shuttle, free parking* ⊟ *AE, DC, MC, V.*

$ ✕🏠 **Casa Elena Hotel.** An attractive lobby paneled with lots of dark wood welcomes you to this centrally located hotel. Just beyond the entrance is a pretty restaurant that lets the breeze in through lace curtains. There's a wide range of dinner options, from fresh fish to grilled steak. The rooms lack the charm of others in the area, but they are clean and comfortable. There are no balconies—for a view, head to the meeting room on the top floor. The pool has a small waterslide that kids seem to love. ⊠ *6 Av.* ☎ *7926–2235* 🖷 *7926–0097* ⊕ *www.casaelena.com* ⇘ *28 rooms* ♿ *Restaurant, cable TV, pool, laundry service, meeting room, free parking* ⊟ *AE, DC, MC, V.*

$$$ 🏠 **Hotel del Patio-Tikal.** Built in traditional Spanish style, this modern hotel is known by its barrel-tile roof. Rooms face a small patio with a trickling fountain. Ask for a room on the first floor, as these have much larger windows. The patio restaurant sits under big arches leading to a grassy courtyard, making it a much more pleasant place to relax than the musty bar. ⊠ *2 Calle and 8 Av., Santa Elena* ☎ *7926–0104* 🖷 *7926–3030* ⇘ *21 rooms* ♿ *Restaurant, cable TV, pool, gym, free parking; no a/c* ⊟ *AE, DC, MC, V* ⦿l *BP.*

Sports & the Outdoors

There are several caves in the hills behind Santa Elena with interesting stalactite and stalagmite formations and subterranean rivers. The easiest to visit is Aktun Kan, just south of town.

☙ **Ixpanpajul Parque Natural** (⊠ Ruta a Santa Elena, Km 468 ☎ 2336–0576 ⊕ www.ixpanpajul.com) is a private nature reserve sitting on a large stand of primary rain forest. Hiking the suspended bridges of the skyway will give you a bird's-eye view of the indigenous flora and fauna that make the rain forest the most biodiverse ecosystem on the planet. The park also offers myriad adventure opportunities from nighttime ATV tours to horseback rides to mountain-bike excursions. The entrance to the reserve is 6 mi (10 km) south of Santa Elena.

El Remate

❹ *18½ mi (30 km) northeast of Flores.*

A mellow little town on the eastern shore of Lago Petén Itzá, El Remate is known mostly for its wood carvings, made by families that have dedicated themselves to this craft for generations. Because it's less than one hour from both Tikal and Yaxhá, El Remate makes a good base for exploring the area.

With more than 1,500 acres of rain forest, **Biotopo Cerro Cahuí** (⊠ West of El Remate 🎫 Q20) is one of the most accessible wildlife reserves in El Petén. It protects a portion of a mountain that extends to the eastern edge of Lago Petén Itzá, so there are plenty of opportunities for hiking. Two well-maintained trails put you in proximity of birds like oscillated turkeys, toucans, and parrots. As for mammals, look up to spot the long-armed spider monkeys or down to see squat rodents called *tepezcuintles.* Tzu'unte, a 4-mi (6-km) trail, leads to two lookouts with views of nearby lakes. The upper lookout, Mirador Moreletii, is known by locals as Crocodile Hill because, from the other side of the lake, it looks like the eye of a half-submerged crocodile. Los Ujuxtes, a 3-mi (5-km) trail, offers a panoramic view of three lakes. Both hikes begin at a ranger station, where English-speaking guides are sporadically available.

Where to Stay & Eat

¢–$ ✕ **La Estancia Cafetería.** Owner Victor Morales's specialty is an exquisite whitefish served with vegetables sautéed in butter on a wooden platter. Every once in a while he cooks up some fresh venison. Even though the driveway is usually filled with cars, this eatery is easy to miss—look for the Orange Crush sign. ✉ *1¼ mi (2 km) south of El Remate* ☎ *No phone* ▭ *No credit cards.*

$–$$ ✕▥ **La Casa de Don David.** As you chat with David Kuhn, the owner of this cluster of bungalows, keep an eye out for his pet parrot. The little fellow sometimes gets jealous. But talking with Kuhn is worth it, as he and his wife, Rosa, have lived in the area for more than 25 years and are a great source of travel tips. Rooms are simple and clean, with private baths. Perhaps La Casa is most famous for its second-story restaurant (¢), which has good home cooking. Have dinner for two in a booth, or eat at the "friendship table" and make some new acquaintances. One meal is included in the room rate—you can choose to have breakfast, lunch, or dinner here. Credit cards are accepted for Internet reservations. ✉ *On road to Biotopo Cerro Cahuí* ☎ *5306–2190 or 7928–8469* ⤳ *15 rooms* ⚕ *Restaurant, fans, free parking; no a/c in some rooms, no room TVs* ⊕ *www.lacasadedondavid.com* ▭ *MC, V* ⑩ *BP.*

Sports & the Outdoors

The fun folks at **Tikal Canopy Tour** (✉ Near entrance to Tikal ☎ 708–0674) have expeditions that take you to the true heart of the rain forest—not on ground level, but more than 100 feet up in the air. In the canopy you'll see monkeys and maybe even a sloth. The tour, which costs US$25 per person, ends with an exhilarating 300-foot-long ride down a zip line.

Shopping

Although most souvenirs here are similar to those found elsewhere in Guatemala, the beautiful wood carvings are unique to El Petén. More than 70 families in this small town dedicate themselves to this craft. Their wares are on display on the side of the highway right before the turnoff for the Camino Real hotel on the road to Tikal.

North Shore, Lake Petén Itzá

❺ *8 mi (13 km) west of El Remate.*

The small villages of San Pedro, San José, and San Andrés, on the northwest shore of Lake Petén Itzá, have beautiful views of the sparkling lake. Several upscale lodges and hotels have opened here, and the area is accessible via bus or car on a dirt road either from El Remate or from Santa Elena.

Where to Stay & Eat

★ $$$$ ×⌂ **Camino Real Tikal.** To experience the natural beauty of the jungles surrounding Lago Petén Itzá without sacrificing creature comforts, many people head to Camino Real Tikal. It's possible to spend several days at the hotel without exhausting the possibilities—kayaking on the lake, hiking in a private reserve, swimming in the pool, lounging in the lakeside hammocks, and experiencing a traditional Mayan sauna. A dozen thatch-roof villas set high on the hillside hold the rooms, all of which have porches with views of the sparkling lake. ⊠ *Lote 77, Parcelamiento Tayasal, 3 mi (5 km) west of El Remate, San José* ☎ *7926–0204* 🖷 *7926–0222* ⊕ *www.caminoreal.com.gt* ↗ *72 rooms* ♨ *Restaurant, coffee shop, fans, cable TV, pool, gym, boating, bar, shop, airport shuttle, car rental, travel services* ▤ *AE, DC, MC, V* ⋈ *BP.*

★ $$$$ ×⌂ **La Lancha.** Francis Ford Coppola's latest lodging venture isn't quite as luxe as his two properties in Belize, but everything is done in exquisite taste. Guatemalan and Balinese textiles and handmade furniture make rooms cozy. All the casitas glimpse Lake Petén Itzá, though the pricier, larger lake-view units have the stunning, splurge-worthy views. ⊠ *8 mi (13 km) west of El Remate, San José* ☎ *7928–8331, 800/746–3743 in U.S.* 🖷 *501/824–4912* ⊕ *www.blancaneauxlodge.com* ↗ *10 casitas* ♨ *Restaurant, fans, pool, boating, bar, shop, travel services* ▤ *AE, MC, V* ⋈ *CP.*

$$$$ ×⌂ **Ni'tun Reserve Ecolodge.** After hiking through the jungle, you'll
FodorsChoice love returning to this charming cluster of cabins. The point is to disturb
★ the environment as little as possible, so the buildings are constructed of stone and wood left behind by farmers clearing land for fields. The common areas, including a massive kitchen downstairs and an airy bar and reading room upstairs are delightful. The owners also run Monkey Eco Tours, so you can choose from itineraries ranging from one-day trips to nearby villages to a seven-day journey to El Mirador. ⊠ *1 mi (2 km) west of San Andres* ☎ *5201–0759* ⊕ *www.nitun.com* ↗ *4 cabins* ♨ *Restaurant, fans, travel services; no a/c, no room TVs, no kids* ▤ *AE, DC, MC, V* ⋈ *All-inclusive* ⊗ *Closed late May–early June.*

OTHER MAYAN SITES IN EL PETÉN

Although Tikal is the most famous, El Petén has hundreds of archaeological sites, ranging from modest burial chambers to sprawling cities. The vast majority have not been explored, let alone restored. Within a few miles of Tikal are several easy-to-reach sites. Because they're in isolated areas, it's a good idea to go with a guide (*see* Tours in Tikal & Environs Essentials, *below*).

Sights to See

Nakúm lies deep within the forest, connected to Tikal via jungle trails that are sometimes used for horseback expeditions. You cannot visit during the rainy season, as you'll sink into mud up to your ankles. Two building complexes and some stelae are visible. ⊠ *16 mi (26 km) east of Tikal.*

The 4,000-year-old city of **Uaxactún** was once a rival to Tikal's supremacy in the region. It was conquered by Tikal in the 4th century and lived in the shadow of that great city for centuries. Inscriptions show that Uaxactún existed longer than any other Mayan city, which may account for the wide variety of structures. Here you'll find a Mayan observatory.

Uaxactún is surrounded by thick rain forest, so the trip can be arduous, but as it's difficult to get here, you most likely won't have to fight the crowds as you do at neighboring Tikal, leaving you free to enjoy the quiet and mystic air of the ruins. The rock-and-dirt road is passable during the drier seasons and nearly impossible at other times without a four-wheel-drive vehicle. You'll need to secure a permit to visit Uaxactún. The administration building in Tikal is on the road between the Jaguar Inn and the Jungle Lodge. Obtaining a permit is sometimes easier said than done, but with a little persistence and perhaps a small *mordida* (bribe), you should be able to get past the guards into the administration area where they grant the free permits. Sometimes police will ask to accompany you on the trip, which is helpful for two reasons: it prevents potential robberies and, most important, will give you an extra person to push if your vehicle gets stuck. The police may ask you for some money; a Q20 tip goes a long way toward making your trip smooth. ⊠ *16 mi (24 km) north of Tikal.*

Overlooking a beautiful lake of the same name, the ruins of **Yaxhá** are divided into two sections of rectangular structures that form plazas and streets. The city was probably inhabited between the Pre-Classic and Classic periods. The ruins are being restored by a German organization. Lake Yaxhá, surrounded by virgin rain forest, is a good bird-watching spot. During the rainy season only a four-wheel-drive vehicle—or setting out on horseback, motorcycle or on foot—will get you to Yaxhá; the rest of the year the road is passable. The CBS TV program *Survivor Guatemala* was shot at Yaxhá in 2005. ⊠ *30 km (48 km) south of Flores, 19 mi (30 km) east of Tikal.*

A popular ecotourism destination, **El Zotz** is where you'll find the remnants of a Mayan city. On a clear day you can see the tallest of the ruins at Tikal from these unexcavated ruins. The odd name, which means "the bat" in Q'eqchí, refers to a cave from which thousands of bats make a nightly exodus. Troops of hyperactive spider monkeys seem to have claimed this place for themselves, swinging through the treetops and scrambling after each other like children playing a game of tag. Unlike those in Tikal, however, these long-limbed creatures are not used to people and will shake branches and throw twigs and fruit to try to scare you away. During the rainy season the mosquitoes can be fierce, so bring your strongest repellent. ⊠ *15 mi (24 km) west of Tikal.*

El Mirador, once equal in size and splendor to Tikal, may eventually equal Tikal as a must-see Mayan ruin. It's just now being explored, but elaborate plans are being laid to establish a huge park four times the size of Tikal. The Mirador Basin contains the El Mirador site itself; four other known Mayan cities that probably were as large as Tikal (Nakbé, El Tintal, Xulnal, and Waxná); and many smaller but important sites—perhaps as many as 80 to 100 cities. The Mirador Basin is home to an incredible diversity of plant and animal life, including 200 species of birds, 40 kinds of animals (including several endangered ones, such as jaguars), 300 kinds of trees, and 2,000 different species of flora. It has been nominated as a UNESCO World Heritage Site. Currently, fewer than 2,500 visitors get to El Mirador annually, as it's a difficult trek requiring five or six days of hiking (round-trip). The jumping-off point for the trek is Carmelita Village, about 50 mi (84 km) north of Flores. There are no hotels in the Mirador Basin, and no roads except for dirt paths. Local tour companies (*see below*) can arrange treks. ⊠ *40 mi (66 km) northwest of Tikal.*

Where to Stay

$ ☷ **El Sombrero Campamento Ecologico.** This cluster of wooden cabins is a restful place to spend the night. There's only three hours of electricity a day, but the lakefront views and ample opportunities for bird-watching more than make up for it. The friendly Italian owner Gabriella Moretti goes out of her way to arrange trips for her guests. There are rooms with shared bathrooms for very reasonable rates. ⊠ *Yaxhá* ☎ *7861–1687 or 7861–1688* ⊕ *www.ecosombrero.com* ⇆ *13 rooms, 7 without bath* ⌂ *Restaurant, boating, horseback riding, bar; no a/c, no room TVs* ⊟ No *credit cards.*

TIKAL & THE MAYAN RUINS ESSENTIALS

Transportation

BY AIR

Aeropuerto Internacional Santa Elena (FRS), often referred to as the Flores airport, is less than ½ mi (1 km) outside town. Taxis and shuttles meet every plane and charge about 20 quetzales to take you into town. The airport has service to and from Guatemala City, Belize City, and Cancun. Continental has nonstop twice-weekly flights from Houston.

Maya Island Air and Tropic Air have two daily flights each way between the international airport near Belize City and Santa Elena–Flores. Flights typically leave in the early morning and in the midafternoon, in each direction. The 45-minute flights cost around US$104 one-way, or US$203–US$208 round-trip.

Note that when flying out of Belize internationally, even to Guatemala, you'll pay the US$35 exit fee; when flying out of Flores internationally, even to Belize, you'll pay the US$30 Guatemalan exit fee.

🚩 **Maya Island Air** ☎ 501/223-1140 in Belize City, 7926-3386 in Flores ⊕ www.mayaairways.com. **Tropic Air** ☎ 501/226-2012 in Belize, 800/422-3435 in U.S. and Canada ⊕ www.tropicair.com.

BY BUS

Linea Dorada runs two daily buses (US$17–US$20 one-way from Belize City) all the way to Flores, via San Ignacio, Belize (you could board/get off at San Ignacio, but there's no formal stop—you have to wave the bus down), and Melchor de Mencos, Guatemala. The trip takes four to five hours, including border crossing. The 42-mi (70- km) paved route between Flores–Santa Elena and Tikal is served by scheduled minibus shuttles, operated by San Juan Travel. They cost around US$5 per person round-trip and leave from the San Juan Hotel, stopping at other hotels. The trip takes about 1½ hours. Buses leave at 5, 6, 7, 8, 9, and 10 AM and 2 PM and return at 12:30, 2, 3, 4, 5, and 6 PM. Please note that schedules are subject to frequent change and you should check with your hotel before making plans. Local buses serving other destinations depart from the market in Santa Elena near Calle Principal. They are inexpensive but very slow.

A less expensive option, but one that requires more time and effort, would be to take regular Belize buses to San Ignacio, and then a bus (or collective or a taxi) to the border just beyond the town of Benque Viejo del Carmen.

Numerous local chicken buses and minibuses run roughly hourly during the day between Melchor de Mencos at the Belize border and Santa Elena–Flores. They're always packed and cost around US$3. These buses won't take you all the way to Tikal, however; for that, you must get off in Ixlu (also known as El Cruce, the crossroads), and change buses. A minibus to Tikal from Ixlu is around US$2.50.

When leaving Belize by land, there's a US$18.75 exit fee.

Linea Dorada ✉ 4a Calle, Santa Elena ☎ 7926-0070 ✉ Calle de la Playa, Flores ☎ 2232-9658. **San Juan Travel** ✉ Calle 2, Santa Elena ☎ 7926-0042.

BY CAR

Roads in El Petén are often in poor repair and not very well marked. Some roads are impassable during the rainy season, so check with the tourist office before heading out on seldom traveled roads, such as those to the more-remote ruins surrounding Tikal. A four-wheel-drive vehicle *doble-tracción,* is highly recommended.

To be on the safe side, never travel at night. If you come upon a fallen tree across the road, do not get out of your car to remove the debris. Robbers have been known to fell trees to get tourists to stop. Turn around as quickly as possible.

If you're not booked on a tour, the best way to get around El Petén is by renting a four-wheel-drive vehicle. The major rental agencies, including Budget and Hertz, have offices at Aeropuerto Internacional Santa Elena. Koka, a local company, also rents vehicles from an office in the airport, as does Tabarini, which usually has a good selection. You need a valid driver's license from your own country to drive in Guatemala. Crystal Auto Rental in Belize City permits its vehicles to be taken into Guatemala (the El Petén/Tikal area only).

Local Agencies Budget ✉ Aeropuerto Internacional Santa Elena ☎ 7950-0741. **Crystal** ✉ Mile 5, Northern Hwy, Belize City ☎ 501/223-1910. **Hertz** ✉ Aeropuerto Internacional Santa Elena ☎ 7950-0204. **Koka** ✉ Aeropuerto Internacional Santa Elena ☎ 7926-1233. **Tabarini** ✉ Aeropuerto Internacional Santa Elena ☎ 7926-0253 or 7926-0277.By Taxi

After you cross the border from Belize into Melchor de Mencos, you can hire a taxi or minivan to take you and your party direct to Tikal or, if you prefer, to Flores–Santa Elena. You'll pay US$30 to US$50 (for the van-taxi, not per person), depending on your bargaining ability and your fluency in Spanish. Taxis from the Santa Elena–Flores airport to Tikal are around US$40.

BORDER FORMALITIES

The Belize border is about 9 mi (15 km) from San Ignacio, just beyond the town of Benque Viejo del Carmen. Belize has built a new customs and immigration building at the border. Border crossings here are usually quick and easy.

Upon arrival at the border, you'll be approached on the Belize side by money changers asking if you want to exchange U.S. or Belize dollars for Guatemalan quetzals. The rate given by money changers will be a little less than you'll get at an ATM or bank, but you may want to exchange enough for your first day in Guatemala. There's a bank in Melchor de Mencos, but it does not have an ATM and doesn't exchange money. While U.S. dollars are usually accepted in El Petén, it's easier to deal in quetzals, and the exchange rate at shops and restaurants may be poor. There also are money changers on the Guatemalan side.

Belize formalities include paying your US$18.75 exit fee. Guatemalan officials often ask for a Q10 or US$2 entrance fee. There's no such fee, but many visitors pay this small bribe just to keep things going smoothly. Most visitors to Guatemala, including citizens of the United States, Canada, and European Union, do not need visas and passports are normally stamped with a permit to enter for 90 days. Customs officials rarely check baggage.

Melchor de Mencos is a scruffy border town with unpaved streets. Shops on the main drag sell Guatemalan crafts. Other than extremely basic hotels (some of which are brothels), the only place to stay nearby is the Río Mopan Lodge (US$70 double). The Swiss owner, Marco Gross, can help smooth any border problems, arrange good tours anywhere in El Petén, exchange money, and provide a good night's sleep at his lodge. Among his tours: a day trip to Tikal, including lunch, entrance fee, guide, and transfers (US$50), and an overnight tour, including a one-night stay at the Jungle Lodge in the park, along with guide, entrance fees, lunch, and transfers (US$100 per person, double occupancy).

There's no safe long-term parking at the border, so if you are driving a rental car, you should arrange to park it elsewhere. Only a handful of Belize rental companies allow their vehicles to be taken into Guatemala (try Crystal in Belize City). Note, however, that Belize insurance isn't valid in Guatemala, and Guatemalan insurance currently isn't sold at the border. The nearest place to buy it is Flores.

🗊 **Tikal Travel at Río Mopan Lodge** ✉ Melchor de Mencos ☎ 7926–5196 🖷 7926–5067 ⊕ www.tikaltravel.com.

Contacts & Resources

BANKS & RESOURCES

Guatemalan currency is called the quetzal, after the resplendent national bird. There are 1-, 5-, 10-, and 25-centavo coins. Bills come in denominations of one-half, 1, 5, 10, 20, 50, and 100 quetzals. At this writing, $1 was worth roughly Q7.6, but at most hotels and money changers in El Petén you'll get a little less.

While U.S. dollars are seldom refused in Guatemala and the U.S. dollar is officially a parallel currency, using quetzals will make transactions easier and less confusing. You can exchange U.S. dollars at any bank and in high-end hotels. It's far more difficult to exchange other currencies. If you're traveling with currency other than U.S. dollars, it would be wise to change the money into dollars or quetzales before you arrive. Traveler's checks are accepted mainly in larger hotels. If you need to exchange money, do so before heading off on your jungle adventure.

There are several banks in Santa Elena, but few anywhere else in the region. Those on Calle 4, the main street, have ATMs that work with foreign ATM cards with MasterCard or Visa logos. You may have to try more than one ATM before you find one that works with your card. Flores has one bank, but it does not have an ATM. Make sure you only have a four-digit pin number, as many ATMs only take four digits.
🏧 Banks **Banrural** ✉ Calle 4 at Av. 3, Santa Elena ☎ 7926-1002.

Banco Industrial ✉ Calle 4, Santa Elena ☎ 7926-0281.

EMBASSIES

Government embassies are in Guatemala City.
🏧 **Canada** ✉ Edificio Edyma Plaza, 8th fl., 13 Calle 8-44, Zona 10, Guatemala City ☎ 2363-4348. **United Kingdom** ✉ 16 Calle 0-55, Edificio Torre Internacional, 11th fl., Guatemala City ☎ 2367-5425. **United States** ✉ Av. La Reforma 7-01, Zona 10, Guatemala City ☎ 2326-4000.

EMERGENCIES

Medical facilities in El Petén are not as modern as in the rest of the country. If you're really sick, consider getting on the next plane to Belize City. Centro Médico Maya in Santa Elena has physicians on staff, though little or no English is spoken.
🏧 **Centro Médico Maya** ✉ Av. 4, Santa Elena ☎ 7926-0180.
🏧 **Pharmacies Farmacia Nueva** ✉ Av. Santa Ana, Flores ☎ 7926-1387.
🏧 **Emergency Services Police** ☎ 7926-1365.

MAIL & SHIPPING

The main post office in Flores is a half block east of the main square. In Santa Elena the post office is a block east of the bridge leading to Flores. Tikal also has a small post office. Mail service is slow, so expect to get back home before your letter does.
🏧 **Post Offices Flores** ✉ Av. Barrios, Flores. **Santa Elena** ✉ Calle Principal, Flores. **Tikal Park** ✉ Near visitor center.

TOURS

Flores-based Martsam Travel, run by Lileana and Benedicto Grijalva, offers many different types of tours in the area. Tikal Travel in Melchor de Mencos at the Belize–Guatemala border has well-priced tours of Tikal and other Mayan sites in El Petén. Flores-based Expedition Panamundo specializes in tours of the Mayan world and bird-watching expeditions. Tip tour guides about 10% of the tour price.

🏕 **Expedition Panamundo** ⊠ 2 Calle and 4 Av., Zona 1, Santa Elena ☎ 7926-0501, 2331-7588 in Guatemala City. **Martsam Travel** ⊠ Calle Centroamérica and Av. 30 de Junio, Flores ☎ 7926-0346 🖶 7926-3225. **Tikal Travel at Río Mopan Lodge** ⊠ Melchor de Mencos ☎ 7926-5196 🖶 7926-5067 ⊕ www.tikaltravel.com.

FROM BELIZE Many tour operators in the San Ignacio, Belize, area operate day and overnight or multinight tours of Tikal. You'll pay more in Belize than in Guatemala, but you reduce the hassle factor—you'll probably be picked up at your Cayo hotel, whisked across the border, provided with a guide to Tikal, and fed lunch (hotel accommodations are arranged if you're staying overnight). You'll typically pay US$75 to US$100 for a day trip to Tikal from San Ignacio, and US$150 to US$200 for an overnight tour.

Air tours from Belize City also are an option. Expect to pay from US$400 to US$700 per person for overnight tours from Belize City, including air, hotel, meals, Tikal entry fee and guide, and transfers in Guatemala.

Tropic Air also has day and overnight tours of Tikal by air from San Pedro, Belize. The day trip costs US$366 per person and includes airfare, ground transportation, guided tour, entrance fee, and lunch. The overnight tour, with a similar tour package, is US$388, plus hotel.

Tours from Belize typically do not include the Belize and Guatemala exit fees.

See The Cayo and Adventure Vacations chapters for more information.

VISITOR INFORMATION

Arcas, which returns illegally captured animals to the wild, is a great resource on the flora and fauna of El Petén. The staff at Inguat, Guatemala's tourism promotion agency, is courteous, professional, and knowledgeable. Inguat has two offices in El Petén, one in Flores and one at Aeropuerto Internacional Santa Elena.

🏕 **Arcas** ⊠ 6 mi (10 km) east of Santa Elena in San Benito 🖶 7926-0946 ⊕ www.arcasguatemala.com. **Inguat** ⊠ On Parque Central, Flores ☎ 7926-0669 ⊠ Aeropuerto Internacional Santa Elena ☎ 7926-0533 at airport.

Mayan Sites

WORD OF MOUTH

"Stay around San Ignacio and see Caracol, see Xunantunitch and enjoy the jungle and river there, find someone to take you up the river and canoe down yourself."

—macnamara

"We had to walk a mile through a jungle trail to get to the [Tikal] ruins. The weather was perfect: 75°, cloudy. Wow, what a site! The courtyard area in the grand Plaza was surrounded by temples and Mayan housing. [We] saw spider monkeys, colorful birds, coatimundis, and finally, howler monkeys. The howlers were so loud. Just amazing how the Mayans built these magnificent temples in 600 AD without our modern ways."

—puckettt

By Lan Sluder   **VISITING BELIZE WITHOUT TOURING ANY** Mayan sites is like going to Greece and not seeing the Acropolis and the Parthenon. For at least five millennia, the Maya left their imprint on what is now Belize, and today some of the Mayan world's most awe-inspiring ruins are yours to explore. Archaeologists have identified more than 600 significant Mayan sites in Belize, and doubtless many more are yet to be discovered. You can choose from among more than a dozen major excavated sites that are open to visitors, in all parts of the country, from Corozal and Orange Walk districts in the north to Cayo in the west and Toledo in the south. Some, such as Cahal Pech or Xunantunich, are by the roadside and easily reached; others, such as La Milpa or Cerros, will have you tramping the bush like Indiana Jones. Even the most accessible sites aren't overrun with hordes of travelers—at some you may be the only visitor, other than perhaps a troop of howler monkeys or a flock of parrots. This chapter fills you in on the fascinating history of the Maya in Belize, exposes some of the secrets of their great architecture, suggests itineraries for visiting the most interesting sites, and provides tips for touring the realm of the Maya.

NOTABLE MAYAN SITES IN BELIZE

The following are our picks for the most notable Mayan sites in Belize. See the destination chapters for detailed information on the sites, including hours and admission fees.

Northern Belize

Altun Ha. The most-visited Mayan site in Belize, though not the most impressive, is popular with cruise ship passengers and for those staying on Ambergris Caye or Caye Caulker. It's a little more than an hour's drive north of Belize City. One of the temples at Altun Ha is prominently pictured on Belikin beer bottles.

Cerros. Although the few remaining original structures here are weathered, and there's no museum or visitor center, Cerros—like Tulum in the Yucatán—enjoys a glorious location right beside the water.

Chan Chich. The lodge of the same name was built literally on top of this minor ceremonial site. It can be reached by car or charter flight and is best visited in connection with a stay at the lodge.

Cuello. It's one of the oldest Mayan sites in the region, settled more than 2,500 years ago. It's on the property of a rum distillery near Orange Walk Town, and you have to get permission in advance to visit it.

Lamanai. Boat your way up the New River to the shores of the New River Lagoon to see this ruin, which has the most beautiful setting of any Mayan site in Belize. You can also reach it by road from Orange Walk Town. Lamanai has a small museum and a resident troop of howler monkeys.

La Milpa. The third-largest Mayan site in Belize (only Caracol and Lamanai are larger), La Milpa is in the early stages of exploration and excavation. It can be visited through advance arrangement with Programme for Belize, on whose land it sits.

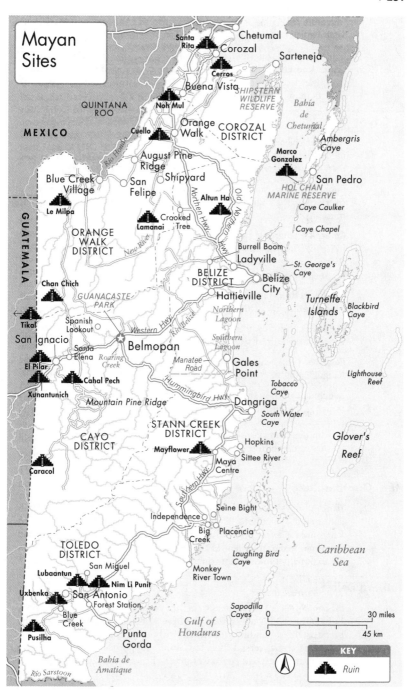

Mayan Sites

Chetumal
Santa Rita
Corozal
Sarteneja
Cerros
Buena Vista
SHIPSTERN
WILDLIFE
RESERVE
Bahía
de
Chetumal
QUINTANA
ROO
Noh Mul
Orange
Walk
COROZAL
DISTRICT
MEXICO
Cuello
Marco
Gonzalez
Ambergris
Caye
August Pine
Ridge
San Pedro
Blue Creek
Village
San
Felipe
Shipyard
HOL CHAN
MARINE RESERVE
Le Milpa
Altun Ha
Caye Caulker
Crooked
Tree
ORANGE
WALK
DISTRICT
Lamanai
Caye Chapel
New River
Burrell Boom
Ladyville
St. George's
Caye
Chan Chich
BELIZE
DISTRICT
Belize
City
Turneffe
Islands
Blackbird
Caye
GUANACASTE
PARK
Hattieville
Tikal
Spanish
Lookout
Northern
Lagoon
Western Hwy
Río Belize
San Ignacio
Santa
Elena
Belmopan
Southern
Lagoon
El Pilar
Roaring
Creek
Manatee
Road
Gales
Point
Lighthouse
Reef
Xunantunich
Cahal Pech
Hummingbird HWY
Tobacco
Caye
Mountain Pine Ridge
Dangriga
South Water
Caye
Glover's
Reef
STANN CREEK
DISTRICT
Hopkins
CAYO
DISTRICT
Mayflower
Sittee River
Caracol
Maya
Centre
Southern Hwy
Seine Bight
Independence
Big
Creek
Placencia
Caribbean
Sea
TOLEDO
DISTRICT
Laughing Bird
Caye
Lubaantun
San Miguel
Nim Li Punit
Monkey
River Town
Uxbenka
San Antonio
Forest Station
Sapodilla
Cayes
Blue
Creek
Pusilha
Punta
Gorda
Gulf of
Honduras
0   30 miles
0   45 km
Bahía de
Amatique
Río Sarstoon

GUATEMALA

KEY

▲ Ruin

Noh Mul. This ruin, settled around 350 BC, is about 10 mi north of Orange Walk Town on private land.

Santa Rita. Corozal Town is built on what was the large Mayan trading center known as Chactemal (or Chetumal, as the capital of Quintana Roo, Mexico, is known today). A part of the ruins, now called Santa Rita, is on a hill on the outskirts of town.

The Cayo

Actun Tunichil Muknal. "ATM" near Belmopan provides the most rewarding Mayan cave experience in Belize. To see the cave, you have to take a 45-minute hike and a brief swim, and be a part of a guided tour.

Cahal Pech. This small Late Classic site, with a lovely location on a hill overlooking San Ignacio, is easily accessible from town. It has a little museum.

Caracol. The largest and most significant site in Belize is a must if you're in Cayo. It's an all-day trip from San Ignacio through the Mountain Pine Ridge, but it's well worth the time. There's a museum and visitor center, and extensive excavations have been underway for more than 20 years.

Che Chem Ha. This cave on private land south of Benque Viejo has artifacts dating back 2000 years.

El Pilar. Set on hills above the Mopan River at the Guatemalan border is one of the largest sites in Belize, but little of it has been excavated.

Pacbitun. Near San Antonio village on the road to the Mountain Pine Ridge, Pacbitun dates back to at least 1000 BC. It's on private land.

Xunantunich. Though it's not one of the largest sites in Belize, Xunantunich is one of the easiest and most pleasant to visit. To reach it, you cross the Mopan River on a quaint, hand-pulled ferry. There's a well-done museum and visitor center. For views of Cayo and part of Guatemala, be sure to climb to the top of El Castillo. It's off the Western Highway, west of San Ignacio.

Petén, Guatemala

Tikal. Along with Copán in Honduras and Palenque in Mexico, Tikal is considered by many to be the most impressive of all Mayan sites. The Petén area is home to several other ruins, including **Nakúm, El Ceibal, Uaxactún, Yaxhá, Yaxchilán, El Zotz,** and **El Mirador.** Some, like El Mirador, are extremely remote, requiring a multiday jungle trek.

Southern Belize

Lubaantun. Occupied for less than 200 years in the Late Classic period, Lubaantun is unusual in that no stelae were ever found here, and the precisely fitted building stones, laid without mortar, have rounded corners. The controversial "Crystal Skull" supposedly was found here. Lubaantun is near San Pedro Columbia village, about 20 mi from Punta Gorda.

GREAT ITINERARY: MAYAN SITES BLITZ

If you want to see the top Mayan sites in one trip, base yourself in Cayo for a few days. Information on tour operators and guides, and on admissions to specific sites, are in destination chapters.

If, after a few days in Western Belize and Guatemala you still haven't had your fill of things Mayan, you can add extensions to northern Belize and to Punta Gorda in southern Belize.

DAY 1: SAN IGNACIO

San Ignacio is an easy jumping-off spot to see several small but fascinating nearby ruins. If you get an early start, you can take in **Xunantunich, Cahal Pech,** and **El Pilar.** Both Cahal Pech and Xunantunich can be reached by bus (albeit with a short hike after the bus ride in both cases), but a taxi or rental car is needed to get to El Pilar. Guided tours of all these sites can be arranged in San Ignacio or at lodges and hotels in the area. (*See* The Cayo, Chapter 4)

DAY 2: CARACOL

Caracol, the most important Mayan site in Belize deserves a full day. You can drive yourself—or go on a tour. There is no bus transportation in the Mountain Pine Ridge. Even if you arrive independently, you can hire a guide to show you around once you're at the site, or you can tour it on your own. There's an informative museum and visitor center. (*See* The Cayo, Chapter 4)

DAY 3 & 4: TIKAL

Tikal is by far the most impressive Mayan site in the region and shouldn't be missed. Many operators offer day tours of Tikal from the San Ignacio area. (*See* Tikal, Chapter 7.)

TIPS

● Altun Ha, the ruin closest to Belize City, gets crowds of cruise ship day-trippers, so if you go, try to avoid days when there are several cruise ships in port.

● Be aware of your surroundings, and before heading anywhere remote by yourself, check with the locals to find out if there have been any recent safety issues.

● On your visit to Tikal, stay at one of the lodges at the park if possible—you'll be able to visit the ruins early in the morning or late in the afternoon, when howler monkeys and other animals are active and most day visitors have left.

● Pack plenty of bug juice with DEET. Mosquitoes are especially bad around Cerros and at the ruins near Punta Gorda.

8

Mayflower. This Classic period site, off the Southern Highway just south of Dangriga, is in the early stages of excavation. Waterfalls nearby make the setting appealing.

Nim Li Punit. Off the Southern Highway north of Punta Gorda is Nim Li Punit ("Big Hat" in Ketchi), a small but pretty site. There's a visitor center.

Pusilha. At a site near Aguacate Village on the Moho River is this collection of extensive but low-lying structures on a small hill. You can also see the remains of a stone bridge. Because of its remote location off the main highway, there aren't many tourists who make the trip out here.

Ambergris Caye

Although there are no large Mayan sites on the cayes, Ambergris Caye has several small ruins. **Chac Balam** can be visited on a boat tour to Bacalar, at the far north end of the island. **Marco Gonzalez,** at the south end of the island, is difficult to find without a local guide.

SEEING THE RUINS

Most visitors to Belize are not serious "Maya buffs" who spend all their time touring ruins. Instead, they opt to visit Mayan sites as just one aspect of their beach or mainland vacation. If this is your first trip to Belize, we recommend you do the same. Following are the sites that are easily visited from the most popular areas.

Ambergris Caye & Caye Caulker. Tour operators on these islands run trips to **Lamanai** (usually a full-day trip by boat and road) and to **Altun Ha** (normally a half-day trip, although it may be longer if it includes lunch and a spa visit at Maruba Spa). You can also visit **Tikal** on an overnight trip by air to Flores, Guatemala, with a change of planes in Belize City. It's also possible to arrange boat tours of small ruins on Ambergris Caye, including **Chac Balam** at Bacalar.

Belize City. Tour operators based in Belize City, most of which cater to cruise ships, offer day trips by road, boat, or air to **Lamanai** and by road to **Altun Ha,** and also by road to **Xunantunich** and other ruins, including **El Pilar** and **Cahal Pech** near San Ignacio. The Altun Ha tour often is combined with a brief tour of Belize City. The tours to San Ignacio may be combined with a stop at the Belize Zoo. You can also visit **Tikal** on a day or overnight trip by air from the international airport in Belize City to Flores.

Corozal Town. Tour operators in Corozal Town can arrange a full-day trip by road and boat to **Lamanai.** They also offer boat trips to **Cerros** or a visit to nearby **Santa Rita** by road. By advance arrangement, tour operators may be able to arrange road tours of **Cuello, La Milpa, Noh Mul,** or other less-visited sites.

San Ignacio, Belmopan & Mountain Pine Ridge. Tour operators in the San Ignacio, Belmopan, and Mountain Pine Ridge areas focus on the many Mayan sites in Cayo, including **Caracol, Xunantunich, Cahal Pech,** and

El Pilar. Tours to Caracol typically require a full day, while the other sites can each be done in a half-day or less. There are also guided tours of notable caves, including **Actun Tunichil Muknal** (full-day) and **Che Hem Ha** (half-day). Day and overnight tours by road to **Tikal** are also offered.

Hopkins & Placencia. Tour operators in Hopkins and Placencia offer half-day tours to the **Mayflower** ruins (sometimes combined, on a full-day trip, with a visit to the Cockscomb Basin Wildlife Sanctuary). They also offer full-day trips by road to the ruins near Punta Gorda, mainly **Lubaantun** and **Nim Li Punit.** You can also fly from Dangriga or Placencia, via Belize City, to Flores to see **Tikal.**

Punta Gorda. Tour operators in Punta Gorda and nearby focus on trips by road to the ruins of **Lubaantun, Nim Li Punit,** and **Pusilha.** These tours usually include visits to modern Maya villages near Punta Gorda. You can also fly from Punta Gorda, with a change of planes in Belize City, to Flores to see **Tikal.**

> **TIPS**
>
> Tour operators in each area offer day or part-day trips (and in a few cases, overnight trips) to the sites. Tours may not operate every day, especially off-season, and there may be a minimum number of participants required for the tour to run. Tour operators may be able to provide tours to lesser-visited sites with an advance arrangement. Except for certain caves such as Actun Tunichil Muknal, which can be visited only with a guide, most Mayan sites can be visited independently—you just need a rental car, or, in a few cases, bus fare.

A MAYAN PRIMER

Chronology

Traditionally, archaeologists have divided Mayan history into three main periods: Pre-Classic, Classic, and Post-Classic. Although some academics question the validity of such a uniform chronology, the traditional labels are still in use.

The **Pre-Classic** (circa 3,000 BC–AD 250) period is characterized by the influence of the Olmec, a civilization centered on the Gulf Coast of present-day Mexico. During this period, cities began to grow, especially in the southern highlands of Guatemala and in Belize, and it's at this time that Belize's Cuello, Lamanai, Santa Rita, Cahal Pech, Pacbitun, and Altun Ha sites were first settled.

By the **Late Pre-Classic** (circa 300 BC–AD 250) period, the Maya had developed an advanced mathematical system, an impressively precise calendar, and one of the world's five original writing systems. In Belize, Cerros was established during the Late Pre-Classic period.

During the **Classic** (circa 250 BC–AD 900) period, Maya artistic, intellectual, and architectural achievements literally reached for the stars. Vast city-states were crisscrossed by a large number of paved roadways, some of which still exist today. The great cities of Caracol (Belize), Palenque

(Mexico), Tikal (Guatemala), and Quirigu (Guatemala) were just a few of the powerful centers that controlled the Classic Maya world. In AD 562, Caracol—which, at its height, was the largest city-state in Belize, with a population of about 150,000—conquered Tikal. Other notable Classic period sites in Belize include Xunantunich, El Pilar, and Lubaantun.

The single largest unsolved mystery about the Maya is their rapid decline during the **Terminal Classic** (AD 800–900) period and the centuries following. Scholars have postulated that climate change, pandemic disease, drought, stresses in the social structure, overpopulation, deforestation, and changes in the trade routes could have been responsible. Rather than a single factor, several events taking place over time could well have been the cause.

The Maya of the **Post-Classic** (AD 900–early 1500s)period were heavily affected by growing powers in central Mexico. Architecture, ceramics, and carvings from this period show considerable outside influence. Although still dramatic, Post-Classic cities such as Chichén Itzá and Uxmal pale in comparison to their Classic predecessors. By the time the Spanish conquest reached the Yucatán, the Maya were scattered, feuding, and easy to conquer. Several sites in Belize, including Lamanai, were continuously occupied during this time, and even later.

Key Dates

Here are some key dates in the history of the Maya in Belize and in the El Petén area of Guatemala. Most of the dates are approximate, and some dates are disputed.

BC

3114	Date of the creation of the world, or 0.0.0.0.0 according to the LongCount calendar
3000	Early Olmec and Mayan civilizations thought to have begun
2500	Cuello established
2000	Santa Rita established
1500	Lamanai established
1000	Cahal Pech established
900	Olmec writing system developed; Caracol established
800	Tikal established
700	First written Mayan language
500	First Mayan calendars carved in stone
250	Altun Ha established
200	First monumental buildings erected at Tikal and El Mirador

AD

400–600	Tikal becomes leading city-state, with population of perhaps 200,000
553	Accession of Lord Water as Caracol ruler
562	Caracol conquers Tikal
599	Accession of Lord Smoke Ahau as Caracol ruler
618	Accession of Kan II as Caracol ruler

631	Caracol defeats Naranjo; Caracol's population is 150,000
700	Lubaantun established
800	Cahal Pech abandoned
895	Xunantunich abandoned
899	Tikal abandoned
900	Classic period of Mayan history ends
900–1500	Maya civilization in decline, many cities abandoned
1000	Southern Belize Mayan centers mostly abandoned
1050	Caracol abandoned
1517	Spanish arrive in Yucatán and begin conquest of Maya
1517–1625	Diseases introduced from Europe cause death of majority of Maya
1524–25	Hernán Cortés passed through Belize en route to Honduras, after leading expeditions to conquer the Aztecs in Mexico
1546–1600s	Maya in Belize rebel against Spanish
1695	Tikal ruins rediscovered by Spanish
1700s	Lamanai continuously occupied over 3,000 years
1724	Spanish abolish *encomienda* system of forced Maya labor
1839	John Lloyd Stephens and Frederick Catherwood visit Belize
1847	Caste Wars in Yucatán begin
1881	Early archaeological work begins at Tikal, by Alfred Maudslay
1894	Thomas Gann begins exploring Xunantunich and other Belize ruins
1936	Caracol ruins rediscovered by a lumberman
1956	William Coe and others begin excavations at Tikal
1992	Rigoberta Menchu, a Maya from Guatemala, wins Nobel Peace Prize
2012	The end of the world, 13.0.0.0.0 in the Long Count calendar

HISTORY IN BRIEF

Anthropologists believe that humans from Asia crossed a land bridge, in what is now the Bering Strait in Alaska, into North America more than 25,000 years ago. Gradually these Paleoindians, or "Old Indians," whose ancestors probably were Mongoloid peoples, made their way down the continent, establishing Native American settlements in what is now the United States and Canada. Groups of them are thought to have reached Mesoamerica, which includes, besides Belize, much of central Mexico, Guatemala, Honduras, and Nicaragua, around 20,000 to 22,000 years ago.

These early peoples were hunter-gatherers. The Olmec civilization, considered the mother culture of later Mesoamerican civilizations including that of the Maya, arose in central and southern Mexico 3,000 to 4,000 years ago. The Olmecs developed the first writing system in the New World, dating from at least 900 BC. They also had sophisticated mathematics and created complex calendars. The Olmecs built irrigation systems to water their crops.

As long ago as around 3000 BC—the exact date is in question and has changed as archaeologists have made new discoveries—the Maya began to settle in small villages in Belize and elsewhere in the region. They developed an agriculture based on the cultivation of maize (corn), squash, and other fruits and vegetables. In Belize, settlements were established as early as 2500 BC at Cuello in what is now Orange Walk District in northern Belize. Then, over the next 1,000 years or so, small settlements arose at Santa Rita in Corozal and Lamanai in Orange Walk, and at Cahal Pech, Caracol, and elsewhere in Cayo District in western Belize. What would become the great city-states of the region, including Tikal in today's Petén region of Guatemala and Caracol in Cayo, were first settled around 900 to 700 BC.

Two or three centuries before the time of Christ, several Mayan villages grew into sizeable cities. The Maya began to construct large-scale stone buildings at Tikal and elsewhere. Eventually, Tikal, Caracol, and other urban centers each would have thousands of structures—palaces, temples, residences, monuments, ball courts, even prisons. Although the Maya never had the wheel, and thus no carts or wagons, they built paved streets and causeways, and they developed crop irrigation systems.

At its height, in what is known as the Classic period (250 BC to AD 900), the Maya civilization consisted of about 50 cities, much like ancient Greek city-states. Each had a population of 5,000 to 100,000 or more. Tikal, the premier city in the region, may have had 200,000 residents in and around the city during its heyday, and Caracol in Belize probably had nearly as many. The peak population of the Maya civilization possibly reached 2 million or more, and as many as a million may have lived in Belize alone—nearly four times the current population.

The Mayan culture put a heavy emphasis on religion, which was based on a pantheon of nature gods, including those of the sun, moon, and rain. The Mayan view of life was cyclical, and Mayan religion was based on accommodating human life to the cycles of the universe.

Contrary to what scholars long believed, however, Mayan society had many aspects beyond religion. Politics, the arts, business, and trade were all important and dynamic aspects of Mayan life. Dynastic leaders waged brutal wars on rival city-states. Under its ruler Lord Smoke Ahau, Caracol, the largest city-state in Belize, conquered Tikal in AD 562, and less than a hundred years later, conquered another large city, Naranjo (also in Guatemala).

The Maya developed sophisticated mathematics. They understood the concept of zero and used a base-20 numbering system. Astronomy was the basis of a complex Mayan calendar system involving an accurately determined solar year (18 months of 20 days, plus a 5-day period), a sacred year of 260 days (13 cycles of 20 days), and a variety of longer cycles culminating in the Long Count, based on a zero date in 3114 BC, or 0.0.0.0.0—the date that the Maya believed was the beginning of the current cycle of the world.

The Mayan writing system is considered the most advanced of any developed in Mesoamerica. The Maya used more than 800 "glyphs," small pictures or signs, paired in columns that read from left to right and top to bottom. The glyphs represent syllables and, in some cases, entire words, that can be combined to form any word or concept. There is no Mayan alphabet. Mayan glyphs can represent either sounds or ideas, or both, making them difficult to accurately interpret. The unit of the writing system is the cartouche, a series of 3 to 50 glyphs, the equivalent of a word or sentence in a modern language.

As in most societies, it's likely that the large majority of the Maya spent much of their time simply trying to eke out a living. In each urban area the common people lived in simple thatch dwellings, similar to those seen in the region today. They practiced a slash-and-burn agriculture. Farmers cleared their small plots by burning the bush, then planting maize, squash, sunflowers, and other crops in the rich ash. After two or three years, when the soil was depleted, the plot was left fallow for several years before it could be planted again.

Beginning around AD 800, parts of the Mayan civilization in Belize and elsewhere in Mesoamerica began to decline. In most areas the decline didn't happen suddenly, but over decades and even centuries, and it took place at different times. For example, the cities in the Northern Lowlands of the Yucatán, such as Chichén Itzá, flourished for several more centuries after Tikal and Caracol were abandoned.

Scholars are still debating the reasons for the decline. Climatic change, lengthy droughts, overpopulation, depletion of arable land, social revolutions by the common people against the elites, pandemic disease epidemics, and the impact of extended periods of warfare all have been put forth as reasons. It may well have been a combination of factors, or there may have been different causes in different regions.

Whatever the reasons, the Mayan civilization in Belize and elsewhere in Mesoamerica never regained its Classic period glory. By the time the Spanish arrived in the early 1500s, only a few of the Mayan cities, mainly in the Highlands of Guatemala, were still thriving. Most of the great cities and trading centers of Belize and Guatemala, including Caracol and Tikal, had long been abandoned. Lamanai and a few other urban settlements were still inhabited.

Seeking gold and other plunder, the Spanish began their conquest of the Maya in the 1520s. Some Mayan states offered fierce resistance, and the last Mayan kingdom, in Mexico, was not vanquished until almost 1700. The Maya in Belize rebelled against the Spanish several times, but there was one enemy against which the Maya were defenseless: European disease. Small pox, chicken pox, measles, flu, and other infectious diseases swept through the Mayan settlements. Scientists believe that within a century, nearly 90% of the Maya had been wiped out by "imported" diseases.

Maya resistance to European control continued from time to time. In 1847 Mayan Indians in the Yucatán rose up against Europeans in the bloody Caste Wars, which lasted until 1904. This had a major impact on Belize, as many Mexican Mestizos (persons of mixed Indian and European heritage) and Maya moved to northern Belize to escape the violence. Sarteneja, Orange Walk Town, and Ambergris Caye were among the areas at least partly settled by refugees from the Yucatán.

Much of the Mayan civilization was buried under the tropical jungles for centuries, and Westerners knew little about it. In the process of trying to convert the Maya to Christianity in the 16th century, the Spanish burned most of the codices, Mayan "books" made of deer hide or bleached fig-tree paper. Only in the last few decades have scholars made progress in deciphering Mayan glyphic writing.

In 1839 two British adventurers, John Lloyd Stephens and Frederick Catherwood, visited Central America, including Belize, and explored a number of the Mayan sites. Their books, especially *Incidents of Travel in Central America, Chiapas, and Yucatán,* with text by Stephens and illustrations by Catherwood, brought the attention of the world to the Mayan past.

In the late 1800s the first systematic archaeological excavations of Tikal and Mayan sites in Belize were begun. Alfred Maudslay, an Englishman, conducted excavations at Tikal in 1881–82, and Harvard's Peabody Museum did fieldwork there between 1895 and 1904. Sylvanus Morley, a well-known Maya expert conducted work at Tikal at times between 1914 and 1928. In 1956 the University of Pennsylvania began the first large-scale excavation project at Tikal. In Belize, Thomas Gann, a British medical officer stationed in what was then British Honduras, carried out the first excavations of several major Belize Mayan sites, including Santa Rita, Xunantunich, Lubaantun, sites on Ambergris Caye, and others, starting in 1894. Since then, many university and museum teams, including ones from the University of Pennsylvania, the Royal Ontario Museum, Tulane University, the University of Texas, the University of California, and the University of Central Florida, have conducted extensive fieldwork in Belize. Drs. Diane and Arlen Chase, of the University of Central Florida, have been at work at the largest site in Belize, Caracol, since 1983.

About 25,000 Maya live in Belize today. In southern Belize they're predominantly Ketchi and Mopan Maya, in western Belize, Mopan Maya, and in northern Belize, Yucatec Maya. The largest concentration of Maya in Belize is in the small villages in Toledo District near Punta Gorda.

The end of the world, or at least its current cycle, will take place on December 21, 2012, according to the Long Count calendar of the ancient Maya.

DOS & DON'TS FOR VISITING RUINS

- **Don't ever take any artifact from a Mayan site, not even a tiny pottery shard.** The theft of Mayan antiquities is a serious crime. Luggage is often searched at the international airport, and if any Mayan artifacts are found, you could be in hot water.

- **Do climb the temples and enjoy the views from the top.** At most sites, you're free to climb the ruins. The views from El Castillo at Xunantunich, from structures at Cerros of Chetumal Bay, and from Lubaantun to the sea, are among the most memorable. Be warned, though: most of the steps are very steep.

- **Do descend into Xilbalda.** The Maya called the underworld Xilbalda. You can experience it by visiting one of the caves once used by the Maya. Actun Tunichil Muknal, "The Cave of the Stone Sepulture," near Belmopan, is our favorite. Che Chem Ha near San Ignacio is another cave with many Mayan artifacts. Both require a guide. Private land, especially in Cayo and Toledo, often contains caves with Mayan artifacts.

- **Do look for wildlife at the ruins and en route.** One of the best things about the ruins and their surroundings is that they're home to many birds and wild creatures. On the long drive to Caracol, for example, you'll pass through pine ridge and broadleaf jungle, and you may see brocket deer, oscellated turkey, and coatimundi. En route to Caracol, we once saw a small crocodile sunning at the bridge over the Mopan River and, on another occasion, a fer-de-lance at DiSilva village. You're sure to see many beautiful butterflies. The trip up the New River to Lamanai is another good opportunity to see birds and wildlife on the riverbanks, and once you get to Lamanai, chances are good that you'll spot howler monkeys.

- **Don't be surprised to find Maya ruins in unexpected places.** There are at least 600 known Mayan sites in Belize, and the number of ruins out there probably runs into the thousands. Nearly every jungle lodge in Belize has some kind of Mayan site on the grounds, and some lodges, such as Pook's Hill, Nabitunich, Chan Chich, and Maya Mountain, have hosted archaeological digs. Mayan artifacts still remain in many caves, and pottery shards can be as common as weeds in the backyards of many private homes. After all, at the height of the Maya kingdoms, there were perhaps a million Maya living in Belize, and their traces are everywhere.

ARCHITECTURE

One look at the monumental architecture of the Maya, and you might feel transported to another world (perhaps that's why Tikal was used as the rebel base in the original 1977 *Star Wars*). The breathtaking structures are even more impressive when you consider that they were built 1,000 to 2,000 years ago or more, without iron tools, wheels, or pulleys. The following is a brief explanation of the architecture you see at a Maya ruin.

Influences

Mayan architecture, even the great temples, may echo the design of the typical thatch hut ordinary Maya used for thousands of years. The rectangular huts had short walls made of a limestone mud and were topped by a steeply tilted two-sided thatch roof. Caves—ever-important Mayan ceremonial sites—were also influential. Many above-ground Mayan temples and other monumental structures have cavelike chambers, and the layout of Mayan cities probably reflected the Mayan cosmology, in which caves played a critical role.

Building Materials

With few exceptions, the large buildings in Mayan cities were constructed mostly from limestone, which was widely available in Belize and the Mexican Yucatán. Quarries were often established close to a building site so that workers didn't have to haul stone long distances. The Maya used limestone for mortar, stucco, and plaster. Limestone was crushed and burned in wood-fired kilns to make lime. A cementlike mortar was made by combining one part lime with one part of a white soil called *sahcab,* and then adding water.

The Maya also used wood, which was plentiful in Mesoamerica. In fact, some of the early temples were probably constructed of wood poles and thatch, much like the small houses of the Maya; unfortunately, these buildings are now lost.

Tools

The Maya were behind the curve with their tool technology. They didn't have iron tools, pulleys to move heavy weights, or wheels to build carts. They didn't have horses or other large animals to help them move materials. Instead, they used large numbers of laborers to tote and haul stones, mortar, and other building materials.

Obsidian, jade, flint, and other hard rocks were used to make axes, knives, and saws. The Maya had mason's kits to cut and finish limestone, and they had the equivalent of a plumb bob and other tools to align and level stones. The Maya were skilled stoneworkers, although the degree of finish varied from city to city.

City Layout

In most Mayan cities, large plazas were surrounded by temples and large pyramids, probably used for religious ceremonies and other important public events. Paved causeways connected the plazas. Away from the city center were sprawls of "suburbs"—smaller stone buildings and traditional thatch huts.

Most cities had ball courts, and although the exact rules are unclear, players used a ball of natural rubber (rubber was discovered by the Olmecs) and scored points by getting the ball through a hoop or goalpost. "Sudden death" had a special meaning—the leader of the losing team was sometimes killed by decapitation.

Adventure
Vacations

9

By Lan Sluder

THESE DAYS MORE TRAVELERS THAN EVER are seeking trips with an active or adventure component, and tour operators are responding with an ever-increasing selection of exciting itineraries. Belize, with its opportunities for many different kinds of activities, is at the leading edge of the adventure-travel trend. In Belize you can select something easy, like cave tubing, snorkeling, fishing, horseback riding, hiking, birding, wildlife spotting, and canoeing. Or you can go for jungle trekking, caving, windsurfing, sea kayaking, or mountain-biking expeditions that require higher degrees of physical endurance and, in some cases, considerable technical skill. You can rough it or opt for comfortable, sometimes even luxurious, accommodations; put adventure at the center of your trip or make it only a sideline; go for a multiweek package, or only a day trip. Study multiple itineraries and packages to find the trip that's right for you.

Choosing a tour package carefully is always important, but it becomes even more critical when the focus is adventure or sports. Below are selected trip offerings from some of the best adventure tour operators, both inside and outside Belize. When wisely chosen, special-interest vacations lead to distinctive, memorable experiences—just pack your curiosity along with the bug spray.

For additional information about a specific activity or destination within Belize, contact the **Belize Tourist Board** (✉ Blue Horizons Bldg., Mile 3½, Northern Hwy. 🕿 Box 325, Belize City, Belize ☎ 501/223–1913 or 800/624–0686 🖷 501/223–1943 ⊕ www.travelbelize.org), or one of the tour operators listed in this section.

Choosing a Trip

With dozens of options for special-interest and adventure tours in Belize, including do-it-yourself or fully guided package trips, it's helpful to think about certain factors when deciding which company or package will be right for you.

- **Are you interested in adventure travel on the sea or the mainland, or both?** Belize offers two very different adventure environments: the sea and the mainland. The Caribbean, various bays and lagoons, the barrier reef that runs 185 mi (303 km) along the eastern coast of the country, and three South Pacific–style atolls are perfect for activities such as fishing, sailing, diving, snorkeling, and windsurfing. Inland, you can rappel hundreds of feet into a limestone sinkhole, explore an underworld labyrinth of caves full of Mayan artifacts, hike the rain forest, ride horses or bikes to remote waterfalls, or tube through underground rivers. Some travelers prefer to concentrate on either water or land activities, but you can combine the two. Just be sure to give yourself enough time.

- **How strenuous a trip do you want?** Adventure vacations commonly are split into "soft" and "hard" adventures. Hard adventures, such as strenuous jungle treks and extended caving trips, usually require excellent physical conditioning and previous experience. Most hiking, biking, canoeing-kayaking, cave tubing, snorkeling, brief cave tours, and similar soft adventures can be enjoyed by persons of all ages who are in good health and are accustomed to a reasonable amount of exercise. A little honesty goes a long way—recognize your own level of physical fitness and discuss it with the tour operator before signing on.

- **Would you like to pick up new skills?** Belize is a great place to pick up new skills, whether it's how to paddle a kayak, how to rappel down a cliff face, or how to dive. For example, you can take a quick resort diving course to see if you like scuba, or you can do a complete open-water certification course, usually in three to four days. Before committing to any program, do some research to confirm that the people running it are qualified. Check to see if the dive shop or resort is certified by one of the well-known international dive organizations, such as the Professional Association of Diving Instructors (PADI), the largest certification agency in the world, or National Association of Underwater Instructors (NAUI), the second-largest. Among the other how-to programs or lessons offered in Belize are kayaking, kayak surfing (riding the sea swells driven through the barrier reef by prevailing trade winds), horseback riding, snorkeling, and windsurfing. The sky's the limit, literally: you can go parasailing and, at times, you can even score skydiving lessons.

- **Do you want an "off-the-shelf" tour package or do you prefer to build your own trip?** You can opt to buy a prepackaged adventure or special-interest trip, complete with full-time guides who will do everything from meet your international flight to cook your meals, or you can go the more independent route, arranging local guides or tour operators on a daily, or even hourly, basis. Because English is the official language in Belize and most tour operators have e-mail and Web sites, it's easy to put together an adventure package à la carte. Many package tour operators also offer you the ability to combine two or more trips or to create a custom itinerary. It all comes down to whether you're happier doing it yourself or having someone else take care of all the logistics and details.

- **How far off the beaten path do you want to go?** As one of the least densely populated countries in the hemisphere—more than two-fifths of the country is devoted to nature reserves and national parks—Belize offers many off-the-beaten-path experiences. Although many trips described in this chapter might seem to be headed into uncharted territory, tour operators carefully check each detail before an itinerary goes into a brochure. You won't usually be vying with busloads of tourists for photo ops, but you'll probably run into occasional small groups of like-minded travelers. Journeys into truly remote regions, such as to Victoria Peak in the Maya Mountains, typically involve camping and the simplest of accommodations, but they reward with more abundant wildlife and locals who are less accustomed to the clicking of cameras. Ask yourself if it's the *reality* or the *image* of roughing it that appeals to you. Stick with the reality.

- **Are you ready for intellectual adventure?** Although Belize delivers great physical adventures, don't overlook the opportunities for cerebral exploration, too. Among the options for stimulating your little gray cells are archaeological digs, ecology and nature programs, elder education, and homestays in a different cultural setting. You'll come back with recharged mental batteries and perhaps some new skills, too.

- **How much are you willing to spend?** Belize has an adventure for nearly every budget. For penny-pinchers, homestay or local guesthouse programs and camping are among the low-cost options. At the high end, yacht charters and upmarket packaged nature tours can cost thousands of dollars per person per week. In general, the more planning, organizing and booking you do yourself, and the more you rely on Belize-based operators, the lower the cost. As always, comparison shopping pays off. The cost of two tours of the same length can vary greatly, depending on accommodations, equipment, transportation options, and amount of hand-holding involved. The Internet has made comparing rates much easier, and nearly all tour operators have Web sites. Use the Web to check recent reviews of tours and tour operators.

Tour Operators

Below is contact information for all tour operators mentioned in this chapter, including international Belize-based operators or those who are based in the United States or elsewhere. As the scope of adventure trips to Belize has widened, the number of tour operators has increased. Although the list below isn't exhaustive by any means, it is selective—we've chosen established firms that offer a good selection of itineraries. Such operators are usually the first to introduce great new destinations, forging ahead before luxury hotels and air-conditioned coaches tempt less hardy visitors.

Action Belize. ⊠ *Mile 3½, Northern Hwy., Belize City, Belize* ☎ *501/223–2987 or 888/383–6319* 🖷 *501/223–2986* ⊕ *www.actionbelize.com.*
Adventure Center. ⊠ *1311 63rd St., #200, Emeryville, CA 94608* ☎ *510/654–1879 or 800/228–8747* 🖷 *510/654–4200* ⊕ *www.adventurecenter.com.*
Adventure Life. ⊠ *1655 S. 3rd. St. W, Suite 1, Missoula, MT 59801* ☎ *406/541–2677 or 800/344–6118* 🖷 *406/541–2676* ⊕ *www.adventure-life.com.*
Amigos del Mar. ⊠ *San Pedro, Belize* ☎ *501/226–2706* 🖷 *501/226–2648* ⊕ *www.amigosdive.com.*
Backroads. ⊠ *801 Cedar St., Berkeley, CA 94710* ☎ *510/527–1555 or 800/462–2848* 🖷 *510/527–1444* ⊕ *www.backroads.com.*
Bak-a-Bush Big Hill Station. 🖃 *Box 698, Belize City, Belize* ☎ *501/223–5194* ⊕ *www.chukkacaribbean.com.*
Banana Bank Lodge & Jungle Equestrian Adventure 🖃 *Box 48, Belmopan City, Belize* ☎ *501/820–2020* 🖷 *501/820–2026* ⊕ *www.bananabank.com.*
Belize Aggressor. ⊠ *7810 Hwy. 182 E, Morgan City, LA 70381* ☎ *985/305–2628 or 800/348–2628* 🖷 *985/384–0817* ⊕ *www.aggressor.com.*
Belize Audubon Society. 🖃 *Box 1001, Belize City, Belize* ☎ *501/223–4988* ⊕ *www.belizeaudubon.org.*
Belize Jungle Dome Adventure Vacations. ⊠ *Banana Bank, Belmopan City, Belize* ☎ *501/822–2124* ⊕ *www.greendragonbelize.com.*
Belize River Lodge. ⊠ *Belize City, Belize* ☎ *888/275–4843* ⊕ *www.belizeriverlodge.com.*
Belize Sailing. ⊠ *Caye Caulker, Belize* ☎ *501/600–2302* ⊕ *www.belize-sailing.com.*

Belize Sailing Charters. ⊠ *Placencia, Stann Creek, Belize* ☎ *501/253–3138* 🖷 *501/523–5251* ⊕ *www.belize-sailing-charters.com.*

Belize Trips. 🗂 *Box 1108, Belize City, Belize* ☎ *501/223–0376* ⊕ *www. belize-trips.com.*

Beyond Touring. ⊠ *3036 Lake Shore Dr., Deerfield Beach, FL 33442* ☎ *954/415–2897* 🖷 *954/360–9387* ⊕ *www.beyondtouring.com.*

Blackbird Caye Resort. 🗂 *Box 13099, Burton, WA 98013* ☎ *206/463–0833 or 888/271–3483* ⊕ *www.islamarisolresort.com.*

Caves Branch Adventure Co. 🗂 *Box 356, Belmopan City, Belize* ☎ *501/822–2800* 🖷 *501/810–1333* ⊕ *www.cavesbranch.com.*

Cave-Tubing in Belize. ⊠ *Belize City, Belize* ☎ *501/605–1575* ⊕ *www. cave-tubing.com.*

Cayo Adventure Tours. 🗂 *Box 88, Santa Elena, Cayo, Belize* ☎ *501/824–3246* 🖷 *501/824–3864* ⊕ *www.cayoadventure.com.*

Chaa Creek Expeditions. 🗂 *Box 53, San Ignacio, Cayo, Belize* ☎ *501/824–2037* 🖷 *501/824–2501 or 800/861–1519* ⊕ *www.chaacreek.com.*

Chan Chich Lodge. 🗂 *Box 37, Belize City, Belize* ☎ *501/223–4419 or 800/353–8009* ⊕ *www.chanchich.com.*

Cornerstone Foundation. ⊠ *90 Burns Ave., San Ignacio, Cayo, Belize* ☎ *501/824–2373* ⊕ *www.peacecorner.org.*

Country Walkers. 🗂 *Box 180, Waterbury, VT 05676-0180* ☎ *802/244–1387 or 800/464–9255* 🖷 *802/244–5661* ⊕ *www.countrywalkers.com.*

Dems Dats Doin'. 🗂 *Box 73, Punta Gorda, Belize* ☎ *501/722–2470.*

Destinations Belize. 🗂 *General Delivery, Placencia, Belize* ☎ *501/523–4018* 🖷 *603/452–4797* ⊕ *www.destinationsbelize.com.*

Discovery Expeditions. ⊠ *5916 Manatee Dr., Belize City, Belize* ☎ *501/223–0748* 🖷 *501/223–0750* ⊕ *www.discoverybelize.com.*

Ecological Tours & Services. 🗂 *Box 473, Belize City, Belize* ☎ *501/223–4874* ⊕ *www.ecotoursbelize.com.*

El Pescador. 🗂 *Box 17, San Pedro, Ambergris Caye, Belize* ☎ *501/226–2398 or 800/242–2017* 🖷 *501/226–2977* ⊕ *www.elpescador.com.*

El Pescador PG. 🗂 *Box 135, Punta Gorda, Belize* ☎ *501/722–0050* 🖷 *501/722–0051* ⊕ *www.elpescadorpg.com.*

Equitours. 🗂 *Box 807, Dubois, WY 82513* ☎ *307/455–3363 or 800/545–0019* ⊕ *www.ridingtours.com.*

Exotic Birding. ⊠ *2424 9th Ave., #1208, Longmont, CO 80503* ☎ *877/247–3371* ⊕ *www.exoticbirding.com.*

Far Horizons Archaeological & Cultural Trips. 🗂 *Box 2546, San Anselmo, CA 94979* ☎ *415/482–8400 or 800/552–4575* 🖷 *415/482–8495* ⊕ *www.farhorizon.com.*

Fishing International. ⊠ *5510 Skylane Blvd., Suite 200, Santa Rosa, CA 95403* ☎ *707/542–4242 or 800/950–4242* 🖷 *707/546–3474* ⊕ *www. fishinginternational.com.*

G.A.P. Adventures. ⊠ *355 Eglinton Ave., E, Toronto, ON M4P 1M5 Canada* ☎ *416/260–0999 or 800/708–7761* ⊕ *www.gapadventures.com.*

Glovers Atoll Resort. 🗂 *Box 2215, Belize City, Belize* ☎ *501/520–5016* 🖷 *501/223–5424* ⊕ *www.glovers.com.bz.*

Green Reef Belize Coral Reef Conservation NGO. ⊠ *100 Coconut Dr., San Pedro, Ambergris Caye, Belize* ☎ *501/226–2833* ⊕ *www.ambergriscaye. com/greenreef/index.html.*

Hamanasi Eco Tours. ✉ *Hopkins/Sittee River, Hopkins, Stann Creek, Belize* ☎ *501/520–7073* 🖷 *501/520–7090* ⊕ *www.hamanasi.com.*

Hidden Valley Inn. ⌁ *Box 170, Belmopan City, Belize* ☎ *501/822–3320 or 866/443–3364* 🖷 *501/822–3334* ⊕ *www.hiddenvalleyinn.com.*

Inglewood Camping Grounds. ✉ *Mile 68¼, San Ignacio, Cayo, Belize* ☎ *501/824–3555* ⊕ *www.inglewoodcampinggrounds.com.*

International Expeditions. ✉ *1 Environs Park, Helena, AL 35080* ☎ *205/428–1700 or 800/633–4734* 🖷 *205/428–1714* ⊕ *www.internationalexpeditions.com.*

International Zoological Expeditions (IZE). ✉ *210 Washington St., Sherborn, MA 01770* ☎ *503/655–1461 or 800/548–5843* 🖷 *503/655–4445* ⊕ *www.ize2belize.com.*

Isla Marisol. ⌁ *Box 10, Dangriga, Belize* ☎ *501/520–2056* ⊕ *www.islamarisolresort.com.*

Island Expeditions. ✉ *368–916 W. Broadway, Vancouver, BC V5Z 1K7 Canada* ☎ *604/452–3212 or 800/667–1630* 🖷 *604/452–3433* ⊕ *www.islandexpeditions.com.*

Jaguar Paw Lodge. ⌁ *Box 1832, Belize City, Belize* ☎ *501/820–2023* 🖷 *501/820–2024* ⊕ *www.jaguarpaw.com.*

Jungle Camp at Chaa Creek. ⌁ *Box 53, San Ignacio, Cayo, Belize* ☎ *501/824–2037* 🖷 *501/824–2501* ⊕ *www.belizecamp.com.*

Maya Centre Women's Group. ✉ *Southern Hwy., Maya Centre* ⌁ *Box 108, Dangriga, Belize* ☎ *501/603–9256.*

Maya Research Program. ✉ *9617 Great Hills Trail, #1632, Austin, TX 78759* ☎ *512/922–5682* ⊕ *www.mayaresearchprogram.org.*

Mayawalk Tours. ✉ *19 Burns Ave., San Ignacio, Cayo, Belize* ☎ *501/824–3070* ⊕ *www.mayawalk.com.*

The Moorings. ✉ *19345 U.S. Hwy. 19N #4, Clearwater, FL 33764* ☎ *727/535–1446 or 888/952–8420* ⊕ *www.moorings.com.*

Mountain Equestrian Trails. ✉ *Mile 8, Mountain Pine Ridge Rd., Cayo, Belize* ☎ *501/820–4041 or 800/838–3918* ⊕ *www.metbelize.com.*

Mountain Travel-Sobek. ✉ *1266 66th St., Emeryville, CA 94608* ☎ *510/594–6000or 888/687–6235* 🖷 *510/594–6001* ⊕ *www.mtsobek.com.*

Nature Photography Adventure. ⌁ *Box 752, Willard, MO 65781* ☎ *417/742–3470* ⊕ *www.naturephotography.us.*

Nature Treks. ⌁ *Box 64805, Tucson, AZ 85728* ☎ *520/696–2002* 🖷 *520/297–0596* ⊕ *www.naturetreks.net.*

Nekton Diving Cruises. ✉ *520 SE 32nd St., Ft. Lauderdale, FL 33316* ☎ *954/463–9324 or 800/899–6753* 🖷 *954/463–8938* ⊕ *www.nektoncruises.com.*

PACZ Tours. ✉ *C/o Eva's, Burns St., San Ignacio, Cayo, Belize* ☎ *501/824–2477* ⊕ *www.evasonline.com.*

Paradise Down. ⌁ *Box 14, Caye Caulker, Belize* ☎ *501/226–0437* 🖷 *501/226–0438* ⊕ *www.paradisedown.com.*

Paradise Expeditions. ⌁ *Box 126, San Ignacio, Cayo, Belize* ☎ *501/824–2772* ⊕ *www.birdinginbelize.com.*

Peter Hughes Diving. ✉ *5273 NW 158th St., Miami, FL 33014* ☎ *305/669–9391 or 800/932–6237* 🖷 *305/669–9479* ⊕ *www.peterhughes.com.*

Protech Belize. ⌁ *Box 130, San Pedro, Ambergris Caye, Belize* ☎ *501/226–3008 or 866/703–9677* ⊕ *www.protechdive.com.*

Raggamuffin Tours. ✉ *Front St., Caye Caulker, Belize* ☎ *501/226–0348* ⊕ *www.raggamuffintours.com.*

River Rat Kayak and Land Expeditions. ✉ *San Ignacio, Cayo, Belize* ⊕ *www.riverratbelize.com.*

Rod & Reel Adventures. ✉ *32617 Skyhawk Way, Eugene, OR 97405* ☎ *541/349–0777 or 800/356–6982* 🖷 *541/338–0367* ⊕ *www. rodreeladventures.com.*

SayLKing. ✉ *Beachfront, Caye Caulker, Belize* ☎ *501/620–6875.*

SeaHorse Dive Shop. ✉ *Placencia, Stann Creek, Belize* ☎ *501/523–3166 or 800/991–1969* ⊕ *www.belizescuba.com.*

Sea Kayaking by Saddle Caye South. ✉ *Placencia, Stann Creek, Belize* ☎ *501/503–3130* ⊕ *www.kayakbelize.com.*

Seakunga Adventures. ☎ *800/781–2269* ⊕ *www.seakunga.com.*

Slickrock Adventures. ⌂ *Box 1400, Moab, UT 84532* ☎ *435/259–4225 or 800/390–5715* 🖷 *435/259–6996* ⊕ *www.slickrock.com.*

South American Experience. ✉ *47 Causton St., Pimlico London, SW1P 4AT U.K.* ☎ *0207/976–5511* 🖷 *0207/976–6908* ⊕ *www. southamericanexperience.co.uk.*

Tabutne Diving. ✉ *19 Front St., Caye Caulker, Belize* ☎ *501/226–0437* ⊕ *www.tabutnediving.com.*

Tanisha Tours. ✉ *Pescador Dr. San Pedro, Belize* ☎ *501/226–2314* ⊕ *www.tanishatours.com.*

TIDE. ✉ *1 Mile San Antonio Rd., Punta Gorda, Toledo, Belize* ☎ *501/ 722–2274* 🖷 *501/722–2655* ⊕ *www.tidebelize.org.*

TMM (Belize) Ltd. ✉ *Coconut Dr., San Pedro, Belize* ☎ *501/226–3026 or 800/633–0155* 🖷 *501/226–3072* ⊕ *www.sailtmm.com.*

Toadal Adventure Belize. ✉ *Pt. Placencia, Placencia, Stann Creek, Belize* ☎ *501/523–3207* 🖷 *501/523–3334* ⊕ *www.toadaladventure.com.*

Toledo Ecotourism Association. ⌂ *Box 157, Punta Gorda, Belize* ☎ *501/ 722–2096* 🖷 *501/722–2196* ⊕ *www.ecoclub.com.*

Tour Belize. ⌂ *Box 281, Belize City, Belize* ☎ *501/223–2089* 🖷 *501/ 223–6422* ⊕ *www.tourbelize.bz.*

Turneffe Flats Lodge. ⌂ *Box 10670, Bozeman, MT 59719* ☎ *623/298– 2783 or 888/512–8812* 🖷 *623/298–5008* ⊕ *www.tflats.com.*

Turneffe Island Lodge. ✉ *400 Louisiana, Suite 900, Houston, TX 77002* ☎ *713/236–7739 or 800/874–0118* 🖷 *713/236–7743* ⊕ *www. turneffelodge.com.*

University of Texas Mesoamerican Archaeological Research Laboratory. ✉ *1 University Station R7500, Austin, TX 78712* ☎ *512/232–7049* 🖷 *512/ 232–7050* ⊕ *http://uts.cc.utexas.edu/~marl/.*

Victor Emanuel Nature Tours. ✉ *2525 Wallingwood R., Suite 1003, Austin, TX 78746* ☎ *512/328–5221 or 800/328–8368* 🖷 *512/328–2919* ⊕ *www.ventbird.com.*

Western Spirit Cycling Adventures. ✉ *478 Mill Creek Dr., Moab, UT 84532* ☎ *435/259–8732 or 800/845–2453* 🖷 *435/259–2736* ⊕ *www. westernspirit.com.*

Wilderness Travel. ✉ *1102 9th St., Berkeley, CA 94710* ☎ *510/558–2488 or 800/368–2794* 🖷 *510/558–2489* ⊕ *www.wildernesstravel.com.*

Windy Hill Tour Co. ⌂ *Box 85, San Ignacio, Cayo* ☎ *501/824–2017* 🖷 *501/824–3080* ⊕ *www.windyhilltours.com.*

ECOTOURISM IN BELIZE

Central America is the original ecotourism destination; as a result, you'll see the term used liberally everywhere. For lodging it can be used to describe a deluxe private cabana on a well-tended beach or a hut in the middle of nowhere with pit toilets. It may also point to environmental conservation efforts by parks or tour companies that are conscious of natural resources and their role in not depleting them. Or it may mean just the opposite. Wildlife parks, butterfly farms, cloud forests, and Maya ruins are some of the incredible ecodestinations in this area. And mountain biking, bird-watching, jungle hiking, scuba diving, cave tubing, fishing, and white-water rafting are just some of the eco-activities.

You can do your part to protect the natural heritage of Belize and the Tikal area of Guatemala by being an ecologically sensitive traveler. Where possible, choose green hotels, those that have taken care to protect the environment and that have energy-efficient cooking, lighting, and cooling systems, and that recycle and dispose of waste responsibly. Be culturally sensitive, as both countries have highly diverse populations, each with different cultural attitudes and perspectives. Also, try to do business with companies that hire local people for positions at all levels, and where possible choose local restaurants and hotels over chain properties. When diving or snorkeling, avoid touching or breaking coral, and don't take part in swim-with-dolphins or swim-with-manatees tours as most naturalists say these programs disturb the animals. Also, use eco-friendly sunscreen. On caving or hiking trips, take nothing but photographs and leave nothing of yours behind. When visiting Maya sites, never remove anything, not even a tiny shard of pottery.

For the most part, Belize has reaped the benefits of the growing tourism industry, drawing in much-needed capital to bolster national coffers. The costs of tourism are less obvious, however. Among other effects, indigenous communities are undermined by increasingly tourist-oriented economies—cultivating a plot of land may no longer support a family, but selling knickknacks in the streets just might. Where tourists come, expats often follow, and land, especially beachfront land, is quickly priced out of the reach of locals. There's no easy solution to this dilemma, and balancing the advantages of tourism against its drawbacks is, and will remain, a constant struggle for Belize. The long-term effects are as much dependent on the attitudes and behavior of visitors as they are on prudent national policies.

CRUISES

Cruises Around the Cayes & Atolls

Few things in life compare with the experience of being on a sailboat in the Caribbean—the caress of the wind and the salt spray on your face, the sun on your back, and all around the mint green, turquoise, and vodka-clear sea. Companies listed below provide day sails as well as longer, multiple-night trips.

Season: Year-round

Locations: Most day sails and longer crewed trips start in San Pedro, Caye Caulker, Belize City, or Placencia. The boats visit nearby islands, snorkel spots, and dive destinations. Generally, they stay inside the barrier reef.

Cost: Day sails on a crewed boat start at BZ$100 per person and may include lunch and drinks. Overnight and longer trips can run BZ$300 to BZ$1,500 or more per day, depending on the size of the boat, the number in your party, and what's included.

Tour Operators: Belize Sailing; Belize Sailing Charters; Raggamuffin Tours

Raggamuffin Tours does day sails around the northern cayes as well as a BZ$500-per-person, two-night/three-day island-hopping trip from Caye Caulker to Placencia. The nights are spent camping on Tobacco and Rendezvous cayes (camping equipment provided), with stops at Goff and Southwater cayes. Belize Sailing runs sail trips from Caye Caulker on the catamaran *Nepenthe,* while the similarly named Belize Sailing Charters does day and longer trips on the *Talisman* out of Placencia. Sailboat owners tend to be free spirits who may pick up and sail to another port at the drop of a yachting cap, so check locally to see what boats are still sailing.

Yacht Charters

A crewed or bareboat sailing charter lets you explore the Belize barrier reef and little-visited cayes at your own pace. Most charters are for a week, though shorter charters may be available off-season. Placencia and San Pedro are the two main sailboat charter bases in Belize. You sail inside the reef, protected from ocean swells. A typical day? Wake to a private sunrise over the Caribbean. Have breakfast and a quick swim. Dive or snorkel all morning, snag a lobster or conch, and then drop anchor at a remote island for a barbecue on the beach. In the afternoon, relax with a rum and tonic and enjoy the warm trade winds. Go ashore to a beachside restaurant for a seafood dinner. Then, relax on your boat before drifting off to sleep under Central American stars.

Season: Year-round

Locations: Inside the barrier reef—either the northern cayes from San Pedro, Ambergris Caye, or the southern cayes from Placencia.

Cost: Bareboat sailing charters range from about BZ$1,000 to BZ$2,000 per night for two to eight people (not all operators permit daily charters), and BZ$6,000 to BZ$16,000 for weeklong charters for two to eight people, plus provisions. For crews, add about BZ$250 a day for a skipper and BZ$200 a day for a cook.

Tour Operators: Belize Sailing Charters; the Moorings; Raggamuffin Tours; TMM Belize

TMM Belize, with bases in San Pedro and Placencia, has around 40 sailboats, mostly catamarans with a few monohulls, for weekly bareboat or crewed charter. The Moorings, with a base in Placencia, has a selection of 37- to 47-foot catamarans. Among the smaller charter operations, Belize Sailing Charters offers crewed charters on the *Talisman* and other sailboats. Raggamuffin Tours provides multiday crewed charters from Caye Caulker to Placencia.

LEARNING VACATIONS

Art & Archaeology

Some travelers want a quick look at a country's major sights, while others prefer to immerse themselves in the culture. In Belize this means participating in a "dig" at a Maya archaeological site, usually under the direction of a university archaeological team.

Season: Sessions run only a few weeks of the year, usually in spring or summer.
Locations: Archaeological digs that accept volunteer workers are mostly in Orange Walk District.
Cost: Archaeological programs start at around BZ$1,250 for one week, and BZ$2,300 for two weeks. These prices don't include transportation to Belize or incidental personal expenses.
Tour Operators: Maya Research Program; University of Texas Mesoamerican Archaeological Research Laboratory

The Maya Research Program, sponsored by the Blue Creek Regional Political Ecology Project, has one- and two-week volunteer programs in the Blue Creek area of Orange Walk District. The University of Texas Mesoamerican Archaeological Research Laboratory (MARL) accepts volunteers at its field station in the Rio Bravo Conservation area of Orange Walk District, located on Programme for Belize lands. Volunteers (who pay a fee to participate) must commit for at least one week and may stay as long as three weeks, and in some cases longer. The program usually runs from February to April, with other options in summer, some for academic credit. Volunteers live in a rustic dorm setting and learn the basics of field archaeology through lectures and hands-on experience.

Cultural Tours

In Belize, you can live with the modern-day Maya or Garifuna at a home-stay or village guesthouse program.

Season: Year-round
Locations: Homestay and village guesthouse programs are in Toledo District near Punta Gorda. There's also a home-stay tour at Indian Church Village in Orange Walk District.

Cost: Village guesthouse programs start at BZ$45 per person per night, including lodging, activities, and meals. Homestays generally cost about the same.

Tour Operators: Beyond Touring; Dems Dats Doin'; Maya Centre Women's Group; Toledo Ecotourism Association

The Toledo Ecotourism Association (T.E.A.) program allows visitors to participate in the village life of the Maya while maintaining some personal privacy. You stay in small guesthouses in one of nine Mopan and Kek'chi Maya villages in Toledo District, including San Antonio, San Miguel, and Blue Creek. Barranco, a predominantly Garifuna village, also has a guesthouse. The guesthouses are very simple, with traditional thatch roofs and outdoor latrines. You take meals in the homes of villagers and participate in the routines of village life. The program, endorsed by the Belize Tourist Board, is a collective owned by more than 200 members and is designed to promote cultural exchange. A separate program, run privately by Dem Dats Doin' (which also operates an eco-farm and a private tourist information office in Punta Gorda) arranges stays for visitors in the homes of Toledo villagers. Again, the accommodations are extremely simple—you may share a room with the family in a small thatch building with dirt floor. Homestays at Maya Centre at the entrance to the Cockscomb Wildlife Sanctuary can be arranged through the Maya Centre Women's Group, a group of about 50 Mopan women who have banded together to sell handicrafts. Beyond Touring also offers some homestay programs at Indian Church Village near Lamanai.

Eco-Oriented Volunteer Programs

If you have more time than money, and want to help Belizeans, you may want to look into eco-oriented volunteer programs.

Season: Year-round
Locations: Throughout Belize
Cost: From BZ$770 a month, including food and lodging, but not including transportation to Belize, mandatory health insurance, and incidental personal expenses.
Tour Operators: Belize Audubon Society; Cornerstone Foundation; Green Reef Belize Coral Caye Conservation NGO

With the Belize Audubon Society (BAS), you can apply for volunteer jobs at its marine or mainland parks or at its office in Belize City. People with education, community development, and conservation experience and skills make especially good candidates. The BAS is Belize's premier conservation organization and manages or comanages eight national parks and monuments. Volunteers must commit for a minimum of three months (one month at marine areas) and in most cases must pay for their own accommodations and food. For example, volunteers at Half Moon Caye National Monument at Lighthouse Atoll pay BZ$30 a day. The nonprofit Cornerstone Foundation, based in San Ignacio, Cayo, provides volunteer opportunities in community development, ecology, health care, and other areas. Volunteers, who live in communal lodging, must commit for a minimum of three months. Green Reef on Ambergris

Caye is a nonprofit dedicated to the sustainable use of Belize's marine resources. It accepts volunteers, who usually pay nothing but must provide their own lodging, food, and transportation expenses.

THE OUTDOORS

Bird-Watching Tours

When selecting a bird-watching tour, ask questions. What species might be seen? What are the guide's qualifications? Does the operator work to protect natural habitats? How large are the birding groups? What equipment is used? (In addition to binoculars and a birding guidebook, this should include a high-powered telescope, a tape recorder to record and play back bird calls, which is a way of attracting birds, and a spotlight for night viewing.)

Season: Year-round, though more common from December to March, when birds from the north winter in Belize and there's less rain.
Locations: Cayo, Orange Walk, Stann Creek, and Toledo Districts
Cost: From BZ$1,600 per person for a six-day birding trip, including guides, lodging, and some meals. On an à la carte basis, short birding hikes with a local guide cost from BZ$30 per person.
Tour Operators: Chan Chich Lodge; Exotic Birding; Hidden Valley Inn; Nature Treks; Paradise Expeditions; Victor Emanuel Nature Tours

More than 575 species of birds have been spotted in Belize, and every year five or more additional species are found in the country. Birders flock to Belize to see exciting species such as the Jabiru Stork, the largest bird in the Western Hemisphere; the Harpy Eagle with its 7-foot wingspan; the beautiful Scarlet Macaw; the Keel-billed Toucan, the national bird of Belize; 21 species of hummingbirds; and endangered or rare species such as the Yellow-headed Parrot, Oscellated Turkey, Orange-breasted Falcon, and Chestnut-breasted Heron. Birding hotspots in Belize include Crooked Tree Wildlife Sanctuary, the Mountain Pine Ridge, the area around Chan Chich Lodge at Gallon Jug, and the Cockscomb Basin. *Birds of Belize*, by H. Lee Jones and Dana Gardner, is the bible of Belize birding, although some complain that the 484-page, 2.2-pound birding guide is heavy and cumbersome in the field. The operators listed above offer trips to the best birding areas in Belize.

Ecotrips

With about two-fifths of Belize dedicated to national parks and reserves, the country is a natural for ecotripping.

Season: Year-round
Locations: Throughout Belize
Cost: From BZ$100 for day trips
Tour Operators: Belize Audubon Society; Chaa Creek Expeditions; Chan Chich Lodge; G.A.P. Adventures; Hamansi Eco Tours; Hidden Valley Inn; International Expeditions; International Zoological Expeditions; TIDE; Victor Emanuel Nature Tours

Park rangers and local guides at Cockscomb Basin Wildlife Sanctuary, managed by the Belize Audubon Society, provide guided nature tours of Cockscomb and can also arrange multiday treks to Victoria Peak, one of the highest mountains in the country. Hamanasi and other resorts in Hopkins and Placencia run day tours to Cockscomb. International Zoological Expeditions has bases at Blue Creek in Toledo District and on South Water Caye off Dangriga; from both areas it runs educational and nature programs for students, teachers, and others. Victor Emanuel Nature Tours runs tours, oriented to birding but including wildlife spotting, at Chan Chich Lodge, Hidden Valley Inn, and at Crooked Tree. TIDE runs nature tours in Bladen Nature Reserve and elsewhere in beautiful Toledo. G.A.P. Adventures' 15- to 60-day trips through Mexico and Central America, which offer a mix of Mayan ruins, cultural tours, birding, and beaching, include time in Belize. The 60-day Mexico & Central America Journey trip, which it calls "the Big Kahuna," includes about five days in Belize. International Expedition's 10-day Rainforest, Reef & Ruins trip has stops at Lamanai, Tikal, and Ambergris Caye. At many jungle lodges, including, notably, Chan Chich, Ek'Tun, Chaa Creek, duPlooy's, Blancaneaux, Lamanai Outpost, Caves Branch, and Pook's Hill (*see individual chapters for details on these lodges*), you can hire a local guide to take you on a guided nature walk or a longer wildlife spotting trip.

Jungle Camping & Lodges

Belize has a few developed campgrounds, and it does offer primitive camping on some cayes and at some national parks on the mainland. Several hotels and lodges also offer a camping option. Because there are dozens of jungle lodges in Belize, most are not covered in this section. See individual chapters for information on lodges.

Season: Year-round
Locations: Throughout Belize
Cost: Camping from BZ$5 per person per night
Tour Operators: Belize Audubon Society; Caves Branch Adventure Co.; Glovers Atoll Resort; Inglewood Camping Grounds; Island Expeditions; Jungle Camp at Chaa Creek; Seakunga Adventures; Slickrock Adventures

Caves Branch Adventure Co. offers camping both at its base camp off the Hummingbird Highway and as a part of its many overnight jungle treks. For a more upscale camping experience, Chaa Creek has small casitas on raised platforms at its Jungle Camp, near its main lodge in Cayo. Several small hotels and lodges, including the Trek Stop in Cayo and Jungle Jeanies and Tipple Tree Beya Inn, both in Hopkins, allow camping for a small fee. Another camping option in Cayo is Inglewood Camping Grounds, which even has RV hookups. Seakunga Adventures specializes in kayaking and camping trips, with base camps in the Sapodilla Cayes, Glover's Atoll, and elsewhere. Both Slick Rock Adventures and Island Expeditions offer camping on the cayes and inland as part of their kayaking and other adventure trips. Glover's Atoll Resort provides primitive camping facilities at its beautiful island, Northeast Caye, on Glover's Atoll. Basic tent camping facilities are available at several national parks and reserves, including Cockscomb and Half Moon Caye, both of which are managed by the Belize Audubon Society. Most of the remote islands off the Belize coast are now privately owned, and camping is allowed only with permission of the owner or caretaker.

Photo Safaris

A photo safari can sharpen your photography skills while letting you visit some of the most scenic spots in Belize.

Season: Year-round
Locations: Cayo District, the Cayes
Cost: From BZ$4,400, plus airfare
Tour Operators: Exotic Birding; Nature Photography Adventure

Nature Photography Adventure runs annual photo safari trips to Belize. Typically, you stay in a midlevel lodge in Cayo and also visit one of the cayes. Exotic Birding, in addition to running birding trips to Belize, offers an annual 10-day Belize Photography Workshop. The trip begins with a class in Houston, then moves to Belize, with stays at Crooked Tree, San Ignacio, and Caye Caulker.

SPORTS

Bicycling

Despite heat, humidity, bad drivers, and rough roads, cycling is a big sport in Belize, and you often see local cyclists risking life and limb to train on the Western or Northern highways. Mountain biking, however, is only beginning to take hold in Belize, mostly in the Mountain Pine Ridge.

Season: Year-round
Locations: Mountain Pine Ridge for mountain biking
Cost: From BZ$150 per person for a full-day mountain-biking expedition; some hotels and lodges rent bikes from BZ$10 to BZ$20 a day, or provide them free for guests. Six-day mountain- biking tour with guide, meals, and accommodations from BZ$4,000.
Tour Operators: Caves Branch Adventure Co.; Western Spirit

Caves Branch offers what they call "jungle biking," a Belize version of mountain biking that involves a full-day bike trip. Western Spirit has six-day bike expeditions in the Mountain Pine Ridge and in other areas of Cayo District.

Canoeing & Kayaking

Belize has some of the best sea kayaking in Central America. Thanks to the barrier reef, a literal barrier to big waves and swells, the sea inside the reef is much calmer than the open ocean. Belize also has good kayaking and canoeing on inland rivers and lagoons.

Season: Year-round
Locations: Sea kayaking around Ambergris Caye, Caye Caulker, and elsewhere along the coast inside the barrier reef; canoeing and kayak-

ing on the Macal, Mopan, Sibun, Swasey, Hondo, New, Belize, and other rivers, and on the Progresso, Placencia, Northern, Southern, New, and other lagoons.

Cost: Day kayaking and canoe trips from BZ$150 a person; kayaking tours from BZ$1,600 per person for four days, BZ$2,800 per person for seven days.

Tour Operators: Caves Branch Adventure Co.; G.A.P. Adventures; International Zoological Expeditions; Island Expeditions; Mountain Travel Sobek; River Rat Kayaking and Land Expeditions; Sea Kayaking by Saddle Caye South; Seakunga; Slick Rock Adventures; Toadal Adventure

There are two types of kayaking trips: base kayaking and expedition kayaking. On a base kayaking trip, you have a home base—usually a caye—from which you take day trips (or longer). On an expedition-style trip, you travel from island to island or up mainland rivers. Typically, base kayaking is easier, but expedition kayaking is more adventurous.

Toadal Adventures, based in Placencia, provides top-notch sea and river expedition kayak trips that usually last for four to six days in southern Belize; they can customize trips to your specific schedule and interests. Island Expeditions and Slick Rock Adventures both do complete expedition packages, several of which combine sea and river kayaking and base and expedition aspects. They both focus on Glover's Atoll and land activities in central and southern Belize. Seakunga also runs both base camp and expedition-style kayaking trips at Glover's Atoll as well as the Sapodilla Cayes in southern Belize, and other locales. International Zoological Expeditions has eight- to ten-day trips, usually with an educational component such as ethnobotanical walks or mapping an island. IZE's trips combine time inland at Blue Creek in Toledo and at South Water Caye. Saddle Caye South offers self-guided kayak trips—in effect, kayak rentals—and five-day island hopping expeditions with guide, kayaks, camping gear, meals, and support boat. About three days of Mountain Travel Sobek's nine-day "Rainforest to Reef" trip are spent kayaking around the Sapodilla Cayes and the Port Honduras Marine Reserve in Toledo District. G.A.P. Adventures has a weeklong island hopping kayak trip, starting and ending in Placencia. You paddle for two to four hours a day, with stops at Pumpkin Caye, the Silk Cayes, and the Sapodilla Cayes. Most of the trips by all operators provide opportunities for snorkeling, fishing, hiking, and caving as well as kayaking. Several Belize-based operators, including River Rat Kayaking, Caves Branch Adventure Co., and a number of the jungle lodges, run day and overnight kayaking trips in Cayo District. In addition, rental kayaks are available in Placencia, San Pedro, Caye Caulker, and elsewhere for do-it-yourselfers. Some hotels also provide kayaks for their guests.

Cave Tubing

An activity you'll find in few places outside Belize is cave tubing. You drift down a river, usually the Caves Branch River in Cayo District, in a large rubber inner tube. At certain points the river goes underground, and you float through eerie underground cave systems, some with Maya artifacts still in place. The only light is from headlamps.

Season: Year-round, though seasonal rains June through November can sometimes raise water levels too high for tubing, and during dry season (February–May), some river levels may occasionally become too low.
Locations: Rivers in Cayo District, primarily the Caves Branch River and Barton Creek
Cost: From BZ$90 per person for a half-day trip
Tour Operators: Action Belize; Belize Cave-Tubing; Belize Jungle Dome Adventure Vacations; Belize-Trips; Caves Branch Adventure Co.; Cayo Adventure Tours; Chaa Creek Expeditions; Discovery Expeditions; Ecological Tours and Services; Ian Anderson's Caves Branch Adventure Co.; Jaguar Paw Lodge; Jungle Dome Adventure Vacations; Mayawalk; Windy Hill Tour Co.

In the last decade since Jaguar Paw Lodge and Ian Anderson's Caves Branch Adventure Co. first introduced it, cave tubing has become one of the most popular soft adventure activities in Belize. It's the number one mainland shore excursion of cruise-ship passengers, and on days when several large ships are docked in Belize City, you should expect inner-tube traffic jams. Several Belize City–based tour operators, including Action Belize, Belize Cave-Tubing, Ecological Tours, and Discovery Expeditions, cater to the cruise-ship day-trippers. In addition, Cayo-based tour operators, including Chaa Creek Expeditions, Ian Anderson's Caves Branch Adventure Co., Jaguar Paw Lodge, Cayo Adventure Tours, Jungle Dome Adventure Vacations, and Windy Hill Tour Co., run cave-tubing day trips. Belize Trips can arrange custom cave tubing trips for individuals or groups. The drill with most of these operations is the same. You pile into a van or bus for a short drive to a parking area near the Caves Branch River off the Western Highway, hike a short distance, and then pop into the Caves Branch with your inner tube for a float on the river and through several caves. Depending on where you're launched into the river, you float through anywhere from three to seven caves, some of which have ancient pottery shards and other artifacts of the Maya. Most of the caverns are very dark, and guides normally provide headlamps. The activity level is usually light, and even some people who can't swim or who are in their seventies and eighties go cave tubing. Caves Branch Adventure Co. offers longer and more active (and more expensive) cave-tubing trips. In the "River of Caves" cave-tubing trip, you float underground for a total of nearly 7 mi. San Ignacio–based tour operators, including Cayo Adventure Tours, also offer tubing at Barton Creek Cave.

Caving

Belize has some of the most extensive cave systems in Central America. One cave system in the Chiquibul Wilderness is 35 mi long. Only serious, highly trained cavers need consider the remote, difficult caves of Belize, but more casual adventurers can find fairly easy day trips to caves like Actun Tunichil Muknal, frequently described by visitors as a highlight of their Belize vacation.

Season: Year-round
Locations: Cayo and Toledo districts.

Cost: Day trips to caves from BZ$70 per person.
Tour Operators: Caves Branch Adventure Co; Mayawalk; PACZ Tours; River Rat Kayak and Land Expeditions

A small number of tour companies, including Mayawalk, PACZ, and River Rat, are permitted to take visitors into Actun Tunichil Muknal (ATM) cave. From a base camp off the Western Highway in Cayo District, you walk about 45 minutes to the "Cave of the Stone Sepulchre" in Roaring Creek Valley. Entering the cave requires a short swim. Once you make your way inside the cave formation, your headlamp reveals hundreds of Maya artifacts—thought to have been used in rituals to *Chac,* the Rain God of the Maya—as well as human remains. Most visitors find visiting ATM an amazing experience. There are several other easy-to-moderate caves in Cayo that can be visited on day tours, including Che Chem Ha, Rio Frio, and Barton Creek. Caves Branch Adventure Co., widely considered the premier jungle guide operation in the country, conducts day and overnight caving trips. Some of the trips are rated moderate and others difficult.

Fishing

Drop your hook in Belize and you're almost guaranteed to catch something. Lagoons and shallow flats are ideal for bonefish. The barrier reef supports grouper, snapper, and jacks. In the blue water beyond the reef, anglers will find tuna, sailfish, and pompano. Some of the world's best permit fisheries are off the coast of southern Belize. The estuaries and river mouths are home to tarpon and snook. It's even possible to achieve a "grand slam" in Belize—that is, catch tarpon, permit, and bonefish, all in one day.

Season: Year-round, with best fishing for tarpon May–September; permit, January–November; snook, November–March; bonefish, April–November; sailfish, January–June.
Locations: All coastal areas and the Cayes
Cost: Local fishing guides charge from BZ$400 per day; complete fishing packages including meals, accommodations, and guides for seven days, from BZ$3,500 per person (not including airfare).
Tour Operators: Belize River Lodge; Blackbird Caye Resort; Destinations Belize; El Pescador; El Pescador PG; Fishing International; Glover's Atoll Resort; International Zoological Expeditions; Isla Marisol; Rod & Real Adventures; Turneffe Flats Lodge; Turneffe Island Lodge

The best-known fishing lodges in Belize aren't skunky fishing camps but high-end resorts catering to affluent anglers who, after a hard day on the water, expect ice-cold cocktails, equally icy air-conditioning, and Sealy Posturepedic mattresses. El Pescador on North Ambergris Caye and its sister fishing lodge, El Pescador PG in Punta Gorda; two lodges on Turneffe Atoll (Turneffe Flats and Turneffe Island Lodge); several beach resorts in Placencia and Hopkins; and some lodges on Lighthouse and Glover's atolls offer fishing with a touch of luxury—everything from guides to cold drinks is included.

ADVENTURES TO GET YOUR HEART RATE UP

Most adventure tours and trips in Belize can be handled by anyone used to a reasonable amount of activity. Even couch potatoes can hack it. But a few are more physically challenging and require a higher level of fitness or skill. Here are three adventures that will send your heart rate soaring:

Climb Victoria Peak. This may be the toughest trek in Belize. You need a guide, and the trip takes a total of four to five days up and back. Though Victoria Peak is only 3,675 feet high, and the top of the mountain is just 17 mi from the visitor center at Cockscomb Basin Wildlife Sanctuary, the going—through tropical jungle—is rough, hot, and humid, with slopes of up to 60 degrees.

Dive the Blue Hole. The bottom of Blue Hole, a large underwater sinkhole at Lighthouse Atoll, is more than 400 feet down. Although not an inherently difficult dive, it's deep, and it's best done only by experienced divers. Hammerhead, tiger, and other sharks prowl the hole. Be forewarned: over the years, at least three divers have died making the dive.

Rappel the Black Hole. Caves Branch Adventure Co. runs a two-day jungle expedition that starts with a rappel more than 200 feet into the Actun Loch Tunich sinkhole, followed by a trip through more than 10 mi (6 km) of underground river. For a longer and even more intense jungle trek, consider Caves Branch's seven-day "Lost World Expedition."

Belize River Lodge, the oldest fishing lodge in Belize (it's been in continuous operation since 1960) operates live-aboard boats including a 58-foot Hatteras yacht. It also runs fishing skiffs from its lodge on the Belize Olde River.

If you want a less-expensive fishing vacation, you can make your own arrangements for lodging and meals and hire your own local fishing guides in San Pedro, Placencia, Hopkins, Punta Gorda, and elsewhere. Mary Toy's Destinations Belize in Placencia is a compromise between a total package and doing it all yourself. She can help you arrange moderate accommodations, some meals, and guides for light-tackle or fly-fishing day trips (or for longer periods). She also puts together moderately priced packages for fishing in Placencia and elsewhere in southern Belize.

Live Aboards

If you're serious about diving and want to hit the best dive spots in Belize, morning, noon, and night, with as many as six dives a day, live-aboard dive boats are your best bet.

Season: Year-round
Locations: Live aboards concentrate on dives around Belize's three

atolls—Lighthouse, Turneffe, and Glovers—with most dives at Lighthouse and Turneffe. The boats depart from Belize City.

Cost: Expect to pay about BZ$3,000 to $5,000 for six days of diving. That price includes all dives, meals, airport transfers, and stateroom accommodations on the dive boat. It does not include airfare to Belize, tips, alcoholic beverages, equipment rentals, Nitrox, marine park fees, and incidentals.

Tour Operators: Belize Aggressor; Nekton Diving Cruises; Peter Hughes Diving; Tabutne Diving

Peter Hughes Diving's 138-foot *Sun Dancer II,* which can hold up to 20 passengers in 10 staterooms, departs from Belize City on Saturday afternoon and moors at either Turneffe or Lighthouse atoll. For the next six days, divers explore these two atolls, getting as many as five dives a day. The ship moves two or three times a day. (Twenty people died during Hurricane Iris in October 2001, near Placencia, when Peter Hughes Diving's *Wave Dancer* liveaboard capsized.) The itinerary of the 18-passenger *Belize Aggressor* is similar to that of the *Sun Dancer II,* with passengers embarking in Belize City on a Saturday and spending time until the next Friday at Turneffe and Lighthouse atolls, with as many as five or six dives each day. Nekton Diving has weekly departures from Belize City on most Saturdays from November to May on the *Nekton Pilot.* Most Nekton cruises visit Turneffe and Lighthouse atolls, but about a third of them, called Belize South itineraries, also include dives at Glover's Atoll. Tabutne Diving has weeklong trips that leave on Saturday from Belize City on the *Tabutne 1,* a 70-foot boat that carries up to 12 divers. It goes to Lighthouse and Turneffe atolls. Tabutne Diving is associated with Paradise Down dive shop on Caye Caulker.

Scuba Diving & Snorkeling

Belize has the largest living coral reef system in the Western and Northern hemispheres, and three of the only four coral atolls outside the South Pacific. Here you can see more than 300 species of tropical fish, 100 types of coral, and many large sea creatures, including hammerheads, whale sharks, manatees, and manta rays. It's no wonder that the scuba diving and snorkeling in Belize are considered among the best in the world. Belize has more than 50 dive shops and snorkel tour operators, so only a representative sample of the top operators are included here. See individual chapters for more information on dive and snorkel shops and on specific dive destinations.

Season: Year-round

Locations: Serious divers focus on the three atolls—Lighthouse, Turneffe, and Glovers—all of which have dedicated dive lodges and are the destinations of most live-aboard dive boats.

Good recreational diving options abound all around the northern cayes and off the southern coast. For snorkeling, Hol Chan Marine Reserve near Ambergris Caye is the most popular spot, and at Shark-Ray Alley, now a part of Hol Chan, you can swim with stingrays and nurse sharks. There's also excellent snorkeling along most of the barrier reef, patch reefs, and at the atolls.

Cost: Snorkel trips from BZ$40 per person; two-tank dives from BZ$90; one-week dive packages, including hotel, meals, and dives, from BZ$2,400 per person.

Tour Operators: Amigos del Mar; Belize Aggressor; Belize Trips; Blackbird Caye Resort; Destinations Belize; Glover's Atoll Resort; Hamanasi Eco Tours; Isla Marisol; Nekton Diving Cruises; Peter Hughes Diving; Paradise Down; Protech; Sea Horse Dive Shop; Tabutne Diving; Turneffe Island Lodge

The largest concentration of dive shops and dive trip operators is on Ambergris Caye. It's a short boat ride to the spur-and-groove formations along the barrier reef. Several San Pedro operators with speedboats, including Amigos del Mar and Protech Belize, can take you to the Blue Hole, the largest ocean sinkhole in the world, with depths of more than 400 feet. Paradise Down and other dive shops on Caye Caulker take divers to the same sites as the dive shops on Ambergris Caye. Almost a dozen dive lodges and hotels are on Belize's atolls, including Turneffe Island Lodge, Blackbird Caye Resort, Isla Marisol, Glover's Atoll Resort, and others. Live-aboard dive boats also cluster here, although the Belize Agressor, Nekton Diving, Peter Hughes, and Tabutne Diving live-aboards leave from and return to Belize City.

Almost a dozen dive lodges and hotels are on Belize's atolls, and live-aboard dive boats also cluster here. Off the southern coast—served by Hamanasi Eco Tours, Sea Horse Dive Shop, and other operators—you can dive less-visited sites such as the Silk Cayes, home to large numbers of whale sharks in spring, and Belize's largest marine park, South Water Caye Marine Reserve.

Hiking, Trekking & Walking

See trips above and other multisport categories for more information.

Horseback Riding

Time to tack up and hit the trail! You can ride to waterfalls in the Mountain Pine Ridge or to Maya ruins and caves in Cayo.

Season: Year-round
Locations: Cayo District
Cost: From BZ$1,400 per person for horseback riding packages for four days; from BZ$80 for a half-day ride.
Tour Operators: Banana Bank Lodge; Equitours; Mountain Equestrian Trails

Two well-established Belize outfits offer horseback-riding tours. At Banana Bank Lodge you can ride one of their 50 horses (predominantly quarter horses) on a 4,000-acre ranch that hugs the banks of the Belize River. At Mountain Equestrian Trails you can take day rides or multinight horseback trips into the Mountain Pine Ridge and the high bush of Cayo District. U.S.-based Equitours offers riding tour packages in Cayo, with extensions to Tikal. The Lodge at Chaa Creek, Cahal Pech Village, Caves Branch Adventure Camp, and duPlooy's Lodge, all in Cayo, as well as Inn at Robert's Grove in Placencia and Maruba Spa off the Old Northern Highway, also arrange horseback-riding trips.

Zip Lining

Zip lines allow you to experience the jungle at canopy level, suspended in a harness 50 to 80 feet in the air, zooming from one platform in the trees to another.

Season: Year-round
Locations: Cayo District
Cost: From BZ$110 per person
Tour Operators: Jaguar Paw Lodge; Bak-a-Bush Big Hill Station

Jaguar Paw Lodge, which opened the first zip line in Belize, has eight platforms. Bak-a-Bush has four platforms. There's also a zip line near the entrance of Tikal park.

Multisport

Multisport simply means that you can take part in a series of different activities—hiking, kayaking, cave tubing, birding, swimming, snorkeling. With so many land and water activities packed into one small country, Belize is ideal for multisporting, and many Belize-based and international tour operators provide trips that exercise nearly every muscle in your body.

Season: Year-round
Locations: Throughout Belize
Cost: Day tours from BZ$100 per person; package tours from BZ$800 for four days, and BZ$2,100 for 15 days.
Tour Operators: Adventure Center; Adventure Life; Beyond Touring; Caves Branch Adventure Co.; Cayo Adventure Tours; Chaa Creek Expeditions; Country Walkers; Destinations Belize; G.A.P. Adventures; Hamanasi Eco Tours; International Zoological Expeditions; Island Expeditions; Mayawalk Tours; Mountain Travel Sobek; Nature Treks; PACZ Tours; River Rat Kayak and Land Expeditions; Seakunga Adventures; Slick Rock Adventures; Toadal Adventure Belize; TIDE; Wilderness Travel; Windy Hill Tour Co.

Many Belize adventure trips include a bunch of different activities. For example, the 15-day Hummingbird Highway trip offered by Adventure Center starts with four days at and around Tikal, touring Maya sites; the next couple of days sends you caving and hiking in Cayo, followed by three days of canoeing on the Macal River, and ending with snorkeling or diving off Caye Caulker. Island Expedition's 10-night Ultimate Adventure trip begins with sea kayaking, diving, snorkeling, and boardsailing at Glover's Atoll, then switches to caving and kayaking on the mainland. Seakunga's multisport tour, Caves to Cayes, combines kayaking, mountain biking, and inflatable river-raft activities. The other tour companies listed above offer a similar variety of activities in many areas of Belize.

UNDERSTANDING BELIZE

BELIZE AT A GLANCE

Fast Facts

Name: Officially changed from British Honduras to Belize in 1973
Capital: Belmopan City
Type of government: Parliamentary democracy
National anthem: *Land of the Free*
Administrative divisions: 6 districts (similar to U.S. states)—Corozal, Orange Walk, Belize, Cayo, Stann Creek, and Toledo
Independence: September 21, 1981; Belize remains a member of the British Commonwealth
Constitution: September 21, 1981
Legal system: Based on English Common Law
Suffrage: 18 years of age; universal
Legislature: An elected House of Representatives and an appointed Senate
Population: 280,000
Population density: 32 people per square mi, the lowest population density in Central America and one of the lowest population densities in the Americas

Median age: Male 18.8, female 19
Life expectancy: Male 65, female 70
Infant mortality: 27.07 deaths per 1,000 live births
Literacy: 94%
Language: English (official). Spanish is widely spoken. Creole, Garifuna, and several Mayan languages also spoken
Ethnic groups: Mestizo, 50%; Creole, 25%; Maya, 11%; Garifuna, 6%; Other, 8%
Religion: Roman Catholic, 50%; Pentecostal, 7%; Seventh Day Adventist, 7%; Anglican 5%; Methodist, 4%; Mennonite, 4%; Jehovah's Witness, 2%
Discoveries & inventions: When Western Europe was still in the Dark Ages, the ancient Maya in Belize and elsewhere in Mesoamerica had developed astronomical, mathematical, agricultural, calendrical, medical, and hieroglyphic writing systems of extraordinary complexity.

Geography & Environment

Land area: 22,966 square km (8,866 square mi); about the size of Massachusetts
Coastline: 386 km (240 mi), bordered on the east by the Caribbean
Terrain: Low-lying coastal plains that give way to low mountains in the south
Islands: More than 400 islands offshore in the Caribbean, the largest of which is Ambergris Caye
Natural resources: Farm land, timber, fish, oil
Natural hazards: Hurricanes (June–November) and coastal flooding
Environmental issues: Deforestation, water pollution from sewage and agricultural runoff, deterioration of coral reefs

If the world had any ends, British Honduras would certainly be one of them.
–Aldous Huxley

The Macal River Valley is sacred land. It's worth fighting for. Everything is connected in the biological world. We have lost too much of the planet, bit by bit, piece by piece. And that is exactly how we have to save it, piece by piece.
–Sharon Matola, director of the Belize Zoo, on the fight against building hydropower dams on the Macal River, a fight lost as the dams were built

Economy

Currency: Belize dollar
Exchange rate: BZ$2 = $1
GDP: US$1.8 billion
Per capita income: BZ$12,700 (US$6,350)
Inflation: 2.9%
Unemployment: 9%
Work force: 90,000 (services 55%, agriculture 27%, industry 18%)
Debt: US$1.5 billion
Major industries: Tourism, agriculture, fishing
Agricultural products: Sugar cane, citrus fruit, bananas
Exports: US$401 million
Major export products: Sugar, bananas, citrus, clothing, fish, cultured shrimp, wood

Export partners: U.S. 37%, U.K. 27%, Jamaica, 5%
Imports: US$580 million
Major import products: Machinery, manufactured goods, fuels, pharmaceuticals, food, beverages
Import partners: U.S. 30%, Mexico 12%, Guatemala, 7%, Cuba, 7%, China 4%, Japan 4%

No wait till de man ded, fu tell am y good. (Creole for "Don't wait until a man is dead to tell him that he is good.")
   –Lucio Alcocer, Belizean songwriter

Political Climate

In an ongoing dispute, Guatemala claims Belize territory in the south and north; an agreement reached in late 2002 to resolve the issue has not yet been brought to a referendum in either country.

Our two countries (Belize and the United States) share the same side of planet Earth. We can draw wisdom and strength from the basic values of a common heritage, the same language and common law, a kindred parliamentary democracy, and a mixed economy.
   –George Cadle Price, prime minister of Belize, 1983, to President Ronald Reagan

Did You Know?

• More than 40% of Belize's land is protected as national parks or reserves.

• Belize has the longest barrier reef in the Western and Northern hemispheres.

• The two tallest buildings in Belize, one at Caracol and one at Xunantunich, date back more than 1,000 years.

• Belize is thought to have the largest population of manatees in the world.

• Belize is the only country in Central America with English as the official language.

• Belize has fewer than 400 mi of paved roads.

• The expanse of *Selva Maya* (Maya Forest), which Belize shares with Guatemala and Mexico, covers some 25,000 square km, the largest block of tropical forest north of the Amazon Basin.

• At the height of the Mayan civilization, Belize may have had a population approaching 1 million people, almost four times the population of the country today.

• Belize is the only country in Central America without a border on the Pacific Ocean.

BELIZE Q&A

Here are answers to the 10 most frequently asked questions we receive about Belize:

Is Belize a safe place to visit? The best answer is "Yes, but . . ." Most visitors say they feel quite safe in Belize (except, they say, in some areas of Belize City). Tourist Police patrol areas of Belize City, Placencia, and Ambergris Caye, and many hotels and jungle lodges have security guards. Out of the hundreds of thousands of visitors the numbers who are victims of any kind of crime is perhaps a few hundred. So, though this is still a developing country, enjoy yourself and and follow standard travel precautions: don't wander into areas that don't feel safe; avoid deserted beaches and streets after dark; and don't flash expensive jewelry or cash. Be aware that there have been a few carjackings and robberies on remote roads or at little-visited parks and Mayan sites; travel in a group or with a guide to less popular places.

Where can we snorkel from shore? Belize has world-class snorkeling, but most of it requires a boat ride to the barrier reef. There are exceptions—the small islands that are on or near the reef, such as South Water, Ranguana, and Tobacco cayes, or the areas around the atolls, especially Glover's. Of course, you can go snorkeling off almost any beach, even if there's no patch of coral nearby.

How much does it rain during the rainy season (May through November)? It depends on where you are in Belize and when you're there. Northern Belize gets about a third as much rain—around 50 inches—as the Deep South, which can get 150 inches or more. The seasonal rains begin in Toledo in early May, progress north over the next couple of months, and usually start in Corozal in late June. The cayes have different microclimates than the mainland and generally get less rain.

The rainy season typically peaks from June through August. By November, rainfall in nearly all areas of Belize averages 8 inches or less a month. The so-called rainy season is actually a good time to visit Belize, and that's not just a Tourist Board answer. Often the rains come overnight or in the early morning, and then the sun comes out. Many old Belize hands say they prefer traveling in summer or fall: prices are lower, hotel rooms are plentiful, the landscape is lush after rains, it's a little cooler than in the dry season months of April and May, and water visibility is usually very good.

Are the beaches in Belize nice? Although there are lovely stretches of beaches, many of the beaches are not as good for swimming or sunbathing as the wide, sandy, beaches of the main Caribbean. Belizean beaches are usually narrow ribbons of sand, with clear but shallow water and an often-mucky sea floor.

Does Belize have "real" jungles? "High bush" in Belize means undisturbed wilderness, and there's plenty of that. However, not all bush in Belize is the kind of canopied, broadleaf jungle that you may be thinking about. The Deep South, with its plentiful rainfall, has lush tropical and semitropical rain forest. The Cayo also has wide swaths of broadleaf bush. Northern Belize and parts of the Cayo have little classic jungle—it's primarily dry rain forest and agricultural lands.

Why are airfares to Belize so high, and how can we find cheaper flights? Belize is not a mass-market tourist destination. Air service is still limited, and service is mostly from a few hubs in the United States. Charter flights are rare, so fares tend to stay high. To find the most affordable flights, stay flexible on your dates, prowl the discount airline reservation services (like Expedia, Orbitz, and Travelocity), avoid peak holiday travel (around Christmas and Easter), and sign up for Internet specials and e-mail fare alerts on the airlines flying to Belize—currently Continental, American, US Airways, Delta, and TACA.

While traveling around the country, should we rent a car, take a bus, fly, or hire a taxi? Each has advantages and disadvantages. With a rental car, you go when and where you want, including remote areas that don't have air or bus service or to sites that would otherwise require an expensive guided tour. However, auto rental costs are high, and gas is around US$5 a gallon. Buses provide a true local experience and fares are dirt cheap, but buses mainly run on the major roads and stop frequently to pick up and drop off passengers. Buses take up to twice as long as a private car. Flying is the fastest way to get around the country; service is frequent on most routes, and the views from low altitudes are often dramatic. The downside? Fares—especially if you're traveling with a family—can add up, and not all destinations have service. In some cases, transfers by taxi can be an option, although taxis generally are quite expensive. For most long-distance trips, there are no set fares, so the rate is a matter of negotiation and can vary considerably, depending on your bargaining skills. Drivers may also ask a little more if there are three or four going together, rather than just one or two. Expect to pay around BZ$3 a mile for longer trips in Belize. Here are some costs for taxi transfers, but remember, your mileage may vary:

International airport to San Ignacio: BZ$180–BZ$220

International airport to Placencia: BZ$300–BZ$400

San Ignacio to Mountain Pine Ridge (lodges): BZ$80–BZ$100

San Ignacio to Placencia: BZ$400–BZ$500

Dangriga to Hopkins: BZ$80–BZ$90

We're on a budget—can we just stay in a cheap hut on the beach or hang a hammock on a palm tree? Maybe. If you're looking for five-dollar rooms on the beach

or free camping on your own private island, you won't find that in Belize. However, there's camping at a few campgrounds in national parks and reserves, including Cockscomb and Half Moon Caye. Some beach hotels and lodges allow camping and may even rent you a tent. Expect to pay BZ$10 and up, per person, per night. Most people find that for only a few dollars more per night, they can stay at a budget hotel and avoid the problems with bugs, snakes, and potential thefts often faced by campers. Caye Caulker, Placencia Village, Hopkins, and San Ignacio all have budget hotels with double rooms starting at around BZ$20 to BZ$30 a night.

We want to spend time at the beach and also in the jungle. Where should we go? On a first and relatively brief visit to Belize, sample the best "surf 'n turf" by splitting your time between one of the popular beach areas—Ambergris Caye, Caye Caulker, Hopkins, or Placencia—and the rest in Cayo, which has the largest concentration of popular mainland activities.

How do we get to the Cayo from the international airport near Belize City? There's currently no scheduled air service from Belize City to San Ignacio. Though jungle lodges offer guest transfers, prices are high—typically BZ$300 or more for one to four people. You may want to try one of three other ways to do it:

• **Rent a car.** It's about two hours from the international airport to downtown San Ignacio. The main roads, like the Western Highway, are in good condition, and directions are well marked. However, if you're going somewhere outside San Ignacio proper, such as Hidden Valley Inn or Blacaneaux Lodge, the roads aren't paved and are extremely difficult to navigate. It's better not to attempt driving them on your own. There are about eight rental car companies at the airport, just across the parking lot from the main terminal.

• **Take a shuttle van.** Several hotels and tour operators, including the Trek Stop, Cahal Pech Village, Aguada, and Discovery Tours, have van service to Cayo from the international airport and other points in Belize City, including the Marine Terminal and the municipal airport. It costs around BZ$70 per person, one-way. Make reservations in advance. For contact information, see The Cayo, Chapter 4.

• **Bus it.** Though this is the cheapest option, it's a hassle, and because it's only about BZ$20 (US$10) less than taking a shuttle van, we recommend the latter.

• **Hire a taxi.** If you're traveling with several people, it may make sense to negotiate with a taxi at the airport to take you to your destination in Cayo. Licensed cabs have green plates. The exact price depends on exactly where you're going and your bargaining skills, but it will likely be less than BZ$200.

RETIRING IN BELIZE

So you fell in love with Belize, met some expats who bought their beachfront lot for a song, and want to do the same for your retirement years? Here's the scoop on what you can really expect if you decide to follow suit.

Belize can be enchanting for potential retirees. The climate is frost free. Land and housing costs are still moderate, especially compared with already popular areas of the Caribbean. The official language is English, and the historical and legal background of the country is more comparable to those in the United States, Canada, and Great Britain than most other parts of Latin America and the Caribbean. Belize has a stable and democratic, if sometimes colorful, tradition. Recreational activities, on land and in the Caribbean, are almost limitless.

But for all those positives, there are some drawbacks: high costs for food, gas, and household items; high import duties; crime and drug problems; culture shock for those unaccustomed to the ways of a semitropical, developing country with a true multicultural society; growing resentment of foreigners; plenty of red tape; increasing taxes; a 15% stamp duty on real estate purchases by foreigners, payable by the buyer; and, most importantly for many retirees, medical care that in many cases isn't up to first-world snuff. Sometimes, too, it's the little things that bother expats: they can't live without the *New York Times* on Sunday or they experience unbearable cravings for a decent slice of pizza.

If retirement in Belize still sounds like a good option for you, there are three options to look into:

The Qualified Retired Persons Incentive Act. It's run by the Belize Tourist Board, and

anyone at least 45 years old is eligible to participate in the program. Contact the tourism board for more information (⊕ travelbelize.org).

Official Permanent Residency. Requirements and benefits are similar to those of the Retired Persons Incentive Act. With official residency, you can work in Belize. Before you can apply, you need to live in Belize for a year first, leaving for no more than two weeks. Permanent Residency approvals are handled by the Belize immigration department and often take a long time.

Regular Tourist Card. Many expats simply stay in Belize on a regular tourist card. Upon entry, you receive a free visitor permit, good for up to 30 days. This permit can be renewed for up to three months at US$25 a month. After that, renewals cost US$50 a month. After 12 months, it's necessary to leave the country for 72 hours and start the process again. Renewals are never guaranteed, and the rules could change at any time.

The best advice for anyone contemplating retiring or relocating? Try before you buy. Living in Belize is quite different from vacationing. If possible, rent an apartment or house for a few months and see how you like daily life. Be cautious about buying property. Real estate agents aren't licensed or regulated, and because the pool of qualified buyers in Belize is small, it's a lot harder to sell than to buy.

Living Abroad in Belize, by Lan Sluder (author of this book), published in late 2005, is a handbook for those considering retiring or relocation in Belize. The author interviewed scores of expats and retirees in Belize to help provide readers with a realistic view of the pros and cons of living there.

WILDLIFE GLOSSARY

An amazing array of creatures make their homes in Belize and Guatemala. Many are not terribly difficult to see, thanks to their brilliant coloring. Others are likely to elude you completely. A rundown of some of the region's most attention-grabbing mammals, birds, reptiles, amphibians—even a few insects—are listed below. Common names, in English and Spanish, are given, so you can understand the local wildlife lingo.

Agouti (*guanta, paca, tepezcuintle*): A 20-inch-long tailless rodent with small ears and a large muzzle, the agouti is known locally as the gibnut. It's reddish brown on Guatemala's Pacific coast, more tawny orange on Belize's Caribbean slope. You might spot one sitting on its haunches and eating large seeds and fruit. Largely nocturnal, the agouti is more likely to be seen on a menu than in the wild. Known as the royal rat, it was served to Queen Elizabeth on her last visit to Belize.

Anteater (*oso hormiguero*): Three species—giant, silky, and collared—are found in this region. Only the collared, or vested, anteater is commonly seen (and too often as a roadkill). This medium-size anteater (30 inches long with an 18-inch tail) has long sharp claws for ripping into insect nests. You may spot one lapping up ants and termites with its long sticky tongue.

Aracari (*cusingo*): These slender toucans, known for their strikingly colored bills, eat ripe fruit. They often travel in groups of six or more. Collared aracaris on the Caribbean coast have a chalky upper mandible.

Armadillo (*cusuco*): These are the same animals that are found in the southern United States. Mostly nocturnal and solitary, this edentate (a mammal with few or no teeth) roots in the soil with its long muzzle for a varied diet of roots, insects, and small animals. They are sometimes found on the menu in local restaurants.

Basilisk (*gallego*): Flaps of skin on their long toes enable the "Jesus Christ lizard" to run across water. The emerald basilisk in the Caribbean lowlands is marked with turquoise and black on its green body. Adult males grow to 3 feet and have crests on their heads, backs, and tails.

Booby: This red-footed bird received its unflattering name because it was unafraid of humans. Because of this it became the easy prey of hungry sailors landing at Belize's Half Moon Caye, where 4,000 now live in a protected nature reserve. Look for nests with fuzzy white chicks.

Caiman (*cocodrilo*): The spectacled caiman is a small crocodile that subsists mainly on fish. It's most active at night (its eyes glow red when illuminated by a flashlight), basking in the sun by day. It's distinguished from its American cousin by its sloping brow and smooth back scales.

Capuchin monkey (*mono carablanca*): With black fur and pink faces surrounded by wisps of white, capuchin monkeys are found singly or in groups of up to 20. They are extremely active foragers, sometimes even coming to the ground to search for food.

Coati (*pizote*): A long-nose relative of the raccoon, the coati has a slender, ringed tail it often holds straight up. Lone males or groups of females with young are active during the day, either on the ground or in the trees. They're omnivorous and feed on fruit and seeds as well as mice and rats. In Belize, they are known as Quash.

Cougar (*puma*): Growing to 5 feet in length, mountain lions are the largest unspotted cats in Central America. Rarely seen, they live in most habitats in the region and feed on vertebrates ranging from snakes to deer.

Crocodile (*lagarto*): Although often referred to as alligators, crocodiles reign supreme in this region. They are distinguished from the smaller caiman by their flat heads, narrow snouts, and spiky scales. The American crocodile can reach 16 feet in length, while the smaller Morelet's crocodile grows to 8 feet. The territories of both species overlap in estuaries and brackish coastal waters, but only the American crocodile is able to filter excess salt from its system, allowing it to venture to the more distant cayes. Crocodiles seldom attack humans, preferring fish, birds, and the occasional small mammal. Both species are endangered and protected by international law.

Ctenosaur (*garrobo*): Known in Creole as the wish willy, this 36-inch-long lizard is mostly tan with four dark bands on its body and a tail ringed with rows of sharp, curved spines. This cousin of the iguana sleeps in burrows or tree hollows and is most commonly seen along the coast of Belize. Though largely vegetarian, it won't turn its nose up to a meal of a small creature.

Dolphin (*delfin*): Several species are frequently spotted off the Pacific shores. They often travel in groups of 20 or more and play around vessels. Look for spotted dolphins, which are 6 feet long and have pale markings on their posterior.

Eagle Ray: One of the Caribbean's most graceful swimmers, these flat-bodied rays range in size from 6 to 8 feet. They have a white underside and numerous white spots and circular markings over their darker backs. Their pronounced heads have flattened, tapered snouts, and their long, thin tails have one to five venomous spines at the base. They prefer cruising sandy areas, occasionally stopping to dig for mollusks.

Fer-de-lance (*barba amarilla*): One of the most dangerous of all pit vipers, the fer-de-lance has a host of names, such as tommygoff in Belize and tomagasse in Guatemala. This aggressive snake grows up to 8 feet in length and is distinguished by the bright yellow patches on its head.

Frigate bird (*tijereta del mar*): These black birds with slender wings and forked tails are some of the most effortless and agile fliers of the avian world. Coastal dwellers,

Frigate birds are more common on the Pacific than on the Atlantic. When mating season approaches, males inflate a scarlet pouch beneath their beaks in an effort to attract females.

Frog (*rana*): Over 30 species of frogs can be found in Belize. Most are nocturnal in an effort to avoid being eaten, but the brightly colored poison dart frogs—whose brilliant red, blue, and green coloration warns predators that they don't make a good meal—can be spotted during the day. Red-eyed leaf frogs are among the showiest of nocturnal species. They firmly attach themselves to plants with neon-orange legs, scarlet eyes bulging out from a metallic green body splashed with white dots and blue patches. Large brown marine toads are also common at night.

Howler monkey (*mono congo*): These chunky-bodied monkeys travel in troops of up to 20. A bit on the lethargic side, they eat leaves, fruits, and flowers. The deep, resounding howls of the males serve as communication among and between troops. Erroneously termed "baboons" by Belizeans, these dark-faced monkeys travel only from tree to tree, limiting their presence to dense jungle canopy. They are increasingly difficult to spot in the wild.

Iguana (*iguana*): The largest lizards in Central America, these scaly creatures can grow to 10 feet. They are good swimmers, and will often plop into a body of water when threatened by a predator. Only young green iguanas are brightly colored; adult females are grayish, while adult males are olive (with orangish heads during mating season). They are considered a delicacy among Belizeans, who call them "bamboo chicken."

Jacana (*gallito de agua*): These birds are sometimes referred to as "lily trotters" because their long toes allow them to walk on floating vegetation. They eat aquatic plants and animals and are found at almost any body of water. They expose their yellow wing feathers when in flight. The liberated females lay eggs in several floating nests tended by males.

Jaguar (*tigre*): The largest feline in the Western Hemisphere grows up to 6 feet long and can weigh up to 250 pounds. Exceedingly rare, this nocturnal predator is most often spotted near the Cockscomb Basin Wildlife Sanctuary in Belize.

Kinkajou (*martilla*): A nocturnal relative of the raccoon, kinkajous are known for their 20-inch-long prehensile tails. They actively and often noisily forage for fruit, insects, and the occasional sip of nectar. (If you're unsure that what you have spotted is a kinkajou, simply look at the picture on Belize's $20 note.)

Leaf-cutter ant (*zompopa*): Called wee wee ants in Creole, leaf-cutter ants are the region's most commonly noticed ants. They are found in all lowland habitats. Columns of these industrious little guys, all carrying clippings of leaves, sometimes extend for several hundred yards from plants to the underground nest. The leaves are used to cultivate the fungus that they eat.

Macaw (*lapas*): The beautiful Scarlet Macaw is the only species of this bird found in Belize. Huge, raucous birds with long tails, macaws use their immense bills to rip apart fruits to get to the seeds. Their nests are in hollow trees. They are endangered because of poachers and deforestation.

Manatee: An immense and gentle mammal, the manatee is often called the sea cow. Living exclusively in the water, particularly in shallow and sheltered areas, manatees are said to be the basis of myths about mermaids. Scarce today, these vegetarians have been hunted for thousands of years for their tasty flesh; their image frequently appears in ancient Maya art.

Margay (*caucel*): This nocturnal, spotted cat is similar to the somewhat larger ocelot, but has a longer tail. Mobile ankle joints allow it to climb down trunks head first. The margay eats small vertebrates.

Morpho (*morfo*): This spectacular butterfly doesn't fail to astound first-time viewers. Easy to overlook when resting, their color is only apparent when they take flight. One species has brilliant-blue wings, while another is distinguished by its intense violet color. Adults feed on fallen fruit, never flowers.

Motmot (*pajaro bobo*): Handsome birds of the forest, motmots sit patiently while scanning for large insects and small vertebrates. The species found in Belize make their nests in burrows.

Ocelot (*manigordo*): These medium-size spotted cats have shorter tails than their cousins the margays. They are active night and day, feeding on rodents and other small animals. Their forepaws are rather large in relation to their bodies, hence the Creole name that translates as "fat hand."

Oropéndola (*oropéndola*): These crow-size birds, members of the oriole family, have bright-yellow tails. They nest in colonies with the female building pendulous nests in isolated trees. Males make unmistakable gurgling calls. They are fairly omnivorous, but subsist mostly on fruit.

Parrot (*loro*): A prerequisite of any tropical setting, there are five species of parrot in Central America. All are clad in green, which means they virtually disappear upon landing in the trees. Most have a splash of color or two on their head or wings.

Pelican (*pelícano*): Their large size, big bills, and flapping throat pouches make brown pelicans unmistakable inhabitants of both coasts (although they are far more abundant on the Pacific side). A white American variety prefers freshwater locations. They often fly in V formations and dive for fish.

Roseate spoonbill (*garza rosada*): Pink plumage and distinctive bills set this wader apart from all other wetland birds. They feed by swishing their bills back and forth in the water while using their feet to stir up bottom-dwelling creatures.

Sea turtle: Sea turtles on the coasts of Belize come in three varieties: green, hawksbill, and loggerhead. All have paddlelike flippers and have to surface to breathe.

Spider monkey (*mono colorado, mono araña*): These lanky, long-tailed monkeys hang out in groups of two to four. Their diet consists of ripe fruit, leaves, and flowers. These incredible aerialists can swing effortlessly through the trees using their long arms and legs and prehensile tails. Caribbean and southern Pacific populations are dark reddish brown, while their cousins in the northwest are blond.

Tapir (*danta*): The national animal of Belize is also known as the mountain cow. Something like a small rhinoceros without the armor, it has a stout body, short legs, and small eyes. Completely vegetarian, it uses its prehensile snout for harvesting vegetation. The shy creature lives in forested areas near streams and lakes, where it can sometimes be spotted bathing.

Toucan (*tucán, tucancillo*): Recognizable to all who have ever seen a box of Fruit Loops, the toucan is common in Belize. The largest are the keel-billed and chestnut-mandibled toucans, growing to 22 inches long. The much smaller and stouter emerald toucanet and yellow-ear toucanet are among the most colorful. All eat fruit with their curved, multihued beaks.

—Elbert Greer

BOOKS & MOVIES

Two histories stand out: *The Making of Modern Belize,* by C. H. Grant, and *A Profile of the New Nation of Belize,* by W. D. Setzekorn. *Jaguar,* by Alan Rabinowitz, an interesting book about the creation of the Cockscomb Basin Wildlife Sanctuary, unfortunately tells you too much about the man and too little about the cat. Aldous Huxley, who wrote *Beyond the Mexique Bay,* is always hard to beat. If you're interested in the Maya, Ronald Wright's *Time Among the Maya* ties past and present together in one perceptive whole. Classic works on the Maya include *The Maya* by Michael Coe, a compendious introduction to the world of the Maya, and *The Rise and Fall of the Maya Civilization,* by one of the grand old men of Maya archaeology, J. Eric S. Thompson.

For natural history enthusiasts, four books belong in your suitcase: *Birds of Belize* by H. Lee Jones and Dana Gardner; *Guide to Corals and Fishes of Florida, the Bahamas and the Caribbean* by I. Greenberg; *The Ecotravellers' Wildlife Guide, Belize and Northern Guatemala* by Les Belesky; and *An Introduction to Tropical Rainforests* by T. C. Whitmore. *Our Man in Belize* is a fascinating memoir of life in British Honduras in the 1950s and '60s. For beach reading, *Belize, a Novel* by Carlos Ledson Miller is a fast-paced saga of a Belizean family over four decades.

Paul Theroux's novel, *The Mosquito Coast,* about an obsessed American who drags his family to Central America, was actually set in Honduras, but the movie by the same name, starring Harrison Ford, was filmed in Belize in 1986. The riproaring *The Dogs of War,* 1981, starring Christopher Walken, about soldiers of fortune in Africa, has wonderful scenes of Belize City, especially the lobby of the Chateau Caribbean Hotel, and Emory King, now film commissioner for the Belize government, has a bit part (as indeed he has in nearly all the TV shows and movies shot in Belize).

Heart of Darkness (1994, starring John Malkovich), and 2001's *After the Storm,* directed by Guy Ferland, were also filmed in Belize. One of the first reality TV shows, *Temptation Island,* was shot mostly on Ambergris Caye, at Mata Chica and Captain Morgan's resorts, in 2000–2001. He hasn't filmed anything in Belize, but Francis Ford Coppola (*The Godfather, Apocalypse Now*) owns two resorts in Belize, Turtle Inn in Placencia and Blancaneaux in the Mountain Pine Ridge, along with a third, La Lancha, in Flores, Guatemala. Although filmed in 2005 and 2006 in Mexico, not Belize, Mel Gibson's *Apocalypto* is notable because all the dialogue is in the Yucatec Maya language.

SMART TRAVEL TIPS

⇨ *For region specifics,* see the Essentials sections at the end of each chapter.

Finding out about your destination before you leave home means you won't spend time organizing everyday minutiae once you've arrived. You'll be more streetwise when you hit the ground as well, better prepared to explore the aspects of Belize that drew you here in the first place. The organizations in this section can provide information to supplement this guide; contact them for up-to-the-minute details, and consult the A to Z sections that end each chapter for facts on the various topics. Happy landings!

ADDRESSES

Belize is as laid-back about street names as it is about so many other parts of life. Some areas, such as remote cayes and the main part of Placencia Village, have no streets at all. (In Placencia, houses sit on the beach and along a mile-long sidewalk.) In a few other areas, including Caye Caulker, some of the sandy streets aren't named. People say, "Go down to such-and-such, and turn right." On Ambergris Caye, the three main streets in the town of San Pedro are still locally called Front Street, Middle Street, and Back Street, although maps will say their names are Barrier Reef Drive, Pescador Drive, and Angel Coral Drive. Except in Belize City and in a few towns, where there is mail delivery to homes and businesses, street numbers are a casual affair; even if a building has a number, it may have fallen off long ago.

AIR TRAVEL

BOOKING

When you book, look for nonstop flights and remember that "direct" flights stop at least once. Try to avoid connecting flights, which require a change of plane. Two airlines may operate a connecting flight jointly, so ask whether your airline operates every segment of the trip; you may find that the carrier you prefer flies you only part of the way. To find more booking tips and to check prices and make on-line flight reservations, log on to www.fodors.com.

Electronic tickets are now standard on most airlines. Since electronic tickets eliminate all paperwork, there's no ticket to pick up or misplace; after passing through security checks, you may be able to go directly to the gate and give the agent your confirmation number, or in some cases use an electronic check-in system.

CARRIERS

American Airlines, Continental, Delta, TACA, and US Airways fly to Belize from the United States. The major departure gateways are Atlanta, with daily flights on Delta to Belize City; Charlotte, with daily nonstops on US Airways to Belize City (flight frequency usually is reduced in the fall); Houston, with daily nonstop service to Belize City on TACA and Continental; Dallas–Fort Worth, with daily nonstop service to Belize City on American (sometimes as a code share with TACA); and Miami, with daily nonstop service on American. TACA also flies to Belize City from several other U.S. cities with a change of planes in San Salvador, El Salvador. Continental has a weekly flight nonstop from Newark.

Continental has twice-weekly nonstop service between Houston and Flores, Guatemala.

Domestic planes in Belize are single- or twin-engine island-hoppers. The main carriers are Tropic Air and Maya Island Air, both of which fly to San Pedro on Ambergris Caye and Caye Caulker as well as Corozal, Dangriga, Independence, Placencia, Punta Gorda. They also fly to Flores, Guatemala, for around BZ$415 round-trip. Tikal Jets, a Guatemalan airline, through an arrangement with Maya Island, also provides jet service between Flores and Belize City at times when demand is high. Belize domestic flights on Maya Island and Tropic from and to the international airport are between BZ$215 and BZ$415 round-trip, and about BZ$120 to BZ$350 round-trip between the municipal airstrip in Belize City and domestic destinations. Charter services such as Javier Flying Service and Cai Bee Air Service will take you almost anywhere for around BZ$400 per hour; Javier has flights to Chan Chich Lodge.

🛪 Major Airlines **American Airlines** ☎ 800/433-7300, 501/223-2522 in Belize ⊕ www.aa.com. **Con-**tinental ☎ 800/525-0280, 501/822-1062 in Belize. **Delta Airlines** ☎ 800/241-4141, 501/225-3423 in Belize ⊕ www.delta.com. **TACA** ☎ 800/535-8780, 501/227-7363 in Belize, 502/261-2144 in Guatemala. **US Air** ☎ 800/428-4322, 501/225-3589 in Belize ⊕ www.usairways.com.

🛪 Belizean Carriers **Cari Bee Air Service** ☎ 501/223-3542. **Javier Flying Service** ☎ 501/223-5360 🖷 501/223-1731 ⊕ www.javiersflying.bz. **Maya Island Air** ☎ 501/226-3838, 800/521-1247 in U.S. 🖷 501/226-2192 ✐ mayair@btl.net ⊕ www.mayaairways.com. **Tropic Air** ☎ 501/226-2012, 800/422-3435 in U.S. 🖷 501/226-2338 ✐ tropicair@btl.net ⊕ www.tropicair.com.

🛪 Guatemalan Airlines **Tikal Jets** ☎ 502/2426-1414 ⊕ www.tikaljets.com.

CHECK-IN & BOARDING

For international flights—except for those smaller flights between Belize and Guatemala, where you should be at the airport at least an hour in advance—you should be at the airport at least two hours before your scheduled departure time; for domestic flights, about half an hour. Assuming that not everyone with a ticket will show up, airlines routinely overbook planes. When everyone does, airlines ask for volunteers to give up their seats. In return, these volunteers usually get a certificate for a free flight and are rebooked on the next flight out. If there are not enough volunteers, the airline must choose who will be denied boarding. In Belize, domestic airlines with more passengers than seats sometimes simply add another flight. The first to get bumped are passengers who checked in late and those flying on discounted tickets, so **get to the gate and check in as early as possible,** especially during peak periods. To avoid delays at airport-security checkpoints, try not to wear any metal. Jewelry, belt and other buckles, steel-toe shoes, barrettes, and underwire bras are among the items that can set off detectors.

Always **bring a government-issued photo ID to the airport.** You'll be asked to show it before you're allowed to check in. The international airport in Belize City has security precautions similar to those in the United States; the domestic airstrips in Belize have limited security systems, but there has never been an airline hijacking in Belize.

CUTTING COSTS

The least expensive airfares to Belize and Guatemala are often priced for round-trip travel and usually must be purchased in advance. Airlines generally allow you to change your return date for a fee; most low-fare tickets, however, are nonrefundable. Airfares to Belize are often twice or more the cost of a ticket to Cancún or Cozumel, Mexico, so, if you have the time, **it pays to fly into the Yucatán and take a bus to Belize.** From the Yucatán, a first-class or deluxe bus costs US$25 or less, and takes five to six hours, to Chetumal, Mexico, a border town where you can transfer to a Belize bus. (If you fly into Cozumel, you'll first have to take a ferry to Playa del Carmen.)

You'll save 10% to 45% on flights within Belize by flying to and from the muncipal airport near downtown Belize City, rather than to or from the international airport north of the city in Ladyville. For example, a flight from municipal to San Pedro is BZ$60 one-way, and almost twice that, BZ$108, from international. Savings to other destinations are somewhat less. If you are arriving at the international airport, a transfer by taxi to the municipal airport is BZ$50 (for up to four persons, not per person), so the savings are small at best for a single traveler or couple; transferring to the municipal airport makes more sense for families or groups traveling together. If you are already in the Belize City area and need to fly to another part of the country, or are flying into Belize City from another part of the country, it is always at least a little cheaper to fly to or from municipal.

On international flights it's smart to **call a number of airlines, check their Web sites, or check the Web sites of reservation services such as Expedia, Orbitz, and Travelocity. When you're quoted a good price, book it on the spot**—the same fare may not be available the next day. Always **check different routings** and look into using different airports. **"Metasearch" engines, such as Sidestep, Mobissimo,**

Cheapflights, Kayak, Farechase, One-Travel, and TravelZoo allow you to search multiple travel sites for fares to a specific destination. However, in Belize the two internal airlines charge about the same price on all flights; there are few if any discounts for advance booking, although discounts are sometimes given for paying cash rather than using a credit card, and round-trip fares are the same as two one-way fares. Travel agents, especially low-fare specialists (⇨ Discounts & Deals, *below*), are helpful.

🔎 Consolidators **AirlineConsolidator.com** ☎ 888/468-5385 ⊕ www.airlineconsolidator.com, for international tickets. **Best Fares** ☎ 800/880-1234 ⊕ www.bestfares.com; $59.90 annual membership. **Cheap Tickets** ☎ 800/377-1000 or 800/652-4327 ⊕ www.cheaptickets.com. **Expedia** ☎ 800/397-3342 or 404/728-8787 ⊕ www.expedia.com. **Fly CheapOL** (☎ 888/702-4242 ⊕ www.flycheapol.com. **Hotwire** ☎ 866/468-9473 or 920/330-9418 ⊕ www.hotwire.com. **Latin Discounters** ☎ 877/426-8676 ⊕ www.latindiscounters.com. **Now Voyager Travel** ☎ 212/459-1616 ⊕ www.nowvoyager.com. **Onetravel.com** ⊕ www.onetravel.com. **Orbitz** ☎ 888/656-4546 ⊕ www.orbitz.com. **Priceline.com** ⊕ www.priceline.com. **Traveland** (☎ 800/321-6336 ⊕ www.traveland.com. **Travelocity** ☎ 888/709-5983, 877/282-2925 in Canada, 0870/111-7061 in U.K. ⊕ www.travelocity.com.

🔎 Metasearch Engines **Cheapflights** (⊕ www.cheapflights.com). **FareChase** (⊕ www.farechase.yahoo.com). **Kayak** (⊕ www.kayak.com). **Mobissimo** (⊕ www.mobissimo.com). **Sidestep** (⊕ www.sidestep.com). **TravelZoo** (⊕ www.travelzoo.com).

🔎 Courier Resources **Air Courier Association/Cheaptrips.com** ☎ 800/211-5119 ⊕ www.aircourier.org or www.cheaptrips.com; $20 annual membership. **Courier Travel** ☎ 303/570-7586 🖷 313/625-6106 ⊕ www.couriertravel.org; $50 annual membership. **International Association of Air Travel Couriers** ☎ 308/632-3273 🖷 308/632-8267 ⊕ www.courier.org; $45 annual membership. **Now Voyager Travel** ✉ 1717 Ave. M, Brooklyn, NY 11230 ☎ 212/459-1616 🖷 718/504-4762 ⊕ www.nowvoyager.com.

ENJOYING THE FLIGHT

State your seat preference when purchasing your ticket, and then repeat it when you confirm and when you check in. For more legroom, you can request one of the few emergency-aisle seats at check-in, if you're capable of moving obstacles comparable in weight to an airplane exit door (usually between 35 pounds and 60 pounds)—a Federal Aviation Administration requirement of passengers in these seats. Seats behind a bulkhead also offer more legroom, but they don't have underseat storage. Some airlines now charge a small extra fee for these coach-class seats with more legroom, or reserve them for their best frequent flyers. Don't sit in the row in front of the emergency aisle or in front of a bulkhead, where seats may not recline. SeatGuru.com has more information about specific seat configurations, which vary by aircraft.

Ask the airline whether a snack or meal is served on the flight. If you have dietary concerns, request special meals when booking. These can be vegetarian, low-cholesterol, or kosher, for example. It's a good idea to pack some healthful snacks and a small (plastic) bottle of water in your carry-on bag. On long flights, try to maintain a normal routine, to help fight jet lag. At night, get some sleep. By day, eat light meals, drink water (not alcohol), and **move around the cabin** to stretch your legs. For additional jet-lag tips consult *Fodor's FYI: Travel Fit & Healthy* (available at bookstores everywhere).

Smoking policies vary from carrier to carrier. Most airlines prohibit smoking on all of their flights; others allow smoking only on certain routes or certain departures. Ask your carrier about its policy.

FLYING TIMES
To Belize City, it's roughly 2 hours from Miami and Atlanta; 2½ hours from Dallas, Houston, and Charlotte.

To Flores, Guatemala, from Houston the flying time is about 2½ hours.

HOW TO COMPLAIN
If your baggage goes astray or your flight goes awry, complain right away. Most carriers require that you **file a claim immediately.** The Aviation Consumer Protection Division of the Department of Transportation publishes *Fly-Rights,* which discusses airlines and consumer issues and is available online. You can also find articles and information on mytravelrights.com, the Web site of the nonprofit Consumer Travel Rights Center.

🔲 Airline Complaints **Aviation Consumer Protection Division** ✉ U.S. Department of Transportation, Office of Aviation Enforcement and Proceedings, C-75, Room 4107, 400 7th St. SW, Washington, DC 20590 ☎ 202/366-2220 ⊕ airconsumer.ost.dot.gov. **Federal Aviation Administration Consumer Hotline** ✉ For inquiries: FAA, 800 Independence Ave. SW, Washington, DC 20591 ☎ 800/322-7873 ⊕ www.faa.gov.

RECONFIRMING
Check the status of your flight before you leave for the airport. You can do this on your carrier's Web site, by linking to a flight-status checker (many Web booking services offer these), or by calling your carrier or travel agent. Always confirm international flights at least 72 hours ahead of the scheduled departure time.

AIRPORTS
International flights to Belize arrive at the Philip Goldson International Airport in Ladyville, 9 mi (15 km) north of Belize City, probably the only airport in the world with a mahogany roof. Small domestic airports (which comprise landing strips with a one-room check-in) in Belize are in Belize City, Corozal, Dangriga, Independence, Placencia, Punta Gorda, San Pedro, and Sarteneja.

The international airports in Guatemala are La Aurora in Guatemala City and Flores–Santa Elena Airport in El Petén near Tikal, which has service to Belize, Mexico, and Guatemala City.

🔲 Belize **Belize Municipal Airstrip** ✉ Belize City ☎ No phone. **Philip Goldson International Airport** ✉ Ladyville ☎ 501/225-2014.

🔲 Guatemala **La Aurora International Airport** ✉ Guatemala City ☎ 502/332-6084 or 502/332-6085. **Flores–Santa Elena International Airport** ✉ Flores–Santa Elena, El Petén ☎ 502/950-1289.

DUTY-FREE SHOPPING
The international airports have several duty-free shops selling liquor, cigars, perfume, and other items. You generally can buy duty-free goods only when departing a country, not in the arrival area.

BIKE TRAVEL

In Belize, the lightly traveled rural byways are good for biking, although the rough roads mean you should be prepared for lots of flats. Mountain Pine Ridge, with hardly any traffic on the miles of old logging roads, is an ideal spot for mountain biking. Bicycle racing has become an important sport in Belize, and you often see teams training.

Road biking is less advisable and common in Guatemala, primarily because Guatemalan highways are narrow and largely insufficient for the growing number of cars and trucks on the road. Most roads in El Petén near Tikal are unpaved.

BIKES IN FLIGHT

Most airlines accommodate bikes as luggage, provided they are dismantled and boxed; check with individual airlines about packing requirements. Some airlines sell bike boxes, which are often free at bike shops, for about $20 (bike bags can be considerably more expensive). International travelers often can substitute a bike for a piece of checked luggage at no charge; otherwise, the cost is about $100. Most U.S. and Canadian airlines charge $40–$80 each way.

BIKE RENTALS

In Belize, you can rent mountain bikes in Cayo and road bikes in the Ambergris Caye and Placencia resort areas. Rates are around BZ$29 to BZ$30 a day or BZ$80 to BZ$100 a week. Many resorts and lodges offer bikes to guests, sometimes on a complimentary basis. In Guatemala, ecolodges and hotels rent bikes or lend them to guests free of charge: however, these are not always in top shape.

BOAT & FERRY TRAVEL

Since Belize has about 200 mi (325 km) of mainland coast and some 400 islands in the Caribbean, water taxis and small ferries are a primary form of transportation here. There is scheduled ferry service six or more times a day from Belize City to Ambergris Caye, Caye Caulker, and Caye Chapel, and also between those cayes. One-way fare from Belize City to Ambergris Caye is BZ$30, and the trip takes 1¼

hours. To Caye Caulker the fare is BZ$20, and the trip takes 45 minutes. A ferry runs daily between Corozal Town and San Pedro; the fair is BZ$45 one-way, and the trip takes 2 hours or longer. To reach the more remote cayes, you're basically left to your own devices, unless you're staying at a hotel where such transfers are arranged for you. The resorts on the atolls run their own flights or boats, but these are not available to the general public.

Note that life jackets are typically not provided on boats and the seas can be rough. Postpone your trip if the weather looks bad, and don't be shy about waiting for another boat if the one offered looks unseaworthy or crowded.

FARES & SCHEDULES

Water taxis accept only cash in U.S. or Belize dollars. Tickets can be purchased at the Marine Terminal in Belize City or at the departure/arrival piers on Ambergris Caye and Caye Caulker. Schedules are posted at these locations and are available online.

🚢 Boat & Ferry Information **Belize Marine Terminal** ✉ N. Front St. at Swing Bridge, Belize City ☎ 501/223-1969. **Caye Caulker Water Taxis** ☎ 501/223-2969 ⊕ www.cayecaulkerwatertaxi.com.

BUSINESS HOURS

BANKS & OFFICES

Belize has three local banks, Alliance Bank, Atlantic Bank, and Belize Bank, and two international banks, First Caribbean International (formerly Barclays), and Bank of Nova Scotia. Hours vary, but banks typically are open Monday–Thursday 8–2 and Friday 8–4. The Belize Bank branch at the international airport in Belize City is open 8:30–4 daily.

In Guatemala, most banks are open 9–4, but sometimes until 7 PM. Major banks, such as Bancafe, Banco Industrial, and Banco Occidente, change travelers checks.

GAS STATIONS

Modern, U.S.-style gas stations—Texaco, Esso, and Shell brands, some of them with convenience stores and 24-hour service—are in Belize City and in major towns. In remote areas, especially in southern Belize, gas up whenever you see a gas station. Premium unleaded gas costs close to BZ$10 a gallon. Attendants who pump gas for you do not expect a tip, though any small change is appreciated. If you're driving in from Mexico, stop at the Free Zone, a duty-free shopping area near Corozal Town, and fill up with gas. It'll save you about 40% of the cost in Belize.

Guatemala's gas prices are a little lower than in Belize. At most gas stations, an attendant will pump the gas and make change. Plan to **use cash,** as credit cards are rarely accepted.

MUSEUMS, SHOPS & SIGHTS

Belize is a very laid-back place that requires a certain amount of flexibility when shopping or seeing sights. Shops tend to open according to the whim of the owner, but are generally open 8–noon and 2–8. Larger stores and supermarkets in Belize City and in towns such as San Ignacio and San Pedro do not close at lunch. Some shops and businesses work a half day on Saturday. On Friday, some shops (and even the Belize Tourism Association main office in Belize City) close early for the weekend, and on Sunday, Belize takes it very easy: few shops are open, and many restaurants are closed, except those in hotels. Most Mayan sites in Belize are open 8–4.

In Guatemala, most shops are open 10–7, with a lunch break 1–3. Museums are typically closed Monday. Tikal is open daily 6–6.

PHARMACIES

Pharmacies in Belize City are normally open from 8 AM to 7 or 8 PM Monday–Friday, with shorter hours on Saturday. They're usually closed on Sunday. The city also has several 24-hour pharmacies. Outside Belize City, pharmacies are typically open from 8 AM to 5 or 6 PM Monday–Friday, with shorter Saturday hours. They're closed on Sunday. In all areas, physicians often either dispense drugs directly or own pharmacies. In an emergency, visit the local hospital or medical clinic, where you may be able to obtain the medicine you need. Many drugs, including antibiotics, sleeping pills, and antimalarials, are available without a prescription. However, most pharmacies in Belize have limited inventories. You should bring an adequate supply of any prescription medicine you take.

BUS TRAVEL

Belize has frequent and inexpensive bus service on the Northern and Western highways, and, also reasonable service to southern Belize via the Hummingbird, Manatee, and Southern highways. Elsewhere, bus service is spotty. There's no municipal bus service in Belize City, although several of Belize's franchised bus companies have terminals in Belize City. In late 2005 the largest bus company in Belize, Novelo's, shut down due to financial problems, and smaller regional companies struggled to take up the slack.

In Guatemala, buses are the transportation of choice for locals and visitors. They can get you just about anywhere cheaply and quickly and are great for day trips, but they can get extremely crowded. Be prepared for tight squeezes—this means three to a two-person seat—and watch for pickpockets. Large bags are typically stowed on top, which may make you nervous, but theft from bus tops is rare. Drivers and *cobradors* or *ayudantes* (fare collectors, who call out the stops) are knowledgeable and helpful, if a bit gruff. They can direct you to the right bus, and tell you when and where to get off. To be sure they don't forget about you, **try to sit near the driver.** Incidents involving foreign travelers on public buses are rare. (⇨ Safety, below.) In fact, the most recent incidents have involved a large group of foreigners using chartered tour buses.

🚍 Belize Companies **Novelo's** ⊠ W. Collet Canal, Belize City ☎ 227/2025. **Southern Transport** ⊠ 3 Havana St., Dangriga ☎ 522/2160.

🚍 Guatemala Companies **Autobuses de Oriente** ⊠ Guatemala City ☎ 2238-3894. **Línea Dorada** ⊠ Calle Principal, Santa Elena ⊠ Calle de la Playa, Flores ☎ 2232-9658. **Transgalgos** ⊠ Guatemala City ☎ 2253-3661.

CLASSES

Expect to ride on old U.S. school buses or retired North American Greyhound buses. On some routes of Belize, there are a few express buses with air-conditioning and other comforts. These cost a few dollars more.

In Guatemala, inexpensive public buses, also of the converted school bus variety, crisscross the entire country, including El Petén, but they can be slow and extremely crowded, with a three-per-seat rule enforced. Popular destinations, such as Tikal or Santa Elena, use Pullman buses, which are as well equipped as American bus lines and are considerably more comfortable. Your hotel or INGUAT office can make bus travel recommendations and arrangements for you.

FARES & SCHEDULES

Belizean buses are cheap (about BZ$2–BZ$20 for intertown trips). Likewise, in Guatemala, fares on public buses are a bargain at US25¢–US$3. Buses from the Belize border to Flores are around US$3. On average, it works out to around US$2 an hour to ride buses in Belize, and only about US$1 an hour of travel time in Guatemala.

In Belize, most buses on main routes run according to more-or-less reliable schedules, although the closing of a large line, Novelo's, in 2005, has meant schedule changes and less frequency on some routes; on lesser-traveled routes the schedules may not mean much. The Belize Tourist Board (see below) sometimes has bus schedules for popular routes. In Guatemala, public buses follow loose schedules, sometimes waiting to leave until the bus fills up. Be aware that on some routes the day's very last bus isn't always a sure thing. Schedules for Pullman buses are usually observed.

PAYING

Buses accept only cash in U.S. or Belize dollars.

The main terminals in Belize City and some towns have ticket windows where you pay in advance and get a reserved seat. If you board at other points, you pay the driver's assistant and take any available seat.

In Guatemalan cities, you pay the bus driver as you board. On intercity buses, a fare collector will pass through the bus periodically to take your fare. They have an amazing ability to keep track of all the paid and unpaid fares in a bus jam-packed with riders. For shuttles, you may be asked to pay in advance, but only do so at legitimate agencies.

RESERVATIONS

Advance-purchase bus tickets and reservations are usually not needed or expected in Belize and Guatemala, even for Pullman departures. Arrive at bus terminals about a half hour before your departure. Reservations are generally required for shuttle service in Guatemala and Belize.

SHUTTLE TRAVEL

Belize has some shuttle service, primarily between Belize City and San Ignacio. San Ignacio Shuttle charges BZ$60 per person from the international or municipal airports in Belize City to San Ignacio. The Aguada Hotel in San Ignacio is one of several Cayo hotels that offers van service to and from Belize City, at BZ$70 per person. Línea Dorada runs twice-daily vans between Belize City and Flores, Guatemala, for BZ$40, and between Chetumal and Flores, for BZ$70 (plus border-crossing fees).

Shuttles in Guatemala are private minivans that hold up to eight passengers. They are faster and more comfortable than public buses. Minivans from the Belize border to Flores or Tikal run US$50 to US$80, depending on your bargaining ability (in Spanish) and the number of passengers. Shuttles between Flores and Tikal charge a flat US$5 per person round-trip and run frequently, starting at 5 AM from Flores.

🚌 Belize Companies **Aguada Hotel** ☎ 501/804–3609. **Línea Dorada** ☎ 502/926–3649. **San Ignacio Shuttle** ☎ 501/823-2265 ⊕ www.sanignacioshuttle.com.

🚌 Guatemala Companies **Atitrans** ☎ 7832-0644 or 2363-0178. **Servicios Turísticos Atitlán** ☎ 7832-1493 or 7762-2075.

CAMERAS & PHOTOGRAPHY

With their incredibly varied landscapes, Belize and Guatemala are a photographer's dream. Frothy waves in a turquoise sea and palm-lined crescents of beach are relatively easy to capture on film if you don't let the brightness of the sun on sand and water fool your light meter. You must compensate or else work early or late in the day when the light isn't as brilliant and contrast isn't such a problem. **Invest in a telephoto lens** if you intend to photograph wildlife: even standard zoom lenses won't capture a satisfying amount of detail. High-speed film can compensate for low light in the jungle. The thick tree canopy blocks out more light than you realize.

Casual photographers should **consider using inexpensive disposable cameras** to reduce the risks inherent in traveling with expensive equipment. One-use cameras with underwater functions make your snorkeling and diving adventures more memorable.

Some Maya and many Mennonites don't like to be photographed. In Guatemala's smaller towns, children may offer to pose for a picture, for which a small tip is expected. Likewise, if you snap a candid shot, they may ask afterward for a few *quetzales*. This is off-putting to some; but on the other hand, the children otherwise receive nothing for their participation, while the traveler gets a nice memento. An alternative is to bring a Polaroid camera, whose instant photos are treats for youngsters who very likely have never seen a picture of themselves.

It's best to **always ask permission before taking pictures of indigenous people,** particularly in market areas and rural villages. Although many are more than happy to comply, others may find it disrespectful, invasive, or possibly threatening (due to the increase in child adoption in Guatemala, many parents don't like their childrens' photos taken). Unless you're given permission or a child approaches you, limit your photographs and videotaping to children accompanied by their parents or to adults who work in the tourism trade.

The *Kodak Guide to Shooting Great Travel Pictures* (available at bookstores everywhere) is loaded with tips.

Photo Help Kodak Information Center ☎ 800/242-2424 ⊕ www.kodak.com.

EQUIPMENT PRECAUTIONS

In Belize, sand and high humidity are enemies to your camera equipment. To be on the safe side, **pack your gear in plastic bags** to protect it from the elements. **Don't pack film or equipment in checked luggage,** where it is much more susceptible to damage. X-ray machines used to view checked luggage are extremely powerful and therefore are likely to ruin your film. Try to ask for hand inspection of film, which becomes clouded after repeated exposure to airport X-ray machines, and keep videotapes and computer disks away from metal detectors. Always keep film, tape, and computer disks out of the sun. Carry an extra supply of batteries, and be prepared to turn on your camera, camcorder, or laptop to prove to airport security personnel that the device is real.

FILM & DEVELOPING

In Belize, there are photo-finishing services in major towns and, in Belize City, one-hour photo labs. Guatemala has reliable and affordable photo-development shops, especially in tourist destinations. Many offer one-hour developing at no extra cost.

CAR RENTAL

Belize City and the international airport in Ladyville have most major carrental agencies, as well as several local operators. Prices vary from company to company, but all are high by U.S. standards (BZ$120–BZ$275 per day). A small four-wheel-drive Suzuki, with unlimited mileage from Budget, for instance, costs about BZ$150 per day, though weekly rates are cheaper (about BZ$900). Off-season, rates are a little lower. Some hotels have all-terrain vehicles with guides for about BZ$400 per day. A few resorts have rental cars for about BZ$150–BZ$180 per day.

For serious safaris, a **four-wheel-drive vehicle is invaluable.** But since unpaved roads, mudslides in rainy season, and a general off-the-beaten-path landscape are status quo here, all drivers will be comforted with a four-wheel-drive vehicle, called *doble-tracción* in Spanish.

Car rental has never really caught on in Guatemala, which, given the narrowness of the roads, is just as well. However, for obvious reasons, a car can be an asset to your trip. You don't have to worry about unreliable bus schedules, you have a lot more control over your itinerary and the pace of your trip, and you can head off to explore on a whim. If you do rent a car, **look for guarded parking lots or hotels with private parking,** to prevent theft or damage. Budget, Hertz, and several local companies have rental cars at the Flores airport, starting at around US$65 for a four-wheel-drive.

🚗 Major Agencies **Alamo** ☎ 800/522-9696 ⊕ www.alamo.com. **Avis** ☎ 800/331-1084, 800/879-2847 in Canada, 0870/606-0100 in U.K., 02/9353-9000 in Australia, 09/526-2847 in New Zealand ⊕ www.avis.com. **Budget** ☎ 800/472-3325, 800/268-8900 in Canada, 1300/794-344 in Australia, 0800/283-438 in New Zealand ⊕ www.budget.com. **Crystal** ☎ 501/223-1600, 800/777-7777 in Belize ⊕ www.crystal-belize.com. **Dollar** ☎ 800/800-6000, 0800/085-4578 in U.K. ⊕ www.dollar.com. **Hertz** ☎ 800/654-3001, 800/263-0600 in Canada, 0870/844-8844 in U.K., 02/9669-2444 in Australia, 09/256-8690 in New Zealand ⊕ www.hertz.com. **National Car Rental** ☎ 800/227-7368 ⊕ www.nationalcar.com.

INSURANCE

When driving a rented car you are generally responsible for any damage to or loss of the vehicle. You also may be liable for any property damage or personal injury that you may cause while driving. Before you rent, see what coverage you already have under the terms of your personal auto-insurance policy and credit cards.

In Belize, unless covered by your credit card or personal insurance policy, Collision Damage Waiver insurance costs BZ$20 to BZ$40 a day, and you may still be liable for the first BZ$1,000–BZ$4,000 in damages.

REQUIREMENTS & RESTRICTIONS

In Belize and Guatemala, rental car companies routinely accept driver's licenses from the United States, Canada, and most other countries without question. Most car-rental agencies require a major credit card for a deposit, and some require you be over 25.

Most Belize agencies do not permit their vehicles to be taken into Guatemala or Mexico. Crystal in Belize City does permit its vehicles to be taken into Guatemala, although without any insurance coverage.

SURCHARGES

Before you pick up a car in one city and leave it in another, ask about drop-off charges or one-way service fees, which can be substantial. In Belize, drop-off charges start at around BZ$100. Also inquire about early-return policies; some rental agencies charge extra if you return the car before the time specified in your contract while others give you a refund for the days not used. Most agencies note the tank's fuel level on your contract; to avoid a hefty refueling fee, return the car with the same tank level. If the tank was full, refill it just before you turn in the car, but be aware that gas stations near the rental outlet may overcharge. It's almost never a deal to buy a tank of gas with the car when you rent it; the understanding is that you'll return it empty, but some fuel usually remains. In Belize, some rental agencies with their own pumps actually charge less for gas than you'd pay at service stations, so ask for fill-ups.

CAR TRAVEL

Your driver's license may not be recognized outside your home country. International driving permits (IDPs) are available from the American and Canadian automobile associations and, in the United Kingdom, from the Automobile Association and Royal Automobile Club. These international permits, valid only in conjunction with your regular driver's license, are universally recognized; having one may save you a problem with local authorities.

EMERGENCY SERVICES

When renting a car, ask the rental agency what they do if your car breaks down in a remote area. Most in Belize send a driver with a replacement vehicle or a mechanic to fix the car. For help in Guatemala, your best bet is to call the National or Tourist Police. In either country, **consider renting a cellular phone**(⇨ Telephones, *below*).

🚗 **Belize Police** ☎ 911. **Guatemalan National Police** ☎ 110. **Guatemalan Tourist Police** ☎ 832-0532 Ext. 35 or 832-0533 Ext. 35.

GASOLINE

Modern, U.S.-style gas stations—Texaco, Esso, and Shell brands, some of them with convenience stores and 24-hour service—are in Belize City and most major towns. In more remote areas, especially in the southern part of the country, **fill up the tank whenever you see a service station.** Premium unleaded gas costs about BZ$7.75 a gallon. Diesel fuel is about one-third less. Attendants who pump gas for you don't expect a tip.

Prices at Guatemala's service stations are as high as in Belize. At most gas stations an attendant will pump the gas and make change. Plan to **use cash,** as credit cards are rarely accepted.

ROAD CONDITIONS

Three of the four main roads in Belize, the Western Highway, Northern Highway, and Hummingbird Highway, are completely paved. These two-lane roads are generally in good condition. The Southern Highway, from Dangriga to Punta Gorda, is completely paved except for a 9-mi (15-km) stretch near Big Falls. Aside from these main highways, expect fair to stupendously rough dirt, gravel, and limestone roads; a few unpaved roads may be impassable at times in the rainy season. The main highways in Belize are now well signed, with large green signs directing you to major sites of interest.

Immense improvements have been made to Guatemala's ravaged roads. A new highway from Río Dulce to Tikal has cut travel time along this popular route significantly. The road from the Belize border toward Tikal is unpaved for the first 19 mi (32 km). Roads in remote areas are frequently unpaved, rife with potholes, and can be treacherously muddy in the rainy season. Four-wheel-drive vehicles are recommended for travel off the beaten path. In cities, expect narrow and brick streets. Road signs are generally used to indicate large towns, although smaller towns may not be clearly marked. Look for intersections where people seem to be waiting for a bus—that's a good sign that there's an important turn-off nearby.

ROAD MAPS

The best available road map to Belize is the *Belize Traveller's Map* published by ITMB, Vancouver, Canada, last updated in 2005. **Buy this map before your trip** as it is not always readily available in Belize. *Emory King's Driver's Guide to Beautiful Belize,* updated annually and available in Belize, is a mile-by-mile guide to most roads in Belize. INGUAT and all major car rental companies have maps of Guatemala.

RULES OF THE ROAD

Driving in Belize and Guatemala is on the right. Seat belts are required, although the law is seldom enforced. There are few speed limit signs, and speed limits are rarely enforced. However, as you approach villages and towns **watch out for "sleeping policemen,"** a local name for raised speed bumps on the road. Belize has about a dozen traffic lights, and only Belize City has anything approaching congested traffic. Despite the relatively small number of private cars in Belize, traffic accidents are the number one cause of death in the country. Belizean drivers aren't always as skilled as they think they are, and drunk drivers can be a problem. Guatemala's narrow roads and highways mean you can be stuck motionless on the road for an hour while a construction crew stands around a hole in the ground. **Always allow extra travel time** for such unpredictable events, and **bring along snacks and water.** Otherwise, if you observe the rules you follow at home, you'll likely do just fine. Just don't expect everyone else to follow them.

CHILDREN IN BELIZE & GUATEMALA

Children are welcomed in most hotels and restaurants, especially on weekends, when families go out for lunch in droves. If you are renting a car, don't forget to arrange for a car seat when you reserve. For general advice about traveling with children, consult *Fodor's FYI: Travel with Your Baby* (available in bookstores everywhere).

FLYING

If your children are two or older, ask about children's airfares. As a general rule, infants under two not occupying a seat fly at greatly reduced fares or even for free. But if you want to guarantee a seat for an infant, you have to pay full fare. Consider flying during off-peak days and times; most airlines will grant an infant a seat without a ticket if there are available seats. When booking, confirm carry-on allowances if you're traveling with infants. In general, for babies charged 10% to 50% of the adult fare you are allowed one carry-on bag and a collapsible stroller; if the flight is full, the stroller may have to be checked or you may be limited to less.

Experts agree that it's a good idea to use safety seats aloft for children weighing less than 40 pounds. Airlines set their own policies: if you use a safety seat, U.S. carriers usually require that the child be ticketed, even if he or she is young enough to ride free, because the seats must be strapped into regular seats. And even if you pay the full adult fare for the seat, it may be worth it, especially on longer trips. Do **check your airline's policy about using safety seats during takeoff and landing.** Safety seats are not allowed everywhere in the plane, so get your seat assignments as early as possible.

When reserving, request children's meals or a freestanding bassinet (not available at all airlines) if you need them. But note that bulkhead seats, where you must sit to use the bassinet, may lack an overhead bin or storage space on the floor.

FOOD

About 80% of meat consumed by Belizeans is chicken. If your kids like chicken, they'll be fine in Belize. Fried chicken is very common and inexpensive, often only BZ$4 to BZ$6 for a large serving with side orders of rice and beans. Pizza, hamburgers, and sandwiches also are widely available. The only fast-food chain in Belize is Subway, and it has one location in Belize City.

LODGING

Many hotels in Belize and Guatemala allow young children to stay in their parents' room at no extra charge, but many charge children older than age 11 or 12 as extra adults; be sure to find out the cutoff age for children's discounts.

Considering a kid-friendly hotel? Nearly all hotels in Belize and around Tikal welcome kids of all ages. At jungle lodges, kids will see and hear monkeys and other wild animals. On Ambergris Caye and in Placencia and other beach destinations, "condotels," small condo developments that let units on a nightly basis, are good choices for families. They often have full kitchens and extra space at about the same price as a comparable hotel.

PRECAUTIONS

Protect children from mosquito bites—in some areas mosquitoes may carry malaria or dengue fever. According to the U.S. Centers for Disease Control, no definitive studies have been conducted on what concentration of DEET is safe for children, but, according to the CDC, no serious illness in children has been reported when DEET is used according to manufacturer's directions. DEET should not be used on infants under 2 months. The CDC also recommends oil of lemon eucalyptus as a mosquito repellent, though it shouldn't be used on children under age 3.

If you are coming to Belize with a minor(s) but without the other parent or legal guardian, you should have a precautionary signed and notarized letter from the other parent or guardian authorizing you to take the minor(s) to Belize. You probably won't need the letter, but airline or immigration officials occasionally ask to see proof.

SIGHTS & ATTRACTIONS

Kids love Belize, especially those who enjoy the beach and water activities. Among the top attractions are the Belize Zoo, Belize's six butterfly farms, and the many Mayan sites where kids can clamber up and down ancient temples. Children may enjoy taking a guided nature tour to see howler monkeys, crocodiles, snakes, and tarantulas in the wild. In Guatemala, the ruins of Tikal will make history come alive for kids of all ages.

Places that are especially appealing to children are indicated by a rubber-duckie icon (🦆) in the margin.

SUPPLIES & EQUIPMENT

Baby formula and diapers are available in Belize and Guatemala, but prices are up to twice those in the United States. Pasteurized milk is available in some groceries, and canned or boxed milk is widely available.

COMPUTERS ON THE ROAD

If you're traveling in Belize with a laptop, be aware that the power supply may be uneven, and most hotels do not have built-in current stabilizers. At remote lodges, power is often from fluctuating generators. Electricity is a little more reliable in Guatemala, however, most international hotels have computers and most cybercafés around the country have PCs and printers for reasonable prices. **Bring your own disks** if you want to save your work. **In Belize, all towns and some villages have cybercafés where you can check your e-mail for BZ$15 an hour or less.**

CONSUMER PROTECTION

Whether you're shopping for gifts or purchasing travel services, **pay with a major credit card** whenever possible, so you can cancel payment or get reimbursed if there's a problem (and you can provide documentation). If you're doing business with a particular company for the first time, contact your local Better Business Bureau and the attorney general's offices in your state and (for U.S. businesses) the company's home state as well. Have any complaints been filed? Finally, if you're buying a package or tour, always consider travel insurance that includes default coverage (⇨ Insurance).

In Belize, a surcharge (usually 5%) may be imposed by some merchants when you pay by credit card. **Make sure you're billed in the right currency** before signing your receipt.

🔝 BBBs **Council of Better Business Bureaus** ✉ 4200 Wilson Blvd., Suite 800, Arlington, VA 22203 ☎ 703/276-0100 🖷 703/525-8277 ⊕ www.bbb.org.

CRUISE TRAVEL

Cruising is an increasingly popular way to see Belize. You can choose a small ship of about 200 passengers or less, which can visit small cayes and atolls such as Turneffe Atoll, Tobacco Caye, and West Snake Caye, along with resort areas such as San Pedro (Ambergris Caye) and Placencia. You can also choose a large cruise ship, which carries thousands of passengers and provides all of the amenities of a large floating resort. These big boats call on Belize City. Because of shallow water near shore, passengers are brought ashore in small boats called tenders. Passengers then can take snorkel or Maya ruin tours, or wander around the historic Fort George area of Belize City, visiting the Fort Point Tourist Village and its shops. The Belize government says that nearly a million cruise passengers visit Belize annually. Carnival Cruise Lines has agreed to build a new US$50 million cruise terminal in Belize City, expected to be completed in 2007.

To learn how to plan, choose, and book a cruise-ship voyage, consult *The Complete Guide to Caribbean Cruises* (available in bookstores everywhere).

🔝 Cruise Lines **American Canadian Caribbean Line** ☎ 800/556-7450 ⊕ www.accl-smallships.com. **Carnival Cruise Lines** ☎ 888/227-6482 ⊕ www.carnival.com. **Celebrity Cruises** ☎ 800/722-5941 ⊕ www.celebritycruises.com. **Holland America** ☎ 877/932-4259 ⊕ www.hollandamerica.com. **Norwegian Cruise Line** ☎ 800/327-7030 ⊕ www.ncl.com. **Princess Cruises** ☎ 800/774-6237 ⊕ www.princesscruises.com. **Royal Caribbean** ☎ 866/562-7625 ⊕ www.royalcaribbean.com. **Windstar Cruises** ☎ 800/258-7245 ⊕ www.windstarcruises.com.

CUSTOMS & DUTIES

When shopping abroad, keep receipts for all purchases. Upon reentering the country, **be ready to show customs officials what you've bought.** Pack purchases together in an easily accessible place. If you think a duty is incorrect, appeal the assessment. If you object to the way your clearance was handled, note the inspector's badge number. In either case, first ask to see a supervisor. If the problem isn't resolved, write to the appropriate authorities, beginning with the port director at your point of entry.

IN AUSTRALIA

Australian residents who are 18 or older may bring home A$900 worth of souvenirs and gifts (including jewelry), 250 cigarettes or 250 grams of cigars or other tobacco products, and 2.25 liters of alcohol (including wine, beer, and spirits). Residents under 18 may bring back A$450 worth of goods. If any of these individual allowances are exceeded, you must pay duty for the entire amount (of the group of products in which the allowance was exceeded). Members of the same family traveling together may pool their allowances. Prohibited items include meat products. Seeds, plants, and fruits need to be declared upon arrival.

🛂 **Australian Customs Service** ⌨ Customs House, 10 Cooks River Dr., Sydney International Airport, Sydney, NSW 2020 ☎ 02/6275-6666 or 1300/363-263, 02/8334-7444 or 1800/020-504 quarantine-inquiry line 🖷 02/8339-6714 ⊕ www.customs.gov.au.

IN BELIZE & GUATEMALA

Duty-free allowances for visitors entering Belize include one liter of liquor and one carton of cigarettes per person. Customs officials will confiscate beer, including beer from Guatemala or Mexico, as Belize protects its domestic brewing industry. All electronic and electrical appliances, cameras, jewelry, or other items of value must be declared at the point of entry. You should have no trouble bringing a laptop computer into Belize. Firearms of any type are prohibited. You cannot bring fresh fruits or vegetables into Belize. Although a couple of dozen food items, including meats, rice, beans, sugar, and peanuts, require an import license to be brought into Belize, grocery items in small amounts for personal use, in their original packages, are usually allowed.

Visitors may enter Guatemala duty-free with a camera, up to six rolls of film, any clothes and articles needed while traveling, 500 mg of tobacco, 3 liters of alcoholic beverages, 2 bottles of perfume, and 2 kg of candy. Unless you bring in a lot of merchandise, customs officers probably won't even check your luggage, although a laptop may be somewhat scrutinized.

ON DEPARTURE

To take home fresh seafood of any kind from Belize, you must first obtain a permit from the Fisheries Department. There's a 20-pound limit.

It's illegal to export most Maya artifacts. If you buy any such goods, do so only at a well-established store, and keep the receipt. You may not take fruits or vegetables out of Guatemala.

🛂 **Belize Fisheries** ☎ 501/224-4552. **U.S. State Department** ⊕ www.travel.state.gov.

IN CANADA

Canadian residents who have been out of Canada for at least seven days may bring in C$750 worth of goods duty-free. If you've been away fewer than seven days but more than 48 hours, the duty-free allowance drops to C$200. If your trip lasts 24 to 48 hours, the allowance is C$50; if the goods are worth more than C$50, you must pay full duty on all of the goods. You may not pool allowances with family members. Goods claimed under the C$750 exemption may follow you by mail; those claimed under the lesser exemptions must accompany you. Alcohol and tobacco products may be included in the seven-day and 48-hour exemptions but not in the 24-hour exemption. If you meet the age requirements of the province or territory through which you reenter Canada, you may bring in, duty-free, 1.5 liters of wine *or* 1.14 liters (40 imperial ounces) of liquor *or* 24 12-ounce cans or bottles of beer or ale. Also, if you meet the local age requirement for tobacco products, you may bring in, duty-free, 200 cigarettes, 50 cigars or cigarillos, and 200 grams of tobacco. You may have to pay a minimum duty on tobacco products, regardless of whether or not you exceed your personal exemption. Check ahead of time with the Canada Border Services Agency or the Department of Agriculture for policies regarding meat products, seeds, plants, and fruits.

You may send an unlimited number of gifts (only one gift per recipient, however) worth up to C$60 each, duty-free, to Canada. Label the package UNSOLICITED

GIFT—VALUE UNDER $60. Alcohol and tobacco are excluded.

🚹 **Canada Border Services Agency** ✉ Customs Information Services, 191 Laurier Ave. W, 15th fl., Ottawa, Ontario K1A 0L5 ☎ 800/461-9999 in Canada, 204/983-3500, 506/636-5064 ⊕ www.cbsa.gc.ca.

IN NEW ZEALAND

🚹 **New Zealand Customs** ✉ Head office: The Customhouse, 17-21 Whitmore St., Box 2218, Wellington ☎ 09/300-5399 or 0800/428-786 ⊕ www.customs. govt.nz.

🚹 **New Zealand Customs** ✉ Head office: The Customhouse, 17-21 Whitmore St., Box 2218, Wellington ☎ 09/300-5399 or 0800/428-786 ⊕ www.customs. govt.nz.

IN THE U.K.

From countries outside the European Union, including Belize and Guatemala, you may bring home, duty-free, 200 cigarettes, 50 cigars, 100 cigarillos, or 250 grams of tobacco; 1 liter of spirits or 2 liters of fortified or sparkling wine or liqueurs; 2 liters of still table wine; 60 ml of perfume; 250 ml of toilet water; plus £145 worth of other goods, including gifts and souvenirs. Prohibited items include meat and dairy products, seeds, plants, and fruits.

🚹 **HM Customs and Excise** ✉ Portcullis House, 21 Cowbridge Rd. E, Cardiff CF11 9SS ☎ 0845/010-9000, 0208/929-0152 advice service, 0208/929-6731, 0208/910-3602 complaints ⊕ www.hmce.gov.uk.

IN THE U.S.

U.S. residents who have been out of the country for at least 48 hours may bring home $600 worth of foreign goods duty-free, as long as they have not used the $600 allowance or any part of it in the past 30 days. This allowance, lower than the standard $800 exemption, applies to the 24 countries in the Caribbean Basin Initiative (CBI)—including Belize and Guatemala. If you visit a CBI country and a non-CBI country, you may bring in $800 worth of goods duty-free, but no more than $600 may be from a CBI country.

U.S. residents 21 and older may bring back 2 liters of alcohol duty-free, as long as one of the liters was produced in a CBI country. In addition, regardless of your age, you are allowed 200 cigarettes and 100 non-Cuban cigars. As a practical matter, busy customs agents often do not levy duty on additional alcohol and tobacco as long as it is for personal use. Antiques, which U.S. Customs and Border Protection defines as objects more than 100 years old, enter duty-free, as do original works of art done entirely by hand, including paintings, drawings, and sculptures. This doesn't apply to folk art or handicrafts, which are in general dutiable. You may also send packages home duty-free, with a limit of one parcel per addressee per day (except alcohol or tobacco products or perfume worth more than $5). You can mail up to $200 worth of goods for personal use; label the package PERSONAL USE and attach a list of its contents and their retail value. If the package contains your used personal belongings, mark it PERSONAL GOODS RETURNED to avoid paying duties. You may send up to $100 worth of goods as a gift; mark the package UNSOLICITED GIFT. Mailed items do not affect your duty-free allowance on your return.

🚹 **U.S. Customs and Border Protection** ✉ For inquiries and complaints, 1300 Pennsylvania Ave. NW, Washington, DC 20229 ⊕ www.cbp.gov ☎ 877/227-5551 or 202/354-1000.

DISABILITIES & ACCESSIBILITY

Wheelchair accessibility in Belize and Guatemala is extremely limited. Outside major cities, roads are unpaved, making wheelchair travel difficult. Exploring Central America's attractions usually involves walking down steep trails, muddy or gravel paths, or cobblestone streets. In Belize, boats and small planes are used to get to the cayes and to remote areas. Airplanes often lack jetways, and passengers must walk down rollaway steps to the pavement. Cruise ship passengers are brought to shore in small boats called tenders. Buses are not equipped to carry wheelchairs, so wheelchair users should hire a van to get around. It's estimated that about three-fourths of government buildings in Belize, including post offices, are not accessible to people with mobility disabilities. Few if any laws require accessibility for those with disabilities. However, there's a growing awareness of the needs of people with disabilities, and the friendly, helpful attitude of the people goes some way toward making up for the lack of provisions. We know of many people with physical limitations who have traveled extensively in Belize and El Petén, overcoming all challenges.

🖪 Local Resources In Belize, **Central American Information Center** ✉ Box 50211, San Diego, CA 92105 ☎ 619/262-6489. In Guatemala, **INGUAT** ✉ 7 Avenida 1-17, Zona 4 ☎ 331-1339 or 331-1333.

RESERVATIONS

When discussing accessibility with an operator or reservations agent, ask hard questions. Are there any stairs, inside *or* out? Are there grab bars next to the toilet *and* in the shower/tub? How wide is the doorway to the room? To the bathroom? For the most extensive facilities meeting the latest legal specifications, opt for newer accommodations. If you reserve through a toll-free number, consider also calling the hotel's local number to confirm the information from the central reservations office. Get confirmation in writing when you can.

SIGHTS & ATTRACTIONS

Few sights in Belize or around Tikal were designed with travelers in wheelchairs in mind, and fewer still have been renovated to meet that need. Newer destinations may have the necessary facilities and accommodations, but don't count on it—it's best to call ahead or get a recommendation from someone who has visited the property.

TRANSPORTATION

The U.S. Department of Transportation Aviation Consumer Protection Division's online publication *New Horizons: Information for the Air Traveler with a Disability* offers advice for travellers with a disability, and outlines basic rights. Visit DisabilityInfo.gov for general information.

🖪 Information & Complaints **Aviation Consumer Protection Division** (⇨ Air Travel) for airline-related problems; ⊕ airconsumer.ost.dot.gov/publications/horizons.htm for airline travel advice and rights. **Departmental Office of Civil Rights** ✉ For general inquiries, U.S. Department of Transportation, S-30, 400 7th St. SW, Room 10215, Washington, DC 20590

☎ 202/366-4648, 202/366-8538 TTY ☐ 202/366-9371 ⊕ www.dotcr.ost.dot.gov. **Disability Rights Section** ✉ NYAV, U.S. Department of Justice, Civil Rights Division, 950 Pennsylvania Ave. NW, Washington, DC 20530 ☐ ADA information line 202/514-0301, 800/514-0301, 202/514-0383 TTY, 800/514-0383 TTY ⊕ www.ada.gov. **U.S. Department of Transportation Hotline** ☐ For disability-related air-travel problems, 800/778-4838 or 800/455-9880 TTY.

DISCOUNTS & DEALS

Be a smart shopper and compare all your options before making decisions. A plane ticket bought with a promotional coupon from travel clubs, coupon books, and direct-mail offers or purchased on the Internet may not be cheaper than the least expensive fare from a discount ticket agency. And always keep in mind that what you get is just as important as what you save.

In Belize, most hotels, even budget ones, have Web sites and e-mail. Discounts between 10% to 20% are often available for direct Internet booking.

DISCOUNT RESERVATIONS

Many of the hotels in Belize and Guatemala—including some budget ones—have Web sites. Discounts, typically 10%–20%, are often available for reservations made online.

To save money, look into discount reservations services with Web sites and toll-free numbers, which use their buying power to get a better price on hotels, airline tickets (⇨ Air Travel), even car rentals. When booking a room, always **call the hotel's local toll-free number** (if one is available) rather than the central reservations number—you'll often get a better price. Always ask about special packages or corporate rates.

When shopping for the best deal on hotels and car rentals, look for guaranteed exchange rates, which protect you against a falling dollar. With your rate locked in, you won't pay more, even if the price goes up in the local currency.

🖪 Hotel Rooms **Accommodations Express** ☎ 800/444-7666 or 800/277-1064. **Hotels.com** ☎ 800/246-8357 ⊕ www.hotels.com. **Turbotrip. com** ☎ 800/473-7829 ⊕ w3.turbotrip.com.

PACKAGE DEALS

Don't confuse packages and guided tours. When you buy a package, you travel on your own, just as though you had planned the trip yourself. Fly/drive packages, which combine airfare and car rental, are often a good deal. In cities, ask the local visitor's bureau about hotel and local transportation packages that include tickets to major museum exhibits or other special events.

DIVING

Belize offers some of the best scuba diving in the world. There are scores of dive sites, though few are accessible from the beach. The cayes and atolls offer world-class diving experiences. The water throughout the Caribbean is crystal clear, often to 200 feet, and the quantity and variety of marine life are astounding.

Resorts often offer guests introductory scuba instruction in a pool, followed by a shallow dive; some hotels have on-site dive shops. All shops offer instruction and certification according to the standards set by either the National Association of Underwater Instructors (NAUI) or the Professional Association of Diving Instructors (PADI). They also have a variety of day and night dives to wrecks, reefs, and underwater walls.

Don't fly within 24 hours after scuba diving.

🔲 Organizations **NAUI Worldwide** ⬭ Box 89789, 1232 Tech Blvd., Tampa, FL 33619 ☎ 800/553-6284 or 813/628-6284 ⊕ www.naui.org. **PADI** ✉ 30151 Tomas St., Rancho Santa Margarita, CA 92688 ☎ 800/729-7234 or 949/858-7234 ⊕ www.padi. com ⬭ 3771 Jacombs Rd., Bldg. C, #535, Richmond, British Columbia, Canada V6V 2L9 ☎ 800/565-8130 ✉ Unit 3, 4 Skyline Pl., French's Forest, New South Wales, Australia 2086 ☎ 2/9451-2300

EATING & DRINKING

The restaurants we list are the cream of the crop in each price category. Properties indicated by an ✕🏠 are lodging establishments whose restaurant warrants a special trip.

MEALS & SPECIALTIES

You can eat well in Belize. The country has no unique cuisine, but a gastronomic gumbo of Mexican, Caribbean, Mayan, Garifuna, English, and American dishes

provides a tasty variety of dining choices. Belize has restaurants serving French, Thai, Indian, Chinese, Mexican, and even Sri Lankan food. On the coast and cayes, seafood—especially lobster, conch, and locally caught fish such as snapper and grouper—is fresh, relatively inexpensive, and delicious. Try creole specialties such as cow-foot soup (yes, made with real cow's feet), "boil up" (a stew of fish, potatoes, plantains, cassava and other vegetables, and eggs), and the ubiquitous "stew chicken" with rice and beans. Many creole dishes are seasoned with red or black *recado*, a paste made from annatto seeds and other spices. In border areas, enjoy mestizo favorites such as *escabeche* (onion soup), *salbutes* (fried corn tortillas with chicken and a topping of tomatoes, onions, and peppers), or *garnaches* (fried tortillas with refried beans, cabbage, and cheese). In Dangriga and Punta Gorda or other Garifuna areas, try dishes such as *sere lasus* (fish soup with plantain balls) or cassava dumplings. In most areas of Belize, you can chow down on American classics like fried chicken, pork chops, and T-bone steaks.

In general, Guatemala does not have a distinguished national cuisine; most of the top restaurants serve continental fare. The classic Guatemalan dish is tasty but unremarkable: eggs, refried black beans, meat (either sliced beef or chorizo), cheese, and Guatemala's thick corn tortillas. There a few standouts though, including *róbalo*, a common and delicious native whitefish called snook elsewhere; ceviche, chilled marinated seafood flavored with lime or a tomato broth; and a few dishes not seen on North American menus, such as *tepisquintle*, (the world's largest rodent) and *sopa de tortuga* (turtle soup). Note that while such animals may be exotic fare, in Central America they're often hunted to extinction. Street vendors typically sell fried chicken and french fries, or *churrosquitos* (sliced beef or chorizo served with pickled cabbage and tortillas). *Huevos motuleños* (layers of fried eggs served on a crispy tortilla with cheese, beans, hot sauce, and sometimes ham) make an amazing breakfast. Vegetarians in both Belize and Guatemala may be "beaned out" after a week or so, although *ensalada aguacate* (avocado salad), *pan de banana* (banana bread), and *flan* (a crème caramel dessert) never get dull. Warning: while eating on the street is as Guatemalan as it gets, many travelers have gotten sick doing so. In Belize, street food is generally safe, although use common sense and don't buy from vendors where the food is covered in flies.

MEALTIMES

In Belize, breakfast is usually served 7 to 9, lunch from 11 to 2, and dinner from 6 to 9. Few restaurants are open late. Remember, though, that small restaurants in Belize may open or close at the whim of the owner. Off-season, restaurants may close early if it looks as if there are no more guests coming, and some restaurants close completely for a month or two, usually in September and October.

In Guatemala, lunch is the biggest meal, or at least the longest, running from noon to 2 or 3. Breakfast starts at 7, and dinner not long after sundown. Restaurants in major tourist areas may stay open later, but most towns are all but deserted by 9 PM.

Unless otherwise noted, the restaurants listed in this guide are open daily for lunch and dinner.

PAYING

Only the more expensive restaurants accept credit cards and traveler's checks.

RESERVATIONS & DRESS

Reservations are rarely needed in Belize or the Tikal area. The exceptions are for dinner at jungle lodges and at small restaurants where the owner or chef needs to know in advance how many people are dining that night, so that the restaurant can be sure to have enough supplies on hand. We mention reservations only when they're essential. We mention dress only when men are required to wear a jacket or a jacket and tie, which is nearly unheard of in Belize.

WINE, BEER & SPIRITS

Many restaurants in Belize serve beer—usually Belikin—and terrific, tropical mixed drinks; a growing number offer wine. Belikin is available in regular, stout, and premium versions (the premium is sold mostly in more expensive bars and restaurants). Lighthouse, a lighter lager, is also available at many bars and restaurants. American and other imported beers are available in some groceries, but prices are high. Due to restrictive import laws, the beers of neighboring Mexico and Guatemala are rarely available in Belize. Several Belize companies manufacture liquors, primarily rum, but also gin and vodka. Traveller's "One Barrel" Rum, with a slight vanilla flavor, is a favorite, and Duurley's Gold or "Parrot" (so called for the parrot on the label) wins the stamp of approval from some aficionados. Imported wines are available in supermarkets and better restaurants, at about twice the price of the same wines in the United States. There are wine stores in Belize City and San Pedro. One restaurant, Rendezvous on North Ambergris Caye, makes its own wines from imported grape juice, and cashew wine and other local wines are sometimes available around the country. The drinking age in Belize is 18, although IDs are rarely checked.

Guatemala has no real wine market to speak of, but top restaurants often have excellent imported bottles. The national beers Gallo and Cabro are decent, while imported liquor and local spirits distilled from sugarcane can be found most everywhere. The official drinking age in Guatemala is 20.

ECOTOURISM

Central America is the original ecotourism destination, and, as a result, you'll see the term used liberally everywhere. With respect to lodging, it can be used to describe deluxe, private cabanas on a tidy beach, or a hut in the middle of nowhere with pit toilets. It may also point to environmental conservation efforts by parks or tour companies who are conscious of natural resources and their role in not depleting them. Wildlife parks, butterfly farms, cloud forests, and trips to Mayan ruins are some of the incredible ecodestinations in this area. And mountain biking, bird-watching, jungle hiking, scuba diving, cave tubing, fishing, and white-water rafting are just some of the ecoactivities.

ELECTRICITY

There's no need to bring a converter or adapter as electrical current in Belize and Guatemala is 110 volts, the same as in the United States, and outlets in both countries take U.S.-style plugs. In a few remote areas, lodges and hotels may generate their own electricity, and after the generators are turned off at night, power, if there is any, comes only from kerosene lanterns or your flashlight.

EMBASSIES

Citizens of Australia and New Zealand may contact the British High Commission.

🇨🇦 Canada **Honorary Consul of Canada** ✉ 83 N. Front St., Belize City ☎ 501/223-1060 🖷 501/223-0060.

🇬🇹 Guatemala **Embassy of Guatemala** ✉ 8 A St., Belize City ☎ 501/223-3150 🖷 501/223-5140.

🇲🇽 Mexico **Embassy of Mexico** ✉ 18 N. Park St., Belize City ☎ 501/223-0194 🖷 501/227-8742.

🇬🇧 United Kingdom **British High Commission** ✉ Belmopan ☎ 501/822-2146 🖷 501/822-2761.

🇺🇸 United States **Embassy of the United States** ✉ 29 Gabourel La., Belize City ☎ 501/227-7161 🖷 501/223-0802.

EMERGENCIES

In an emergency, call 911 or 90 nationwide. There are police stations in Belize City and in Belmopan City, in the towns of Benque Viejo, Corozal, Dangriga, Orange Walk, Punta Gorda, San Ignacio, and San Pedro, and in Placencia Village and a few other villages. Police generally respond quickly to emergencies, although lack of equipment, supplies, and training may sometimes reduce their effectiveness. Police are generally polite, professional, and will do what they can to help. In Belize City and in most tourist areas, including Placencia and San Pedro, there are special tourist police whose job is to patrol areas where visitors are likely to go and to render any assistance they can, including providing directions.

Most Belizeans are extremely solicitous of the welfare of visitors to the country. In an emergency, it's likely that bystanders or people in the area will gladly offer to help, usually going out of their way to render any assistance they can.

In a medical emergency, your hotel can provide the names of nearby physicians and medical clinics. You can also go to the emergency room of public hospitals, which are located in Belize City, Belmopan City, and major towns; or, in larger villages around the country, the local medical clinic. Don't worry about payment—in an emergency, public hospitals and clinics will treat you regardless of your ability to pay. Afterward, you may be asked to pay what you can, but in any event the charges likely will be a small fraction of what you would pay in the United States. Private hospitals (there are two in Belize City and one in San Ignacio) may ask for some guarantee of payment. *For more information, see the health section below.*

ENGLISH-LANGUAGE MEDIA

BOOKS

Due to import taxes and high shipping costs, books are more expensive in Belize than in North America or Europe. There are small bookstores in Belize City, and used books are available in San Pedro and Corozal Town. Almost every major tourist destination in Guatemala has one or two stores with used paperbacks in English. Some are willing to trade books or lend books, too.

NEWSPAPERS & MAGAZINES

Belize has no daily newspapers, but it has a number of brash weeklies. As in most countries, crime and politics make the front pages, often in sensational headlines. *The Reporter,* published in Belize City, is the best independent newspaper. For visitors, the chatty *San Pedro Sun,* one of two weeklies on Ambergris Caye, is a good source of information, as is the monthly *Placencia Breeze* in Placencia.

Belize Magazine is published quarterly online at (⊕ www.belizemagazine.com).

Belize First has a Web edition (⊕ www.belizefirst.com), and is a good resource for cultural, dining, lodging, and service information.

The monthly Guatemalan journal **Revue** (✉ 4 Calle Oriente 23, Antigua,

Guatemala ☎ 832–4619) is more of an advertisement with a few articles on local trends than a guidebook. *Lugares y Destinos* is a free bilingual guide produced by INGUAT, the Guatemalan Tourist Commission. *Destination Guatemala* and *Central America Guide* are detailed visitor and business guides, and are available in most upscale hotels.

The better or international chain hotels usually have fairly current editions of a few major U.S. and European newspapers, typically *USA Today, The Economist,* and *Newsweek.*

RADIO & TELEVISION

Belize's most informative television news is on Channel 5, which also offers its daily news summaries on the Web at ⊕ www.channel5belize.com. Another station in Belize is Channel 7, with an online version of its evening news at ⊕ www.7newsbelize.com. Many hotels have cable or satellite TV, with 50 or more channels from the U.S. and Mexico. Love-FM Radio (95.1 Mhz) is the nation's leading radio station, playing standards and soft rock.

Cable TV is a popular amenity in Guatemalan hotels. You can expect HBO, Showtime, ESPN, TNT, the Discovery Channel, MTV (a Spanish variety), and one or two feeds from regional stations in the United States (usually from Denver, curiously). Radio stations generally play a mix of American pop, rock, and Latin favorites.

ETIQUETTE & BEHAVIOR

Belizeans and *Chapins* (the nickname for a Guatemalan) are incredibly kind and friendly. Let them know you are, too, and always greet someone with a "Good morning" or "Buenos dias" before asking for directions, for a table in a restaurant, or when entering a store or museum, for example. It will set a positive tone and you'll be received much more warmly for having done it.

Don't take pictures inside churches. Do not take pictures of indigenous people without first asking their permission. Offering them a small sum as thanks is customary.

Since the civil war ended, Guatemala has become a popular country for North Americans looking to adopt children. Although most adoptive parents go through perfectly legal channels, it's also believed by some Guatemalans that many children may be adopted illegally or even stolen from birth mothers, since it's often a lucrative process. Guatemalans, particularly those in rural areas who may interact less with travelers on the whole, may be sensitive to foreigners approaching their children, no matter how amiable one's intentions. For this reason, **always be respectful when interacting with children,** and never pick them up or attempt to unless you're invited to do so by the child's parents. In April 2000 two visitors were killed in a market area of Todos Santos Cuchumatan when villagers feared that their children were in danger of abduction.

With the exception of Pullman buses and shuttles, the seats on Guatemalan buses are expected to fit three abreast. Though tourists are often larger than the average local, you should respect the rule, and make room for others. It's perfectly fine to step into the aisle to let someone take a middle or window seat. Also in Guatemala, as rude as it may seem, a quick hiss or whistle is an acceptable way to get someone's attention—you may even take up the habit yourself, particularly with waiters. Unfortunately men may catcall women in this way as well, which is not considered terribly rude either.

BUSINESS ETIQUETTE

Business dress in Belize is casual. Men rarely wear suits and ties, and even the prime minister appears at functions in a white shirt open at the neck. The business environment is more formal in Guatemala, where suits are more the norm.

GAY & LESBIAN TRAVEL

Most Belizeans have a very conservative view of sexual orientation. There are no openly gay or lesbian clubs or bars. However, many gay and lesbian travelers visit Belize and report no problems at all. Likewise, Guatemala is also conservative.

⚑ Gay- & Lesbian-Friendly Travel Agencies **Different Roads Travel** ✉ 1017 N. LaCienega Blvd.,

Suite 308, West Hollywood, CA 90069 ☎ 310/289-6000 or 800/429-8747 (Ext. 14 for both) 🖷 310/855-0323 📧 lgernert@tzell.com. **Kennedy Travel** ✉ 130 W. 42nd St., Suite 401, New York, NY 10036 ☎ 800/237-7433 or 212/840-8659 🖷 212/730-2269 🌐 www.kennedytravel.com. **Now, Voyager** ✉ 4406 18th St., San Francisco, CA 94114 ☎ 415/626-1169 or 800/255-6951 🖷 415/626-8626 🌐 www.nowvoyager.com. **Skylink Travel and Tour/Flying Dutchmen Travel** ✉ 1455 N. Dutton Ave., Suite A, Santa Rosa, CA 95401 ☎ 707/546-9888 or 800/225-5759 🖷 707/636-0951; serving lesbian travelers.

HEALTH

Belize has a high standard of health and hygiene. You can drink the water in Belize City, the Cayo, Placencia, on Ambergris Caye, and in most other areas you are likely to visit, though many visitors prefer the taste of bottled water. In remote villages, however, water may come from shallow wells or cisterns and may not be safe to drink. The water on Caye Caulker often smells of sulfur. Assume, while in Guatemala, that the water is not safe to drink except at the best hotels. Bottled water, *agua mineral* or *agua pura* in Spanish, is available even at the smallest *tiendas* (stores) and is cheaper than in North America.

HIV/AIDS is an increasing concern in Central America, especially in Belize, where the incidence on a per capita basis is the highest in the region.

FOOD & DRINK

The major health risk in Belize is sunburn, not digestive distress. In Guatemala, the risk is Montezuma's Revenge, or traveler's diarrhea, caused by eating contaminated fruit or vegetables or drinking contaminated water. So **watch what you eat.** Avoid ice: in Guatemala, ask for your drinks *sin hielo*, without ice. In most resort areas in Belize, the ice is perfectly safe. Also skip uncooked food and unpasteurized milk and milk products, and in Guatemala **drink only bottled water** or water that has been boiled for at least 20 minutes, even when brushing your teeth. Mild cases may respond to Imodium (known generically as loperamide) or Pepto-Bismol (not as strong), both of which can be purchased

over the counter, although you should bring along your own stash. Also, drink plenty of purified water or tea—chamomile is a good folk remedy. In severe cases, rehydrate yourself with a salt-sugar solution: ½ teaspoon salt (*sal*) and 4 tablespoons sugar (*azucar*) per quart of water.

MEDICAL PLANS

No one plans to get sick while traveling, but it happens, so consider signing up with a medical-assistance company. Members get doctor referrals, emergency evacuation or repatriation, hotlines for medical consultation, cash for emergencies, and other assistance.

🔢 Medical-Assistance Companies **International SOS Assistance** 🌐 www.internationalsos.com ✉ 3600 Horizon Blvd., Suite 300, Trevose, PA 19053 ☎ 215/942-8000 or 800/523-6586 🖷 215/354-2338 ✉ Landmark House, Hammersmith Bridge Rd., 6th fl., London, W6 9DP ☎ 20/8762-8008 🖷 20/8748-7744 ✉ 12 Chemin Riantbosson, 1217 Meyrin 1, Geneva, Switzerland ☎ 22/785-6464 🖷 22/785-6424 ✉ 331 N. Bridge Rd., 17-00, Odeon Towers, Singapore 188720 ☎ 6338-7800 🖷 6338-7611.

OVER-THE-COUNTER REMEDIES

Many medicines requiring a doctor's prescription at home don't require one in Belize; drugstores often sell prescription antibiotics, sleeping aids, and painkillers. However, most pharmacies have only a very small inventory, and only the most commonly prescribed drugs are available. In Belize, private physicians often own an associated pharmacy, so they sell you the medicine they prescribe. Pharmacies in Guatemala sell a wide range of medications, including U.S. prescription-only drugs. Ask for what you want with the generic name. Some pharmacies are open 24 hours, and deliver directly to hotel rooms. Most hotel proprietors will direct you to such services.

PESTS & OTHER HAZARDS

Sand flies (also sometimes referred to as no-see-ums, or as sand fleas, which are a different insect) are common on many beaches, cayes, and in swampy areas. They can infect their victims with leishmaniasis, a disease that can cause the skin to develop sores that can leave scars. In rare cases, the visceral form of leishmaniasis, if untreated, can be fatal. Use repellent containing a high concentration of DEET or try Cactus Juice insect repellent to help deter sand flies. Some say lathering on Avon's Skin So Soft or any oily lotion such as baby oil helps, too, but we found better luck with the strong stuff.

The botfly or beefworm is one of the most unpleasant of Central American pests. Botfly eggs are deposited under your skin with the help of a mosquito, where one can grow into larva, a large living worm. To rid yourself of your unwanted pal, cover the larva's airhole in your skin with Vaseline, and after it suffocates you can remove it with a sterile knife. Or see your doctor.

Virtually all honeybees in Belize and Guatemala are Africanized. The sting of these killer bees is no worse than that of regular bees, but the hives are much more aggressive. If attacked by Africanized bees, try to get into a building, vehicle, or under water.

Scorpions are common in Belize and around Tikal. Their stings are painful, but not fatal. There are many poisonous snakes in Belize and lowland Guatemala, including the notorious fer-de-lance and small but deadly coral snakes. However, most visitors never even see a snake, and if bitten, medical centers do stock antivenom. Crocodiles (called alligators by Belizeans) are present in many lagoons and rivers, but very rarely are they known to attack humans.

Divers and snorkelers may experience "itchy itchy" or pica pica, a skin rash, in spring and early summer, when the tiny larvae of thimble jelly fish may get on the skin. Putting Vaseline or other greasy lotion on the skin before entering the water may help prevent the itch, and applying Benadryl, vinegar, or even Windex to the affected area may help stop the itch.

If you're a light sleeper, you might want to pack earplugs. Monkeys howling through the night and birds chirping at the crack of dawn are only charming on the first night of your nature excursion.

SHOTS & MEDICATIONS

According to the U.S. Centers for Disease Control and Prevention, there's a limited risk of malaria, hepatitis A and B, dengue fever, typhoid fever, and rabies in Central America. In most urban or easily accessible areas you need not worry. However, if you plan to spend a lot of time in the jungles, rain forests, or other remote regions, or if you want to stay for more than six weeks, **check with the CDC's International Travelers Hotline.**

In areas where malaria and dengue are prevalent, **sleep under mosquito nets.** Pack your own—it's the only way to be sure there are no tears. Although most hotels in Belize have screened or glassed windows, your room probably will not be completely mosquito-proof. Wear clothing that covers your arms and legs, apply repellent containing at least 30% DEET, and spray for flying insects in living and sleeping areas. Also **consider taking antimalarial pills**; chloroquine (the commonly recommended antimalarial for Belize and Guatemala) is sold as Aralen in Central America. It must be started a week before entering an area with malaria risk. Malarone is prescribed as an alternative, and it can be started only two days before arrival in a risk area. In Belize there are fewer than 1,000 reported cases of malaria a year, mostly in the far south. In Guatemala, El Petén is a risk area. There's no vaccine for dengue.

Rabies is always a concern when you get bitten by a stray dog or other wild animal; scrub the wound under clean, running water with soap or iodine—or, failing those, some local rum—and get antirabies shots immediately.

Travelers should have up-to-date shots for tetanus and hepatitis A and B. Children traveling to Central America should have current inoculations against measles, mumps, rubella, hepatitis, and polio.

🚺 Health Warnings **National Centers for Disease Control and Prevention** (CDC) ✉ Office of Health Communication, National Center for Infectious Diseases, Division of Quarantine, Travelers' Health, 1600 Clifton Rd. NE, Atlanta, GA 30333 ☎ 877/394–8747 international travelers' health line, 800/311–

3435 other inquiries, 404/498-1600 Division of Quarantine and international health information ☏ 888/232-3299 ⊕ www.cdc.gov/travel. **Travel Health Online** ⊕ tripprep.com. **World Health Organization (WHO)** ⊕ www.who.int.

HOLIDAYS

New Year's Day (January 1); Baron Bliss Day (officially March 9, but date may vary); Good Friday; Holy Saturday; Easter Monday; Labour Day (May 2); Sovereign's Day (May 24); National Day (September 10); Independence Day (September 21); Columbus Day (October 12); Garifuna Settlement Day (November 19); Christmas Day; Boxing Day (December 26).

INSURANCE

The most useful travel-insurance plan is a comprehensive policy that includes coverage for trip cancellation and interruption, default, trip delay, and medical expenses (with a waiver for preexisting conditions).

Without insurance you'll lose all or most of your money if you cancel your trip, regardless of the reason. Default insurance covers you if your tour operator, airline, or cruise line goes out of business—the chances of which have been increasing. Trip-delay covers expenses that arise because of bad weather or mechanical delays. Study the fine print when comparing policies.

If you're traveling internationally, a key component of travel insurance is coverage for medical bills incurred if you get sick on the road. Such expenses aren't generally covered by Medicare or private policies. U.K. residents can buy a travel-insurance policy valid for most vacations taken during the year in which it's purchased (but check preexisting-condition coverage). British and Australian citizens need extra medical coverage when traveling overseas. British citizens need extra medical coverage when traveling abroad.

Always **buy travel policies directly from the insurance company**; if you buy them from a cruise line, airline, or tour operator that goes out of business you probably won't be covered for the agency or operator's default, a major risk. Before making any purchase, review your existing health and home-owner's policies to find what they cover away from home.

▣ Travel Insurers In the U.S.: **Access America** ✉ 2805 N. Parham Rd., Richmond, VA 23294 ☏ 800/284-8300 ⎙ 804/673-1469 or 800/346-9265 ⊕ www.accessamerica.com. **Travel Guard International** ✉ 1145 Clark St., Stevens Point, WI 54481 ☏ 800/826-1300 or 715/345-1041 ⎙ 800/955-8785 or 715/345-1990 ⊕ www.travelguard.com. ▣ In the U.K.: **Association of British Insurers** ✉ 51 Gresham St., London EC2V 7HQ ☏ 020/7600-3333 ⎙ 020/7696-8999 ⊕ www.abi.org.uk. In Canada: **RBC Insurance** ✉ 6880 Financial Dr., Mississauga, Ontario L5N 7Y5 ☏ 800/387-4357 or 905/816-2559 ⎙ 888/298-6458 ⊕ www.rbcinsurance.com. In Australia: **Insurance Council of Australia** ✉ Level 3, 56 Pitt St., Sydney, NSW 2000 ☏ 02/9253-5100 ⎙ 02/9253-5111 ⊕ www.ica.com.au. In New Zealand: **Insurance Council of New Zealand** ✉ Level 7, 111-115 Customhouse Quay, Box 474, Wellington ☏ 04/472-5230 ⎙ 04/473-3011 ⊕ www.icnz.org.nz.

LANGUAGE

English is Belize's official language. Spanish also is widely spoken especially in northern and western Belize. Several Maya dialects and the Garifuna language are also spoken. Some Mennonite communities speak German. Creole, which uses versions of English words and a West-African–influenced grammar and syntax, is spoken by many Belizeans, especially around Belize City.

Around Tikal, wherever tourist traffic is heavy, you'll find a few English speakers; you'll have considerably less luck in places off the beaten path. In general, very little English is spoken in El Petén, and in some small villages in the region, absolutely none. In addition, many Guatemalans will answer "yes" even if they don't understand your question, so as not to appear unkind or unhelpful. To minimize such confusion, try posing questions as "Where is so-and-so?" rather than asking "Is so-and-so this way?"

LANGUAGES FOR TRAVELERS

A phrase book and language-tape set can help get you started. *Fodor's Spanish for Travelers* (available at bookstores everywhere) is excellent.

LODGING

In Belize, you'll likely stay in one of four types of lodging: a traditional hotel, a jungle lodge, a beach resort, or a lodge on a remote caye. Traditional hotels, usually found in Belize City and in larger towns, can be basic budget places or international-style hotels such as the Radisson Fort George in Belize City. Jungle lodges are concentrated in the Cayo and Orange Walk districts, but they can be found most anywhere. Jungle lodges need not be spartan; most have electricity (though the generator may shut down at 10 PM), a number have swimming pools, and a few even have air-conditioning. The typical jungle lodge has a roof of bay-palm thatch and may remind you of a Maya house gone upscale. Beach hotels also come in various levels of luxury, from a basic seaside cabin on Caye Caulker to a small, deluxe resort such as the Inn at Robert's Grove on the Placencia peninsula or Hamanasi near Hopkins. On Ambergris Caye, many resorts are "condotels"—small, low-rise condominium complexes with individually owned units but managed like a hotel. Lodging choices on remote cayes appeal to the diving and fishing crowd. Amenity levels vary greatly, from cabins with outdoor bathrooms to simple cottages with composting toilets to comfortable villas with air-conditioning. Regardless of the kind of lodging, you'll almost invariably stay at a small place of 2 to 25 rooms where the owners actively manage the property. Thus, Belize accommodations usually reflect the personalities of their owners, for better or worse.

Although hotels in Belize have published rates, in the off-season at least you may be able to negotiate a better rate, especially if you're staying more than one or two nights. Walk-in rates are usually lower than prebooked rates, and rooms booked direct on the Internet may be lower than those booked through agents.

Unlike 20 years ago, Guatemala now has lodging options that go well beyond the needs of the backpacker, in the form of reliable international hotels, classy colonial charmers, and rustic retreats with local flair. Most of the hotels in Flores and elsewhere near Tikal are small, locally owned inns. A few international chain hotels in El Petén like the Camino Real have rooms and facilities equal to those at home.

The lodgings we list are the cream of the crop in each price category. We always list the facilities that are available, but we don't specify whether they cost extra; when pricing accommodations, always ask what's included and what costs extra. Properties are assigned price categories based on the range between their least and most expensive standard double rooms at high season (excluding holidays). Properties marked ✕🏨 are lodging establishments whose restaurants warrant a special trip.

Assume that hotels operate on the European Plan (EP, with no meals) unless we specify that they use either the Continental Plan (CP, with a continental breakfast), Breakfast Plan (BP, with a full breakfast), or the Modified American Plan (MAP, with breakfast and dinner) or are all-inclusive (including all meals and most activities).

APARTMENT & VILLA RENTALS

If you want a home base that's roomy enough for a family and comes with cooking facilities, consider a furnished rental. These can save you money, especially if you're traveling with a group. Home-exchange directories sometimes list rentals as well as exchanges.

In Belize, you can most easily find vacation rentals on Ambergris Caye. The Ambergris Caye Web site (⊕ www.ambergriscaye.com) has a good selection of rental houses and condos. There also are some vacation rental houses in Placencia and Hopkins and on Caye Caulker. Individual chapters in this guide direct you to vacation rental sources.

🛈 **International Agents** Hideaways International ⊠ 767 Islington St., Portsmouth, NH 03801 ☎ 603/430-4433 or 800/843-4433 📠 603/430-4444 ⊕ www.hideaways.com; annual membership $185. **Vacation Home Rentals Worldwide** ⊠ 235 Kensington Ave., Norwood, NJ 07648 ☎ 201/767-9393 or 800/633-3284 📠 201/767-5510 ⊕ www.vhrww.com. **Villas International** ⊠ 4340 Redwood Hwy., Suite D309, San Rafael, CA 94903 ☎ 415/499-9490 or 800/221-2260 📠 415/499-9491 ⊕ www.villasintl.com.

CAMPING

If you don't mind a few mosquito or sand-fly bites, you can camp in Belize. It's generally prohibited in the national parks and preserves but is allowed at Cockscomb Preserve and at Half Moon Caye National Monument. A number of hotels and lodges in Cayo district, including Clarissa Falls, Trek Stop, and Ian Anderson's Caves Branch Adventure Camp permit camping. One lodge, Chaa Creek, has a safari camp, permanent camp sites on platforms. There are only a few RV campgrounds with hookups in Belize—two are in Corozal District in northern Belize, the Lagoon Campground and Caribbean Village and one, Inglewood Camping Grounds, is in San Ignacio in Cayo District—but some hotels in rural areas, especially in Cayo, allow those with RVs or trailers to park (no or limited hookups) on their property.

Camping is popular among the back-packer crowd in Guatemala, and there's camping available at Tikal.

HOME EXCHANGES

If you would like to exchange your home for someone else's, join a home-exchange organization, which will send you its updated listings of available exchanges for a year and will include your own listing in at least one of them. It's up to you to make specific arrangements.

🛃 **Exchange Clubs HomeLink USA** ⊠ 2937 NW 9th Terrace, Wilton Manors, FL 33311 ☎ 954/566-2687 or 800/638-3841 🖷 954/566-2783 ⊕ www.homelink.org; $75 yearly for a listing and online access; $45 additional to receive directories. **Intervac U.S.** ⊠ 30 Corte San Fernando, Tiburon, CA 94920 ☎ 800/756-4663 🖷 415/435-7440 ⊕ www.intervacus.com; $128 yearly for a listing, online access, and a catalog; $68 without catalog.

HOSTELS

No matter what your age, you can save on lodging costs by staying at hostels. In some 4,500 locations in more than 70 countries around the world, Hostelling International (HI), the umbrella group for a number of national youth-hostel associations, offers single-sex, dorm-style beds and, at many hostels, rooms for couples and family accommodations. The Belize Tourist Board discourages hostel accommodations, but hostel-type budget hotels are available on Caye Caulker and Ambergris Caye and in Belize City, Punta Gorda, San Ignacio, and elsewhere.

Membership in any HI national hostel association, open to travelers of all ages, allows you to stay in HI-affiliated hostels at member rates; one-year membership is about $28 for adults (C$35 for a two-year minimum membership in Canada, £15 in the U.K., A$52 in Australia, and NZ$40 in New Zealand); hostels charge about $10–$30 per night. Members have priority if the hostel is full; they're also eligible for discounts around the world, even on rail and bus travel in some countries.

🛃 **Organizations Hostelling International–USA** ⊠ 8401 Colesville Rd., Suite 600, Silver Spring, MD 20910 ☎ 301/495-1240 🖷 301/495-6697 ⊕ www.hiusa.org. **Hostelling International–Canada** ⊠ 205 Catherine St., Suite 400, Ottawa, Ontario K2P 1C3 ☎ 613/237-7884 or 800/663-5777 🖷 613/237-7868 ⊕ www.hihostels.ca. **YHA England and Wales** ⊠ Trevelyan House, Dimple Rd., Matlock, Derbyshire DE4 3YH, U.K. ☎ 0870/870-8808, 0870/770-8868or 0162/959-2600 🖷 0870/770-6127 ⊕ www.yha.org.uk. **YHA Australia** ⊠ 422 Kent St., Sydney, NSW 2001 ☎ 02/9261-1111 🖷 02/9261-1969 ⊕ www.yha.com.au. **YHA New Zealand** ⊠ Level 1, Moorhouse City, 166 Moorhouse Ave., Box 436, Christchurch ☎ 03/379-9970 or 0800/278-299 🖷 03/365-4476 ⊕ www.yha.org.nz.

HOTELS

All hotels listed have private bath unless otherwise noted.

RESERVING A ROOM

Most hotels in Belize, and many in Guatemala, are now on the Internet, and 80% or more of bookings are made by e-mail. Use ⊕ www.fodors.com to find the Web address of hotels in mentioned in this book.

🛃 **Toll-Free Numbers Best Western** ☎ 800/528-1234 ⊕ www.bestwestern.com. **Choice** ☎ 800/424-6423 ⊕ www.choicehotels.com. **Clarion** ☎ 800/424-6423 ⊕ www.choicehotels.com. **Holiday Inn** ☎ 800/465-4329 ⊕ www.ichotelsgroup.com. **Marriott** ☎ 800/228-9290 ⊕ www.marriott.com. **Radisson** ☎ 800/333-3333 ⊕ www.radisson.com. **Ramada** ☎ 800/228-2828, 800/854-7854 international reservations ⊕ www.ramada.com or www.

ramadahotels.com. **Westin Hotels & Resorts**
☎ 800/228-3000 ⊕ www.starwood.com/westin.

MAIL & SHIPPING

When sending mail to Central America, be sure to include the city or town and district, country name, and the words "Central America" in the address. Belizean mail service is very good, except to and from remote villages, and the stamps, mostly of wildlife, are beautiful. An airmail letter from Belize City takes about a week to reach the United States, longer from other areas.

Guatemala's postal service has been privatized, and efficiency is improving. From Guatemala, letters to the United States take one to two weeks, and slightly longer to Canada and the United Kingdom.

OVERNIGHT SERVICES

If you have to send something fast, use DHL, which is expensive but does the job right.

🗐 **Major Services DHL** ⊠ Belize: 38 New Rd., Belize City ☎ 501/223-4350 ⊠ Guatemala: 7 Avenida 2-42, Zona 9, Guatemala City ☎ 502/332-3023.

POSTAL RATES

In Belize, an airmail letter to the United States is BZ60¢, a postcard, BZ30¢; to Europe, BZ75¢ for a letter, BZ40¢ for a postcard.

A letter or postcard from Guatemala to anywhere in the Americas costs 40¢; to Europe, Asia, and the Pacific it's 80¢.

RECEIVING MAIL

In Belize you can receive mail sent Poste Restante or General Delivery at the **main post office** (⊠ Front St. at northern edge of Swing Bridge, Belize City, Belize ☎ 501/227-2201), where it will be kept for at least a month (bring a passport or other ID to pick it up). The post office is open Monday–Thursday 8–5 and Friday 8–4:30. **American Express** (⊠ Belize Global Travel, 41 Albert St., Belize City, Belize ☎ 501/227-7363) handles mail for cardholders free of charge.

SHIPPING PARCELS

In Belize, parcels have to be standard, wrapped in brown paper, and, if you're in Belize City, sent from a special post office,

which is on Front Street next to the regular post office.

🗐 Shipping Contacts **Belize City parcel post office** ⊠ N. Front St. next door to main post office ☉ Mon.–Thurs. 8–noon and 1–4:30, Fri. 8–noon and 1–4.

MONEY MATTERS

There are two ways of looking at the prices in Belize: either it's one of the cheapest countries in the Caribbean or it's one of the most expensive countries in Central America. A good hotel room for two will cost you upward of BZ$200; a budget one, as little as BZ$20. A meal in one of the more expensive restaurants will cost BZ$50–BZ$75 for one, but you can eat lobster and salad in a small seafood restaurant for as little as BZ$25–BZ$30 or the classic creole dish of stew chicken and rice and beans for BZ$8. Prices are highest in Belize City and on Ambergris Caye.

Guatemala can be remarkably inexpensive, but prices for first-class hotels approach those in developed countries. Trips into remote parts of the jungle or specialty travel like river rafting and deep-sea fishing are also relatively expensive. Sample costs: a cup of coffee, 4 quetzals; bottle of beer, 8 quetzals; ½-mi taxi ride, 25 quetzals.

Prices throughout this guide are given for adults. Substantially reduced fees are almost always available for children, students, and senior citizens. For information on taxes, *see* Taxes.

ATMS

Most Belizean banks have ATMs, but not all accept foreign cards. ATMs at Belize Bank's dozen offices around the country do take ATM cards issued outside Belize on the CIRRUS/MasterCard, PLUS, and Visa Electron networks. There are no Belize Bank offices on Caye Caulker or in Placencia. Atlantic Bank ATMs, including those in Placencia, Caye Caulker, and the international airport (near the American Airlines check-in area) accept foreign cards on the Visa Electron network. First Caribbean International Bank ATMs (only in Belize City, Belmopan, and Dangriga) also accept foreign cards with Visa and MasterCard logos. ScotiaBank and Alliance Bank ATMs currently do not accept ATM cards issued outside Belize, but this could change. Do NOT go to Belize expecting to get all your cash from ATMs, as machines frequently are down or out of money. ATMs in Belize give cash in Belize dollars. If you are in northern Belize, you can cross into Mexico and get money from one of the many ATM machines in Chetumal, although you will get your dough in pesos, which you will then have to exchange for U.S. or Belize dollars.

In Guatemala, banks with a "Credomatic" symbol accept most ATM cards, including those in the CIRRUS/MasterCard and PLUS/Visa networks. Ask your home bank to recommend a bank in Guatemala for you to use, as it may have a particular "sister bank." Also, your PIN should have no more than four digits; you can change your PIN at your local branch.

CREDIT CARDS
Throughout this guide, the following abbreviations are used: **AE**, American Express; **DC**, Diners Club; **MC**, MasterCard; and **V**, Visa.

In Belize, Master Card and Visa are widely accepted, American Express less so, and Discover hardly at all. Hotels and shops in Belize sometimes levy a surcharge for credit card use, usually 5% but ranging from 2% to 10%. If you use a credit card, ask if there's a surcharge.

🛈 Reporting Lost Cards In Belize, the American Express representative is **Belize Global Travel Services, Ltd.**, (41 Albert St., Belize City). For American Express cardmember services call 501/227-7363. For American Express traveler's check refunds call collect 801/945-9163. To report a lost or stolen Visa, MasterCard, or other credit or ATM card, call the issuing bank or other institution.

CURRENCY
The Belizean dollar (BZ$) is pegged to the U.S. dollar at a rate of BZ$2 per US$1, although private money changers at border areas may give a different rate. Most hotel prices are quoted in U.S. dollars, while most restaurant prices are in Belize dollars. In this guide, all Belize prices are quoted in Belize dollars. To convert to U.S. dollars, just divide the Belize dollar figure by 2. Be-

cause misunderstandings can happen, if it's not clear, **always ask which currency is being used.** When leaving Belize, you can exchange Belizean currency back to U.S. dollars (up to US$100) at Belize Bank at the international airport, or use whatever you have left to pay the airport exit tax of BZ$70. The Belize dollar is difficult if not impossible to exchange outside of Belize.

The quetzal, named after Guatemala's national bird, is divided into 100 centavos. There are 1-, 5-, 10-, and 25-centavo coins, and a 1 queztal coin. Bills come in denominations of ½, 1, 5, 10, 20, 50, and 100 quetzals. In early 2006, the quetzal was worth about 13¢; or 7.6 quetzals to the U.S. dollar. Unless otherwise stated, in the Tikal & Environs chapter, prices are quoted in U.S. dollar amounts.

CURRENCY EXCHANGE
If you're not from the United States, it's best to convert your money to U.S. currency before arriving in Belize. Other currencies, including Canadian dollars, are not widely accepted in Belize, and you'll have a hard time finding a place that will exchange your money. Because the U.S. dollar is gladly accepted everywhere, there's little need to exchange it. When paying in U.S. dollars, you may get change in Belize or U.S. currency, or in both.

Money changers at Belize's Mexico and Guatemala borders operate on a free-market system and pay a rate depending on the demand for U.S. dollars, sometimes as high as BZ$2.15 to US$1. Banks generally exchange at BZ$1.98 or less. The best place to exchange Belize dollars for Mexican pesos is in Corozal, where the exchange rate is quite good. At the Guatemala border near Benque Viejo del Carmen, you can exchange Belizean or U.S. dollars for quetzales—money changers will approach you on the Belize side and also on the Guatemala side.

In Guatemala, it seems, U.S. currency is never turned away in shops and restaurants. You can exchange cash on the street in the area around the central post office for slightly more than the official rate, but it's illegal, and you run the risk of being shortchanged.

Although ATM transaction fees may be higher abroad than at home, ATM rates are excellent because they're based on wholesale rates offered only by major banks. You won't do as well at exchange booths in airports or rail and bus stations, in hotels, in restaurants, or in stores.

🛈 Exchange Services **International Currency Express** ✉ 427 N. Camden Dr., Suite F, Beverly Hills, CA 90210 ☎ 888/278-6628 orders 🖷 310/278-6410 ⊕ www.foreignmoney.com. **Travel Ex Currency Services** ☎ 800/287-7362 orders and retail locations ⊕ www.travelex.com.

TRAVELER'S CHECKS

Do you need traveler's checks? It depends on where you're headed. If you're going to rural areas and small towns, go with cash; traveler's checks are best used in cities. Lost or stolen checks can usually be replaced within 24 hours. To ensure a speedy refund, buy your own traveler's checks—don't let someone else pay for them: irregularities like this can cause delays. The person who bought the checks should make the call to request a refund.

In Belize, your traveler's checks should be in U.S. dollars.Most hotels and travel operators in Belize accept traveler's checks, and some restaurants and gift shops do. However, even in Belize City and popular tourist areas such as San Pedro, clerks at groceries and other shops may be reluctant to accept traveler's checks or will have to get a supervisor's approval to accept it. Some places charge a small fee, around 1% or 2%, if you pay with a traveler's check. Most banks will cash them for a fee of 1% to 2%, but it may require a long wait in line. In all cases, you will need your passport in order to use or cash a traveler's check.

PACKING

Pack light—baggage carts are scarce at Central American airports and international luggage limits are increasingly tight—and bring casual, comfortable, hand-washable clothing. T-shirts and shorts are acceptable near the beach and in tourist areas; more modest attire is appropriate in smaller towns and the same long sleeves and pants will protect your skin

from the ferocious sun and mosquitoes. Bring a hat to block the sun from your face and neck. If you're heading into the Cayo, the mountains, or the highlands, especially during the winter months, bring a light sweater, a jacket, and something warm to sleep in, as nights and early mornings can be chilly. Sturdy sneakers or hiking shoes or boots with rubber soles for rocky underwater surfaces are essential. A pair of sandals (preferably ones that can be worn in the water) are good, too.

Be sure to bring insect repellent, sunscreen, sunglasses, and an umbrella. Other handy items include tissues, a plastic water bottle, and a flashlight (for occasional power outages or use in areas without street lights). A mosquito net for those roughing it is essential. Snorkelers should consider bringing their own equipment if there's room in the suitcase. Sand and high humidity are enemies of your camera equipment. To protect it, consider packing your gear in plastic ziplock bags. Also bring your own condoms and tampons. You won't find either easily or in familiar brands.

In your carry-on luggage, pack an extra pair of eyeglasses or contact lenses and enough of any medication you take to last a few days longer than the entire trip. You may also ask your doctor to write a spare prescription using the drug's generic name, as brand names may vary from country to country. In luggage to be checked, **never pack prescription drugs, valuables, or undeveloped film.** And don't forget to carry with you the addresses of offices that handle refunds of lost traveler's checks. Check *Fodor's How to Pack* (available at online retailers and bookstores everywhere) for more tips.

To avoid customs and security delays, carry medications in their original packaging. Don't pack any sharp objects in your carry-on luggage, including knives of any size or material, scissors, nail clippers, and corkscrews, or anything else that might arouse suspicion.

To avoid having your checked luggage chosen for hand inspection, don't cram bags full. The U.S. Transportation Security

Administration suggests packing shoes on top and placing personal items you don't want touched in clear plastic bags.

CHECKING LUGGAGE

You're allowed to carry aboard one bag and one personal article, such as a purse or a laptop computer. Make sure what you carry on fits under your seat or in the overhead bin. Get to the gate early, so you can board as soon as possible, before the overhead bins fill up.

Baggage allowances vary by carrier, destination, and ticket class. On international flights, you're usually allowed to check two bags weighing up to 70 pounds (32 kilograms) each, although a few airlines allow checked bags of up to 88 pounds (40 kilograms) in first class. Some international carriers don't allow more than 66 pounds (30 kilograms) per bag in business class and 44 pounds (20 kilograms) in economy. If you're flying to or through the United Kingdom, your luggage cannot exceed 70 pounds (32 kilograms) per bag. On domestic flights, the limit is usually 50 to 70 pounds (23 to 32 kilograms) per bag. In general, carry-on bags shouldn't exceed 40 pounds (18 kilograms). Most airlines won't accept bags that weigh more than 100 pounds (45 kilograms) on domestic or international flights. Expect to pay a fee for baggage that exceeds weight limits. Check baggage restrictions with your carrier before you pack.

In Belize, Tropic Air and Maya Island Air officially have 70-pound (32-kilogram) weight limits for checked baggage. However, in practice the airlines rarely weigh luggage, and if you're a little over it's usually no problem. Occasionally, if the flight on the small Cessna or other airplane is full and there's a lot of luggage, some bags may be sent on the next flight, usually no more than an hour or two later.

Airline liability for baggage is limited to $2,500 per person on flights within the United States. On international flights it amounts to $9.07 per pound or $20 per kilogram for checked baggage (roughly $640 per 70-pound bag), with a maximum of $634.90 per piece, and $400 per passenger for unchecked baggage. You can

buy additional coverage at check-in for about $10 per $1,000 of coverage, but it often excludes a rather extensive list of items, shown on your airline ticket.

Before departure, itemize your bags' contents and their worth, and label the bags with your name, address, and phone number. (If you use your home address, cover it so potential thieves can't see it readily.) Include a label inside each bag and **pack a copy of your itinerary.** At check-in, make sure each bag is correctly tagged with the destination airport's three-letter code. Because some checked bags will be opened for hand inspection, the U.S. Transportation Security Administration (TSA)recommends that you leave luggage unlocked or use the plastic locks offered at check-in. TSA screeners place an inspection notice inside searched bags, which are resealed with a special lock.

If your bag has been searched and contents are missing or damaged, file a claim with the TSA Consumer Response Center as soon as possible. If your bags arrive damaged or fail to arrive at all, file a written report with the airline before leaving the airport.

⚐ Complaints **U.S. Transportation Security Administration Contact Center** ☎ 866/289-9673 ⊕ www.tsa.gov.

PASSPORTS & VISAS

When traveling internationally, carry your passport even if you don't need one. Not only is it the best form of ID, but it's also being required more and more. As of December 31, 2005, for instance, Americans need a passport to reenter the country from Bermuda, the Caribbean, and Panama. Such requirements also affect reentry from Canada and Mexico by air and sea (as of December 31, 2006) and land (as of December 31, 2007). **Make two photocopies of the data page** (one for someone at home and another for you, carried separately from your passport). If you lose your passport, promptly call the nearest embassy or consulate and the local police.

U.S. passport applications for children under age 14 require consent from both parents or legal guardians; both parents must appear together to sign the application. If only one parent appears, he or she must submit a written statement from the other parent authorizing passport issuance for the child. A parent with sole authority must present evidence of it when applying; acceptable documentation includes the child's certified birth certificate listing only the applying parent, a court order specifically permitting this parent's travel with the child, or a death certificate for the nonapplying parent. Application forms and instructions are available on the Web site of the U.S. State Department's Bureau of Consular Affairs (⊕ travel.state.gov).

ENTERING BELIZE & GUATEMALA

To enter Belize, only a valid passport is necessary for citizens of Australia, Canada, CARICOM member states, Great Britain, Hong Kong, European Union countries, Mexico, New Zealand, Norway, the United States, and Venezuela; no visa is required. Nationals of about 30 other countries require a visa, and nationals of about two dozen countries require both a visa and clearance by the immigration office. Visas for nationals of several Asian countries, including Pakistan, Bangladesh, Nepal, Myanmar, and the People's Republic of China, are very expensive, costing up to US$2,000. Check the Belize Tourist Board Web site at ⊕ www.travelbelize.org for the latest updates on visas. You can also contact **Belize Immigration and Nationality Department** (Belmopan, Cayo District, Belize, 501/822–2423).

If, upon arrival, the customs official asks how long you expect to stay in Belize, give the longest period you might stay—you may legally stay for up to 30 days on the tourist card you'll receive on entry—otherwise, the official may endorse your passport with a shorter period. You can renew your entry permit at immigration offices for a fee of BZ$50 per month for the first six months; after six months, it costs BZ$100 a month for up to six more months, at which time you must leave the country for 72 hours to start the process over. (Note that renewals are not guaranteed.) If you're young and entering Belize

by land from Mexico or Guatemala, you may be asked to prove you have enough money to cover your stay. You're supposed to have US$60 a day, though this requirement is rarely enforced.

Visa requirements for Guatemala were relaxed in 2004, and nationals of most countries in North and South America don't need visas to stay for up to 90 days. However, nationals of many Asian countries and some European countries do need visas issued in advance. Check the requirements on Guatemala's immigration Web site, in English and Spanish. Citizens of the United States, Canada, and most other Western countries do not need a visa when entering Guatemala from Belize.

🚩 Visa & Entry Information **Belize Tourist Board** ☎ 800/624-0686 ⊕ www.travelbelize.org.

REST ROOMS

You won't find many public rest rooms in Belize, but hotels and restaurants usually have clean, modern rest rooms with American-style—indeed American-made—toilets. Hot-water showers in Belize often are the on-demand type, powered by butane gas.

Rest rooms in Guatemala use Western-style toilets, although bathroom tissue generally should not be flushed but discarded in a basket beside the toilet.

SAFETY

There's considerable crime in Belize City, but it rarely involves visitors. When it does, Belize has a particularly rapid justice system for such crimes, meaning that the offender often gets a trial within hours and, if convicted, can be sent to prison ("the Hattieville Ramada") the same day. Tourist police patrol Fort George and other areas of Belize City where visitors convene. Police are particularly in evidence when cruise ships are in port. If you avoid walking around at night (except in well-lighted parts of the Fort George area), you should have no problems in Belize City. Outside of Belize City, and possibly the rougher parts of Dangriga and Orange Walk Town, you'll find Belize to be safe and friendly.

Pickpockets are probably the most common threat in Guatemala—but by using common sense and taking certain precautions, crime shouldn't interfere with your trip. Pickpockets and other thieves typically work in pairs or threes; one will distract or disrupt you in some way, while another slips a hand into your pocket or backpack during the commotion. This typically happens in a crowded market or street corner, especially if your hands are full with your luggage or purchases. They are so skilled, you often you won't realize you've been robbed until quite some time later. If you know you'll be passing through a crowded area (entering or leaving the bus terminal, for example) carry only the money you'll need for the bus or taxi to your hotel, and stow the rest in your money belt, and carry your backpack in front of you. There have been a few ugly incidents of robbery and rape of foreign tourists on buses, so it's best to avoid traveling at night, particularly in remote areas. If you're returning late to your hotel, avoid going alone, and use a taxi—if you have to ring the bell to enter the hotel, ask the driver to wait until you are safely inside.

In 2005 there were sporadic incidents in Belize–Guatemala border areas. In two or three cases, masked men believed to be from Guatemala held up tourist vehicles in the Mountain Pine Ridge in western Belize. Other incidents in recent years include the late 2001 killing of three machete-wielding Guatemalan farmers by Belize Defence Forces soldiers near San Ignacio, robberies and carjackings on the Hummingbird Highway and near El Pilar Mayan ruins in El Cayo, and the murder of a young tourist in Stann Creek District in 2005. Thefts from hotel rooms, especially in Placencia Village, occur occasionally. Given the hundreds of thousands of visitors to Belize, however, these incidents are isolated, and the vast majority of travelers never experience any crime in Belize.

The road from the Belize border toward Tikal has long been an area where armed robbers stopped buses and cars, and there also have been incidents at Tikal Park itself. The number of incidents has declined, due to increased patrols by the Guatemalan military, but you should ask locally about crime conditions before traveling to Tikal.

Don't wear a waist pack, which pegs you as a tourist. Distribute your cash and any valuables (including your credit cards and passport) between a deep front pocket, an inside jacket or vest pocket, and a hidden money pouch. Do not reach for the money pouch once you're in public.

LOCAL SCAMS

Most Belizeans and Guatemalans are extremely honest and trustworthy. It's not uncommon for a vendor to chase you down if you accidentally leave without your change. That said, most organized scams arise with tours and packages, in which you're sold a ticket that turns out to be bogus. **Arrange all travel through a legitimate agency,** and always get a receipt. If a problem does arise, the Belize Tourist Board or INGUAT may be able to help mediate the conflict.

WOMEN IN BELIZE & GUATEMALA

Many women travel alone or in small groups in Belize without any problems. Machismo is not as much a factor in the former British Honduras as it is in Latin countries in the region. Unfortunately in the past, Guatemala has been the site of some disturbing assaults on women. These have occurred on buses, usually late at night in remote areas. Women should avoid making such trips alone. A more common complaint is catcalling, which is typically more of an annoyance than a legitimate threat. Most women, locals and foreigners alike, try to brush it off. That said, however, women make up a large percentage of the travelers in Guatemala, and the vast majority have positive experiences.

If you carry a purse, choose one with a zipper and a thick strap that you can drape across your body; adjust the length so that the purse sits in front of you at or above hip level. (Don't wear a money belt or a waist pack.) Store only enough money in the purse to cover casual spending. Distribute the rest of your cash and any valuables between deep front pockets, inside jacket or vest pockets, and a concealed money pouch.

SENIOR-CITIZEN TRAVEL

Discounts for seniors in Belize and Guatemala are rare, unless you travel with a North American tour company or educational program that offers them. Of course, it doesn't hurt to ask, following the protocol used at home: To qualify for age-related discounts, mention your senior-citizen status up front when booking hotel reservations (not when checking out) and before you're seated in restaurants (not when paying the bill). Be sure to have identification on hand. When renting a car, ask about promotional car-rental discounts, which can be cheaper than senior-citizen rates.

🎏 Educational Programs **Elderhostel** ⊠ 11 Ave. de Lafayette, Boston, MA 02111 ☎ 877/426-8056, 978/323-4141 international callers, 877/426-2167 TTY 🖷 877/426-2166 ⊕ www.elderhostel.org. **Interhostel** ⊠ University of New Hampshire, 6 Garrison Ave., Durham, NH 03824 ☎ 603/862-1147 or 800/ 733-9753 🖷 603/862-1113 ⊕ www.learn.unh.edu.

SHOPPING

If you're a shop-'til-you-drop type, you won't be happy in Belize. At their best, stores offer mundane merchandise at prices higher than at home. Belize imports most of what it consumes, and import duties and shipping charges add to the cost. Guatemala, on the other hand, has a strong arts and handicraft tradition, and most shops focus on these goods. However, there's little in the way of fashionable stores.

SMART SOUVENIRS

Belize does not have the rich crafts tradition of its neighbors Guatemala and Mexico. Gift shops offer the usual collection of off-color T-shirts and bad-taste gewgaws, but there are handicrafts, furniture, Belize music (punta rock), local foods and drinks, and other items that make good souvenirs or gifts from Belize. Don't buy items that contribute to the destruction of endangered wildlife or the reef, such as items made from coral, including black coral, and turtle or tortoise shells. Some gift shops in Belize also carry high-quality

textiles and other items from Guatemala. Local rum, Belikin beer, Marie Sharp's hot sauces and jams, Belizean coffee from Gallon Jug, colorful Belize postage stamps, carvings from ziricote wood, and high-quality chairs and other furniture made from tropical hardwoods make good buys.

For souvenir seekers, Guatemala's handicrafts, called *artesanía* or *típica* always draw the most attention, particularly the handwoven tapestries, carved wooden masks, handblown glass, and traditional indigenous clothing, such as women's *huipiles*. Such goods are beautiful and inexpensive, and they're sold throughout the country. Miniature wooden or ceramic frames make great little keepsakes, as do small hand-painted wooden jewelry boxes or masks. More exclusive items including jade carvings and jewelry, antiques, and particularly complex weavings, especially those made of silk instead of cotton, are available but are best purchased in Guatemala City, Antigua, and to a lesser extent Quetzaltenango, rather than around Tikal.

WATCH OUT

The sale of some items contributes to the destruction of the natural environment, so **avoid items made from coral** and turtle or tortoise shells. **Never purchase items pilfered from archaeological sites,** particularly stone carvings. They may be confiscated when you leave the country, and perhaps worse, your souvenir shopping aids in the destruction of irreplaceable historical and cultural relics. The export of Mayan artifacts is strictly prohibited.

SIGHTSEEING GUIDES

In Belize, all tourist guides are required to take a series of training courses and must be licensed by the government. If in doubt about the credibility of a guide, ask to see the guide's license.

A guide's license in Guatemala means little. Here, nothing beats a personal recommendation. Ask other travelers first, and your hotel second. Otherwise, stick to the established agencies to avoid getting cheated. Tikal is an exception: official guides wear a "Carnet de Guía de Turismo" (Tourist Guide ID), and can be hired at the visitor center. Many hotels also arrange guided tours to the ruins and surrounding sights.

SPORTS & OUTDOORS

Nearly everything worth doing in Belize involves the outdoors. Diving and snorkeling are the number-one reasons why visitors come to the cayes and coast of Belize. Fishing for tarpon, bonefish, and permit, along with larger fish on the reef and beyond, is another good reason to visit. Birding, wildlife spotting and photography, and hiking are world-class attractions of Belize's mainland rain forests, lagoons, and landscapes. Canoeing and sea kayaking are growing sports in Belize. There's no surfing in Belize—the offshore barrier reef limits wave action—but windsurfing and kite surfing are excellent off many cayes and mainland beach areas, thanks to prevailing 15- to 20-mph winds. A mountains-to-the-sea canoe race, La Ruta Maya, is held each year in March. With miles of limestone caves, Belize has some of the best caving in the region, and mountain biking is popular in the Mountain Pine Ridge and elsewhere. Golf is limited in Belize; a championship 18-hole course with a spectacular seaside setting is on Caye Chapel, and a 9-hole "jungle course" is near Belmopan. Two small 9-hole courses are being developed near Corozal Town. At least two 18-hole courses have been announced for the Placencia and Hopkins area, but it may be years before they are built, if at all. Tennis is not big in Belize, but you can play on hotel courts on Ambergris Caye, on Caye Chapel, and in Placencia. Among Belizeans, soccer (called football in Belize) and basketball are the most popular sports, and bicycle racing has many fans. The British colonial legacy didn't succeed in leaving many cricket fans, but the game is played here and there.

Hiking is surely Guatemala's greatest outdoor attraction. Whether it's amid Maya ruins or in dense rain forest, a pair of sturdy shoes and a sense of adventure are well rewarded in Guatemala. More specialized ecotourism is expanding, with a few tour operators offering bird-watching, white-water rafting, caving, and mountain-biking trips. Soccer and basketball are popular sports among Guatemalans.

STUDENTS IN BELIZE & GUATEMALA

Central America is a fantastic place for students and those on a budget. You can live well on $15 a day in Guatemala. Belize is more expensive; expect to shell out BZ$60–BZ$90 a day. There are few hostels as such, but Guatemala and Belize are packed with cheap lodging possibilities. Any option near a bus station is usually affordable. Belize, Caye Caulker, San Ignacio, Hopkins, and Placencia Village have sizeable concentrations of budget hotels. One of the cheapest ways to spend the night, of course, is camping, and as long as you have your own tent or hammock, and the permission of the land owner or caretaker, it's easy to set up camp in many areas. In Belize, some hotels rent tents or hammocks and camping space, starting at around BZ$10 a day. To get good tips and advice on traveling within a budget, look for informational bulletin boards and talk to other backpackers.

Belize has several college campuses where students hang out; the largest, but still quite small, is the University of Belize campus at Belmopan. Galen University is a small private university near San Ignacio. There are four off-shore medical schools. These small med schools (most have fewer than 100 students) are in San Pedro, Belmopan, Belize City, and Corozal Town.

IDs & Services STA Travel ⌧ 10 Downing St., New York, NY 10014 ☎ 212/627-3111, 800/777-0112 24-hr service center ⎙ 212/627-3387 ⊕ www.sta. com. **Travel Cuts** ⌧ 187 College St., Toronto, Ontario M5T 1P7, Canada ☎ 800/592-2887 in the U.S., 416/979-2406 or 866/246-9762 in Canada ⎙ 416/979-8167 ⊕ www.travelcuts.com.

TAXES

At this writing, the Belizean government planned to increase the hotel tax from 9% to 10% in mid-2006. Check to find out if the airport-departure tax of BZ$70, which must be paid in cash (in either U.S. or Belize dollars) when you leave the country, is included in your airline ticket charges. Guatemala and Mexico charge a land border exit fee of BZ$30, plus a conservation fee of BZ$7.50. For departures by boat to Guatemala or Honduras, you pay only the BZ$7.50 conservation fee. If you're leaving Belize by land or water and then returning to later fly out of Belize, **ask that your conservation fee be applied toward your airport-departure tax** as credit. The BZ$30 land-exit fee can't be applied to your international air-departure fee.

For most consumer goods and services in Belize, including restaurant meals, tours, rental cars, and diving, there's a 10% Goods and Services Tax (GST), introduced in mid-2006.

Most Guatemalan hotels and some tourist restaurants charge an additional 10% tourist tax. The airport-departure tax is US$30. Guatemalan customs officials at the border will often ask for a 10 quetzal fee when you enter at Melchor de Mencos. There's no such official fee, but to avoid delays, it's probably best to pay.

VALUE-ADDED TAX

In mid-2006 a new V.A.T.-style tax in Belize, called the Goods and Services Tax (GST), of 10% was implemented, replacing the 9% national sales tax. Guatemalan stores, restaurants, and hotels charge a 10% V.A.T.

TELEPHONES

AREA & COUNTRY CODES

The country code for Belize is **501**; for Guatemala, **502.** The country code is 1 for the United States, 61 for Australia, 64 for New Zealand, and 44 for the United Kingdom.

All Belizean numbers are seven digits. The first digit is the district area code (2 for Belize District, 3 Orange Walk, 4 Corozal, 5 Stann Creek, 6 for mobile phones, 7 Toledo, and 8 Cayo). The second digit indicates the type of service (0 for prepaid services, 1 for mobile, 2 for regular landline). The final five digits are the customer's telephone number. Thus a number such as 22x-xxxx means that it's a regular telephone in Belize District. To dial any

Belize number in Belize, local or long distance, you must dial all seven digits. When dialing from outside Belize, dial the international access code, the country code for Belize (501), and all seven digits. When calling from the United States, dial 011/501–xxx–xxxx.

CELLULAR PHONES

You can rent a cell phone in Belize starting at BZ$10 a day. Check at the BTL office at the international airport, across the parking lot near the rental car offices, or contact BTL (⇨ *above*). It's also possible to use your own cell phone in Belize, if it's on the GSM 1900 digital system, but you'll have to have a new SIM chip installed. This costs about BZ$50 and can be done at the BTL office at the international airport or in some cell phone stores in Belize City and San Pedro. BTL also has "unregistered" roaming for visitors with cell phones, even those not on Belize's GSM 1900 system. When you try to make a call in Belize using your cell phone, you're automatically connected to a recording offering the option of a live operator to make the call, charging it to your credit card, or calling collect, but before you accept, ask the cost per minute.

DIRECTORY & OPERATOR ASSISTANCE

To obtain directory information in Belize, dial 113; for operator assistance, dial 115. You can get telephone numbers in Belize on the Web site of Belize Telecommunications Ltd., ⊕ www.btl.net. For Guatemalan operator assistance (Spanish) dial 121; for information (Spanish) dial 124.

E-MAIL & INTERNET ACCESS

Belize is wired. DSL high-speed Internet is available in most populated areas, and cable Internet is offered in Belize City. In more remote areas, there's the option of satellite Internet. An increasing number of hotels offer broadband, either wired or wireless, in rooms, and others have high-speed Internet in an Internet room. There may, or may not, be an extra charge. Internet cafés can be found in San Pedro, Caye Caulker, Belize City, San Ignacio, Placencia, Hopkins, Corozal Town, Punta

Gorda, and other areas. Rates are usually BZ$10 to BZ$20 an hour.

Business-friendly hotels in Guatemala have Internet access in their rooms and in computer rooms where they charge guests by the hour for access. Cybercafés are everywhere, too, and are best for checking e-mail and for surfing. Rates are low, usually US$2 to US$3 an hour, or less.

INTERNATIONAL CALLS

Calling internationally from Belize is easy, but expensive. You'll pay around BZ$1.50 a minute for calls to the United States. To call the United States, dial 001 or 10-10-199 plus the area code and number. Pay phones accept only prepaid Belize Telecommunications Ltd. phone cards, available in shops at BTL offices in denominations from BZ$5 to BZ$50. "USA Connect" prepaid cards, for sale in some stores in Belize City and elsewhere, come in denominations of BZ$5 and BZ$20 and claim discounts of as much as 57% for calls to the United States only. BTL blocks many foreign calling cards. By far, the cheapest way to call internationally is to use a Web phone at a cybercafé.

In Guatemala, there are direct phones to AT&T U.S. operators at Telgua, the telephone company of Guatemala, located in most towns. They generally close for a few hours at lunch. Calls are cheapest from a cybercafé or private telephone company. To make a collect call (*llamar por cobrar*), dial 147120 from a Telgua phone. Guatemala's public pay phones use prepaid calling cards, which you can purchase at small grocery markets, pharmacies, and Telgua offices. Ask for a *tarjeta telephónica*. They come in denominations of 20, 30, and 100 quetzales; calls within Guatemala cost 15 to 50 centavos per minute.

☎ International Calling Contacts **Belize Telecommunications Limited (BTL)** ✉ 1 Church St. ☎ 501/223-2868.

☎ Resources **Belize Telecommuncations Ltd.** ☎ 501/227-7960 ⊕ www.btl.net). **Telgua** ⊕ www.telgua.com.gt.

LONG-DISTANCE SERVICES

AT&T, MCI, and Sprint access codes make calling long distance relatively con-

venient, but you may find the local access number blocked in many hotel rooms. First ask the hotel operator to connect you. If the hotel operator balks, ask for an international operator, or dial the international operator yourself. One way to improve your odds of getting connected to your long-distance carrier is to travel with more than one company's calling card (a hotel may block Sprint, for example, but not MCI). If all else fails, call from a pay phone. If you are travelling for a longer period of time, consider renting a cell phone from a local company.

☎ Belize Access Codes **AT&T Direct** ☎ 811 from pay phones, 555 from hotels. **MCI WorldPhone** ☎ 815 from pay phones, 557 from hotels. **Sprint International Access** ☎ 812 from pay phones, 556 from hotels.

☎ Guatemala Access Codes **AT&T Direct** ☎ 190. **MCI WorldPhone** ☎ 189. **Sprint International Access** ☎ 195.

PUBLIC PHONES

Belize has a good nationwide phone system. There are pay phones on the street in the main towns. All pay phones in Belize now require a prepaid phone card (*above*), rather than coins. Local calls cost BZ25¢; calls to other districts, BZ$1.

In Guatemala, it's easier to make local calls from your hotel. Telgua is the phone company (formerly the only phone company, but it now has competition), and every decent-size town has a Telgua office, most of which are open daily 7 AM–midnight. You usually have to wait to submit your number to the cashier, and then wait again to be called to use a phone. Do not use the black, red, or blue wall-mounted phones with signs that read "Free Collect Call." They charge a whopping $10 per minute and have a five-minute minimum.

TIME

Belize and Guatemala time is the same as U.S. Central Standard Time. Daylight Savings Time is not observed.

TIPPING

Belize restaurants rarely add a service charge, so in better restaurants, tip 10%–15% of the total bill. At inexpensive restaurants, leave small change or tip 10%.

Many hotels and resorts add a service charge, usually 10%, to bills, so at these places additional tipping is not necessary. In general, Belizeans tend not to look for tips. It's not customary to tip taxi drivers.

In Guatemala, restaurant bills do not typically include gratuities; 10% is customary. Bellhops and maids expect tips only in the expensive hotels. Guards who show you around ruins and locals who help you find hotels or give you little tours should also be tipped. Children will often charge a quetzal to let you take their photo (⇨ Cameras & Photography, *above*).

TOURS & PACKAGES
Please see the Adventure Vacations chapter for information on tours and packages.

TRAIN TRAVEL
There's no train service in Belize or Guatemala.

TRAVEL AGENCIES
A good travel agent puts your needs first. Look for an agency that has been in business at least five years, emphasizes customer service, and has someone on staff who specializes in your destination. In addition, **make sure the agency belongs to a professional trade organization.** The American Society of Travel Agents (ASTA) has more than 10,000 members in some 140 countries, enforces a strict code of ethics, and will step in to mediate agent-client disputes involving ASTA members. ASTA also maintains a directory of agents on its Web site; ASTA's TravelSense.org, a trip-planning and travel-advice site, can also help to locate a travel agent who caters to your needs.

🔂 Local Agent Referrals **American Society of Travel Agents (ASTA)** ✉ 1101 King St., Suite 200, Alexandria, VA 22314 ☎ 703/739-2782, 800/965-2782 24-hr hotline 🖶 703/684-8319 ⊕ www. astanet.com and www.travelsense.org. **Association of British Travel Agents** ✉ 68-71 Newman St., London W1T 3AH ☎ 020/7637-2444 🖶 020/7637-0713 ⊕ www.abta.com. **Association of Canadian Travel Agencies** ✉ 130 Albert St., Suite 1705, Ottawa, Ontario K1P 5G4 ☎ 613/237-3657 🖶 613/237-7052 ⊕ www.acta.ca. **Australian Federation of Travel Agents** ✉ Level 3, 309 Pitt St., Sydney, NSW 2000 ☎ 02/9264-3299 or 1300/363-416 🖶 02/

9264-1085 ⊕ www.afta.com.au. **Travel Agents' Association of New Zealand** ✉ Level 5, Tourism and Travel House, 79 Boulcott St., Box 1888, Wellington 6001 ☎ 04/499-0104 🖶 04/499-0786 ⊕ www. taanz.org.nz.

VISITOR INFORMATION
Learn more about foreign destinations by checking government-issued travel advisories and country information. For a broader picture, consider information from more than one country.

🔂 Tourist Information **Belize Tourist Board (BTB)** ✉ Lower Flat, New Horizon Investment Building Mile 3½, Northern Hwy., Box 325, Belize City, Belize, Central America ☎ 501/223-1913 or 800/624-0686 🖶 501/223-1943 ✍ info@travelbelize.org ⊕ www. travelbelize.org. For information on Guatemala, contact **INGUAT**, the Guatemala tourism board ☎ 800/464-8281 in U.S., 613/233-2339 in Canada, 020/7351 3042 in U.K. ⊕ www.visitguatemala.com.

🔂 In the U.K. For information on Belize, contact the **Belize High Commission** ✉ 10 Harcourt House, 19A Cavendish Sq., London W1M 9AD ☎ 0207/499-9725. For information on Guatemala, contact the **Guatemalan Embassy** ✉ 13 Fawcett St., London SW10 9HN ☎ 020/7351 3042.

🔂 In the U.S. **Belizean Embassy** ✉ 2535 Massachusetts Ave. NW, Washington, DC 20008 ☎ 202/332-9636 🖶 202/332-6888. **Guatemalan Embassy** ✉ 2220 R St. NW, Washington, DC 20008 ☎ 202/745-4952 🖶 202/745-1908.

🔂 Government Advisories **U.S. Department of State** ✉ Bureau of Consular Affairs, Overseas Citizens Services Office, 2201 C St. NW Washington, DC 20520 ☎ 202/647-5225 or 888/407-4747, 317/472-2328 for interactive hotline ⊕ www.travel.state.gov. **Consular Affairs Bureau of Canada** ☎ 800/267-6788 or 613/944-6788 ⊕ www.voyage.gc.ca. **U.K. Foreign and Commonwealth Office** ✉ Travel Advice Unit, Consular Directorate, Old Admiralty Building, London SW1A 2PA ☎ 0870/606-0290 or 020/7008-1500 ⊕ www.fco.gov.uk/travel. **Australian Department of Foreign Affairs and Trade** ☎ 300/139-281 travel advisories, 02/6261-1299 Consular Travel Advice ⊕ www.smarttraveller.gov.au or www.dfat. gov.au. **New Zealand Ministry of Foreign Affairs and Trade** ☎ 04/439-8000 ⊕ www.mft.govt.nz.

WEB SITES
Do check out the World Wide Web when planning your trip. You'll find everything from weather forecasts to virtual tours of

famous cities. Be sure to visit Fodors.com (⊕ www.fodors.com), a complete travel-planning site. You can research prices and book plane tickets, hotel rooms, rental cars, vacation packages, and more. In addition, you can post your pressing questions in the Travel Talk section. Other planning tools include a currency converter and weather reports, and there are loads of links to travel resources.

For information on Belize, visit: ⊕ www.travelbelize.org, the official site of the Belize Tourist Board, or ⊕ www.toucantrailcom, a site also developed by the Belize Tourist Board focusing on budget accommodations. In addition to hotel information, both sites, and especially Toucan Trail, have excellent general information on Belize. Also, visit ⊕ www.belizefirst.com. At this site, Lan Sluder, the author of this guide and the author of five other books on Belize, offers to answer any reasonable question about Belize by e-mail, usually within 48 hours, a free service. He has so far answered more than 10,000 questions for readers. For destination-specific information, check out ⊕ www.ambergriscaye.com for San Pedro; ⊕ www.gocayecaulker.com or ⊕ www.cayecaulker.org for Caye Caulker; ⊕ www.belizex.com for the Cayo district and elsewhere; ⊕ www.placencia.com or ⊕ www.destinationsbelize.com for Placencia; ⊕ www.southernbelize.com or ⊕ www.puntagordabelize.com for Punta Gorda and southern Belize; ⊕ www.hopkinsbelize.com for the Hopkins area; and ⊕ www.northernbelize.com, ⊕ www.corozal.com, or ⊕ www.belizenorth.com for northern Belize.

For general information on Guatemala, go to ⊕ www.guatemala.travel.com.gt.

INDEX

PHOTO CREDITS

Cover Photo (Belize Barrier Reef): *Jeff Hunter/The Image Bank/Getty.* 10, *Cayo Espanto Island Villas.* 11, *Danita Delimont/Alamy.* **Color Section:** Snorkeling above the Belize Barrier Reef: *Stephen Frink Collection/Alamy.* Lamanai, a Maya ruin on the banks of a lagoon: *Rainer Kiedrowski/Bildarchiv Monheim/age fotostock.* Toucan: *Peter Arnold, Inc./Alamy.* Scuba diver with Hawksbill Turtle, Half Moon Caye: *Stuart Westmorland/age fotostock.* Fishing on the beach: *Mark Lewis/Alamy.* Comparsas dancers at the San Pedro Carnival, Ambergris Caye: *Joe Viesti/viestiphoto.com.* Horseback riding through the forest in Chaa Creek: *Jon Cruys-Williams/Alamy.* Ice-cream street vendor: *Angelo Cavalli/age fotostock.* Snorkeler off Half Moon Caye: *Brandon Cole Marine Photography/Alamy.* Deep Sea Fishing Pier in San Pedro: *David Hoey/viestiphoto.com.* Canoeing on the Macal River, Cayo District: *David Hoey/viestiphoto. com.* Garifuna musician on turtle shell drums: *Bruno Morandi/age fotostock.* Conch shells on Ambergris Caye: *Brandon Cole Marine Photography/Alamy.* Jaguar perched in tree: *Jerry Short/viestiphoto. com.* Snorkeling off the Cayes: *Stephen Frink Collection/Alamy.*

NOTES

NOTES

NOTES

NOTES

ABOUT OUR WRITER

Belize First magazine founder Lan Sluder has been banging around Belize since 1991. In addition to authoring *Living Abroad in Belize, San Pedro Cool,* and other books on Belize, he has written about the country for *Caribbean Travel & Life,* the *Bangkok Post,* and Canada's *Globe & Mail* among other publications. His favorite part of Belize? Corozal Town and Punta Gorda. His children, though, prefer San Pedro.